D0500467

NEW TESTAMENT COMMENTARY

NEW TESTAMENT COMMENTARY

By

WILLIAM HENDRIKSEN

Exposition

of

Colossians and Philemon

BAKER BOOK HOUSE

GRAND RAPIDS, MICHIGAN

1964

COPYRIGHT, 1964, BY WILLIAM HENDRIKSEN

Library of Congress Catalog Card Number: 54–924

All rights in this book are reserved. No part may be reproduced in any manner without permission in writing from the copyright holder, except brief quotations used in connection with reviews in a magazine or newspaper.

PRINTED IN THE UNITED STATES OF AMERICA

TABLE OF CONTENTS

LIST OF ABBREVIATIONS

The letters in book-abbreviations are followed by periods. Those in periodical-abbreviations omit the periods and are in italics. Thus one can see at a glance whether the abbreviation refers to a book or to a periodical.

A. *Book Abbreviations*

A.R.V.	American Standard Revised Version
A.V.	Authorized Version (King James)
Gram.N.T.	A. T. Robertson, *Grammar of the Greek New Testament in the Light of Historical Research*
Gram.N.T.Bl.-Debr.	F. Blass and A. Debrunner, *A Greek Grammar of the New Testament and Other Early Christian Literature*
I.S.B.E.	*International Standard Bible Encyclopedia*
L.N.T. (Th.)	Thayer's *Greek-English Lexicon of the New Testament*
L.N.T. (A. and G.)	W. F. Arndt and F. W. Gingrich, *A Greek-English Lexicon of the New Testament and Other Early Christian Literature*
M.M.	*The Vocabulary of the Greek New Testament Illustrated from the Papyri and Other Non-Literary Sources,* by James Hope Moulton and George Milligan (edition Grand Rapids 1952)
N.N.	*Novum Testamentum Graece,* edited by D. Eberhard Nestle and D. Erwin Nestle (most recent edition)
N.E.B.	New English Bible
N.T.C.	W. Hendriksen, *New Testament Commentary*
R.S.V.	Revised Standard Version
S.H.E.R.K.	*The New Schaff-Herzog Encyclopedia of Religious Knowledge*
Th.W.N.T.	*Theologisches Wörterbuch zum Neuen Testament* (edited by G. Kittel)
W.D.B.	*Westminster Dictionary of the Bible*
W.H.A.B.	*Westminster Historical Atlas to the Bible*

B. *Periodical Abbreviations*

ATR	*Anglican Theological Review*
BA	*Biblical Archaeologist*

BibZ	*Biblische Zeitschrift*
ET	*Expository Times*
Exp	*The Expositor*
GTT	*Gereformeerd theologisch tijdschrift*
HTR	*Harvard Theological Review*
Int	*Interpretation*
JBL	*Journal of Biblical Literature*
JTS	*Journal of Theological Studies*
TSK	*Theologische Studien und Kritiken*
TZ	*Theologische Zeitschrift*
WTJ	*Westminster Theological Journal*

Please Note

In order to differentiate between the second person singular (see Philem. 4) and the second person plural (see Col. 1:2), we have indicated the former as follows: "you"; and the latter as follows: "y o u."

Introduction
to
Colossians and Philemon

I. Why Should We Study Colossians and Philemon?

The basic reason for the study of any Bible-book is given in II Tim. 3:16, 17. In addition we may well ask, Why should we, *especially today*, study these letters?

1. First of all because we are living in *the space-age*.

We hear and read about space-programs, galaxies, lunar probes, men-in-orbit. To a certain extent we can even see orbital flights on the television-screen. We discuss the prospects of inter-stellar flight. So, we as Christians naturally ask, "How is our Lord and Savior, Jesus Christ, related to this vast universe of space and of star-systems? Or does he, perhaps, stand outside of it?" For the great comfort of all believers this basic question is answered in Colossians (see especially on 1:16, 17, 20).

2. Again, this is the age of *ecumenicity*.

Today in religious circles *interdenominational Christian fellowship* — also called *ecumenicity* — is making headway. As many see it, this interdenominational fellowship must become organic union. They dream about a super-church. Will this be a body without a head? And if there is to be a head, will it be an earthly head? Today this question is very real, for not only Protestantism but also Roman Catholicism is looking forward toward ultimate ecclesiastical union. Even while this book is being written Protestant leaders are meeting in an ecumenical council at the invitation of the pope. Has he not loudly proclaimed that "the separated brothers" should be gathered, that they should return to the fold and recognize the supreme authority of . . . Rome? But must the Church have an earthly head at all? Who, after all, is the Head of the Church, both organic and ruling? Yes, and not of the Church alone but of all things? Colossians answers *this* question too (see on 1:18, 19, 24; 2:10, 19). May its teaching never be rejected or compromised in any way.

Now in the ecumenical movement there are men who are earnestly desirous of promoting the type of spiritual oneness of which Christ would approve; in fact, which he has commanded (see N.T.C. on John 17:21). Accordingly, it is their intention that members of various denominations and backgrounds shall sit down together and discuss their differences, in order, *without any sacrifice of essentials*, to resolve them if possible, to merge denominations wherever that can be done with spiritual benefit to all concerned, and in any event to investigate possible avenues of co-operation for philanthropic and cultural enterprises. All this is to be encouraged. Ecu-

3

menicity in that sense is not something to be avoided but to be welcomed.

There are others, however, who seem to have surrendered — if they ever had it! — the idea of *the finality of the Christian religion* and of *the all-sufficiency of Christ*. Their purpose seems to be to establish a *world-church*, that is, not only to merge the Protestant, Roman Catholic, and Russian Orthodox groups, but even to wed Christianity and the non-Christian religions. They seem to feel that Christ, to be sure, has something, in fact, has *much* to offer, but *not everything*. Rama, Vishnu, Zoroaster, Buddha, Confucius, Moses, and Mohammed have made their contributions too. It has been reported that Gandhi accepted all great religions as his. The extremists in the present ecumenical movement seem to be imitating Gandhi.

Now this virtual denial of the all-sufficiency of Christ was the very heresy — though presented in a different form — which Paul faced when he wrote Colossians. Is the Christian religion final or is it not? Is Christ all-sufficient or do we need other Saviors to supplement him? Colossians answers that question. The entire epistle is really an answer, but see especially 1:18; 2:9, 10.

3. The present era calls for basic reflection on *Christ's deity*.

The very emphasis on ecumenicity confronts the Church with the necessity of re-examining its basic beliefs regarding the Christ. If Christ is really God in the same sense in which the Father (and the Spirit) is God, then must the Unitarian, the Jew, and the Mohammedan be excluded from the ecumenical movement, or is there a possibility of compromise here? Reflection upon similar basic questions with respect to Christ — such questions as, "Are there three *persons* in the one, divine essence?" — is also forced upon us by the influence of the theology of Karl Barth. We see, therefore, that this space-age, this age of ecumenicity, is also *the age which forces upon us re-examination of our historical and confessional beliefs regarding the relation of Christ to the Father and to the Trinity.* And on this point, too, Colossians speaks with great clarity (see on 1:15a; 2:9).

4. This is the age of *pragmatism*.

It must be granted that by no means every one is interested in meditation and reflection upon deep theological truths. Today's slogan is: "Ideas must be tested by their practical value." Not, "Is it true?" but "Does it work?" is what people generally want to know. Colossians points out that these two questions cannot be separated. To be sure, Christianity is a life, but it is *a life based upon a belief*, a mighty energizing doctrine. He who is the Object of our faith is also the Source of our life. a. What this *faith* amounts to, and b. how this Christian *life* is lived, is here set forth with such surpassing beauty and grandeur that the remark of A. Deissmann was to the point, "When I open the chapel door of the epistle to the Colossians it is as if Johann Sebastian [Bach] himself sat at the organ." For a. see especially Col. 1; for b. especially 3:5-17.

4

5. The age in which we are living is also marked by a re-emphasis on the great truth of *the equality of all men in relation to their Maker.*

There are many who agree that all men are equally helpless by nature, all equally in need of salvation, all equally duty-bound to live a life to God's glory; and that consequently no man has a right to oppress his fellow-man. Now if this be true then what should be the relation between race and race, husband and wife, parents and children, master and slave, employer and employee? And if the relationships be strained, how can the tension be removed? There is much disagreement on this score. Here, too, Colossians comes to the rescue. The teaching of Col. 3:18–4:1 cannot be neglected without harm.

It is, however, especially in Philemon that we have a practical illustration — an example in actual life, for all to see — of the manner in which such a problem is to be solved. The lesson there taught is of immense practical significance for the age in which we are living. As a bonus this little epistle also grants us a fascinating insight into the soul of Paul, *the man, the warm-hearted, practical Christian.*

6. Finally, as the signs of the return of our Lord are beginning to multiply there is today *a renewed interest in the doctrine of the last things.*

With longing eyes believers are looking forward to "the inheritance of the saints in the light" (Col. 1:12). On this point too Colossians has much to offer. It is Paul's aim "to present every man perfect in Christ" (1:22, 28). To his fellow-Christians in Colosse he holds out the hope — a hope steadfast and sure — that "when Christ is manifested they, too, will be manifested with him in glory" (3:4). This *must* be true, for is not their life even now "hid with Christ in God"? That living Lord is "Christ in y o u, the hope of glory."

Viewed from every angle, therefore, this gem of an epistle is abreast of and even in advance of present-day discussion and reflection. It is timely. It is this because it presents the Christ who is the same yesterday, today, and forever, and who is:

    a. the Architect and Sustainer of the universe;

    b. the Head of all things, and especially the organic and ruling Head of his own Body, the Church, its all-sufficient, one and only Savior;

    c. the image of the invisible God, the embodiment of all the divine fulness;

    d. the Source of the Christian's life and peace and joy;

    e. the Rewarder of those who strive to be a blessing to others, regardless of social position; and

    f. as present within us, our "Hope of glory."

II. The City of Colosse

A. *Geography*

Essential to an understanding of Paul's Epistle to the Colossians is an acquaintance with the general features of the territory in which Colosse was located. The letter makes mention of three cities: Hierapolis (4:13), Laodicea (2:1; 4:13-16), and Colossae or Colosse (1:2). Though originally these were Phrygian cities, in Paul's day they had become part of the Roman province of "Asia." Their ancient site is included in today's Turkey in Asia (Minor). A few simple sketches, proceeding from the familiar to the less familiar and purposely omitting all unnecessary detail, may be helpful. Everyone is acquainted, of course, with the shape of western Asia Minor. Hierapolis, Laodicea, and Colosse are shown in this first sketch, in relation to the entire region and particularly to Ephesus which was Paul's center of missionary activity for this part of the third missionary journey during which the *three* churches, and probably also others, must have been established (Acts 19:10; Rev. 1:11). Distances are easy to see at a glance, since the side of each square represents 100 miles. Accordingly, Ephesus was located approximately 100 miles west of the three cities.

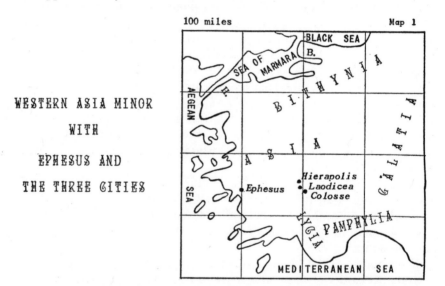

WESTERN ASIA MINOR

WITH

EPHESUS AND

THE THREE CITIES

100 miles   Map 1

About 900 air-miles WNW of the three cities was Rome. By actual travel it was well over 1000 miles away from the triad, the exact distance varying according to the route taken. Far to the East, by slightly south, of the three cities was Paul's birthplace, Tarsus, to the SE of which lay Antioch in Syria, from which Paul started out on his third missionary journey. Also with respect to the places to the east of the three cities it must be borne in mind that the actual *travel* distances were usually considerably greater than the direct or flying distances indicated on the map. In those days there was nothing like our Pennsylvania Turnpike with its seven tunnels. Lesser obstacles, too, had to be skirted. If one wished to travel by land from Antioch in Syria to Tarsus, he had to go around the Cilician Gulf, as indicated by the dotted line.

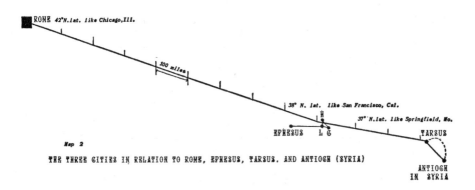

Map 2

THE THREE CITIES IN RELATION TO ROME, EPHESUS, TARSUS, AND ANTIOCH (SYRIA)

The three cities were situated in the Lycos (or -us) Valley. The Lycus River, also known as "The Little Maeander," branches off from the Maeander, shown on present-day maps as the Menderes River. The valley of the Lycus is in the form of a right triangle, with the mountains of Mossyna as its *hypotenuse,* the Salbakus and Cadmus ranges as *base,* and the Maeander Valley as *altitude.* Hierapolis and Laodicea were located one on one side and the other on the opposite side of the river. A distance of about six miles separated them. Colosse straddled the river, and was situated eleven or twelve miles farther east and slightly to the south. The acropolis of the city was on the south bank; the tombs and buildings on the north. Colosse therefore occupied a narrow glen of the upper Lycus. It was beautifully and strategically located, with the Cadmus Range rising very steeply to the south, and the Mossyna Range to the north. The Eastern Highway passed through Colosse, for roads naturally follow valleys.

Note that in Map 3, which follows, the side of each square represents 10 miles.

The question arises, "When Paul traveled from Antioch in Syria to Ephesus in the Roman province of Asia, what road did he take?" Did he or did he not touch Colosse? Bible atlases offer a variety of possibilities:

1. L. H. Grollenberg, *Atlas of the Bible,* map inside back cover, seems to have adopted the Northern Galatia view, and makes the apostle travel to the far north. Even when Paul at last wends his way toward Ephesus, he is too far north to come into contact with Colosse. Discussion of this theory

7

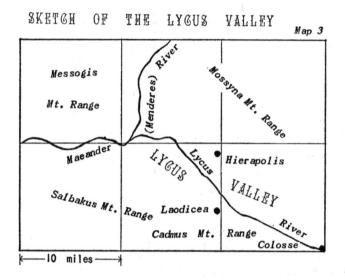

SKETCH OF THE LYCUS VALLEY

Map 3

does not belong to the present Commentary. Those who are interested in the reasons why I reject this Northern Galatia theory can find them stated in my book *Bible Survey,* pp. 334-336.

2. Others — such as J. L. Hurlbut, *A Bible Atlas,* p. 121; G. E. Wright and F. V. Filson, *The Westminster Historical Atlas to the Bible,* Plate XV — send Paul across the hills from Pisidian Antioch to Ephesus, an unusual and difficult way of travel. This road, too, avoids Colosse, being too far north.

3. The most natural route for Paul to have taken is the one indicated among others by Emil G. Kraeling, *Rand McNally Bible Atlas,* Map 20. It is the road from Antioch in Syria, over Tarsus, Derbe, Lystra, Iconium, Antioch in Pisidia, Apamea, Colosse, Laodicea, and thus, following for a while the Maeander Valley, to Ephesus. This road passes right through Colosse. It is the route illustrated on the next sketch. The idea of the sketch is *not* to suggest that this has now been established — Paul *may* have taken the route indicated under Number 2 above — but that room should certainly be left for this possibility since it was the more natural way of travel.

When the question is asked, "Why do most maps scrupulously avoid Colosse in routing Paul's third journey?" the answer could well be that this is the result, in part, of the influence of that great scholar, to whom the entire world of biblical scholarship is deeply indebted, namely, Sir William Mitchell Ramsay (see especially his *Historical Geography of Asia Minor;* and his *Cities and Bishoprics of Phrygia*) . Now Ramsay himself admits that "the ordinary and frequented route for trade between Antioch and the west coast passed through Apamea and Colosse." Why then does he not follow this lead? Here is his own statement, "But it would appear from the Epistle

FIRST PART OF
PAUL'S THIRD MISSIONARY JOURNEY

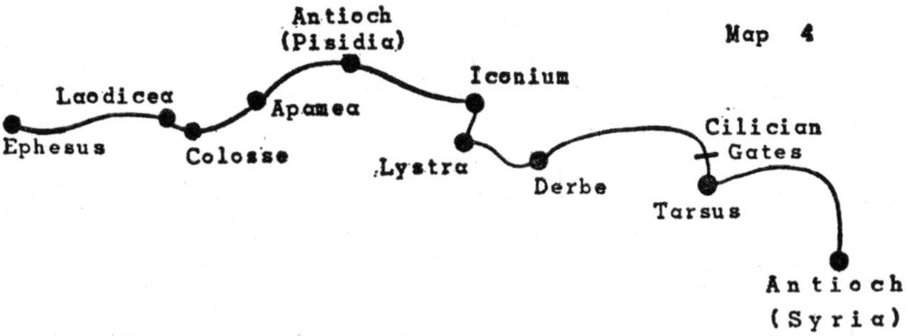

Map 4

Laodicea · Ephesus · Colosse · Apamea · Antioch (Pisidia) · Iconium · Lystra · Derbe · Cilician Gates · Tarsus · Antioch (Syria)

to the Colossians (2:1) that the Christians at Colosse and Laodicea had not seen his [Paul's] face." But does it actually follow from the indicated reference (Col. 2:1) that Paul *never passed through* Colosse? Is not this a case of basing too much on too little? Is it not possible that Paul passed through *the place* though he never personally founded *the church?* More careful, therefore, it would seem to me, is the statement of L. Berkhof, "Though Paul may have gone into the Lycus Valley, he certainly did not find nor found the Colossian church there since he himself says in Col. 2:1 that the Colossians had not seen his face in the flesh." [1] And as to the mountain-road on which many commentators and geographers send Paul, Sherman E. Johnson states, "But this is an unnatural and unlikely route." [2] The *present* highway and railroad are where we would expect them to be: in the valleys of the Menderes and Lycus rivers (see "Lands of the Bible Today," published by the National Geographic Society, December, 1956). Contrary to what happened on the *second* journey, when Paul's itinerary was changed by divine direction (Acts 16:6-8), on the *third* journey the trip from Antioch in Syria to Ephesus was carried out according to his own previous plan, as Acts 18:21 indicates (cf. that verse with 19:1), the divine approval resting upon it. It may be safely assumed, therefore, that he may have taken the easier and more usual route.[3]

---

[1] L. Berkhof, *New Testament Introduction,* p. 214.
[2] "Laodicea and its Neighbors," *BA,* Vol. XIII, No. 1 (Feb. 1950), pp. 1-18. The quotation is from p. 4.
[3] Lightfoot's observation that Paul "would not be deterred by any rough or unfrequented paths" can be answered by the counter-remark that one does not ordinarily choose such paths unless there be a special reason to do so. And as to other routes that have been suggested, such as require considerable detours, why would Paul take them when his purpose, namely, to confirm the churches already established, and continue on his way to Ephesus according to promise, did not require this?

B. *History*

The valley of the Lycus was plagued by many an earthquake.[4] Asia Minor is included in a belt of volcanic activity. Now earthquakes and volcanic activity spell disaster; think, for example of what the earthquake *circa* A. D. 60 did to Laodicea and Hierapolis! Nevertheless, volcanic ground is also fertile ground. It is excellent for grass and vegetation. Hence, on the rich meadows of the Lycus Valley grazed great flocks of sheep, bringing riches to the manufacturers of garments. This was all the more true because the waters of this valley were impregnated with chalky deposits. Now although these chalk-formations rendered parts of *the soil* barren, *the chalky waters* were just right for the purpose of dyeing cloth. This was an additional reason why the garment-industry flourished here. The trade of the dyer was practiced in all the three cities. It is not surprising, therefore, that the cities in this valley prospered, though in course of time their fortunes varied widely, as will be indicated.

1. *Colosse*

No one knows when Colosse (or Colossae) was founded. All we do know is that already in the days of Xerxes, king of Persia (485-465 B. C.), it was a thriving community. This Xerxes was the "Ahasuerus" of the book of Esther, who deposed Queen Vashti because she refused to yield to his unreasonable demand. He was the despot who commanded the waters of the Hellespont to be scourged with 300 lashes and the workmen to be beheaded because, due to a violent storm, the first attempt to bridge the narrow channel ended in failure. Having conquered Egypt, this terrible dictator had made extensive preparations for the invasion of Greece.

Now it was while he and his army were on their way toward the Hellespont that, seeking to avoid more difficult terrain, they passed through Colosse and the Lycus Valley. The Greek historian Herodotus, who in his *History* has given us a vivid — though not always thoroughly trustworthy — account of this ill-fated expedition, in this connection describes Colosse of the year 480 B. C. as "a great city of Phrygia" (VII.30).

Xerxes was followed by Artaxerxes I (465-425 B. C.), who allowed Ezra to

---

Here, too, I must beg to differ with Lightfoot when he states, "On the second occasion, St. Paul's primary object is to visit the Galatian churches which he had planted on the former journey (Acts 18:23), and it is not till after he has fulfilled this intention that he goes to Ephesus." On the contrary, Ephesus, too, was clearly in the plan from the beginning, as has been indicated. See J. B. Lightfoot, *Saint Paul's Epistles to the Colossians and to Philemon*, pp. 24-28.

[4] Strabo (*Geography* XII.viii.16) describes it as *seismic, subject to earthquakes*. J. B. Lightfoot on pp. 38-40 of his book, *Saint Paul's Epistles to the Colossians and to Philemon*, gives documentary evidence for the many earthquakes which visited Laodicea and the surrounding region in the years preceding and subsequent to the birth of Christ.

lead a number of Jews back to Jerusalem and sanctioned the building of the walls under the direction of Nehemiah. Shortly afterward Darius II began to reign over the tottering empire (423-404 B. C.). Now "Darius [II] and Parysatis had two sons born to them: the elder Artaxerxes and the younger Cyrus" (Xenophon, *Anabasis* I.i.1). Darius II, then, was succeeded by his oldest son Artaxerxes II (404-358). But the latter's younger brother, Cyrus, because of his conviction that he himself should have been the heir to the throne and also by reason of a personal grievance against Artaxerxes, in all secrecy planned a revolt, gathering allies from various regions and under various pretexts. A contingent of roundly "10,000" Greeks attached itself to Cyrus. However, at Cunaxa, near the gates of Babylon, Cyrus, the very able and handsome pretender, was killed (Xenophon, *op. cit.*, I.viii.24-29). In connection with this campaign Xenophon, a bright young Athenian, gained for himself lasting fame, and this in two areas: a. as leader of the retreat of the "10,000," proving his rapidly acquired and amazing military skill, and b. as a master of narrative, in his *Anabasis* giving to posterity a brilliant account of the march.

Now it was very shortly after the beginning of this expedition, while marching south-eastward from Sardis, that the army reached Colosse and remained there seven days. It is in this context that Xenophon calls the Colosse of the year 401 B. C. "a city inhabited and prosperous and great" (I.ii.6). And Colosse was great indeed, and this not only in relative size and population, but also in strategic importance. Was it not situated on a highway that linked East and West Asia? Was it not the key to the entrance of the Lycus Valley and at the same time to the road eastward toward Apamea and the Cilician gates? But in course of time in this same valley other cities were founded, so that Colosse received competitors, as will now be set forth.

2. *Laodicea*

The march of the "ten thousand" had demonstrated the weakness of Persia's vast but unwieldy and antiquated army. Accordingly, Alexander the Great (336-323 B. C.) saw and grasped his opportunity. In the symbolic language of Daniel 8, very suddenly the he-goat (Greco-Macedonia under Alexander) comes from the west, storming across the earth and charging the two-horned ram (the Medo-Persian Empire), throwing it to the ground and trampling upon it. Even the wrath of man was praising God: Alexander brought not only Greek dominion but also the Greek language to the regions which he conquered, with the result — unforeseen by Alexander but included in God's plan — that at a later time this language could be used as a very effective vehicle for the spread of the gospel. God's ways are wonderful.

Sometime after Alexander's death his empire was divided into four parts (Dan. 8:8). Lysimachus received Thrace; Cassander, Macedonia; Ptolemy Soter, Egypt; and Seleucus, Syria and a vast region to the east of it. After some time Antiochus II (Theos) ruled over Syria (261-247 B. C.); Ptolemy II Philadelphus (283-246 B. C.) — builder of cities, patron of art and literature — over Egypt. These two kings entered into an agreement whereby Syria's king was to divorce his wife and marry the Egyptian king's daughter Berenice. The execution of the unholy plan brought nothing but trouble (Dan. 11:6). Now the name of this scheming, crafty, vindictive divorced wife was *Laodice*. It was for this woman that the new city of *Laodicea,* which replaced a smaller town, was named.

Though Laodicea did not prosper immediately, once the Roman province of Asia was founded (190 B. C.) the city began to flourish as a mighty center of industry. Soon Laodicea became famous for the fine, black wool of its sheep. Besides, due to a change in the road-system, it became a very important highway-junction, a place where the Eastern Highway met four other roads. The combination of these favorable factors meant trade, commerce, banking operations, riches (cf. Rev. 3:14-22) and political prestige; also the latter, for by the Romans Laodicea was made the capital of a political district embracing twenty-five towns.

3. *Hierapolis*

In a volcanic region there are generally many chasms out of which arise vapors and springs. These springs, supposedly, have healing power. They are by many considered of value in the treatment of such conditions as rheumatism, gout, dyspepsia, etc. Hence, resorts are often established in the vicinity of such springs. For present-day examples think of such European resorts as those at Aachen, Baden-Baden, Bath, Spa; or of similar places in the United States: Hot Springs, Las Vegas Springs, White Sulphur Springs. And so Hierapolis, too, became a famous spa, a city "full of self-made baths." By the thousands people would gather here to drink the healing waters and to bathe in them. The "flowing rills" of the city became its "jewels."

Besides, Hierapolis had its Charonion or Plutonium, which was a hole reaching far down into the earth whence issued a vapor reportedly so dreadful that it even poisoned the birds that flew over it. Naturally these springs and this deep cave were by the superstitious people of that age connected with and dedicated to divinities that were worshiped here. Hence, Hierapolis had a multitude of temples. In this connection it is often said that the original meaning of the name Hierapolis is *holy city*. This possibility must be granted. It is also possible, however, that the name was derived from the mythical Amazon queen Hiera.

4. *The Further History of Colosse in Relation to Laodicea and Hierapolis*

In view of the facts as related it is not surprising that in the long run Colosse was not able to keep abreast of its younger and more lavishly endowed competitors. In fact even the earthquake which did such damage to Laodicea and Hierapolis *circa* A. D. 60 could not reverse the trend. The prosperous citizens of Laodicea immediately rebuilt their city, and that without accepting aid from the government. Hierapolis, too, was restored, though not immediately. But long before A. D. 60 Colosse had already lost the race. If one was looking for health, pleasure, or relaxation, he would go to Hierapolis; if he was interested in trade or politics, he would direct his steps to Laodicea. But as for Colosse, the Greek historian and geographer Strabo, writing about two generations before Paul wrote Colossians, calls the Colosse of his day "a small town" (*Geography* XII.viii.13).

Today the ruins of Laodicea are still rather extensive. However, when nearby Denizli was built, some of these ruins were used as a quarry, and more recently many of the remaining stones were used in the construction of a railroad. But here is still that little hill tenderly embraced by two small tributaries of the Lycus River. On this hill Laodicea once stood. Here may be seen the ruins of the two theaters, one still rather well preserved; also what is left of the gymnasium, aqueduct, a large necropolis, and stones from the Eastern gate.

Hierapolis is more conspicuous. It stood on a lofty terrace. Over the precipitous cliffs which support this terrace glistening cataracts of pure white stone, the chalky deposits of the streams, come tumbling down into the plain below. In the autumn these frozen falls, glistening in the sunlight and visible from a distance, afford a beautiful sight. The ruins of Hierapolis are extensive. On the lofty plateau the city-walls can still be traced; also the pillars of the ancient gymnasium, the remains of what may well have been the statuary hall, ruins of arches, of a temple, churches, and baths. Especially remarkable are the ruins of two theaters, the smaller one from the Hellenistic age and the larger one from the Roman period. The latter stands at the east edge of the city, on the hill-side. As seen even today it can be described as one of the most perfect theaters of Asia Minor.

Now compare with all this what is left of Colosse. Though it is true that in the year 1835, when the archaeologist W. J. Hamilton visited the site, a few foundations of buildings, some pillars, fragments of cornices, and a necropolis with stones of a peculiar shape could still be seen, there was nothing to compare with the extensive and well-marked ruins of the other two cities. And today much of what was still there in 1835 has disappeared, having been used for building operations in Honaz and elsewhere.

It is a wonderful thought that to a church located in a town which in Paul's day was already so insignificant, a church which in all probability was small in membership, the very important Epistle to the Colossians was sent. What may seem small in the eyes of man is frequently great and important in the eyes of God.

Let us now consider the people to whom this Epistle was addressed.

C. *People*

Colosse, situated farther to the east than Laodicea and Hierapolis, was the most Phrygian of the three. It was populated by natives of Phrygia, pagans who worshiped various deities, as will be pointed out later. Nevertheless, a rather considerable number of Jews mingled with this heathen population, for Antiochus the Great (223-187 B. C.) had transported two thousand families from Mesopotamia and Babylon to Lydia and Phrygia.[5] These Jews prospered in the Lycus Valley and attracted others of their country-men. The traffic in dyed wools and other business prospects acted like a magnet. Inscriptions in Phrygia have furnished ever so many indications of Jewish settlers there.[6] Thus, by the year 62 B. C., in the single district of which Laodicea was the capital there lived at least eleven thousand Jewish freemen. The entire Jewish population (including women and children) was, of course, far larger than that.[7] We know from the second chapter of the book of Acts that Jews from Phrygia were among those present at the feast of Pentecost described there.

It would be an error to infer from the preceding that the Jews who had emigrated to the Lycus Valley, and their descendants, were interested in this region only because it offered good prospects for business. To some of them the baths of Hierapolis were even more of an attraction than the com-merce of Laodicea and (for a while) of Colosse. Listen, for example, to the complaint of the Talmudist: "The wines and the baths of Phrygia have separated the ten tribes from Israel." [8]

Now since, as has been shown, Colosse was a typically pagan city, with a strong intermingling of Jews, we cannot be surprised if we discover that the danger to the church that was planted here stemmed from two sources, namely, pagan and Jewish and even from a mixture of these two.

The Lycus Valley belonged to the Roman Empire from 133 B. C. During the seventh and eighth centuries A. D. it was overrun by the Saracens. About this time too the city became deserted. An earthquake was probably a contributing factor. The population moved to Chonas (the later *Honaz*), a little to the south, near the foot of Mt. Cadmus. In the twelfth century the city of Colosse disappears completely.[9]

---

[5] Josephus, *Ant.* XII.iii.4.
[6] See William M. Ramsay, *Cities and Bishoprics of Phrygia,* the chapter on "The Jews in Phrygia."
[7] For the evidence see Lightfoot, *op. cit.,* pp. 20, 21.
[8] *Talm. Babl.* Sabbath 147 b.
[9] For studies with respect to the Geography and Archaeology of Colosse and its sur-roundings see General Bibliography at the end of this volume.

III. The Church at Colosse

A. *Its Founding*

Was Paul ever in Colosse? According to some he never set foot there.[10] According to others not only did he spend some time there but he himself in person founded the church.[11] Now it has already been shown that Paul may have passed through Colosse on his third missionary journey, traveling from Antioch in Syria to Ephesus in Asia Minor. But the book of Acts (18:23; 19:1) gives no hint that the apostle founded any churches on this trip. So far as it traversed the country where no churches had as yet been established, the journey must have been to a large extent uninterrupted, for "there is no allusion to preaching in new places, but only to the confirming of old converts" (Ramsay). And it cannot be proved that during his stay at Ephesus Paul visited Colosse *with a view to founding or meeting with a church there.* Moreover, according to what is probably the best interpretation of Col. 2:2, at the time when Paul wrote his letter to the Colossians the membership as of then had not seen his face. Though this may have been intended as a general statement, allowing for exceptions, it was the truth.

Within this framework of established facts there is room for various possibilities, none of which should be entirely excluded. But however it may have been, it is certain that among the many who came to hear the apostle when he labored in his headquarters at Ephesus there were people from the Lycus Valley (Acts 19:8-10). It must have been during this period (A. D. 54-56) that also the church at Colosse was established.

Now in this church Paul had many notable friends:

1. *Epaphras. This man,* probably of heathen extraction,[12] having been converted through the instrumentality of Paul, *was in all probability the actual founder of the churches of the Lycus Valley* (Col. 1:7). He was a Colossian (Col. 4:12), a servant of Christ Jesus (again Col. 4:12), Paul's fellow-prisoner in Christ Jesus (Philem, 23; for explanation see on Col. 4:10a), and a hard worker in the three neighboring congregations of the Lycus Valley (Col. 4:13). He was vigilant in prayer and loyal to the point of being willing to suffer whatever hardships were in store for him as Christ's ambassador.

---

[10] Herman Ridderbos, *De Brief van Paulus aan de Kolossenzen (Commentaar op het Nieuwe Testament)*, p. 104. H. C. Thiessen, *Introduction to the New Testament*, p. 231.

[11] F. Wiggers, "Das Verhältniss des Apostels Paulus zu der christlichen Gemeinde in Kolossä," *TSK* (1838), pp. 165-188.

[12] For the meaning of his name and for any possible connection with the Epaphroditus who is mentioned in the letter to the Philippians see N.T.C. on Philippians, pp. 138, 139, footnote 116.

2. *Philemon, Apphia, and Archippus.* Since these three are mentioned in one breath (Philem. 1, 2) as the addressees of Paul's smallest extant letter, and since we are told that the church (evidently the one at Colosse; cf. Col. 4:9 with Philem. 10, 16; Col. 4:12 with Philem. 23; and Col. 4:17 with Philem. 2) was wont to meet at Philemon's home, the conclusion is warranted that Philemon, Apphia, and Archippus were closely connected. They may even have belonged to the same family: Philemon the husband and father, Apphia the wife and mother, Archippus the son.

3. *Onesimus* (in later years). He was Philemon's slave. Around his escape, conversion, and return centers Paul's letter to Philemon. See Section IV B; also Commentary on Philemon in this volume.

These, then, were some of Paul's friends and helpers in the congregation at Colosse which was established during his ministry at Ephesus. After this ministry had been completed Paul left for Troas. Then, having crossed the Aegean Sea, he came to Macedonia, and from there went to Corinth. From there he reversed his course and proceeded back toward Jerusalem by way of Macedonia. Tychicus, a Christian from the province of Asia, was one of those who traveled on in advance of Paul from Macedonia to Troas, and was waiting for the apostle in that city (Acts 20:4). His name will come up again at the close of section B.

When Paul arrived in Jerusalem, at the close of his third missionary journey, he was falsely accused and apprehended. Soon his imprisonment began. It lasted about five years, and was endured first at Caesarea and then at Rome. Now it was during this imprisonment in the empire's capital that Epaphras, the minister of the Colossian church, made a trip to Rome, traveling anywhere between 1000 and 1300 miles (the distance depending upon the route he took) to reach that city. On the whole the report which he brought was favorable (Col. 1:3-8), yet not entirely. Paul was made painfully aware of the fact that the church faced a twofold danger.

B. *Its Perils*

In order to understand the nature of the dangers that faced this church it is well to bear in mind that it consisted either entirely or well-nigh entirely of converts from the Gentile world (Col. 1:21, 22, 27; 2:11-13; 3:5-7). Paganism of almost every then-known variety thrived in this region. Such deities as the Phrygian Cybele Sabazius, Men, Isis and Serapis, Helios and Selene, Demeter and Artemis, were worshiped here. Accordingly, the basic evil with which the young church was confronted was

1. *The Danger of Relapse into Paganism with its Gross Immorality*

A careful reading of Col. 3:5-11 proves that this peril was basic. The members of the Colossian church were, at least for the most part, rather recent converts from the darkness and coarse sensuality of heathendom. As such the danger of relapse into their former multiform licentiousness was very real, and this for the following reasons:

There was first of all the cable of their evil past. A habit is like a cable. A person weaves a thread every day until it becomes well-nigh impossible to break the cable.

Secondly, there was the current of a wicked environment. It is hard to row against such a current, and to oppose the opinion and the will of the majority.

Thirdly, there was also the undertow of passion in hearts not wholly consecrated. Though the Colossians had accepted Christ, they had not become "perfect" overnight.

And finally, there was the lure of Satan, seeking by means of ever so many clever devices, to snatch the sheep out of the hand of the Shepherd (cf. John 10:28).

In view of all this we can understand Paul's repeated admonition that the Colossians must continue in their newly acquired faith, must not be moved from the gospel which rather recently they had accepted, must not return to their evil works, must "put to death" such things as immorality, impurity, passion, evil desire, greed, wrath, anger, malice, slander, shameful language, and the telling of untruths (Col. 1:21-23; 2:6; 3:5-11).

2. *The Danger of Accepting the Colossian Heresy*

Now what does the so-called "Colossian Heresy" have to do with all this? Clearly it was exactly the purpose of the teachers of error to show the Colossians how they would be able to triumph over the sins just mentioned, that is, over "the indulgence of the flesh." It was as if they were saying, Are y o u putting up a tremendous but losing battle against the temptations of y o u r evil nature? We can help y o u. Faith in Christ, though fine as far as it goes, is not sufficient, for Christ is not a *complete* Savior."

There is a distinct possibility that in this connection they made use of the word *fulness* (see below, footnote 56), as if to say, "Christ will not give y o u *fulness* of knowledge, holiness, power, joy, etc. Therefore, in order to attain such *fulness,* in addition to believing in Christ y o u must follow our rules and regulations. If y o u do this, y o u will conquer and will attain to maturity, to ultimate happiness and salvation." [13]

That this was actually the connection is clear from the fact that Paul, having summarized "the philosophy of empty deceit" of these peddlers of lies with their persuasive arguments about rules and regulations and their boasting about visions they had seen, concludes his criticism by saying, *"Regulations of this kind* have indeed a show of wisdom . . . (but) *are of no value,*

---

[13] C. F. D. Moule has shown that "the Colossian rules were meant to combat indulgence" (*The Epistles to the Colossians and to Philemon,* in *The Cambridge Greek Testament Commentary,* p. 110). The entire context points in this direction.

serving only to indulge the flesh" (Col. 2:23). In other words, they will *hurt* y o u rather than help y o u. He then proceeds to indicate a far better way — in fact, the *only* way — in which the battle against the flesh can be won (chapters 3 and 4), the way epitomized so strikingly by himself in Rom. 12:21b: "Overcome evil with good," and in Rom. 13:14 (the passage that meant so much to a great leader of the early Church, namely, Augustine), "Put on the Lord Jesus, and make no provision for the flesh."

"The Colossian Heresy" was accordingly a second danger added to the first, and to a certain extent an outgrowth of it. It may be characterized as follows:

a. *False Philosophy* (Col. 2:8) which, though claiming to have discovered secrets and to have seen visions (2:18), denied the all-sufficiency and pre-eminence of Christ. Paul states that the reason why he sets forth the greatness of Christ is that there are those who deny it and are trying to delude others into denying it also (2:2b-4; 2:8, 9; 2:16, 17). The sovereign majesty and complete adequacy of Christ as the perfect Savior and Lord is stressed in such passages as 1:13-20; 1:27, 28; 2:2-4; 2:8-10; 2:16, 17; 2:19; 3:1-4. This is basic to all that follows.

b. *Judaistic Ceremonialism* (Col. 2:11, 16, 17; 3:11), which attached special significance to the rite of physical circumcision, to food-regulations, and to observance of such special days as pertained to the economy of the old dispensation. All such things, says Paul, are but "shadows." They have lost their significance now that *the object casting the shadow,* namely Christ, has himself arrived (Col. 2:17).

c. *Angel-worship* (Col. 1:16; 2:15; 2:18), which also would detract from the uniqueness of Christ, as if he were insufficient for complete salvation.

d. *Asceticism* (Col. 2:20-23), which in its unsparing treatment of the body went beyond Judaism. The apostle exposes its utter futility and points to Christ as the real answer to the problems of doctrine and life that vex the Colossians (2:20-23, contrast 3:1-4).

Questions arise to which the letter does not supply the answer; for example, What is the larger context of this Colossian Heresy? How did this false philosophy originate? Was it an offspring of incipient gnosticism of the ascetic type? Could it be an outgrowth, perhaps, of the theories of the Essenes, in this case covered with a varnish of Christian belief? Was it an intermixture of incipient gnosticism, Essenism (itself already infected with gnostic error), and Christianity? Do the recently discovered Dead Sea Scrolls shed any further light on it?

Here we must tread very carefully. We are perhaps safe in stating that the Colossian Heresy was a syncretism, that is, a weird mixture of Jewish and pagan elements. Gnosticism, with its stress on "knowledge," seems to have had something to do with it, for it is evident from the epistle that the false teachers placed undue emphasis on such things as "knowledge," "wisdom,"

18

"philosophy," "mystery" and "mystic insight." Yet, the evidence for this is usually indirect, that is, it is often not directly stated but to be inferred from Paul's insistence that the *real* knowledge, wisdom, mystery, etc., is to be found in Christ, in him alone (1:26, 27; 2:2; 4:3). Once in a while, though, the errorists are clearly exposed from this particular point of view (2:4, 8a, 18, 23). It is also known that gnostics exalted the spirit, and viewed matter as the seat of evil. To some of them this meant that the body should be neglected, that its natural cravings should be suppressed, if one were ever to reach the goal of *fulness*. There are those, accordingly, who see a reflection of this fallacy in Paul's rather stern rebuke, "Why . . . do y o u submit to regulations, 'Do not handle, Do not taste, Do not touch' " (2:20, 21). They also see the gnostic doctrine of *emanations* reflected and refuted in the apostle's warning against angel-worship (2:18).

A word of caution may, however, well be in order, for (1) we do not as yet have a reasonably *complete* description of gnosticism in the *first* century A. D., (2) neither was it Paul's intention to present *a full account* of the heresy which he is combating. When, therefore, certain authors, taking their cue from the expression "rudiments of the world" (2:8), which they translate "elemental spirits of the universe," present a more or less complete and detailed reconstruction of the heresy, we may well hesitate to accept this. It is all very interesting to picture these "astral spirits" or "planetary lords" as being also guardians of the Mosaic law. It is fascinating to describe them as entering into combat with Christ who, however, "despoils" them (2:15); to present them further as having instituted sacred days by means of the very planets over which they exercise control, and as laying down elaborate rules of abstinence so that by means of obedience to these rules the spirit of man may become disinfected with earthliness and may begin to ascend through various "spheres" to God. But have we any right to form all these conjectures, and to fill the gaps which Paul has left wide open?

There is another objection: Granted that in the Colossian Heresy it is proper to detect some influence exerted by incipient gnosticism of whatever origin — and to grant this seems altogether reasonable —, it still remains true that, all in all, the falsehood which Paul scores so severely had a definitely Jewish background. It insisted on the rite of circumcision (2:11-13) and on the strict observance of the law of Moses with its stipulations regarding foods and feasts (2:14, 16). That this is really what Paul has in mind is clear from the fact that he views the law as fulfilled in Christ (2:16, 17).

It is true that the heresy, while Judaistic, went beyond the Judaism which Paul exposes in Galatians. This is clear especially from its rigorous asceticism, that is, its insistence on obedience to rules which were nothing but "precepts and doctrines *of men*" (2:20-23). Are we dealing here with an extreme form of Pharisaism, or with the doctrines of the Essenes, perhaps?

With respect to the Essenes see Josephus, *The Life* (autobiography) 7-12;

Jewish War II.119-161; Pliny the Elder, *Natural History* V.73; Philo, *Fragment of the Apology for the Jews* XI.1-17; Lightfoot, *op. cit.*, pp. 82-94, 355-419.

Josephus, who at one time himself belonged to this sect, has many fine things to say about it. He calls its members "masters of their temper, champions of fidelity, ministers of peace," etc. His description also shows, however, that the very errors which marked the Colossian Heresy were found among them. They were infected with a strain of incipient gnosticism for, as he tells us, "It is their fixed belief that the body is corruptible and its constituent matter impermanent, but that the soul is immortal and imperishable." They looked upon the soul as "having become entangled in the prison-house of the body." As to Judaistic Ceremonialism and Asceticism, he relates that "after God they hold most in awe the name of their lawgiver [Moses], any blasphemer of whom is punished with death." Also, "They are stricter than all the Jews in abstaining from work on the sabbath day." He refers to "their invariable sobriety and the limitation of their allotted portions of meat and drink." He implies that they were divided into two groups: *celibate* and *marrying*. As to the first group: "Marriage they disdain. . . . They do not on principle condemn wedlock . . . but they wish to protect themselves against women's wantonness," etc. As to the second group, "They give their wives a three-year probation." Further, "Riches they despise." As to attitude toward angels, "They carefully preserve the names of the angels."

Must we conclude from this that the false teachers who vexed the Colossians with their sinister doctrines were Essenes who had nominally turned to Christ, but had retained many of their former beliefs? It is held by some that this is impossible because no Essenes lived in Asia Minor. However, Josephus also states, "They occupy no one city, but settle in large numbers in every town." Pliny the Elder fixes their headquarters "on the west side of the Dead Sea." Philo adds, "They live in many cities of Judea and in many villages and are grouped in great societies of many members." That author also seems to make the Essenic view of marriage a springboard for his own rather uncomplimentary estimate of women, "No Essene takes a wife, because a wife is a selfish creature, excessively jealous, and adept at beguiling the morals of her husband and seducing him by her continued impostures," etc. It is clear at any rate that Essenic influence can easily have reached as far as Colosse. It has been shown earlier that many Jews lived in that particular region.

Now inasmuch as the Qumran sect, which gave us the Dead Sea Scrolls, shows many of these same characteristics, and had its headquarters in the same locality, it is today the conviction of many that the Qumran sect is to be identified with the Essenes. Its *Manual of Discipline* is probably our best source of information with respect to them. In reading it one cannot help wondering whether perhaps Paul's warning, "If with Christ y o u died to the rudiments of the world, why, as though y o u were (still) living in the world, do y o u submit to regulations, Do not handle, Do not taste, Do not touch" was his answer to the Manual's repeated admonitions in the form of, "He shall not touch," and "He shall not taste."

Here we must carefully distinguish between the actual *teaching* of the New Testament, on the one hand, and *the current ideas and beliefs* which it reflects and against which it reacts on the other. As to *teaching*, the New Testament is, of course, entirely distinctive, in the sense that "Jesus Christ spake unlike any other man, for the simple reason that he was unlike any other man," as E. J. Young has stated in a fine article, "The Teacher of Righteousness and Jesus Christ," *WTJ*, Vol. XVIII, No. 2 (May, 1956), p. 145. But as to the *errors* which it combats, there is no principial reason why these could not include the asceticism of the Essenes. This does not mean, however, that we are certain that the apostle Paul in writing Colossians was combating a party of Essenes who claimed to have been converted to Christ. We know too little about conditions that prevailed in Asia Minor during the first century A. D. to draw such a risky conclusion. I agree with the statement of Millar Burrows, "What the Dead Sea Scrolls actually demonstrate has been well summed up by Albright: they show that the writers of the New Testament 'drew from a common reservoir of terminology and ideas which were well known to the Essenes and' — this I would emphasize — 'presumably familiar also to other Jewish sects of the period' " (*More Light on the Dead Sea Scrolls*, p. 132). We can, however, state that the available sources do give us such a picture of the state of syncretistic religion in the days of Paul that the error which he combats in Colossians no longer seems so strange. See also on Col. 2:8, 18, 21; 3:18; footnote 76; and N.T.C. on I Tim. 4:3. The chief point to remember is that the errorists, by riveting so much attention on *man-made* remedies for relapse into paganism, were in reality denying the all-sufficiency of Christ for salvation.

Now, in order to combat this doubleheaded danger — the peril of relapse into paganism with its gross sensuality, and that of accepting the wrong solution — Paul wrote his letter to the Colossians. A more detailed statement as to the purpose of this epistle is found in the next Section (IV).

The one who delivered the letter to its destination was Tychicus, mentioned earlier. He was accompanied by Onesimus, the converted slave who was to be returned to his master Philemon (Col. 4:7-9). They also carried with them for delivery the letter to Philemon regarding Onesimus (Philem. 10-17) and the letter that has been transmitted to us as "The Epistle of Paul to the Ephesians" (Eph. 6:21, 22); but see also on Col. 4:16.

C. *Its Later History*

Paul was released from his first Roman imprisonment, the imprisonment during which he wrote Colossians, Philemon, Ephesians, and Philippians. For proof of this release see N.T.C. on I and II Timothy and Titus, pp. 23-27. Having regained his freedom he probably journeyed to Ephesus and from there to Colosse, just as he had intended (Philem. 22). What happened during his visit with the Colossians has not been revealed. He must have returned to Ephesus soon afterward. With respect to his further travels, all of them conjectural as to their sequence, see N.T.C. on I and II Timothy and Titus, pp. 39 and 40.

As to the congregation at Colosse, its further history is obscure. It would seem that the gradual decay of the church went hand in hand with that of the city. For a while the church had a bishop of its own. However, when the population moved to Honaz, the episcopal see followed the population, until at length, with the coming of the Turkish conquest, "the golden candlestick was removed forever from the Eternal Presence" (J. B. Lightfoot, *op. cit.*, p. 72).

IV. Paul's Purpose in Writing Colossians and Philemon

A. *Colossians*

One day, during his first Roman imprisonment, Paul received a visit from the "minister" of the Colossians, Epaphras (already discussed). The latter informed the apostle about the condition of the church. To a large extent the report was favorable: faith, love, and hope were in evidence. The gospel was bearing fruit increasingly (Col. 1:1-6; 2:5). Yet, there was always the danger of slipping back into the former grossly sinful habits. Moreover, right at this moment false teachers were trying to delude the church by offering a solution which was no solution at all but would make matters worse ("the Colossian Heresy" already described). A letter must therefore be written so that the church may not depart from the pure teaching of its faithful pastor.

In accordance with this background the purpose of this letter was as follows:

1. To warn the Colossians against relapse into their former state with all its soul-destroying vices (Col. 1:21, 23; 3:5-11) and against the "solution" urged upon them by those who refuse to recognize Jesus Christ as the complete and all-sufficient Savior (chapter 2).

2. To direct their attention to "the Son of God's love," so that they may trust, love, and worship him as the very image of the invisible God, the first-born of all creation, the Head of the Church, the One who is in all things

pre-eminent and in whom — in whom *alone* — believers attain their fulness (1:13-18; 2:8, 9).

3. To this very end to enhance among them the prestige of their faithful minister, Epaphras (1:7; 4:12, 13), who, though now with Paul in Rome, joins others in sending greetings, is ever wrestling for them in prayer, and is filled with the deepest concern for them.

In view of the fact that Tychicus was the bearer of the letter to the Colossians and also of the one to Philemon, a member of the Colossian church and owner of the slave Onesimus who was being returned to his master, to the three points already mentioned a fourth must now be added, namely,

4. To emphasize among the Colossians the virtue of forgiveness and kindness. Not too strong is the statement of John Knox, "The whole of Colossians is more or less overshadowed by Paul's concern about Onesimus" (*Philemon among the Letters of Paul*, p. 35). This may well account, at least in part, for the fact that the apostle writes somewhat at length about the importance of showing *tenderness of heart* (3:12-14) and also for the fact that he devotes much space to the relation between slaves and masters (3:22-4:1, 5 verses, 4 of them lengthy), while he says far less about the relation between wives and husbands and about that between children and fathers (3:18-21, *together* only 4 short verses; in contrast with Eph. 5:22-6:4, *16* verses!).

B. *Philemon*

1. A Theory That Departs from the Traditional

Point 4 of the preceding section shows the close relation between Colossians and Philemon. Accordingly, when Herman Baker, the publisher of this *New Testament Commentary*, suggested that Colossians and Philemon be treated in *one* volume his advice was excellent. These two letters, the one written to a church and the other primarily to a family in that church, should not be separated. Much credit for having stressed this truth is due to the labors of such exegetes as Edgar J. Goodspeed and John Knox.

This, however, does not mean that we can agree wholeheartedly with the position which these men have taken with respect to the Purpose of Philemon. Having carefully studied their writings and the books and articles of those who either agree or disagree with them,[14] it has become our convic-

---

[14] See the following: E. J. Goodspeed, *New Solutions to New Testament Problems; The Meaning of Ephesians; The Key to Ephesians;* J. Knox, *Philemon among the Letters of Paul;* criticized by C. F. D. Moule in his valuable work, *The Epistles of Paul the Apostle to the Colossians and to Philemon,* see especially pp. 14-21, which criticism J. Knox tries to answer in the Revised (1959) edition of his aforementioned book. From Knox is also *The Epistle to Philemon* (Introduction and Exegesis, in *The Interpreter's Bible,* Vol. XI). Further: P. N. Harrison, "Onesimus and Philemon," *ATR,* XXXII (1950), pp. 286-294. C. L. Mitton, *The Epistle to the Ephesians; The Formation of the Pauline Corpus of Letters;* Heinrich Greeven, "Prüfung der Thesen von J. Knox zum Philemonbrief," *TZ,* 79 (1954), pp. 373-

tion that while we owe them a debt of gratitude for the light which they have shed on the closeness of the relationship between Colossians and Philemon, we cannot accept their reconstruction of history. What is at best merely probable is at times presented as if it were well-nigh certain, what is merely possible as if it were probable, and what is very questionable as if it were at least possible. Since there are minor differences between Knox and Goodspeed the presentation given below is (unless otherwise stated) substantially that of Knox.

Briefly, then, according to his view the primary purpose of Paul's letter to Philemon is *not* that Onesimus shall be forgiven his offense of having run away from his master and having probably defrauded him besides, but rather *that this slave shall be set free and returned to Paul for the service of the gospel.*

As Knox reconstructs the events pertaining to Onesimus they become a very fascinating story, a kind of romance appropriate for dramatization:

a. Here, then, is this slave who though bearing the name *Profitable* (Onesimus) was not profitable to his superior. He lived with his owner in Colosse, but the latter's name was *not* Philemon but Archippus (*Philemon among the Letters of Paul,* p. 58). This Archippus was a befriender and member of the Colossian church. Church-members would gather in his house for worship. Philemon, though also mentioned in the opening verses of the small epistle, lived elsewhere; see point d.

b. Onesimus, not being in favor with his master, may have run away, though this is not expressed in so many words. And he may have visited Paul in the place of the latter's imprisonment, though also this is not specifically stated. Paul, at any rate, was in prison, perhaps in Ephesus (p. 33), not very far from Colosse.

c. Through the ministry of Paul the slave becomes a Christian. The once useless one becomes very useful. In fact so helpful does he become that the apostle would have liked to have kept him with him, and this not for personal reasons but for evangelistic work. However, after due consideration Paul decides to return the slave to his owner Archippus in order that the latter may of his own free will emancipate him and return him to Paul for kingdom work (p. 29).

d. However, will Archippus really consent to release his slave? If Onesimus has actually defrauded his master, will he not receive severe punishment? Paul finds a solution. In the company of faithful Tychicus the slave will be sent to his owner. In the hand of Tychicus there will also be a letter from Paul in the interest of the slave. It is to Archippus that the body of

---

378. Earlier: E. R. Goodenough, "Paul and Onesimus," *HTR,* 22 (1929), pp. 181-183; and Albert E. Barnett, *The New Testament: Its Making and Meaning,* pp. 79-92; 184-185.

the letter is addressed (p. 62). Now, in order to add weight to his request the apostle puts forth efforts to get others to support his appeal. Was not Laodicea located very close to Colosse? And did not the churches of the Lycus Valley look for leadership to a man — namely, Philemon — who had his headquarters in Laodicea (p. 70)? Let Philemon read the letter, therefore, and let him attach his support to Paul's request. Then let this letter, thus endorsed, be read to the church at Colosse. Having reached Colosse via Laodicea it can now be properly designated as "the letter from Laodicea." In his epistle to the Colossians (4:16) the apostle requests that this small letter which concerns Onesimus be read to the Colossians. Says Knox, "In my opinion there is a probability approaching certainty that this letter [the one "from Laodicea"] was our Philemon" (p. 45).

e. In Col. 4:17 Paul states, "And say to Archippus, See that you fulfil the ministry that you have received." *This "ministry" is the charge to release Onesimus and to send him back to Paul for gospel-activity.* The letter which we call Philemon is therefore "a letter to an individual, the reading of which, it was desired, should be *overheard* by a group to which the individual belonged and which was able to exercise some control over his conduct" (p. 60).

The plan works. In the company of Tychicus the slave travels to Laodicea. There Philemon endorses Paul's request. Slave and letter finally reach Colosse. The church supports Paul's Christian demands upon one of its members (p. 53). Thus Onesimus goes back to Paul.

f. And now the most interesting turn of all. Paul uses Onesimus as he had planned. And lo and behold, the one-time slave at a later time becomes nothing less than *bishop of the church at Ephesus!* Ignatius, bishop of the church of Syrian Antioch, on his way to Rome and martyrdom, stops at Smyrna in Asia Minor. He writes a letter to the Ephesians, in which he expresses his gratitude for the visit of Onesimus and others. In that letter Ignatius says, "Since then in the name of God I received your entire congregation in the person of Onesimus, a man of inexpressible love and your bishop, I beseech you in Jesus Christ to love him and all those who are like him. For blessed is he who granted you to be worthy to receive such a bishop" (Ephesians, I.1; cf. VIII.2).

The climax of this exegetical embroidery is the suggestion that after Paul's death Bishop Onesimus, the ex-slave who was so deeply indebted to the apostle, made a collection of the Pauline epistles; that is, the publication of the corpus of Paul's letters was done under his oversight (p. 107). Goodspeed leans to the conclusion that Philemon himself wrote Ephesians as a covering letter (*The Key to Ephesians,* xvi). Knox seems to endorse this position (p. 96). But the discussion of this theory belongs not here but in a Commentary on Ephesians.

2. Criticism

In what follows, paragraphs a, b, etc., respectively answer paragraphs a, b, etc., above.

a. The most natural interpretation of Philemon 1, 2 is that which views Philemon, Apphia, and Archippus as belonging to one and the same household, together with the slave Onesimus. They lived in Colosse (Col. 4:9). The owner of the slave, moreover, was *not* Archippus but Philemon, the one addressed first and throughout.

b. In all probability Paul was in Rome, not in Ephesus, when he wrote Colossians and Philemon. See V in *this* Commentary. Also, N.T.C. on Philippians, pp. 21-30.

c. In verse 14 the apostle is not asking that Onesimus be returned to him. The very next verse (verse 15b) seems rather to imply that Onesimus will remain in the company of Philemon ("that you should have him forever") who will, however, no longer regard him as a slave but as a brother beloved (verse 16). Moreover, Paul, who has his mind set on leaving the place of his imprisonment and who is already asking that at his destination a lodging be prepared for him (Philem. 22), would hardly be requesting that Onesimus be returned to him.

d. Col. 4:16, though admittedly difficult, seems to refer to an *exchange of letters addressed to churches* (see further on that verse).

e. It is surely more natural to interpret the words, "Attend to the ministry which you have received in the Lord" (Col. 4:17) as referring to the duty of Archippus to carry out a spiritual mission than as referring to his obligation to free a slave, be it even for evangelistic work. See comments on this verse.

f. If about a half century later Ignatius in his letter to the Ephesians had been actually referring to the ex-slave on behalf of whom Paul had made his marvelous plea, a *clear* reference to this previous letter by the great apostle would have been natural; just as, for example, Polycarp, writing to the Philippians, *clearly* reminds them of Paul's earlier letter. The fact that Ignatius had read Paul's Philemon and supplies the evidence of this in his *Ephesians,* does not in any way prove that Bishop Onesimus was the ex-slave.

Thus, it has been shown that Knox's theory, though valuable in showing the close connection between Colossians and Philemon, as a historical reconstruction lacks proof. No damage has been done to the traditional view.

3. Real Purpose of Paul's Letter to Philemon

The real background, then, is as follows:

Philemon was one of the pillars of the church at Colosse. He loved the Lord and the brethren, and had given concrete evidence of this fact again and again (Philem. 7). He was Paul's spiritual son, for, whether directly or indirectly (see on Philem. 19) God has used Paul to change him. His new life had affected not only himself but also his household. It is considered probable that Apphia was his wife, and Archippus their son. Friends who had accepted the Lord regularly gathered for worship at their home (Philem. 2). In the absence of Epaphras, Archippus would probably have charge of the service (Col. 4:17). He may have been a young man who, like Timothy, was in need of encouragement (cf. I Tim. 4:12).

Now, Onesimus was one of the slaves of Philemon's household. This slave ran away, journeying all the way to Rome. In Rome he came into contact with Paul. Just as the Lord had formerly blessed the work of the great missionary to the heart of the master so he now blessed it to the heart of the slave. So dear did the latter become to the apostle that Paul calls him "my child, whom I have begotten in my bonds" (verse 10), "my very heart" (verse 12), "a brother beloved especially to me but how much more to you, both in the flesh and in the Lord" (verse 16), "the faithful and beloved brother" (Col. 4:9). Gladly would Paul have kept Onesimus at his side as an assistant, for his character had finally caught up with his name. In this connection read Philemon 11, and notice the play on a synonym of the name of this slave:

"Onesimus who formerly to you was useless, but now both to you and to me is useful." Cf. also verse 20 in the original.

But Paul does not deem it right to keep Onesimus in Rome. He decides to send him back to his master with the very carefully and politely worded request that the latter accept him as one who is no longer merely a slave but a brother beloved. If he in any way has defrauded his master, Paul is ready to assume full responsibility for the payment of the debt. With insurpassable tact the great apostle adds:

"not to mention to you that you owe me your very self besides," verse 19.

Paul does not command, though, as he himself states, he has a *right* to do so; he rather *appeals* to the heart of Philemon (verse 9). He is fully confident that the latter will do "even better than" what is asked of him (verse 21). The apostle entertains hopes of being released from his present imprisonment and trusts that Philemon will "prepare a guest room" for him (verse 22).

It is hardly necessary to add that although this fully inspired epistle does not in so many words condemn the institution of slavery it strikes at its very spirit and transforms the slave into a brother beloved.

Accordingly, Paul's purpose in writing Philemon may be summarized as follows:

1. To secure forgiveness for Onesimus.
2. To strike at the very heart of slavery by tactfully requesting that, in accordance with the rule of Christ, love be shown to all, including slaves.

3. To provide for himself a place of lodging after his release from imprisonment.

V. The Place and the Time of Writing
Colossians and Philemon

Colossians and Philemon, as well as Ephesians and Philippians, are Prison Epistles. The place of origin and in general the date of *one* determines the date of *all four*. See detailed discussion in N.T.C. on Philippians, pp. 21-30.

Colossians, Philemon, and Ephesians are carried to their destination by Tychicus and Onesimus, all on one trip (cf. Col. 4:7-9, Philem. 10-12; and Eph. 6:21, 22).

As to Paul's circumstances, he is a prisoner (Col. 1:24; 4:3, 10, 18; Philem. 1, 9, 23). In addition to Onesimus other names are mentioned both in Colossians and Philemon. These are Paul's companions: Luke, Aristarchus, Mark, Epaphras, and Demas (Col. 4:10-14; Philem. 23, 24); also Timothy, mentioned together with Paul in the *opening* verse of both letters. Jesus Justus is also with Paul (Col. 4:11), but is not mentioned in Philemon. Paul is enjoying a measure of freedom to preach the gospel (Col. 4:3, 4). He hopes to be released (Philem. 22).

In all this there is nothing that contradicts the traditional view of the Roman origin of these letters. The measure of freedom which Paul enjoys harmonizes with the report of his circumstances in Rome (Acts 28:30, 31), but not with that of his imprisonment in Caesarea (Acts 24-26). Luke's presence is unaccountable if these letters were sent from a prison in Ephesus, for Luke has given us a rather detailed narrative of Paul's ministry in that city (Acts 19) but says nothing about any imprisonment there, and, in fact was not with Paul at that time. But Luke did definitely go with Paul to Rome (Acts 27:1; 28:16). And so did Aristarchus (Acts 27:2). Furthermore, if Rome is the place of Paul's imprisonment when Colossians and Philemon were written, then, in view of I Peter 5:13, Mark's presence is readily understandable, for Mark seems to have been in this "Babylon" shortly afterward.

And as to time, everything points to a date during the period A. D. 61-63, perhaps somewhere in or near the middle of this period, at least *before* the writing of Philippians.[15]

---

[15] See N.T.C. on Philippians, pp. 29 and 30; and for a discussion of the entire Pauline chronology see W. Hendriksen, *Bible Survey*, pp. 62-64, 70.

VI. The Authorship of Colossians and Philemon [16]

A. *Colossians*

In the main three arguments have been urged against the Pauline authorship of Colossians. It has been shown by many commentators that all three are rather readily answered when the facts are examined. The "objections," [17] then are as follows:

(1) *Language and Style show that Paul cannot have been the author.*

  a. *Words Used and Words Omitted*

Colossians contains thirty-four words not found elsewhere in the New Testament and several additional words that occur nowhere else in Paul's epistles. On the other hand, such familiar Pauline words as *righteousness* (δικαιοσύνη), *salvation* (σωτηρία), *revelation* (ἀποκάλυψις), and *to abrogate* (καταργεῖν) are not found in Colossians.

Answer: The percentage of such exceptional words found in Colossians but not elsewhere is comparable to that in other epistles, for example Romans (in a section of similar length) and Philippians. *A different subject requires different words.* Hence many of these words are found in Colossians 1 and 2, where the author combats a unique heresy; see especially 2:16-23.[18] This also accounts for the fact that other words, used in other epistles, in the discussion of other themes, are not found *here*. Why should they be? Percy is entirely correct when he states, "It can be safely affirmed, therefore, that from the aspect of lexicography no serious argument against the genuine character of this epistle can be advanced" (*op. cit.,* p. 18) .

---

[16] See the detailed discussion in Ernst Percy's important work, *Die Probleme der Kolosser-und Epheserbriefe,* 1946.

[17] E. Th. Mayerhoff began the attack. See his work, *Der Brief an die Colosser mit vornehmlicher Berücksichtigung der drei Pastoralbriefe kritisch geprüft.* He regarded Colossians as an imitation of Ephesians which he viewed as written by Paul. F. C. Baur and his followers, the Later Tübingen School, denied the authenticity of all the letters passing under the apostle's name, except Galatians, I and II Corinthians, and most of Romans. But Baur's denial is vitiated by the Hegelian bias upon which it rests. For Baur the question whether or not an epistle is characterized by the anti-Judaistic line of argumentation seems to settle everything. Thus all of Paul's thinking is forced into one groove. This is manifestly unfair. H. J. Holtzmann in his work *Kritik der Epheser-und Kolosserbriefe,* views the letter which has come down to us as Colossians as being in reality an original shorter authentic Colossians plus interpolations from Ephesians which was composed by a Paulinist who in the process of writing it made use of the original and genuine Colossians. A. S. Peake is certainly correct when he states, "The complexity of the hypothesis tells fatally against it" (*Critical Introduction to the New Testament,* p. 52) . Another and more recent author who finds a genuine nucleus in our Colossians is Charles Masson, *L'Épitre de Saint Paul aux Colossiens* (in *Commentaire du Nouveau Testament X,* 1950, pp. 83 ff).

[18] And some of these words are probably borrowed from the technical terminology of the false teachers.

b. *Stylistic Characteristics*

Colossians contains well-nigh endless sentence-chains. Thus, chapter 1 has only five sentences in the original, and one of these, verses 9-20, is a sentence of 218 words.

Also, this letter heaps up synonyms: pray and ask (1:9), endurance and longsuffering (1:11), holy, faultless, and blameless (1:22), founded and firm (or "grounded and stedfast," 1:23), ages and generations (1:26), rooted, built up, and established (2:7).

Again, it is rich in appositional clauses, such as, "the Father . . . who rescued us . . . and transferred us into the kingdom of the Son of his love, in whom we have our redemption (1:12-14), . . . who is the image of the invisible God," etc. (1:15-20).

And finally, certain particles that are of frequent occurrence in Paul's genuine epistles (γάρ, οὖν, διότι, ἄρα, διό) are rarely used here or do not even occur at all in Colossians.

Answer: It should be freely admitted that some of these stylistic characteristics are found in Colossians in a somewhat greater degree than elsewhere in Paul's epistles. Yet, the difference is by no means striking, as the following will indicate:

Lengthy sentences are also found in other Pauline epistles. Thus, Rom. 1:1-7 has 93 words in the original; 2:5-10 has 87. Phil. 3:8-11 has 78.

Synonyms abound in Romans; see 1:18, 21, 25, 29, etc. Also in other epistles; for example, in Philippians: full knowledge and keen discretion (Phil. 1:9), pure and blameless (1:10), glory and praise (1:11), envy and rivalry (1:15), eager expectation and hope (1:20), and so one could easily continue.

Appositional clauses, particularly those descriptive of the deity, are often of a liturgical nature. They are frequently found in ancient hymns in praise of Jehovah, God, Christ, in brief confessions of faith, and in doxologies. Paul has many of them. So have the prophets. And they abound in the liturgies of the synagogue even to the present day. When believers — either individually or collectively — are filled with gratitude to God, they will give humble and enthusiastic expression to this feeling of thankfulness and adoration by describing in clause upon clause God's greatness, faithfulness, wisdom, and love. Does not Romans begin with such an outburst of joyful testimony (1:3-5)? Add the following as a few of the clearest examples: II Cor. 1:3, 4; I Tim. 3:16; and then going back to the Old Testament: Isa. 44:24-28; Ps. 103:2-5; 104:2-5; 136. Besides, Col. 1:15-20, with its appositional clauses, may be a hymn which Paul quotes. See on that passage.

And finally, as to these particles, the argument based upon them has very little if any value: ἄρα does not occur at all in Philippians; διό only once in Galatians; διότι only once in the entire lengthy first epistle of Paul to the

Corinthians, not at all in II Corinthians; hence only once in the entire twenty-nine chapters of Paul's Corinthian correspondence that has come down to us! Hence, not much of an argument for rejecting Colossians as a genuine epistle of Paul can be based on the fact that in the 4 chapters of that letter διότι is not found. And the relative infrequency of οὖν in Colossians as contrasted with its frequency in Romans and in I Corinthians is easy to explain. It arises from the fact that in these epistles of earlier date the apostle is arguing with those whom he addresses, whereas in Colossians he is warning against a heresy.

One of the most recent to deny the Pauline authorship of Colossians — and of all the epistles which tradition ascribes to Paul, with the exception of Galatians, Romans, I and II Corinthians — is Andrew Morton. He bases his "proof" on the use which Paul makes of the conjunction *kai,* meaning *and, also, even,* etc. By the aid of an electronic computer he was strengthened in his hunch that an author will show a consistent pattern in the use of this conjunction. Hence, granted that the Pauline authorship of Galatians, etc., is beyond dispute but that the *kai*-pattern in *Colossians* differs from that in *Galatians,* etc., this would prove that tradition is wrong in regarding Paul as the author of *Colossians.*

Now if Morton could show that every Greek author, no matter in what sense he employs *kai* (whether in the sense of *and, also, even* or in some adversative sense such as *and yet, nevertheless*), no matter what be the contents or nature of his composition (whether it be narrative, descriptive, didactic, hortatory, or doxological), no matter when, why, or to whom he writes, and no matter whom he employs as his secretary and how much latitude he allows his secretary in the use of *kai,* reveals a consistent pattern in his use of this conjunction, his argument would have some value. As it is, he is basing too much on too little. There is, accordingly, truth in the criticism of the William Toedtman: "So *kais* are the most unreliable *figures* to pour into a computer" (*Time,* March 29, 1963, p. 8).

When all the facts are examined, therefore, it is clear that nothing in the language or style of Colossians can be used as an argument against its authenticity.

(2) *The heresy here combated was that of second century gnosticism. Hence, first century Paul cannot have been its author.*

The use of such words as *fulness* (πλήρωμα, 1:19; 2:9), *mystery* (μυστήριον, 1:26, 27; 2:2; 4:3), *ages* (αἰῶνες, 1:26), *wisdom* (σοφία, 1:9, 28; 2:3, 23; 3:16; 4:5), and *knowledge* (γνῶσις, 2:3), as well as the conception of a whole series of angels (1:16; 2:10; 2:15) points to the heresy of Valentinus.

For detailed explanation of these terms see commentary proper.

Answer: It suffices to affirm that the second century Gnostics did not view Colossians as directed against their beliefs. In fact, they make extensive use of it. Also, the evidence which indicates that *incipient* forms of Gnosticism were already present in the first century is increasing.[19]

(3) *The "high Christology" found in Colossians is un-Pauline. It rather reminds one of the doctrine of the Logos in the Gospel according to John.*

Answer: It is certainly true that nowhere else in those epistles which the Church recognizes as having been written by Paul do we find the doctrine of Christ's pre-eminence and his relation to the Father, the universe, the angels, and the Church in such an expanded form as here in Colossians. But is it not altogether probable that this emphasis upon Christ's uniqueness, his supremacy over all, arose from the implied or expressed denial of the same on the part of the Colossian heretics? Surely, the Christology found here, though more detailed, is not any "higher" than that found in other epistles written by Paul, both earlier (Rom. 9:5, according to the correct reading; I Cor. 8:6; II Cor. 4:4), very shortly afterward (Phil. 2:6), and somewhat later (I Tim. 3:16; Titus 2:13).

Indeed, the arguments against the Pauline authorship of Colossians are rather superficial. Not only does the letter claim to have been written by Paul (1:1; 4:18) but the character of Paul, as revealed in his other letters, is also clearly expressed here:

First, Colossians bears close resemblance to Ephesians. He who wrote Ephesians also wrote Colossians. This argument, however, has little value for those who reject the Pauline authorship of Ephesians even more emphatically than they do that of Colossians. To avoid repetition and for the sake of good order the relation between Colossians and Ephesians is accordingly reserved for a Commentary on Ephesians, D.V.

Secondly, Colossians pictures the same kind of author as the one who addresses us from the pages of such almost universally recognized Pauline epistles as Romans, I and II Corinthians, and Galatians. Philippians, moreover, being like Colossians a Prison epistle, also has the identical hall-mark. Note the items of comparison in the table on pages 33, 34.

Therefore, if the Pauline authorship of *Philippians* be granted, as it certainly should be (see N.T.C. on Philippians, pp. 31-37), the conclusion that Paul also wrote *Colossians* would seem to be logical. Note, therefore, the close resemblance in mode of expression. In addition to the similarity already pointed out (see columns 1 and 3 in the table), I call attention *thirdly* to the following:

Verses 9-11 of *the first chapter* in both epistles (Colossians and Philip-

---

[19] See J. M. Bulman, "Valentinus and his School," in S.H.E.R.K. (20th century Extension), pp. 1146, 1147, and the literature there mentioned; also F. L. Cross (editor), *The Jung Codex: A Newly Discovered Gnostic Papyrus.* For a brief summary of second and third century Gnosticism see A. M. Renwick's article, "Gnosticism," in *Baker's Dictionary of Theology,* pp. 237, 238.

	1	2	3
		Romans, I and II Corinthians, Galatians	
	Colossians		Philippians
1. The author is deeply interested in those whom he addresses	1:3, 9; 2:1	Rom. 1:8, 9; I Cor. 3:1, 2; II Cor. 1:6, 23; Gal. 4:19, 26	1:3-11, 25, 26; 2:25-30
2. He loves to encourage and praise them	1:4-6; 2:5	Rom. 1:8; 15:14; 16:19; I Cor. 1:4-7; II Cor. 8:7; Gal. 4:14, 15; 5:7	4:1, 15-17
3. He traces every virtue of those whom he addresses to God, ascribing all the glory to him alone	1:5, 12, 29	Rom. 8:28-30; I Cor. 1:4; 12:4-11; II Cor. 1:3, 4; 2:14; Gal. 5:22-25	1:6; 3:9; 4:13
4. He writes touchingly about the supremacy of love	3:12-17	Rom. 12:9-21; I Cor. 13; II Cor. 5:14; 6:6; 11:11; 12:15; Gal. 5:6, 13, 14, 22	1:9, 16; 2:1, 2
5. He is filled with gratitude to God who laid hold on him and made him, though unworthy, a minister of the gospel	1:23, 25	I Cor. 15:9; II Cor. 11:16; 12:10; Gal. 1:15-17	3:4-14
6. He lists virtues and vices	3:5-9, 12-14	Rom. 1:29-32; I Cor. 5:9, 10; 6:9, 10; Gal. 5:22, 23	3:2, 19; 4:8

	1	2	3
		Romans, *I and II* *Corinthians,*	
	Colossians	*Galatians*	*Philippians*
7. He is never afraid to assert his authority	2:1-4:6	Rom. 12-16; I Cor. 5:13; 16:1; II Cor. 13:1-5	2:12-18; 4:1-9
8. When conditions are at all favorable he thanks God for those addressed and at times assures them of his constant prayer for them	1:3-12	Rom. 1:8-12; I Cor. 1:4-9; II Cor. 1:3-7	1:3-11
9. He warns earnestly against those who are seeking to lead others astray	ch. 2	Rom. 16:17, 18; I Cor. 1:10-17; 5:1; 6:1; ch. 11; II Cor. 13; Gal. 1:6-10, etc.	ch. 3
10. He loves "the gospel"	1:5-7, 23	Rom. 1:16, 17; 2:16 ("*my* gos-pel"); I Cor. 15:1 Gal. 1:6-9	1:5, 7, 12, 16, 27, etc.

pians) contains a summary of the prayer the apostle uttered for those addressed. Note that although the two prayers are by no means the same, there is a striking resemblance: the author prays that his friends may *grow or abound* in grace, may *bear fruit* abundantly, and may possess ever increasingly the true, experiential *knowledge* of God.

With respect to those who have been reconciled to Christ Col. 1:22 shows that it is God's purpose to present them to himself *without blemish (faultless)*. Phil. 2:15 indicates that this quality of being *without blemish,* not only by and by but even here and now, must be the aim of every believer. An important means to this end is *the word or message of God,* as is clear from Col. 1:25 and Phil. 1:14. *Perfection* is ever the goal (Col. 1:28; cf. Phil. 3:12). *Christ's Spirit* is the Energizer (Col. 1:8; and see verse 29; cf. Phil. 1:19, and see 3:21). As for himself, Paul is *supplying whatever is lacking* in the sufferings of Christ (Col. 1:24), as Epaphroditus *supplied what was lack-*

ing in the service which the Philippians had been rendering to Paul (Phil. 2:30) . Note the *sufferings* or *afflictions* of Christ of which Colossians speaks. Philippians, too, speaks about the desire of the apostle to know *the fellowship of his sufferings* (Phil. 3:10) . Of course, if the Colossians are going to be increasingly fruitful they must cling to the truth *as they learned* it from Epaphras (Col. 1:7) , just as the Philippians must continue in the truth *as they learned it* from Paul (Phil. 4:9) .

Turning now to *the second chapter* of Colossians we note that Paul is having a gigantic *conflict* for the Colossians, etc. (Col. 2:1) . In Philippians he also makes mention of a *conflict* in which they and he were jointly engaged (Phil. 1:30) . Paul's physical *absence* does not prevent his spiritual fellowship with the Colossians (Col. 2:5) and should not prevent the Philippians from remaining steadfast (Phil. 1:27) . There is a reference to a kind of *circumcision* that rises above the merely physical (Col. 2:11) . This reminds us immediately of Phil. 3:3. In the writings that have been traditionally ascribed to Paul it is only in these Prison epistles (Col. 2:18, 23; 3:12; Eph. 4:21; Phil. 2:3) that a word is used ($\tau\alpha\pi\epsilon\iota\nu o\varphi\rho o\sigma\acute{\upsilon}\nu\eta$) which, depending upon the context in any particular case, has been translated variously as *self-abasement, humility, lowliness.* Note also the frequent use of the verb *I make full, fill* or *fulfil* ($\pi\lambda\eta\rho\acute{o}\omega$). In the second chapter of Colossians it occurs in verse 10 (see also 1:9, 25; 4:17) . This reminds us of Phil. 1:11; 2:2; 4:18, 19. The number of times this verb is used in Colossians, Ephesians, and Philippians contrasts sharply with its far lower frequency in the other epistles (see also on Col. 1:19, including footnote 56) .

The *heavenward* direction in which, according to *Col. 3*:1, 2, the yearning of the heart should be turned is certainly in line with the *heavenward* call which according to Phil. 3:14 the believer has received. *The things that are upon the earth* (Col. 3:2) which should not absorb our interests are in line with *earthly things* on which the enemies of the cross of Christ set their minds (Phil. 3:19) . The *heart of compassion* demanded of us in Col. 3:12 is similar to the *tender mercy and compassion* mentioned in Phil. 2:1. The beautiful reference to *the peace of God* (Col. 3:15) recalls the similar comforting passage in Philippians (4:7) .

Finally, as to *Col. 4,* peculiar to the epistles of Paul's first Roman imprisonment (except for one occurrence in II Tim. 2:9) is the mention of *bonds* (4:18; cf. Phil. 1:7, 13, 14, 17; Philem. 10, 13) . And the terseness of the command, "And say to Archippus, Attend to the ministry which you have received in the Lord, that you fulfil it" (Col. 4:17) reminds us of the words, similarly crisp, "I entreat Euodia and I entreat Syntyche to be of the same mind in the Lord" (Phil. 4:2) .

The testimony of the early church is in harmony with the conclusion which has been derived from the epistle itself.

Thus Eusebius, having made a thorough investigation of the literature at his command, states: "But clearly evident and plain are the fourteen (letters) of Paul; yet it is not right to ignore that some dispute the (letter) to the Hebrews" (*Ecclesiastical History* III.iii.4,5). Obviously Eusebius, writing at the beginning of the fourth century, knew that the entire orthodox church accepted Colossians as having been written by Paul.

From Eusebius we can go back to Origen (fl. 210-250), who states in his work *Against Celsus,* "And in the writings of Paul . . . the following words may be read in the Epistle to the Colossians, Let no one arbitrarily rob y o u of y o u r prize," etc., quoting Col. 2:18, 19. Note that here *Paul* is specifically mentioned as the author of this letter. Origen, in his several works, quotes from every chapter of Colossians.[20]

From Origen we can go back still farther, to his teacher, Clement of Alexandria (fl. 190-200). In his work *Stromata* or *Miscellanies* he more than once either refers to or quotes from each chapter. To him the author of Colossians is "the apostle." Also in his *Paedagogos* or *Instructor* he quotes from Colossians again and again.

About the same time Tertullian (fl. 193-216) quotes the warning against "philosophy and vain deceit" (Col. 2:8) and ascribes this warning to "the apostle," the very person whom he calls "the same Paul" (*Prescription against Heretics* VII, and cf. VI). Again and again, moreover, he quotes from Colossians such passages as refer to the greatness of Christ. See especially his work *Against Marcion.*

Earlier by a few years, but still for a long time a contemporary of Clement of Alexandria and of Tertullian, was Irenaeus. That he regards Paul as the author of Colossians is clear from his words, "Paul has himself declared. . . . 'Only Luke is with me.' . . . And again he says in the Epistle to the Colossians, 'Luke, the beloved physician greets y o u'" (Col. 4:14, see *Against Heresies* III.xiv.1). Not a single chapter of Colossians remains unquoted or not referred to in the works of Irenaeus. Now when Irenaeus ascribes Colossians to Paul, this testimony should carry considerable weight. He had traveled widely, was intimately acquainted with almost the entire church of his day, and was living in a day and age in which the earliest apostolic traditions were still very much alive.

The Muratorian Fragment (about 180-200), a survey of New Testament books, definitely names Paul as the author of Colossians.

Shortly before this Theophilus of Antioch draws a distinction between the Logos internal and the Logos emitted, and he calls this Logos in his emitted state "the firstborn of all creation" (*To Autolycus* XXII), which strongly reminds one of Col. 1:15. This phrase also occurs in Justin Martyr's *Dialogue with Trypho* LXXXV. Justin Martyr wrote some time between 155

---

[20] For detailed references for Origen and also for earlier writers see the Indices of Texts in *Ante-Nicene Fathers.*

and 161.[21] The Epistle to the Colossians was also included in Marcion's Canon, in the Old Latin, and in the Old Syriac. The witness in favor of Paul's authorship is therefore overwhelming. Testimony, both internal and external, yields but one conclusion, namely, that it was Paul who wrote Colossians.

B. *Philemon*

Since the little letter to Philemon is closely linked with Colossians (Col. 4:10-17; cf. Philem, 2, 23, 24) the Pauline authorship of the latter is a strong argument in favor of identical authorship of the former. Moreover, not only does the writer call himself *Paul,* and this no less than three times (verses 1, 9 and 19), but the request which he presents, and which is the very theme and substance of the letter, is of such a definite and personal character that no good reason can be shown why a forger would have composed it. Moreover, the personality of Paul — combining such traits as deep interest in others, delight in mentioning their good qualities, the conviction that back of every human virtue is God as the Giver, emphasis on the spirit of kindness and pardon — marks this little gem of a letter as strikingly as it does Colossians.

It is not surprising, therefore, that Eusebius gave it a place in his list of acknowledged books (*Ecclesiastical History* III.xxv; cf. III.iii), and that he regarded it as one of the letters of Paul "true, genuine, and recognized." Origen, too, accepts it as a letter of Paul (*Hom. in Jer.* 19). Tertullian was well acquainted with it, and because of his testimony we know that even Marcion accepted it though that heretic rejected I and II Timothy and Titus (Tertullian, *Against Marcion* V.xxi). It is probable that Ignatius borrowed his play on the proper name Onesimus from Paul (cf. Philem. 10, 11, 20 with Ignatius, *To the Ephesians,* chapter 2). The letter is also found in the Muratorian Fragment and in the Old Latin and Old Syriac versions.

The fact that the external evidence for the letter to Philemon is not as extensive as it is for some of Paul's other epistles is easy to understand: the request for the kind reception of the fugitive slave is very brief and contains little material that could be used in doctrinal controversies. From the beginning, however, its acceptance has been almost universal. An attack against it in the fourth and fifth centuries — on the ground that it was unworthy of the mind of Paul and of no value for edification — was answered by Jerome (*Comm. on Philem. pref.*), Chrysostom (*Argum. on Philem.*), and others. A much later attack by F. C. Baur was in line with his rejection of the

---

[21] It is probable that there is an echo of Colossians in such very early writings as *The Epistle of Barnabas* and in Ignatius, *Epistle to the Ephesians,* but why look for merely probable references when so much clear proof has already been furnished?

authenticity of most of the epistles that are traditionally ascribed to Paul (see footnote 16 above), and resulted from the same philosophical bias. He called the little letter "the embryo of a Christian romance," and referred to the fact that whoever wrote it used a few words which the real Paul never uses. His arguments are so easily answered that they hardly deserve comment. One author not unjustly calls this attack on the Pauline authorship of Philemon "one of Baur's worst blunders." Everything in this letter so clearly points to Paul that today those who think otherwise are a very small minority.

Commentary

on

The Epistle to the Colossians

Outline of Colossians

Theme: *Christ, the Pre-eminent One, the Only and All-Sufficient Savior*

I. This Only and All-Sufficient Savior Is the Object of the Believers' Faith, chapters 1 and 2
  A. This Truth Expounded Positively, chapter 1
    1. Opening Salutation
    2. Fervent Thanksgiving and Prayer
    3. The Son's Pre-eminence
      a. In Creation
      b. In Redemption
    4. His Reconciling Love toward the Colossians, and Their Resulting Duty to Continue in the Faith
    5. The Apostle's Share in Proclaiming "the Mystery," namely, "Christ in y o u the hope of glory"
  B. This Truth Expounded Not only Positively but Now Both Positively and Negatively, chapter 2, the Latter over against "the Colossian Heresy" with Its:
    1. Delusive Philosophy
    2. Judaistic Ceremonialism
    3. Angel-worship
    4. Asceticism

II. This Only and All-Sufficient Savior Is the Source of the Believers' Life, and Thus the Real Answer to the Perils by Which They Are Confronted, chapters 3 and 4
  A. This Truth Applied to All Believers, 3:1-17
    1. Believers should be consistent. They should live in conformity with the fact that they were raised with Christ, who is their life
    2. Therefore, they should "put to death" and "lay aside" the old vices; and
    3. They should "put on" the new virtues
  B. This Truth Applied to Special Groups, 3:18-4:1
    1. Wives and their husbands
    2. Children and their fathers
    3. Servants and their masters
  C. Closing Admonitions, Greetings, etc., 4:2-18
    1. Prayer urged
    2. Wise conduct and gracious speech stressed

3. A good word for Tychicus and Onesimus, who have been sent with tidings and encouragement
4. Greetings
5. Exchange of letters requested
6. Crisp directive for Archippus
7. Closing salutation

Outline of Chapter 1

Theme: *Christ, the Pre-eminent One, the Only and All-Sufficient Savior*

I. This Only and All-Sufficient Savior Is the Object of the Believers' Faith, chapters 1 and 2

    A. This Truth Expounded Positively, chapter 1

1:1, 2   1. Opening Salutation

1:3-14   2. Fervent Thanksgiving and Prayer

1:15-20 3. The Son's Pre-eminence

        a. In Creation (verses 15-17)

        b. In Redemption (verses 18-20)

1:21-23 4. His Reconciling Love toward the Colossians, and Their Resulting Duty to Continue in the Faith

1:24-29 5. The Apostle's Share in Proclaiming "the Mystery," namely, "Christ in y o u the hope of glory"

CHAPTER I

COLOSSIANS

1 **1** Paul, an apostle of Christ Jesus through the will of God, and Timothy our brother, 2 to the saints and believing brothers in Christ at Colosse; grace to y o u and peace from God our Father.

1:1, 2

I. *Opening Salutation*

1. Though Paul is in the world and uses the world, he is not of the world. As a letter-writer he makes use of the literary devices of the world but in the process of adopting them he transforms them, raising them to a higher level. In Paul's day a man of the world would often begin a letter by jotting down: a. the name of the writer, b. the name of the person (or persons) addressed, c. the words of greeting. The apostle follows the same method, but he beautifies and sanctifies everything by immediately relating both *sender* and *persons addressed* to Christ ("an apostle *of Christ Jesus*," "brothers *in Christ*"), and by speaking about the work of Christ ("grace and peace") in the very opening salutation.

The apostle writes, **Paul, an apostle of Christ Jesus.** He presents himself as being, in the fullest sense of the term, an official representative of the Anointed Savior, the latter's spokesman. To Christ Jesus he owes his appointment and his authority. Through Paul no one less than Christ Jesus himself is addressing the church. It was from the risen and exalted Lord that Paul had received his difficult but glorious assignment to be *an apostle,* yes, *the* apostle to *the Gentiles,* not *exclusively* but *especially* to them (Acts 9:5, 6, 15, 16; 22:10-21; 26:15-18; Rom. 1:1, 5; Gal. 1:1; 2:9).

Paul continues, **through the will of God.** He had attained his high office neither through *aspiration* (see Acts 9:11), nor through *usurpation* — that was not like Paul! —, nor yet through *nomination* by other men (Gal. 1:1, 16, 17), but by divine *preparation* (Gal. 1:15, 16), having been set apart and qualified by the activity of God's sovereign will (I Cor. 1:1; II Cor. 1:1; Gal. 1:1; Eph. 1:1; II Tim. 1:1; cf. Rom. 15:32; II Cor. 8:5).

Paul adds, **and Timothy our brother** (cf. II Cor. 1:1; Phil. 1:1; I Thess. 1:1; II Thess. 1:1; Philem. 1:1). This is not surprising, since right now Timothy was evidently in Paul's vicinity and wished to extend greetings. Moreover Timothy had spent some time with Paul in Ephesus during the

43

third missionary journey (Acts 19:1, 22), and may thus have become acquainted with some of the people of Colosse who at that time presumably came to hear Paul (Acts 19:10). By calling Timothy "our brother," Paul, though *implying* that his younger associate was not in the full sense of the term an apostle, *was rather emphasizing* the closeness of the relationship between himself and his associate. The apostle loved Timothy deeply and tenderly (Phil. 2:19-23). Paul, Timothy, and the members of the Colossian church all belonged to the same spiritual family. It is, however, Paul, Paul *alone,* who is to be considered the real author of the letter (notice the words "I Paul," in Col. 1:23; cf. 1:24–2:5; 4:3, 7-18), not Paul and Timothy.

Paul continues, **to the saints and believing brothers in Christ at Colosse.** Saints are those who by the Lord have been *set apart* to glorify him. They are *the consecrated ones,* and here the Israel of the new dispensation, whose task it is to proclaim God's excellencies (I Peter 2:9). Saints, then, are persons upon whom the Lord has bestowed a great favor and who have been entrusted with a weighty responsibility. Ideally, saints are *believers.* So also nere: the phrase "to the saints and believing brothers" (note the fact that the definite article *the* is not repeated before the second noun) expresses *one* thought, for saints who are true to their calling are, of course, believing brothers, and that "in Christ," *by virtue of union with him.* The addition of the words "at Colosse" shows that this letter was meant primarily for that congregation, though in a secondary sense it was intended also for the church at nearby Laodicea (4:16), and in fact, for every church throughout the entire dispensation.

The salutation proper is as follows, **grace to y o u and peace from God our Father.** Thus, there is pronounced upon all the saints and believing brothers in Christ at Colosse *grace,* that is, God's spontaneous, unmerited favor in action, his sovereign, freely bestowed lovingkindness in operation, and its result, *peace,* that is, the assurance of reconciliation through the blood of the cross, true spiritual wholeness and prosperity, these two blessings (grace and peace) flowing down from "God our Father." Thus the Greek salutation, "greeting" (*chaírein,* cf. Acts 15:23) and the Hebrew, "peace" (*shālōm,* cf. Judg. 19:20) are here combined, deepened and enriched. The *grace* (*cháris*) is that referred to in Eph. 2:8, "For by grace have y o u been saved through faith, and that not of yourselves; it is the gift of God." The *peace* (*eirēnē*) is that great blessing which Christ as a result of his atoning death has bequeathed to us (John 14:27). It surpasses all understanding (Phil. 4:7). Note the brevity of this opening salutation. It is next to the shortest in all of Paul's epistles (I Thess. 1:1 contains the fewest words; Rom. 1:1-7 has the most). Here in Colossians the usual additional reference to the second Person of the Trinity: "and the Lord Jesus Christ" (as in Rom., I and II Cor., Gal., Eph., Phil., II Thess., and Philem.), "and Christ Jesus our Lord" (as in I and II Tim.), "and Christ Jesus our Savior" (as in Titus), is lacking in the best manuscripts. The reason for this is not known. One thing is certain: the apostle is not in any way detracting from the glory and majesty of Christ. He is not trying to exalt the Father at the expense of the Son, for this is the very epistle in which the deity of the second Person of the Trinity, his pre-eminence above all creatures including all the hosts of angels, and his all-sufficiency for salvation, are set forth in the clearest manner and emphasized most strongly. Is it possible that any mention of the Lord Jesus Christ is here purposely omitted in order by way of contrasting effect to single him out for special discussion in the immediately following verses? Note the specific mention of "our Lord Jesus Christ" in verse 3, and further references to him in verses 4, 7, and especially in the paragraph about the Son of God's love in verses 15-20.

For further details about certain aspects of Paul's opening salutations see N.T.C. on I and II Thessalonians, pp. 37-45; on Philippians, pp. 43-49; and on I and II Timothy and Titus, pp. 49-56; 339-344.

---

3 While praying for y o u we are always thanking God, the Father of our Lord Jesus Christ, 4 because we have heard of y o u r faith in Christ Jesus and of the love which y o u cherish for all the saints, 5 by reason of the hope laid up for y o u in the heavens, of which y o u have previously heard in the message of the truth, namely, the gospel, 6 which made its entrance felt among y o u, as indeed in the entire world it is bearing fruit and growing — so also among yourselves from the day y o u heard and came to acknowledge the grace of God in its genuine character, 7 as y o u learned it from Epaphras our beloved fellow-servant who is a faithful minister of Christ on our behalf, 8 and has made known to us y o u r love in the Spirit.

9 And for this reason, from the day we heard it we never stopped praying for y o u, asking that y o u may be filled with clear knowledge of his will (such clear knowledge consisting) in all spiritual wisdom and understanding, 10 so as to live lives worthy of the Lord, to (his) complete delight, in every good work bearing fruit, and growing in the clear knowledge of God; 11 being invigorated with all vigor, in accordance with his glorious might, so as to exercise every kind of endurance and longsuffering; 12 with joy giving thanks to the Father who qualified y o u for a share in the inheritance of the saints in the light 13 and who rescued us out of the domain of darkness and transplanted us into the kingdom of the Son of his love, 14 in whom we have our redemption, the forgiveness of our sins.

1:3-14

II. *Fervent Thanksgiving and Prayer*

1:3-8

A. *Thanksgiving*

3. While praying for y o u we are always thanking God. In letters of that day the opening greeting was frequently followed by thanksgiving. Thus an

45

ancient letter reads, "I thank the Lord Serapis that when I was in peril on the sea he saved me immediately." [22] This sequence — salutation followed by thanksgiving — is also Pauline.[23] However, Paul does not thank any pagan deity but the only true God. Paul's spontaneous thanksgiving, in which Timothy joins,[24] and which according to the apostle's explicit testimony, is *always* [25] an element in prayer for the Colossians, is offered to God **the Father of our Lord Jesus Christ** (cf. Rom. 15:6; II Cor. 1:3; 11:31; Eph. 1:3; 3:14). Our *Lord,* who has a right to that name because he purchased his people with his blood and is their Sovereign Master, and to whom, as the Anointed Savior, Paul gladly ascribes this honor, is in his very essence God's only Son. He is *Son by nature.* We are children *by adoption.* He has the right to call God *"my* Father" (Matt. 26:39, 42) and to make the majestic claim, "I and the Father, we are one" (John 10:30; cf. 14:9). Calling God "the Father of our Lord Jesus Christ" has a very practical purpose, as the apostle shows plainly in II Cor. 1:3. In his capacity as Father of our Lord Jesus Christ he is "the Father of mercies and God of all comfort." Via Christ every spiritual blessing flows down to us from the Father. And if Christ is "the Son of God's love," as Paul says in this very chapter (Col. 1:13), then God must be the Father of love, the loving Father. Note also that beautiful word of appropriating faith, namely, *our:* "the Father of *our* Lord Jesus Christ." Hence, in the sublimest and most comforting sense, he is *our* Father. What a reason for thanksgiving!

---

[22] A. Deissmann, *Light From the Ancient East* (translated from the German by L. R. M. Strachan, fourth edition, 1922, pp. 179, 180).

[23] Commentators are agreed that in nearly every one of his letters Paul's thanksgiving and/or doxology follows the salutation. On the details there is some confusion. According to some otherwise thoroughly conservative commentators, in *all* of Paul's letters "except Galatians" the opening salutation is followed by thanksgiving. Are these commentators unaware of the fact that, by implication, they are surrendering the Pauline authorship of Titus? This should not be done. See N.T.C. on I and II Timothy and Titus, pp. 4-33, 377-381 (footnote 193). According to others, however, the thanksgiving is omitted not only in Galatians and Titus but also in I Timothy. Now it is true, indeed, that in that letter the opening salutation is not *immediately* followed by thanksgiving or doxology. After an intervening paragraph (I Tim. 1:3-11) there is, however, also here a thanksgiving, beginning with verse 12. A correct summary of this matter, accordingly, would point out that in *all* of Paul's epistles, with the exception of Galatians and Titus, the opening salutation is followed, either immediately or very shortly, by a thanksgiving and/or doxology. For the doxology see II Cor. 1:3 ff.; for the doxology and thanksgiving, Eph. 1:3 ff., and 1:15 ff.

[24] Since both Paul and Timothy are mentioned in the immediately preceding context (verse 1) it is natural to interpret the "we" of verse 3 as a reference to them rather than as an epistolary plural. See N.T.C. on I and II Thessalonians, p. 82, footnote 65.

[25] Though it is grammatically possible (with A.V. and A.R.V.) to construe *always* with *praying,* it is better to join it with *thanking.* This is true in view of the immediately following context (verses 4-8) in which reasons for thanksgiving are given, and also in view of I Cor. 1:4; Eph. 1:16; Phil. 1:3; I Thess. 1:2; II Thess. 1:3; and Philem. 3.

4, 5a. Paul says, "While praying for y o u we are always thanking God, the Father of our Lord Jesus Christ" **because we have heard of y o u r faith in Christ Jesus and of the love which y o u cherish for all the saints.** The simplest construction of verses 4-8 is surely that which regards this section in its entirety as setting forth reasons for *thanksgiving.* The actual *petition* starts in verse 9. Both thanksgiving and petition belong to the essence of *prayer* (Phil. 4:6). Now the *early* mention of reasons for thanksgiving to God with respect to certain basic conditions in Colosse is also excellent Christian psychology. There were dangers threatening the church. Certain weaknesses, moreover, are clearly implied (3:5-11; cf. 2:4, 8, etc.). But before Paul even begins to refer to these things he first of all assures those to whom this letter is sent that he is convinced that the work of God's grace is evident in their lives. What a lesson for every parent, counselor, teacher, and pastor, especially in cases where warning or even rebuke would appear to be in order! There is such a thing as Christian tact (see appendix). And *this* tact is in complete harmony with honesty.

Paul mentions the fact that he and Timothy *have heard* (see on verse 8) of *the faith* of the Colossians in Christ Jesus, that is, of their abiding trust in and personal surrender to the Anointed Savior.[26] With *faith* in Christ Jesus he associates *love* for all the saints. These two always go together, for faith is ever operating through love (Gal. 5:6). The same Magnet, Christ Jesus,[27] who attracts sinners to himself and changes them into saints simultaneously draws them into closer fellowship with each other. Thus, ideally speaking, every believer enshrines his fellow-believers — wherever they may dwell and of whatever race they may be — in his heart (John 13:34; Phil. 1:7, 8; I John 4:7-11). Paul continues, **by reason of the hope laid up for y o u in the heavens.** Thus, to faith and love he now adds hope, completing the familiar triad.[28] In the New Testament this triad is not confined to Paul's writings. It also occurs frequently in the sub-apostolic literature. It is entirely possible that Paul did not invent it. It may have belonged to the common stock of earliest Christianity. In fact, these very graces stand out in the teaching and ministry of Jesus. Again and again the Lord while on earth stressed the importance of *faith* (Matt. 6:30; 8:10, 26; 9:2, 22, 29; 14:31; 15:28; 16:8; 17:20; 21:21; 23:23, etc.). His very presence, words of cheer, bright and beautiful promises, and deeds of redemption inspired *hope,* even when he did not use

---

[26] Some are of the opinion that since the preposition ἐν is used, not εἰς, Christ cannot be regarded as the object of faith, but must be viewed as the sphere in which faith is exercised. This interpretation disregards flexibility of use with respect to the verb πιστεύω and its prepositions and cases. See Gram. N.T. Bl.-Debr. sections 187 (6), 206 (2), 233 (2), 235 (2), 397 (2).

[27] The question, "Why *Christ Jesus* instead of *Jesus Christ?*" has been discussed in N.T.C. on I and II Timothy and Titus, p. 51, footnote 19.

[28] See A. M. Hunter, "Faith, Hope, Love — A Primitive Christian Triad," *ET* xlix (1937-1938), p. 428 f.

the very word (Matt. 9:2; 14:27; Mark 5:36; 6:50; 9:23; John 11:11, 23, 40; I Peter 1:3, etc.). He placed great emphasis on *love* and certainly regarded it as the very essence of both law and gospel, the greatest of the triad (Matt. 5:43-46; 19:19; John 13:34, 35; 14:15, 23; 15:12, 13, 17; 17:26; 21:15, 16, 17, etc.). Often, in a most natural manner, he combined these three. A striking instance of this is found in John 11:

1. *Love*

"Now Jesus loved [or: was holding in loving esteem] Martha and her sister, and Lazarus" (verse 5).

"So the Jews were saying, See how he (constantly) loved him" (verse 36).

2. *Hope*

"This illness is not unto death . . ." (verse 4).

"Our friend Lazarus has fallen asleep, but I go in order to wake him up" (verse 11).

"I am the resurrection and the life; he who believes in me, though he die, yet shall he live, and everyone who lives and believes in me shall never, never die" (verses 25, 26a).

Though none of these sayings contain the word *hope,* they are all hope-inspiring.

3. *Faith*

"Do you believe this?" (verse 26b). (Note how closely hope and faith are related.)

"Did I not say to you that if you would believe you would see the glory of God?" (verse 40).

Another striking instance of the combination love, faith, and hope is found in Christ's Upper Room Discourse during the night in which he washed the feet of his disciples, instituted the Lord's Supper and was betrayed. "Having *loved* his own in the world, he loved them to the uttermost" (John 13:1). By washing the feet of his disciples and issuing the new commandment ("that y o u keep on *loving* one another") he underscored the importance of love (13:34). Immediately afterward he exhorted his disciples to have abiding *faith* in God and in himself: "Let not y o u r hearts any longer be troubled. Continue *to trust* in God, also in me continue *to trust*" (14:1). And hard upon this he inspired them with *hope* by assuring them, "In my Father's house there are many dwelling-places. If it were not so, I would have told y o u; for I go to prepare a place for y o u. And when I go and prepare a place for y o u, I come again and will take y o u to be face to face with me, in order that where I am y o u may be also" (14:2, 3).

Hence, it is not surprising to find this triad in the inspired writings of those who had caught the spirit of Christ's example and teachings. It is found in several variations of sequence, though the three members of the triad do not always occur in immediate succession:

a. faith, hope, and love (Rom. 5:1-5; I Cor. 13:13 [the best-known of all the passages in which the triad occurs]; Heb. 10:22-24; I Peter 1:21, 22).

b. faith, love, and hope (Col. 1:4, 5; I Thess. 1:3; 5:8).

c. hope, faith, and love (I Peter 1:3-8).

d. love, hope, and faith (Eph. 4:2-5; Heb. 6:10-12).

Some have experienced difficulty, however, with the fact that Paul here in Col. 1:4, 5, in which he follows sequence b., seems to be saying that the *faith* of the Colossians and their *love* are based on *hope.* Note the words, "by reason of the hope." How can hope ever be the reason for faith and love? Many interpreters, apparently despairing of finding any other way out of this difficulty, resort to the device of reconstructing the sentence or at least the ideas expressed in it, so as to get rid of the idea that faith and love could be based on hope.[29] However, such a virtual re-wording of the sentence is not at all necessary. Christian mental and moral attitudes and activities such as believing, hoping, and loving, always react upon each other. In general, the more there is of the one the more there will be of the other. This holds too with respect to hope. It reacts mightily and beneficially on faith and love.[30] Christian hope is not mere wishing. It is a fervent yearning, confident expectation, and patient waiting for the fulfilment of God's promises, a full *Christ-centered* (cf. Col. 1:27) assurance that these promises will indeed be realized. It is a living and sanctifying force (I Peter 1:3; I John 3:3). How

---

[29] Some read verses 3-5 as if these meant: "While praying for y o u we are always thanking God . . . because we have heard of y o u r *faith* in Christ Jesus and of the *love* which y o u cherish for all the saints, and because (we have also heard) of y o u r *hope.*" Others translate: "We give thanks to God . . . (praying always for y o u, having heard of y o u r faith . . . and of y o u r love . . .) because of the hope." Thus hope, and it *alone,* is viewed as reason for thanksgiving. Lenski is right when he states: "But this construction yields a strange resultant thought, namely that after hearing of *the faith and love* of the Colossians Paul and Timothy are thanking God, *not* for this faith and love as we should expect but only for *the hope* laid away for the Colossians. . . . No ordinary reader would refer the διά- phrase back so far in order to get such a thought and then pass on." In one form or another this construction which connects *hope* with the apostle's thanksgiving, and avoids the difficulty of making it the reason for faith and love, is advocated by G. G. Findlay ("A Biblical Note," *Exp,* first series, 10 [1879], pp. 74-80), Athanasius, Calovius, Conybeare, Eadie, Hofmann, Michaelis, Storr, etc. Opposed to them are Bruce, Calvin, De Wette, Ellicott, Erasmus, Lenski, Lightfoot, C. F. D. Moule, Ridderbos, Robertson, etc. Commentators of this latter group believe that it makes good sense to say that faith and love are based on hope. With this judgment I am in agreement, and this also for the grammatical reason that the words "by reason of the hope" are in the original joined more closely with "faith . . . and love" than with "always thanking God."

[30] The interaction of the elements in Christian experience has been discussed in N.T.C. on John 7:17, 18.

then should not the hope of glory, a glory of which we have already received the first instalment (II Cor. 1:22; 5:5; Eph. 1:14), strengthen our *faith* in the One who merited all these blessings for us, namely, the Lord Jesus Christ? And how should it not enhance our *love* for those with whom we are going to share this bliss everlastingly? How should it not intensify our sense of oneness with the saints of all the ages? And if this be true even with respect to hope as an attitude and activity of heart and mind, it is surely not less true with respect to hope as an objective reality, namely, *the thing hoped for,* which is the sense in which the word is used here in Col. 1:5a, as also in Gal. 5:5 and Titus 2:13 (to which some interpreters would add Heb. 6:18). As the very context indicates, this hope is "the inheritance of the saints in the light" (Col. 1:12). Therefore we read here that it is "laid up for y o u in the heavens," an expression which immediately reminds one of the heavenly treasure of which Jesus speaks in Matt. 5:20, and of the "inheritance imperishable, undefiled, and unfading reserved in heaven for y o u" of which Peter speaks (I Peter 1:4). It is the glory which shall be revealed to us (Rom. 8:18), the peace and joy that pertains to "our homeland in heaven" (Phil. 3:20; cf. John 14:1-4). This realization of our *hope,* this glory, is so entrancing that as we see it from afar we greet it (Heb. 11:13), with our *faith* in the Giver strengthened, and our *love* for all his children with whom we shall share it enlarged and intensified.

5b-8. Now with respect to this hope Paul continues, **of which y o u have previously heard in the message of the truth, namely, the gospel.** Since the apostle himself explains this statement in verse 7, little comment is needed here. The *main idea* is still thanksgiving for the blessings bestowed upon the Colossians. Note, however, that though this is Paul's chief thought, there is here a certain implication. A warning can easily be read between the lines, to this effect, "O Colossians, I gratefully testify that with respect to this glorious hope y o u have heard a message that was true, uplifting, and fruitbearing (5b, 6). Hence, do not allow yourselves to be led astray by teachers of false doctrine. Cling to the truth that was proclaimed to y o u in the gospel." On the meaning of *gospel* see N.T.C. on Philippians, pp. 81-85. This is the gospel **which made its entrance felt among y o u,**[31] **as indeed in the entire world it is bearing fruit and growing.** The Colossians are being reminded of the power (cf. Rom. 1:16) and successful course of the gospel, as a reason for gratitude. Here, too, there is the implication, "Don't y o u remember the mighty change that occurred when the message of God's redemptive truth made its first appearance among y o u? That gospel needs no addition or supplement. Its influence is being felt in ever-increasing measure, both extensively, invading region after region, and intensively, pro-

---

[31] Thus rather than simply, "which came to y o u." See Oepke, art. παρουσία, πάρειμι, Th.W.N.T., p. 863 ff.

ducing fruit upon fruit in hearts won for Christ. Do not attempt to exchange God's powerful work for man's beggarly elements" (cf. 2:8).

The rapid progress of the gospel in the early days has ever been the amazement of the historian. Justin Martyr, about the middle of the second century, wrote, "There is no people, Greek or barbarian, or of any other race, by whatever appellation or manners they may be distinguished, however ignorant of arts or agriculture, whether they dwell in tents or wander about in covered wagons, among whom prayers and thanksgivings are not offered in the name of the crucified Jesus to the Father and Creator of all things." Half a century later Tertullian adds, "We are but of yesterday, and yet we already fill y o u r cities, islands, camps, y o u r palace, senate, and forum. We have left y o u only your temples." R. H. Glover (*The Progress of World-Wide Missions*, p. 39) states, "On the basis of all the data available it has been estimated that by the close of the Apostolic Period the total number of Christian disciples had reached half a million."

Now, under God, no human individual was a more effective agent in proclaiming the glorious tidings of salvation than was Paul himself. Rescued by Christ, the very One whom he had formerly bitterly opposed, his heart was filled with love and holy zeal for the truth. He gave his very life for it. He reasoned with Jew and Gentile, pleaded with them (cf. II Cor. 5:20, 21), performed miracles among them, visited them in their homes, wept over them. In short, he loved them. When *present* among them, his example — working with his hands to earn a living, admonishing and encouraging them, dealing with them like a father with his children — made a deep impression. He was always pointing away from self to Christ. When *absent* from them, they were on his mind and he would send them messages, vibrant and throbbing, from the heart to the heart. Circumstances permitting, he would revisit them or would send a delegate to help them solve their problems. In his prayers he carried their burdens to the throne of grace. It causes no surprise that from far and near people came to see and hear him. And those who heard told others, and these still others, etc. The following passages serve to explain how, through the ministry of Paul and of those who gave heed to his preaching, the gospel was bearing fruit and growing:

"All those of (the Roman province of) Asia heard the word of the Lord, both Jews and Greeks" (Acts 19:10).

"The word of the Lord grew and increased mightily" (Acts 19:20).

"From y o u (Thessalonians) the word of the Lord has echoed forth, not only in Macedonia and Achaia, but in every place y o u r faith in God has gone forth, so that it is not necessary for us to say anything, for they themselves are reporting about us what kind of entering in we had among y o u, and how y o u turned to God from those idols of y o u r s, to serve God, the living and real One" (I Thess. 1:8, 9).

"Now I want y o u to know, brothers, that the things that have happened to me have in reality turned out to the advantage of the gospel; so that it has become clear throughout the whole praetorian guard and to all the rest that my bonds are for Christ" (Phil. 1:12, 13).[32]

But though Paul took this leading part in the spread of the gospel, he himself, here in Col. 1:6, is placing all the emphasis upon the fact that by God's power and grace it is *the gospel itself* that is thus bearing fruit and growing. He is saying, as it were, "Do not underestimate the vitality of the seed that is scattered upon the ground (see Mark 4:26-29; cf. Isa. 55:11). That seed is germinating, growing, and bearing fruit." The gospel never *depends* on man, not even on Paul. It is *God's* work in which he is pleased to use man.

What has been said implies also *intensive or inner* growth and fruitbearing, gospel-influence on the lives of the people who heard it and gave heed to it. Think of such fruits as faith, love, and hope (verses 4 and 5), with re-emphasis on love (verse 8). And add to this the several fruits mentioned with such striking beauty in verses 9-12 (cf. Gal. 5:22, 23). Fruits for eternity were in evidence everywhere. And this *everywhere* most definitely also included the Lycus Valley, with re-emphasis now on the church at Colosse. That the gospel was not fruitless there had already been stated in verses 4 and 5 and by implication reaffirmed at the very beginning of verse 6 ("which made its entrance felt among y o u"). To this specific instance of fruitbearing the apostle now returns by continuing, **so also among yourselves from the day y o u heard and came to acknowledge the grace of God in its genuine character.** The *main* note is still thanksgiving. The inference is, "So, Colossians, do not destroy this fruit-bearing tree. Do not listen to those who are trying to deprive y o u of the great blessing that has come to y o u." Not only had they come *to know* the truth, they had come *to acknowledge* it, and this from the very day they had first heard it. Such acknowledgment is more than abstract, intellectual knowledge. It is a joyful acceptance and appropriation of the truth centered in Christ. This truth concerns nothing less than the grace of God, his sovereign love in action, his favor toward the undeserving. They had come to acknowledge this grace of God "in its genuine character," unattenuated by philosophical vagaries or Judaistic admixtures.[33]

With reference to this true gospel of grace which as everywhere so also among the Colossians had been bearing fruit increasingly since the day they had heard and accepted it Paul continues, **as y o u learned it from Epaphras**

---

[32] For a summary of Paul's Mission Strategy see the author's *Bible Survey*, pp. 199-207.

[33] Though something can be said for the rendering, "came to acknowledge truly," it would seem to be best to connect the words ἐν ἀληθείᾳ directly with the immediately preceding τὴν χάριν τοῦ θεοῦ. I favor this construction for two reasons: a. the mention of "the message (or *the word*) of *the truth*" in verse 5; and b. the purpose of the letter, namely, to place *the truth* as to Christ's pre-eminence and all-sufficiency over against the lie that was being propagated by the false teachers.

our beloved fellow-servant, who is a faithful minister of Christ on our [34] behald. On Epaphras, the "minister" of the church at Colosse, etc., who had come to see Paul in Rome, among other things in order to report to the apostle about conditions in that church and to secure his help in the battle against worldliness and heresy, see *Introduction* III A and IV A. By calling him "our beloved fellow-servant" and "faithful minister of Christ on our behalf" Paul is doing three things: a. he is placing the stamp of his approval on Epaphras and the gospel the latter had taught the Colossians; b. he is by implication condemning any system of thought that is in conflict with this one and only true gospel; and c. he is saying, "Those who reject the gospel according to the teaching of our beloved Epaphras are also rejecting us (Paul and Timothy) and our teaching . . . and remember, we, in turn, represent Christ (see on verse 1) just as also Epaphras is Christ's *faithful minister.*" Of course, the *main idea* is *gratitude to God* for the fact that from the mouth of this faithful servant Epaphras the Colossians have heard and have accepted that glorious gospel which is bearing fruit among them. The words of verse 3, "While praying for y o u, we are always thanking God," control everything that follows in verses 4-8. With reference to Epaphras the apostle continues, **and has made known to us y o u r love in the Spirit.** This statement takes up the thought expressed earlier (see verse 4b). That Paul and the other apostles regarded love as the most precious fruit of God's grace is evident not only from I Cor. 13:13 ("and the greatest of these is love") but also from such passages as:

Col. 3:14   I John 4:8
I John 3:14   .   I Peter 4:8

And was not this the very emphasis of Christ himself? See John 13:1, 34, 35; 15:12; cf. Mark 12:28-31. Probably in order to prevent the impression from taking root that Epaphras had painted too somber a picture of conditions among the Colossian believers the apostle stresses the fact that his worthy fellow-worker had given him an enthusiastic account of their *love.* This is the love "for all the saints," of which Paul had just spoken. It can never be divorced from the love of which God himself is the object. It indicates that intelligent and purposeful delight in the triune God, that spontaneous and grateful outgoing of the entire personality to him who has re-

---

[34] With A.R.V., R.S.V., Bruce, C. F. D. Moule, Ridderbos, Robertson, etc., I accept the reading ἡμῶν instead of ὑμῶν. It is true that either reading would make sense. Yet, the phrase "minister . . . on *our* behalf" would seem to harmonize most exactly with the words "*our* fellow-servant." Epaphras, who probably owed his conversion to Paul, had been the apostle's representative to the churches at Colosse, Laodicea, and Hierapolis (cf. 4:13). Another reason for adopting this reading is the fact that it has stronger textual support, "well-distributed and early witnesses" (thus C. F. D. Moule), which cannot be said in the same degree with reference to the alternative reading.

vealed himself in Jesus Christ, which issues in deep and steadfast yearning for the true prosperity of all his children. With respect to the latter aspect of this love — on which according to the present context the emphasis falls — it makes itself manifest in the three graces of oneness, lowliness, and helpfulness (Phil. 2:2-4) ; hence, in kindness, true sympathy, and the forgiving spirit (Col. 3:12-14) . Note the modifier, "y o u r love *in the Spirit.*" Although there are those who maintain that this simply means "spiritual love" without any reference to the Holy Spirit, this opinion runs counter to the fact that in such passages as Rom. 15:30; Gal. 5:22; and Eph. 3:16, 17 Christian love is decidedly regarded as the fruit of the indwelling Spirit. It is implanted and fostered by him. Also, it is rather characteristic of Paul that, having made mention of God the Father (verses 2 and 3) and of Christ Jesus the Son (verses 3, 4, 7) , he should now refer to the third person of the Trinity, namely, the Spirit. Cf. Rom. 8:15-17; II Cor. 13:14; Eph. 1:3-14; 2:18; 3:14-17; 4:4-6; 5:18-21.[35]

1:9-14

B. *Prayer*

9. Paul's 218-word sentence starts here at verse 9 and reaches through verse 20. Beginning at verse 15, however, and continuing through verse 20, Christ's Pre-eminence is set forth. Hence, 1:9-14 can be considered a unit of thought all by itself, a touching description of the prayer of Paul and his associates for the Colossians. In the original this part of the sentence — six verses in all — has 106 words.[36] It begins as follows: **And for this reason, that**

---

[35] The phrase ἐν πνεύματι, though not always referring to the Holy Spirit, frequently does so (Rom. 8:9; cf. 8:16; Eph. 2:22; 5:18; 6:18; cf. Jude 20; I Tim. 3:16; see N.T.C. on I and II Timothy and Titus, p. 140) . For the reasons given I cannot agree with Lenski's comments on pp. 31 and 32 of his *Interpretation of Colossians, Thessalonians, Timothy, Titus, Philemon.*

[36] The apostle has been accused of "rambling" or of uttering thoughts that reveal no definite sequence. It is true that ideas crowd his mind in such a manner that logical order is not always *immediately* apparent. Accordingly, interpreters are by no means agreed on the grammatical construction of verses 9-14. Some are of the opinion that the apostle is following a zig-zag course, starting out with thanksgiving in verse 3, changing to earnest petition in verse 9, but turning back to the giving of thanks in verse 12. Now even were this true it would be entirely unobjectionable. How often does not this happen to any believer? I am of the opinion, however, that this view of what the apostle is writing is erroneous. In verse 12 it is not Paul who is giving thanks but the Colossians who will be giving thanks if they "walk worthily of the Lord" (verse 10) . Grammatically I view the construction of verses 9-14 as follows:

Verse 9

The conjunction καί does not mean, "Not only other people but also we," nor, "Not only are y o u praying for us but also we for y o u." But rather, "We are not only *thanking* God (as in verses 3-8) but we are *also* praying for y o u."

The participles προσευχόμενοι and αἰτούμενοι (though the former indirectly) have

is, not only because of the love mentioned in the immediately preceding verse but on the basis of *all* the evidences of God's grace in the lives of the Colossians as described in verses 3-8, **from the day we heard it we never stopped praying for y o u.** Paul means that he and those associated with him (Timothy, see verse 1; Epaphras and others mentioned in 4:10-14) started to pray now "as they had never prayed before"; that is, granted that there had been prayer for this church before, the news which had reached the apostle upon the recent arrival of Epaphras had brought about a remarkable upsurge in prayer, in fervent intercession, and this with great regularity ("never stopped praying"). It reminds us of the upsurge in Paul's preaching at Corinth after the arrival of Silas and Timothy (Acts 18:5).[37]

The apostle was a firm believer in "the fellowship of prayer": a. he (and those associated with him) praying for those addressed, and b. the latter in turn being requested to pray for him. For a. see Column 1; for b. Column 2. Note that in each of the following instances *the assurance* that Paul prays for those addressed and *the request* (expressed or implied) that they pray for him occurs *in the same letter.*

---

as their object-clause (non-final) $\tilde{\iota}\nu\alpha$ $\pi\lambda\eta\rho\omega\theta\tilde{\eta}\tau\epsilon$ κ.τ.λ. What Paul was asking for was that the Colossians might be filled with clear knowledge of God's will.

Verse 10a

The infinitive $\pi\epsilon\rho\iota\pi\alpha\tau\tilde{\eta}\sigma\alpha\iota$ introduces a "contemplated result" statement: "so as to live lives worthy of the Lord," or more literally, "to walk worthily of the Lord" as A.R.V. has it.

Verses 10b-12a

The four participles $\kappa\alpha\rho\pi\omega\phi\rho\rho\tilde{\upsilon}\nu\tau\epsilon\varsigma$, $\alpha\dot{\upsilon}\xi\alpha\nu\dot{\omega}\mu\epsilon\nu\omega\iota$, $\delta\upsilon\nu\alpha\mu\omega\dot{\upsilon}\mu\epsilon\nu\omega\iota$, $\epsilon\dot{\upsilon}\chi\alpha\rho\iota\sigma\tau\omega\tilde{\upsilon}\nu\tau\epsilon\varsigma$, describe what happens when people live lives worthy of the Lord, so that the Colossians (and in fact all believers everywhere then and now) may know whether they are living such lives and how they may attain to greater perfection in reaching this goal. These participles may therefore be considered *supplementary* to $\pi\epsilon\rho\iota\pi\alpha\tau\tilde{\eta}\sigma\alpha\iota$ and in that sense *in apposition* with the meaning of the infinitive.

Verses 12b, 13

Mention of the Father in verse 12a leads to the participial modifier $\tau\tilde{\omega}$ $\iota\kappa\alpha\nu\dot{\omega}\sigma\alpha\nu\tau\iota$ κ.τ.λ., and to the relative-clause modifier $\dot{\omega}\varsigma$ $\dot{\epsilon}\rho\rho\dot{\upsilon}\sigma\alpha\tau\omega$ κ.τ.λ. of verse 13. These are not merely *descriptive* but also *causal,* supplying reasons for thanksgiving.

Verse 14

Mention of "the Son of his love" in verse 13 gives rise to the relative modifier $\dot{\epsilon}\nu$ $\tilde{\omega}$ $\dot{\epsilon}\chi\omega\mu\epsilon\nu$ κ.τ.λ., setting forth *in summary* the redemptive significance of Christ, a fact on which the apostle is going to expatiate.

Conclusion: there surely is no rambling here. The thoughts follow each other in excellent sequence.

[37] Sometimes more meaning is poured into these simple words than would seem to be warranted. Paul's statement is used in order to strengthen the view that he had never been in Colosse, that he knew nobody there, that the church had just now been founded, etc. See what has been said about this in the *Introduction*, II. The City of Colosse, A. Geography; and see also on 2:1.

1.	2.
Rom. 1:9	15:30
Eph. 1:16	6:18, 19
Phil. 1:4	3:17a; 4:9 (implied)
Col. 1:9	4:3
I Thess. 1:2	5:25
II Thess. 1:11	3:1
Philem. 4	22

On the basis of blessings already received the apostle asks for additional favors. Encouraged by evidences of God's grace already present he requests increasing proofs. That is the meaning of "And for this reason," etc. The Lord does not want his people to ask for too little. In the *spiritual* sphere he does not want them to live frugally, parsimoniously. Let them live richly and royally, in harmony with Psalm 81:1!

Now the prayer which is reported here in verses 9b-14 should be compared with Paul's prayers found in the other epistles of his first Roman imprisonment (Eph. 1:17-23; 3:14-21; Phil. 1:9-11). Combining them we notice that the apostle prays that those addressed may abound in such matters as wisdom, knowledge, power, endurance, long-suffering, joy, gratitude, and love. Also, that Jesus Christ (here "the Son of his love") is regarded as the One through whom these graces are bestowed upon the believer, and that the glory of God (here "the giving of thanks to the Father") is recognized as the ultimate purpose. Truly, one cannot afford to ignore Paul's lessons in prayer-life.

Paul had just used the word *praying*. He now adds **asking**. Praying is the more general and comprehensive term. It indicates any form of reverent address directed to the Deity, whether we "take hold of God" by means of intercession, supplication, adoration, or thanksgiving. *Asking* is more specific. It refers to making definite, humble requests. See also Phil. 4:6; I Tim. 2:1 on various synonyms for prayer. The sentence continues, **that y o u may be filled with** [38] **clear knowledge of his will (such clear knowledge consisting) in all spiritual wisdom and understanding**. It is vain to try to serve God without *knowing* what he desires of us (Acts 22:10, 14; Rom. 12:2). Now the knowledge here referred to is no abstract, theoretical learning. Such merely theoretical knowledge might be possessed by any nominal Christian, and in fact to a certain extent by a professed unbeliever and even by Satan himself. Neither does Paul have in mind a store of occult information, such

---

[38] "Filled with" is correct, even though the verb $\pi\lambda\eta\rho\acute{o}\omega$ is here used with the accusative, as in Phil. 1:11 (cf. II Thess. 1:11). Elsewhere the apostle uses it with the dative (Rom. 1:29; II Cor. 7:4) or with the genitive (Rom. 15:13, 14). This simply shows that there is no fixed rule with respect to the case that follows this verb. The tendency, moreover, was toward the accusative.

as acquaintance with passwords. It is not the kind of mysterious *gnosis* which teachers of the *gnostic* type claimed for their "initiates." On the contrary, it is penetrating insight into God's wonderful, redemptive revelation in Jesus Christ, a discernment with fruits for practical life, as the immediately following context (verse 10) also indicates. It results from fellowship with God and leads to deeper fellowship. Hence, this *clear knowledge* (ἐπίγνωσις) is heart-transforming and life-renewing. All the instances of the use of this word in the New Testament point in this definite direction: Rom. 1:28; 10:2; Eph. 1:17; 4:13; Phil. 1:9, 10; Col. 1:9, 10; 2:3; 3:10; I Tim. 2:4; II Tim. 2:25; 3:7; Titus 1:1; Philem. 6; Heb. 10:26; II Peter 1:2, 3, 8; II Peter 2:20; and cf. the cognate verb in I Cor. 13:12. Compare also the Old Testament background: "The fear of Jehovah is the beginning of knowledge" (Prov. 1:7; cf. 9:10; also Ps. 25:12, 14; 111:10). Paul prays that those addressed may *be filled* with such rich, deep experiential knowledge of God's will. No doubt we have here an intentional allusion to the gnostic error with which false teachers were striving to lead the Colossians astray. It is as if Paul were saying: "The *clear knowledge* of God's will which is our basic petition for y o u is incomparably richer and more satisfying than the *knowledge* or *gnosis* that is held out to y o u by the advocates of heresy." The penetrating knowledge which is part of the Christian's spiritual equipment consists in "all spiritual wisdom and understanding." Such *wisdom* is the ability to use the best means in order to reach the highest goal, a life to God's glory. It amounts to *understanding* that is at once spiritual and practical. It is not deceived by the wiles of Satan, the lure of the flesh, or the pretentious claims of false teachers. Such *wisdom and understanding* — for the combination of these two words see Ex. 31:3; 35:31, 35; Isa. 10:13; 11:2; etc. — is the work of the Holy Spirit in human hearts. On the characteristics of true wisdom see also the beautiful passage, James 3:17.

10-12. The practical purpose or contemplated result of this clear knowledge which is the starting-point in Paul's prayer for the Colossians is now stated: **so as to live lives worthy of the Lord** (cf. Eph. 4:1; Phil. 1:27; I Thess. 2:12; III John 6). The apostle and those who are with him pray that the Colossians may "walk" (cf. Gen. 5:22, 24; 6:9, etc.) or conduct themselves in harmony with the responsibilities which their new relationship to God imposes and with the blessings which this new relationship brings. There must be nothing half-hearted about this manner of life. On the contrary, it must be **to (his) complete delight** (see further on 3:22), a conscious striving to please God in everything (cf. I Cor. 10:31; I Thess. 4:1). That this God-glorifying conduct will actually be the result of being filled with *clear knowledge* of his will is easy to see, for the more God's children know him, the more they will also love him; and the more they love him, the more they will also wish to obey him in thought, word, and deed.

By means of four participles the apostle now describes this life of sanctification:

(1) **in every good work bearing fruit.**

Paul attaches high value to good works viewed as the fruit — not the root — of grace. Eph. 2:8-10 is his own commentary.

(2) **and growing in the clear knowledge of God.**[39]

Note that the apostle makes the clear knowledge of God both the starting-point (verse 9) and the resulting characteristic (verse 10) of the God-pleasing life. This is not strange: true, experiential knowledge of God brings about an ever-increasing measure of this very commodity. Thus, though at the very beginning of the story Job already knew God, at a much later time he was able to testify:

> "I had heard of thee by the hearing of the ear;
> But now my eye sees thee;
> Therefore I abhor myself,
> And repent in dust and ashes" (Job 42:5, 6).

Of similar import are such passages as, "They go from strength to strength" (Ps. 84:7). "The path of the righteous is as the dawning light, that shines more and more unto the perfect day" (Prov. 4:18). The very apostle Paul, even when he already knew Christ, is still praying for increased knowledge: "that I may know him" (Phil. 3:10).

(3) **being invigorated with all vigor.**

The maxim, "Knowledge is power" is true in spiritual life more than anywhere else. When a person grows in the clear knowledge of God, his strength and courage increase. The divine indwelling presence enables him to say, "I can do all things in him who infuses strength into me" (Phil. 4:13). Paul adds, **in accordance with his glorious might.** "In accordance with" is stronger than "of" or "by." When the multimillionaire gives "of" his wealth to some

---

[39] What is said of the gospel in verse 6 — bearing fruit and growing — is said of believers here. But this does not rule out the idea that here in verse 10 each participle has its own modifier. Since, in view of Gal. 5:19, 22; Phil. 1:22, it is not unnatural that "bearing fruit" should take as its modifier "in every good work," and since, in view of II Peter 3:18, it is not illogical that "growing" or "increasing" be associated with "in the clear knowledge of God," and finally, since here in Col. 1:10 these two modifiers (ἐν παντὶ ἔργῳ ἀγαθῷ and τῇ ἐπιγνώσει τοῦ θεοῦ) are rather widely separated, there is no compelling reason to depart from those English renderings (A.V., A.R.V., R.S.V., N.E.B.) which associate the first modifier with καρποφοροῦντες, the second with αὐξανόμενοι. The only slight change I suggest (see my rendering) is to retain the chiastic word-order that is found in the original; hence,

modifier	participle
participle	modifier

good cause he may be giving very little; but when he donates "in accordance with" his riches, the amount will be substantial. The Holy Spirit gives not only "of" but "in accordance with." Eph. 1:19-23 shows why God's might is indeed "glorious." What this *strength in action* (κράτος) enables believers to do is stated in the words **so as to exercise every kind of endurance and longsuffering.** Endurance is the grace to bear up under, the bravery of perseverance in the performance of one's God-given task in spite of every hardship and trial, the refusal to succumb to despair or cowardice. It is a human attribute and is shown in connection with *things,* that is, *circumstances* in which a person is involved: affliction, suffering, persecution, etc. *Longsuffering* characterizes the person who, in relation to those who oppose or molest him, exercises patience, refusing to yield to passion or to outbursts of anger. In the writings of Paul it is associated with such virtues as kindness, mercy, love, goodness, compassion, meekness, lowliness, forbearance, and the forgiving spirit (Rom. 2:4; Gal. 5:22; Eph. 4:2; Col. 3:12, 13). In distinction from *endurance* this *longsuffering* is not only a human but also a divine attribute. It is ascribed to God (Rom. 2:4; 9:22), to Christ (I Tim. 1:16), as well as to man (II Cor. 6:6; Gal. 5:22; Eph. 4:2; Col. 3:12, 13; II Tim. 4:2). Another distinction is that longsuffering is shown in one's attitude *not* to things but to persons. Considered as human virtues both endurance and longsuffering are divine gifts (Rom. 15:5; Gal. 5:22), and both are inspired by hope, by trust in the fulfilment of God's promises (Rom. 8:25; I Thess. 1:3; II Tim. 4:2, 8; Heb. 6:12).

(4) **with joy [40] giving thanks to the Father.**

Due to strength imparted by God, believers are able, even in the midst of tribulation, to give thanks with joy and to rejoice with thanksgiving (cf. Matt. 5:10-12; Luke 6:22, 23; Acts 5:41; II Cor. 4:7-17; Phil. 1:12-21). It is to the Father that this thanks is given, for it is he who through "the Son of his love" (verse 13) freely gives us all things (Rom. 8:32). Paul stresses the necessity of thanksgiving again and again (II Cor. 1:11; Eph. 5:20; Phil. 4:6;

---

[40] I follow N.N.'s punctuation here. The thought expressed in verse 11 probably does not need one more modifier dragging on behind. Besides, by separating the phrase "with joy" from the participle "giving thanks," the latter would be the only participle (of the four) having no modifier.

Lightfoot's argument to the effect that "with joy" when added to "giving thanks" would be meaningless because thanksgiving "is in itself an act of rejoicing" is hardly convincing. Authors, both sacred and secular, frequently add such modifiers in order to stress a certain aspect of the word modified. If "with joy" added to "giving thanks" is pleonastic, why should not the same be true in the immediately preceding verse with respect to the modifier "with all vigor" added to "being invigorated"? The New Testament has numerous similar examples. This phenomenon when not overdone serves to make a writer's style interesting and vivid.

It must be admitted, however, that whether one says "so as to exercise every kind of endurance and longsuffering with joy, giving thanks," etc., or "so as to exercise every kind of endurance and longsuffering, with joy giving thanks," etc., makes little difference in resultant meaning.

Col. 3:17; I Thess. 5:18). In the present connection the reasons why the Colossians should thank the Father are given in verses 12b, 13. Here it is pointed out that the Father is the One who qualified y o u [41] for a share in the inheritance of the saints in the light. Just as in the old dispensation the Lord provided for Israel an earthly inheritance, which was distributed to the various tribes and smaller units of national life *by lot* (Gen. 31:14; Num. 18:20; Josh. 13:16; 14:2; 16:1, etc.), so he had provided for the Colossians *an allotment* or *share* in the better inheritance. These people, drawn mainly from the Gentile world (see *Introduction* III B), had been at one time "separated from Christ, alienated from the commonwealth of Israel, and strangers to the covenants of the promise, having no hope and without God in the world." But "now in Christ Jesus those who were once far off" had been "brought near in the blood of Christ" (Eph. 2:12, 13).

The fact that this share in the inheritance is a matter of *sovereign grace* and has nothing to do with human merit is clear first of all from the very word used, namely, *inheritance:* one *receives* an inheritance as a gift; one does not *earn* it. It is emphasized by the words, "who *qualified* y o u." The best comment on this verse is Paul's statement in II Cor. 3:5: "our sufficiency is from God." It is God who *makes worthy* [42] those who in themselves are not worthy, and who thus *enables* them to have a share in the inheritance.

The inheritance *of the saints* means the inheritance of redeemed believers, that is, of those human individuals who, having been drawn out of darkness and having been brought into the light, are consecrated to God. Though some commentators are of the opinion that here in Col. 1:12 *saints* refers to *angels,* there is no basis for this view. Paul loves the word *saints,* using it again and again in his epistles. Not once does he employ it to indicate the angels, always the redeemed (see Rom. 1:7; 8:27; 12:13; 15:25, 26, 31; 16:2, 15; I Cor. 1:2; 6:1, 2; 14:33; etc.). Even I Thess. 3:13 is no exception; see N.T.C. on that passage.

This inheritance "of the saints" is at the same time the inheritance "in the light." This is "the light of the *knowledge* of the glory of God in the face of Jesus Christ" (II Cor. 4:16). It is "the *love* of God poured out in our hearts through the Holy Spirit" (Rom. 5:5); "the *peace* of God that surpasses all understanding" (Phil. 4:7); "the *joy* inexpressible and full of glory" (I Peter 1:8).

The fact that in Scripture the word *light* is actually used metaphorically to symbolize all of these ideas and more besides is clear from the following passages, in every one of which the word *light* is used in an interpretive context:

---

[41] The textual support for ἡμᾶς is weaker. It is probably due to assimilation: see ἡμᾶς in verse 13.
[42] In the Dutch language the basic idea of the verb can be brought out by the verb *verwaardigen.*

The word *light* used in close connection with:

(1) *holiness, being sanctified* (Acts 20:32; 26:18, 23). These passages are especially important since they occur in Paul's own speeches.

(2) *the divine revelation: truth,* and *insight into that revelation: knowledge* (Ps. 36:9; II Cor. 4:4, 6)

(3) *love* (I John 2:9, 10)

(4) *glory* (Isa. 60:1-3)

(5) *peace, prosperity, liberty, joy* (Ps. 97:11; Isa. 9:1-7).

Since God himself is in his very being holiness, omniscience, love, glory, etc., and since to his people he is the Source of all the graces and blessings mentioned above under (1)-(5), he is himself *light*. "God is light, and in him is no darkness at all" (I John 1:5). Jesus said, "I am the light of the world" (John 8:12). As such God is in Christ his people's *salvation. Light* and *salvation* are therefore synonyms (Ps. 27:1; Isa. 49:6). So is *light* and the divine *grace* or *favor* (Ps. 44:3).

The opposite of light is *darkness,* which, accordingly, is symbolical of *Satan* and *his angels;* hence, also of sin, disobedience, rebellion, ignorance, blindness, falsehood, hatred, wrath, shame, strife, lack, bondage, and gloom, as is shown by several of the very passages referred to above, under (1)-(5), and by many others.

What the apostle is saying, therefore, here in Col. 1:12, is that the Father of his beloved Son Jesus Christ — hence, also our Father — has in his sovereign grace made the Colossians worthy of, and competent to receive, a share of the inheritance of the saints in the realm of *salvation* full and free. The further question, "Is this realm present or future?" is not difficult to answer. *In principle* the Colossians have already entered it. They have already been "transferred into the kingdom of the Son of his love" (Col. 1:13; cf. Eph. 2:13). The *full possession,* however, pertains to the future. It is "the hope that is laid up for them in the heavens" (Col. 1:15). From the Lord they will receive the reward, namely, the inheritance (Col. 3:24). See also Eph. 1:18; Phil. 3:20, 21; and cf. Heb. 3:7–4:11.[43] Paul *prays* — for it must be borne in mind that this is still part of the prayer — that for all this the Colossians may be constantly and joyfully thanking God.

13, 14. Verses 13 and 14 *summarize* the divine work of redemption. The details follow in verses 15-23. This reminds us of Romans, where 1:16, 17 summarizes what is described in greater detail in Rom. 1:18–8:39.

Paul's heart was in his writing. He never wrote in the abstract when he discussed the great blessings which believers have in Christ. He was ever deeply conscious of the fact that upon *him,* too, though completely unworthy, the Father had bestowed these favors. Hence, it is not surprising that, deeply

---

[43] The futuristic reference of Col. 1:12 does not receive its due in Lenski's interpretation of the passage.

moved by what he is writing, he changes the wording, from "y o u" to "us":
verse 13, "who qualified *y o u* . . ."; verse 14, "and who rescued *us*. . . ."
Besides, note how all the main ideas of verses 12-14 — *darkness, light, inheritance, remission of sins* [44] — occur also in Acts 26:18, 23, passages that
record *Paul's own* experience and predict the experience of the Gentiles to
whom he was now sent. The apostle, accordingly, in describing the kind-
nesses which had been conferred upon the Colossians and upon himself and
his associates, yes, even upon all rescued sinners, echoes the very words
which the Savior had used in addressing him, even "Saul," the great and
dreadful persecutor:

"I am Jesus whom you are persecuting. But rise and stand upon your
feet since for this purpose I have appeared to you . . . delivering you from
the people and from the Gentiles, to whom I am sending you, to open their
eyes that they may turn from *darkness* to *light* and from the power [or:
jurisdiction] of Satan to God, that they may receive *remission* of sins and an
inheritance among those who are sanctified by faith in me" (Acts 26:15b-18,
quoted in part) .

So Paul writes: **and who rescued** [45] **us.** He drew us to himself, delivering
us from our condition of wretchedness. The verb *rescued* in the present context implies both the utterly hopeless darkness and misery in which, apart
from God's mercy, "we" (the Colossians, Paul, etc.) had been groping
about, and the glorious but arduous redemptive work that was necessary to
emancipate us from our wretched state. The Father rescued us by sending
his Son into the flesh (Col. 1:22; 2:9; cf. Gal. 1:15, 16; 4:4, 5) in order:

a. to die for our sins on the cross (Col. 1:22; 2:14; cf. Gal. 2:20; 6:14) , and

b. to rise and ascend to heaven, whence he poured the Spirit into our
hearts (Col. 3:1; cf. II Thess. 2:13; John 16:7) , so that we, having been
called (Col. 1:6, 7; cf. Gal. 1:15, 16; Phil. 3:14) , were "made alive" (Col.
2:13; cf. Eph. 2:1-5; John 3:3; Acts 16:14) , and by an act of genuine conversion accepted Christ Jesus as Lord and were baptized (Col. 2:6, 12; cf. Acts
9:1-19) .

This entire process is covered by the words, "He rescued us," [46] and this,

---

[44] Notice even ἐξουσίας in Acts 26:18 and here in Col. 1:13.

[45] In the original "who qualified y o u," etc. (verse 12) is a participial modifier, but
"who rescued us," etc. (verse 13) is a relative clause. The latter gives to the thought
expressed a degree of independence, so that it is not so closely joined with that which
precedes. The *prayer* begins to merge with a *description* of the generosity of the
Father (verse 13) and with a summarizing statement regarding the redemptive
work accomplished by means of the Son (verses 13b, 14) .

[46] It is sometimes argued that since ἐρρύσατο is aorist, the reference must be to one
definite act. On this assumption some commentators are of the opinion that the
expression "He rescued us" refers solely to Christ's death on the cross; others,
solely to conversion and baptism. But the aorist tense does not necessarily refer
to just *one act*. On the contrary, the aorist *summarizes*, viewing all that happened
as *one fact*. See also N.T.C. on John 2:20.

out of the domain of darkness, the sphere in which Satan **exercises** his usurped jurisdiction (Matt. 4:8-11; Luke 22:52, 53; cf. Acts 26:18) over human hearts, lives, activities, and over all "the powers of the air," "the spiritual hosts of wickedness in the heavenly places" (Eph. 2:2; 6:12). (For the meaning of *light* and *darkness* see above on verse 12.) Helpless, hopeless slaves were we, chained by our sins in Satan's prison . . . until the Conqueror came to our rescue (cf. II Cor. 2:14). It was God in Christ who rescued us **and transplanted us into the kingdom of the Son of his love.** He brought us out of the dark and dismal realm of false ideas and chimerical ideals into the sun-bathed land of clear knowledge and realistic expectation; out of the bewildering sphere of perverted cravings and selfish hankerings into the blissful realm of holy yearnings and glorious self-denials; out of the miserable dungeon of intolerable bonds and heart-rending cries into the magnificent palace of glorious liberty and joyful songs.

> "Out of my bondage, sorrow and night,
> Jesus, I come, Jesus, I come;
> Into Thy freedom, gladness and light,
> Jesus, I come to Thee;
> Out of my sickness into Thy health,
> Out of my want and into Thy wealth,
> Out of my sin and into Thyself,
> Jesus, I come to Thee.
>
> "Out of the fear and dread of the tomb,
> Jesus, I come, Jesus, I come;
> Into the joy and light of Thy home,
> Jesus, I come to Thee;
> Out of the depths of ruin untold,
> Into the peace of Thy sheltering fold,
> Ever Thy glorious face to behold,
> Jesus, I come to Thee."
>
> (W. T. Sleeper)

It is probable that the underlying figure is one which those addressed — both Gentile and Jew — readily understood. These people knew that earthly rulers would at times transplant a conquered people from one country to another (II Kings 15:29; 17:3-6; 18:13; 24:14-16; 25:11; II Chron. 36:20; Jer. 52:30; Dan. 1:1-4; Ezek. 1:1; see also above: *Introduction,* II. *The City of Colosse,* C). So also "we" have been transplanted, and this *not* from liberty into slavery but from slavery into liberty. Let us then stand in that liberty. Let us not think that our deliverance is only of a partial character, or that by means of mystic rites, painful ceremonies, worship of angels, or any other means (then or now) we must slowly work our way up from sin to holiness. *Once for all* we have been delivered. We have been transplanted not out of darkness into semi-darkness, but out of dismal darkness into "marvelous light" (I Peter 2:9). We have *even now* arrived in "the kingdom of the Son of his (the Father's) love." [47] Here is what may truly be called "realized eschatology." *In principle* we already in this present life partake of the promised glory. God has already begun a good work in us, and as to the future each one of us is able to testify:

"The work thou hast in me begun
Shall by thy grace be fully done" (cf. Ps. 138:8; Phil. 1:6).

"We" have received the Holy Spirit. And his indwelling presence is the "earnest" (first instalment and pledge) of our inheritance (Eph. 1:4; cf. II Cor. 1:22; 5:5). It is the guarantee of still greater glory to come. This follows also from the fact that the Christ who merited this glory for us is "the Son of the Father's love." He is both the Object of this love (Isa. 42:1; Ps. 2:7; Prov. 8:30; Matt. 3:17; 17:5; Luke 3:22) and its personal manifestation (John 1:18; 14:9; 17:26). How then shall not the Father "together with him" freely give us all things? (Rom. 8:32). We have been transplanted into the Kingdom of the Son of God's love, **in whom we have our redemption,** that is, our *deliverance as the result of the payment of a ransom.* Just as according to Israel's ancient law the forfeited life could be ransomed (Ex. 21:30), so our life, forfeited through sin, was ransomed by the shedding of Christ's blood (Eph. 1:7). [48] Besides, as A. Deissmann remarks, "When anybody heard the

---

[47] We must be careful at this point not to burden the exegesis with unworkable distinctions; for example, the one according to which "the kingdom of the Son" pertains to the present, but that "of God" to the future. See O. Cullmann, *Königsherrschaft Christi und Kirche im N.T.* Over against that view, which bases too much on I Cor. 15:23 f., Karl L. Schmidt correctly states that it is impossible to speak about the kingdom of Christ without also speaking about the kingdom of God (article βασιλεία in Th.W.N.T., Vol. I, p. 582). A careful examination of such passages as Eph. 5:5, Rev. 12:10, and a comparison of Rom. 14:17 with John 18:36 and with I Cor. 4:20 shows that no sharp distinction, to be applied wherever these two terms or their synonyms are used, is possible. The kingdom of God, to be sure, is everlasting. But so also is the kingdom of the Son (Luke 1:33; Heb. 1:8; II Peter 1:11).

[48] Though, according to the best textual evidence, the *words* "through his blood" (cf. Eph. 1:7) must not be inserted in Col. 1:14, the *idea,* cannot be excluded. Büchsel. to be sure, *denies* that in *any* biblical reference to redemption the idea of a payment of a ransom is present (article ἀπολύτρωσις, Th.W.N.T., Vol. IV, pp. 354-359). But the evidence is clearly on the other side. Matt. 20:28; Mark 10:45 show that Christ came to give his life as a ransom for many. The words "through the redemption that is in Christ Jesus," (Rom. 3:24), in the light of the verse that immediately follows, indicates the payment of a blood-ransom. The same idea is expressed not only in Eph. 1:7, as already mentioned, but also in Heb. 9:15 (cf. verse 12). It is true that by means of a semantic shift a more general connotation — *deliverance, emancipation, release, restoration,* dropping the idea "through the payment of a ransom" — attaches to the word in Luke 21:28; Rom. 8:23; I Cor. 1:30; Eph. 1:14; 4:30; Heb. 11:35. But it is not fair to generalize. Each passage has to be studied in its own specific context. Paul again and again stresses the idea that our

Greek word λύτρον, *ransom* [on which the word ἀπολύτρωσις, *redemption* is based] . . . it was natural for him to think of the purchase-money for manumitting slaves." Hence, "in him," that is, *through spiritual union with him* (Col. 3:1-3) , *redemption* full and free is ours. This redemption is, accordingly, emancipation from the curse (Gal. 3:13) , particularly from enslavement to sin (John 8:34; Rom. 7:14; I Cor. 7:23) , and release to true liberty (John 8:36; Gal. 5:1) . Through *Christ's* payment of a ransom and *our* faith in him we have obtained from the Father **the forgiveness** or *remission* (cf. Ps. 103:12) **of our sins.** The chain that held us fast has been broken. Though the apostle uses this *expression* "forgiveness of sins" (which is of such frequent occurrence elsewhere in the New Testament) ,[49] only here and in Eph. 1:7 (forgiveness of . . . *trespasses*) , and though he generally conveys a similar idea by words and phrases that belong to the "justification by faith" family, he was, nevertheless, well acquainted with the *idea* of forgiveness of sins, as is shown by Rom. 4:7; II Cor. 5:19; and in Colossians by 2:13 and 3:13. In fact, in Colossians the idea of forgiveness is even emphasized. See footnote 131.

Justification and remission are inseparable. So are also redemption and remission, though this was at times denied. Thus Irenaeus in his work *Against Heresies* I.xxi.2, written about A. D. 182-188, tells us about certain heretics in his day who taught that here in this life salvation occurs in the following two stages:

a. *Remission of sins* at baptism, instituted by the visible, human Jesus;

b. *Redemption* at a later stage, through the divine Christ who descended on Jesus. In this second stage the person whose sins have already been forgiven attains to *perfection* or *fulness.*

It is *possible,* in view of such passages as Col. 2:9, 10; 4:12, that the errorists at Colosse were already spreading this or a similar notion. In any event, it was through the Holy Spirit, who knows all things even *before* they happen and is therefore able to issue warnings that apply to the future as well as to the present, that the apostle wrote these words. They clearly indicate that when a sinner is transplanted out of the power of darkness into the kingdom of light, he is to be regarded as having been *redeemed,* and that this *redemption* implies *the remission of sins.*

Lord paid an enormous price to obtain redemption for his people. It is in the light of such passages as I Cor. 6:10; 7:23; Gal. 3:13; 4:5; I Tim. 2:6; that Col. 1:14 must be explained. Other relevant passages are Ps. 49:8; Matt. 20:28; Mark 10:45; John 1:29; 3:17; I Peter 1:18, 19; Rev. 5:6, 9, 12; 7:14; 12:11.

[49] See Matt. 26:28; Mark 1:4; Luke 1:77; 3:3; 24:47; Acts 2:38; 5:31; 10:43; 13:38; 26:18. Cf. for a fuller account E. Percy, *Die Probleme der Kolosser und Epheserbriefe,* pp. 85, 86. Also B. B. Warfield, *The Person and Work of Christ,* pp. 429 ff., and E. K. Simpson, *Words Worth Weighing in the Greek New Testament,* p. 8 f.

1:15-20

III. *The Son's Pre-eminence*

Verses 15-20 form a unit. If it was not a literary gem composed by the apostle himself, it was probably a hymn or other fixed testimony of the early church adopted by Paul and reproduced here by him either without change or with alterations suitable to the needs of the Colossian church. It is, in any case, a unit and for that reason is here printed in its entirety. And since it clearly consists of two parts these have been reproduced here in parallel columns.[50] The relation of the theme to its two divisions is as follows. The Son's Pre-eminence is shown:

A. In Creation (verses 15-17)	B. In Redemption (verses 18-20)
15 Who is the image of the invisible God, The firstborn of every creature,	18 And he is the head of the body, the church; Who is the beginning, the first-born from the dead, That in all things he might have the pre-eminence,
16 For in him were created all things In the heavens and on the earth, The visible and the invisible, Whether thrones or dominions or principalities or authorities, All things through him and with a view to him have been created;	19 For in him he [God] was pleased to have all the fulness dwell, 20 And through him to reconcile all things to himself, Having made peace through the blood of his cross, Through him, whether the things on the earth Or the things in the heavens.
17 And he is before all things, And all things hold together in him.	

Very striking and solemn are these lines. Note the following points of correspondence between A. and B.:

	A.	B.
(1) "Who is" in verse	15	18
(2) "The firstborn" in verse	15	18
(3) "For in him" in verse	16	19
(4) "In the heavens and on the earth" in verse	16	cf. 20

[50] In order to emphasize the formal correspondence between A. and B., section B. is often printed as beginning with 18b. Thus both A. and B. would begin with the words "Who is." On the other hand as to *content*, B. should begin as printed, namely, with verse 18a, which clearly pertains to Christ's pre-eminence in the realm of redemption.

Not only do *the same expressions occur* in both columns but they occur *in the same sequence!* There is a definite idea-and-form parallelism. The glory of Christ in Creation is balanced by his majesty in Redemption. There are also other items of resemblance; for example, the expression "all things," occurring four times in verses 15-17 and twice in verses 18-20. And the words "through him" of verse 16 are repeated twice in verse 20.

As to the origin and nature of these impressive, solemn, and carefully balanced lines, there are *two main* views. See, however, footnote.[51]

---

[51]   A. *Various Views*

(1) Verses 12-20 are to be regarded as a primitive Christian baptismal liturgy, which in verses 15-20 make use of a hymn of Gnostic origin. Ernst Käsemann, "Eine urchristliche Taufliturgie," *Festschrift Rudolf Bultmann zum 65. Geburtstag überreicht* (1949), pp. 133-148.

(2) Col. 1:15-20 is part of a eucharistic liturgy. G. Bornkamm, *Theol. Blätter,* 1942, p. 61.

(3) Col. 1:13-29 shows us a primitive Christian worship-service. There is a definite pattern of arrangement of clauses according to a 3-7, 3-7 numerical scheme. Ernst Lohmeyer, in *Meyer Commentary* (8th ed., 1930).

(4) Col. 1:15-20 constitutes one of the earliest Christian hymns. Paul included this hymn in his letter to the Colossians. O. A. Piper, "The Savior's Eternal Work; An Exegesis of Col. 1:9-29," *Int* 3 (1949), pp. 286-298.

(5) The passage is a Christological confession composed by Paul. This was the opinion to which Martin Dibelius finally arrived. See his commentary, *An die Kolosser, Epheser, an Philemon,* in *Lietzmann's Handbuch zum Neuen Testament,* 3rd ed. revised by H. Greeven, 1953. Ernst Percy also believed that the lines were written by Paul. For proof he pointed to style similarity; cf. Col. 1:16 with I Cor. 3:21; 12:13; and Gal. 3:26-28. See his well-known work *Die Probleme der Kolosser- und Epheserbriefe,* p. 65.

(6) The lines embody traditional forms of predication, Jewish periods, and a Stoic omnipotence-formula. Eduard Norden, *Agnostos Theos,* 1913.

(7) They owe their origin to the Jewish Wisdom literature (Prov. 8:22-31; Ecclus. 1:4; 43:26). H. Windisch, "Die göttliche Weisheit der Juden und die paulinische Christologie," in *Neutest. Studien für Heinrici,* 1914, pp. 220-234. Closely related to this is the suggestion of C. F. Burney that these lines might be a meditation on Prov. 8:22 in connection with Gen. 1:1. See his article, "Christ as the ARXH of Creation," *JTS* xxvii (1925, 1926), pp. 160 ff. Another related view is that the passage, Col. 1:15-20, is "by St. Paul himself, though possibly in words drawn in part from some Hellenistic hymn to the Wisdom or Word of God." C. F. D. Moule, *The Epistle of Paul the Apostle to the Colossians and to Philemon,* p. 61.

(8) They embody an early Christian hymn of praise to Christ, augmented by the words "and he is the head of his body, the Church." The passage is to be regarded as a non-Pauline composition. C. Masson, *Comm. du NT,* Vol. X. By eliminating certain words he arrives at a parallelism that adheres to strict and definite rules.

(9) Whatever be their origin, they show a definite stylistic pattern, a strophic arrangement. But just what was this *strophic* arrangement? Various attempts at reconstruction have been made. In addition to those by Käsemann, Lohmeyer, Norden, and Masson (see above for references to their writings), there are those by P. Benoit, *La Sainte Bible traduite en français sous la direction de l'Ecole Biblique de Jérusalem;* G. Schille, "Liturgisches Gut im Epheserbrief" (doctoral dissertation, Göttingen, 1952); C. Maurer, "Die Begründung der Herrschaft Christi über die Mächte nach Kolosser 1, 15-20," *Wort und Dienst, Jahrbuch der Theologischen Schule Bethel,* n.F.IV (1955), pp. 79-93; and, last but not least, J. M. Robinson, "A

The first of these two acceptable theories is this: Paul himself composed and dictated the lines. Those who favor this view generally add that Col. 1:15-20 is not a hymn.

The second is this: the passage is a pre-Pauline hymn or well-known and oft-repeated early saying or testimony. Paul, having learned this "hymn" or "saying" which had endeared itself to his heart, made it a part of his letter, either with no addition or alteration or else with slight changes to suit his own purpose.

The following arguments have been advanced in favor of *the first* alternative:

(1) Recognizable quantitative meter such as one might expect in a hymn is found here only after considerable conjectural reconstruction.

(2) It was natural for Paul, a highly emotional person who was writing on a lofty theme (Christ's Pre-eminence) to express himself in such a solemn way. And since many Old Testament passages, very familiar to Paul, praised *Jehovah's* majesty in parallelistic phraseology (Ps. 93; 96; 103; 121; 136; 145-150; etc.) , the apostle, under the guidance of the Spirit, would almost

---

Formal Analysis of Colossians 1:15-20," *JBL,* Vol. LXXVI, Part IV (Dec., 1957) , pp. 270-288.

(10) Although the formal style and the correspondence between Col. 1:15-18a and 18b-20 do give to these lines a striking and solemn aspect, these characteristics do not prove whether, on the one hand, we are dealing here with a hymn or other liturgical unit or whether, on the other hand, we have here an example of Paul's own preaching concerning the glory of Christ. A hymnal unit is obtained only after considerable reconstruction of the text. H. Ridderbos, *Aan De Kolossenzen,* in *Commentaar op het Nieuwe Testament, p.* 151. He does, however, definitely favor a division of Col. 1:15-20 into *two* — and not into *four* — parts.

B. *Criticism*

Several of these thories are open to serious objection. Thus, in a letter which combats incipient Gnosticism one would hardly look for the incorporation of a Gnostic hymn. Again, though *all things* were created in and through and with a view to Christ and though *all things* cohere in him, there is no need to see any Stoic influence in this idea. As to the possible influence of Wisdom literature, *if* there be any such influence it would pertain to the manner of expression, not directly to the essence. It is at the most marginal, affecting form rather than content. Besides, the poetic personification of Wisdom found in Wisdom literature is not *directly* the Son of God himself whom Paul in Colossians has *immediately* in mind. As to those theories which, *without any textual support,* leave out entirely or re-arrange words, phrases or whole lines, in order to arrive at this or that *precise* strophical scheme, in which everything will be perfectly balanced, I cannot accept them. The very fact that so many of them have been tried out, each claiming to be better than the others, condemns them. As to finding here either a baptismal or a eucharistic liturgy, this, too, is very subjective. It is "found" by those who put it there.

The true reason for Col. 1:15-20 lies ready at hand. That reason is the Christ himself in very person, the One who existed from all eternity, became incarnate, fulfilled his amazingly glorious earthly ministry, suffered and died vicariously, rose from the grave, ascended to heaven, and from the Father's right hand sent forth the Spirit.

naturally express himself in similar language in setting forth the majesty of *Christ.*

(3) There is nothing in this passage that can be considered foreign to Paul's main theme in Colossians.

(4) The Paul of I Corinthians and Galatians writes in similar style. See footnote 51,A.5 above.

Those who disagree might answer as follows:

With respect to (1). Does every hymn have recognizable quantitative meter?

With respect to (2). Would anyone, writing spontaneously in the freely flowing style of a letter, compose a passage consisting of two parts which contain not only the same phrases, but even these same phrases arranged in the same sequence?

With respect to (3). True, but this is not in conflict with either theory.

With respect to (4). At best the passages to which Percy refers furnish only partial proof. They do not contain a true and full stylistic parallel to what is found in Col. 1:15-20.

Now though the first theory may, after all, be correct, there would seem to be a stronger argument in support of *the second.* Note the following:

(1) The primitive Church had not only its Old Testament Psalms but also other hymns. Cf. I Cor. 14:26. Paul loved "psalms and hymns and spiritual songs."

Is not this clearly stated in Col. 3:16?

Very vividly illustrated in I Tim. 3:16?

And also clearly motivated by John 3:16?

The early church also had its famous "reliable sayings" (I Tim. 1:15; 3:1; 4:8, 9; II Tim. 2:11-13; Titus 3:4-8). All such sayings, testimonies, confessions, and songs were passed from mouth to mouth and from heart to heart, until they had embedded themselves in the very soul of the community, where all the fears, hopes, struggles, and joys of believers played around them. It would not be strange, therefore, if Paul here in Col. 1:15-20 were actually quoting, either exactly or with some additional word of application, a saying or hymn which had already secured for itself a place of prominence in the life of the Church.

Note, moreover, that Col. 1:15-20 bears testimony to the greatness of Christ, which is the very theme of I Tim. 3:16. That passage, as already indicated, in all probability was another hymn. In this connection it may be of some significance that a generation after Paul's death Pliny the Younger, describing the Christians of his day to the emperor Trajan, states, "They affirmed, moreover, that the sum-total of their guilt or error was this, that they were in the habit of meeting on a certain fixed day before it was light, when they sang in alternate verses a hymn to Christ as to a God . . ." (*Letters* X.xcvi).

(2) The relative pronoun "who" in "who is" (verses 15, 18, especially the latter) "is not obviously natural" (C. F. D. Moule, *op. cit.,* p. 62). It has all the appearance of having been borrowed from a hymn in which it may have been preceded by such words as, "We thank our glorious Lord Jesus." This is comparable to the antecedant presupposed by the hymn quoted in I Tim. 3:16. See N.T.C. on I and II Timothy and Titus, pp. 137, 138.

(3) The carefully constructed nature of the passage, Col. 1:15-20, the parallelistic correspondences pertaining to its two parts, the recurrence of words and phrases *in the same sequence* in these two sections, is more natural in a hymn than in the free-flowing style of a letter.

Before attempting a study of the separate parts, the passage should be seen in its entirety. The following points should be noted:

(1) The passage indicates *at least* the following, namely, that only about thirty years after Jesus had suffered a shameful death on the cross divine honor was ascribed to him. His pre-eminence both in Creation and Redemption, his exaltation above every creature, was being clearly proclaimed by the apostle Paul. However, if the passage is a quotation from an earlier source, as is distinctly possible, it would mean that the recognition of Jesus as God even antedated Paul! See John 20:28; cf. 1:1-18.

(2) By insisting so strongly on the greatness of Christ, this passage implies that he is able to grant to the Colossians the things which Paul, in his beautiful prayer (verses 9-14), had requested for them. That is the connection between the prayer and the "hymn" or testimony. Such assurance was necessary, for the apostle had asked nothing less than *clear* knowledge of God's will, *all* spiritual wisdom and understanding, bearing fruit in *every* good work, and *all* vigor so as to exercise *every* kind of endurance and long-suffering.

(3) Col. 1:15-20 pictures a Christ who holds in his almighty hand and embraces with his loving heart both the realm of creation and that of redemption. He who is "the firstborn of all creation" is also "the firstborn from the dead." He who died on the cross knows by name the most distant star. He not only knows it but guides it. Still better: he controls it in such a manner that it will serve the interests of his people (Rom. 8:28). The so-called "laws of nature" have no *independent* existence. They are the expression of *his* will. And because he delights in *order* and not in confusion it is possible to speak of *laws*. He who in answer to prayer grants assurance of salvation is also able in answer to prayer to grant rain!

The present-day application of this truth is immediately evident. Since the Christ of Calvary rules the heavens and the earth in the interest of his kingdom and to the glory of his Name, always over-ruling evil for good, neither automation nor bomb nor communistic menace nor depression nor economic unbalance nor fatal accident nor gradual decline in mental vigor nor hallucination due to nervous disorder nor any invader from outer space (about which some people have nightmares!) will ever succeed in separating us from his love (Rom. 8:35, 38). He who tells us how to go to heaven and actually brings us there, also knows how the heavens go; for he, all things having been created and "holding together" in him, through him, and unto him, causes them to perform their mission and to go to the place predestined by him.

(4) Over against the heretics who threatened the Colossian church and proclaimed Christ's *in*sufficiency, this passage sets forth his *all*-sufficiency for salvation. This salvation implies not only being saved from the wrath of God, from the sentence of condemnation, and from eternal punishment, but also being spiritually regenerated and strengthened so that one is able to lay aside his old nature with its many vices (Col. 3:5-9) and to put on the new nature with its many virtues (Col. 3:1-3, 12-17). It is the *all*-sufficient Christ, he and he alone, who brings his people to glory. Thus the apostle, even in this grand passage, Col. 1:15-20, is really dealing with the practical implications of faith in Christ. In contrast with this faith the notions of the errorists fade away into worthlessness.

(5) The passage also clearly teaches that Christ's redemptive activity is universe-embracing. In Christ God was pleased to reconcile *all things* to himself. See on 1:20.

Turning now to the first of the two parts into which the section, verses 15-20, is divided we note the Son's Pre-eminence

A. *In Creation*

15. Paul writes, **Who is the image of the invisible God.** This reminds us of Gen. 1:27 which reports that man was created as God's image. As such man was given dominion over the rest of creation. It is significant that Psalm 8, in which this dominion is described in some detail, is by the author of the epistle to the Hebrews interpreted Messianically (Heb. 2:5-9). But though this reference to man's creation as God's image and consequent dominion may well have been in the background, it does not do full justice to the idea conveyed here in Colossians with respect to the Son. *Man,* though God's image, *is not God.* But, as the image of the invisible *God, the Son is,* first of all, *himself God.* "In him all the fulness of the godhead dwells bodily" (Col. 2:9; cf. Rom. 9:5). "In him all the treasures of wisdom and knowledge are hidden" (2:3). Secondly, as the *image* of the invisible God, *the Son is God Revealed.* In Paul's writings this identification of the Son with God himself, the Son being *God's image* or *God made manifest,* is not new. Also in a letter to the Corinthians, written earlier by several years, the apostle had called Christ "the image of God" (II Cor. 4:4) . With this should be compared the apostle's description of his Lord in Philippians (a letter written probably shortly after Colossians) , namely, "existing in the *form* of God" (see N.T.C. on Phil. 2:6) . We have here in Col. 1:15 the same teaching as is found in Heb. 1:3, where the Son is called "the effulgence of God's glory and the very impress of his substance." In different language the apostle John expresses the same thought: "In the beginning was the Word, and the Word was face to face with God, and the Word was God. . . . God himself no one has ever seen. The only begotten God, who lies upon the Father's breast, it is he who made him known" (John 1:1, 18) . Cf. also John 10:30, 38; 14:9; Rev. 3:14. It is in the Son that the invisible God has become visible, so that man sees him who is invisible (cf. I Tim. 1:17; 6:16) .

Now if the Son is the very image of the invisible God, and if this invisible God is from everlasting to everlasting, it follows that the Son, too, must be *eternally* God's image. With respect to his deity he cannot belong to the category of time and space. He cannot be a mere creature, but must be in a class by himself, that is, raised high above every creature. Accordingly, the apostle continues, **the firstborn of every creature,**[52] that is, *the One to whom belongs the right and dignity of the Firstborn in relation to every creature.* That the phrase "the firstborn of every creature" cannot mean that the Son himself, too, is a creature, the first in a very long line, is clearly established by verse 16. He is prior to, distinct from, and highly exalted above every creature. As the firstborn he is the heir and ruler of all. Note Psalm 89:27:

> "I will also make him my firstborn,
> The highest of the kings of the earth." Cf. Ex. 4:22; Jer. 31:9.

The same thought is expressed in Heb. 1:1, 2, "God . . . has spoken to us in his Son, whom he appointed heir of all things, through whom he also made the worlds."

16. The interpretation just given brings verse 15 in harmony with verse 16 which again stresses *Christ's pre-eminence above every creature.* And *that,* let it be re-emphasized, was after all Paul's main theme over against the teachers of error who were disturbing the church at Colosse. We read:

> **For in him were created all things**
> **In the heavens and on the earth,**
> **The visible and the invisible.**
> **Whether thrones or dominions or principalities or authorities,**
> **All things through him and with a view to him have been created.**

---

[52] It makes little difference in resultant meaning whether πάσης κτίσεως be rendered "of all creation" (cf. Rom. 8:22) or "of every creature" (cf. Rom. 8:39) . In favor of "of every creature" is the absence (here in Col. 1:15) of the article. In connection with πάσης one would expect the article if the sense is "of all creation."

All things — it makes no difference whether they be material or spiritual — were created *in him,* that is, *with reference to* the Son, the firstborn. As two walls and the bricks in these walls are arranged *in relation to* the corner-stone, from which they derive their angle of direction, so it was *in relation to* Christ that all things were originally created. He is their Point of Reference. Moreover, it is *through* him, as the *Agent* in creation, and *with a view to* him or *for* him as creation's *Goal* that they owe their settled state ("have been created") . *All* creatures, without any exception whatever, must contribute glory to him and serve his purpose. But is not God the Father — or else the Triune God — rather than the Son, the One for whom all things were brought into being? And do not passages such as Rom. 11:36, I Cor. 10:31, and Eph. 4:6 point in that general direction? Here it must be borne in mind, however, that the apostle's very emphasis in this letter is that the Son, too, is fully divine. In him all the fulness of the godhead dwells bodily (Col. 2:9) . Hence, it is entirely reasonable for him to say that the Son is not only the One to whom all things owe their origin, as the divine Agent in their creation, but is also the Goal of their existence. Of all creatures he is Sovereign Lord. Hence, there is absolutely no justification for trusting in, seeking help from, or worshiping any mere creature, even though that creature be an angel. Angels, too, however exalted they may be, are creatures, and as such are subject to Christ. The *region* to which they or any other created beings belong or which they are thought to occupy, whether that region be heaven or earth or some place in-between, makes no difference. Note the crisscross or chiastic manner in which this thought is expressed:

"For in him were created all things"

In the heavens   and   on the earth

The visible   and   the invisible.

Here clearly the visible creatures are those viewed as on earth; the invisible as in heaven.

Paul is thinking especially of *thrones or dominions or principalities or authorities.* The teachers of error were constantly referring to these angelic beings. The apostle does not deny their existence (Eph. 1:21, 22) . Neither does he reject the idea that they are able to exert influence for good, if still unfallen (on this see N.T.C. on I Tim. 5:21) or for evil, if fallen (Eph. 6:12) . The apostle's idea is rather this: angels have no power apart from Christ. In fact, apart from him they cannot even exist. They are *creatures,* nothing more. To the salvation or perfection of the Colossians they, in and by themselves, can contribute naught whatever. They can only *render service* and this always in subjection to Christ and through *his* power. The *good* angels cannot *add* anything to the fulness of riches and resources which believers have in Christ. The *evil* angels cannot separate them from his love (Rom. 8:35-39). In fact, through his death these sinister powers were basically vanquished (Col. 2:15). They are approaching the day when even their ability to do harm in God's universe and in the hearts and lives of earth-dwellers will be ended once and for all (I Cor. 15:24, 25).

The enumeration "thrones or dominions or principalities or authorities" is not necessarily an arrangement of angels in four distinct groups, either in an ascending or in a descending scale of eminence, as if there were these four sharply differentiated classes. It is possible, nevertheless, that *thrones* and *dominions* must be viewed as *throne-spirits,* that is, such spirits as are dwelling in the immediate vicinity of God's throne (cf. the cherubim, Rev. 4:6). On this assumption *principalities and authorities,* generally mentioned together (Col. 1:16; 2:10, 15; Eph. 1:21; 3:10; I Cor. 15:24), could be spirits of lesser rank. But, however that may be, what Paul is saying is this: *"These angelic beings* of which false teachers are making so much, *call them by whatever names y o u wish* (Eph. 1:21; Phil. 2:9, 10), *are mere creatures,* and having been created through and for Christ, are subject to him." The inference, of course, is this, also for salvation y o u should expect everything from *him,* from him *alone,* not from him *and the angels!* [53]

17. Now if all things have been created through him and with a view to him (verse 16), it stands to reason that he preceded all created beings in time. In fact, "there never was a time when he was not." He was "begotten of the Father before all worlds" (Nicene Creed). Accordingly, the "hymn" continues, **And he is before all things.** He is, accordingly, the Forerunner. The doctrine of Christ's pre-existence from eternity is taught or implied in such passages as John 1:1; 8:58; 17:5; II Cor. 8:9; Phil. 2:6; Rev. 22:13. He is indeed the Alpha and the Omega, the first and the last, the beginning and the end. And this temporal priority in turn suggests pre-eminence and majesty in relation to all creatures: **And all things hold together in him.** The central position of Christ is defended here over against those who rejected it. The One with reference to whom, through whom, and with a view to whom all things were created is also the One who maintains them. The unity, order, and adaptation evident in all of nature and history can be traced to the Upholder or Sustainer of all (cf. Heb. 1:1-3).

---

[53] On these thrones, dominions, etc. see also the following: Slav. Enoch 20:1; Test. Levi 3 (*Ante-Nicene Fathers,* Vol. VIII, p. 13); and in Th.W.N.T. the following articles: Schmitz, θρόνος, III, pp. 160-167, especially p. 167; Michel, κυριότης, III, p. 1096; Delling, ἀρχή, I, pp. 477-488, especially pp. 481-483; and Foerster, ἐξουσία, II. pp. 559-571, especially pp. 568-571.

All things *hold together;* that is, they *continue and cohere.*[54]

There is, accordingly, unity and purpose in all of Nature and History. The world is not a chaos but a cosmos. It is an orderly universe, a *system.* This, to be sure, does not always appear on the surface. Nature seems to be "raw in tooth and claw," without harmony and order. Yet, a closer look soon indicates a basic plan. There is adaptation everywhere. For their perpetuation certain plants need certain definite insects. These insects are present, and so wondrously constructed that they can perform their function. The polar bear is able to live where there is ice and snow. It is kept from slipping on the ice by having fur even on the soles of its feet. The yucca plant can live in the hot, dry desert because not only does it have roots reaching down deeply into the soil for water but also leaves so formed that evaporation is very slow. Our lungs are adapted to the air we breathe, and our eyes to the light by which we see. Everywhere there is *coherence.*

This is true also in the daily events of History. Here, too, things are not as they seem. Often Confusion seems to be rampant. A Guiding Hand is nowhere visible. Instead, we hear the cry of battle, the shriek of anguish. The newspapers, moreover, are filled with accounts of burglary, murder, rape, and race-clash. If we compare the wheel of the universe to a machine, we might say that its gear-teeth seem not to mesh. To be sure, one day in the far-flung future, all will be harmony: the wolf shall dwell with the lamb, and the leopard shall lie down with the kid; and the calf and the young lion and the fatling together; and a little child shall lead them. . . . They shall not hurt nor destroy in all my holy mountain; for the earth shall be full of the knowledge of Jehovah, as the waters cover the sea" (Isa. 11:6-9). But that time has not yet arrived. All is chaos now. But is it really? Should we not rather compare our world to a weaving, whose underside forms no intelligible pattern, but whose upperside reveals beauty and design? Or to an international airfield? Though its planes, constantly coming and going, make us dizzy, so that we expect a collision any moment, we need not really hold our breath, for the man in the control-tower directs each take-off and landing. Thus, too, all creatures in all their movements throughout history are being *held together.* And that which holds them together is not Chance or Fate or the laws of Nature or even the "nine orbs, or rather globes" of

---

[54] The verb συνίστημι (alongside of which συνιστάνω and συνιστάω are used) means (transitive): *I cause to stand together, I bring together; I bring someone to someone else;* hence, *I introduce someone to someone else, I recommend* or *commend* a person (Rom. 16:1) or thing. In the sense of *commending* it is sometimes used favorably — as in the well-known passage Rom. 5:8 — ; sometimes with unfavorable overtones (for both unfavorable and favorable sense respectively, see the two occurrences of this verb in II Cor. 10:8). Here in Col. 1:17 it is used intransitively. The form here is 3rd person s. perf. act. indic. Cf. also for intransitive use: Luke 9:32 (*standing with*) and II Peter 3:5 (*continuing and consisting of*). See also on this verb L.N.T. (A. and G.), p. 798.

Scipio's Dream. On the contrary, "all things hold together *in him.*" It is the Son of God's love who holds in his almighty hands the reins of the universe and never even for one moment lets them slip out of his grasp (cf. Rev. chs. 4 and 5). Though the man of flesh regards this as so much pious twaddle, the man of faith proclaims with the inspired author of the Hebrews, "Now we see not yet all things subjected to him. But we behold . . . Jesus . . . crowned with glory and honor" (2:9). The believer knows that while the *rule* of Christ has not been established in every human heart, the *over-rule* is an actual fact even now (Rom. 8:28; cf. N.T.C. on Phil. 1:12). And at the sea of crystal the Church Triumphant will forever praise and glorify God for his mighty works and ways (Rev. 15:1-4).

Summarizing, the hymn has shown that with respect to all creatures, Christ is Firstborn (verse 15), Point of Reference, Agent, Goal (verse 16), Forerunner, and Sustainer — Governor (verse 17).

B. *In Redemption*

18. The section showing the Son's pre-eminence in the sphere of Creation has ended. Here, at verse 18, begins the paragraph describing his equal sovereignty in the realm of Redemption. We read: **And he is the head of the body, the church.** In the writings of Paul this expression is something new, whether we view it as original with him or as *here* taken over by him from a familiar hymn or saying. It is nowhere found in the earlier epistles such as Galatians, I and II Thessalonians, I and II Corinthians, or Romans. Yet, it would be unwise on this account to say that Paul cannot have been either the author or confirmer of the idea that Christ is, indeed, the head of the body, namely, the church. To be sure, in the earlier letters the apostle wrote not about Christ as the head of the church but about the church as the body of Christ (Rom. 12:5; I Cor. 12:12-31, especially verse 27). His purpose was to show that in that *one* body there were many *members* ("foot," "hand," "ear," "eye"); in other words, that in the one organism of the church there were many functions and talents distributed among a large number of believers, and that each "member" should use his gifts to benefit the entire body. He did not then specifically state that the head of this body was Christ. That was not the point at issue in these earlier letters. At Colosse, however, this headship or pre-eminence of Christ was distinctly the truth in need of emphasis, as has already been shown. It is for this reason that this particular aspect of the doctrine is set forth here in Colossians rather than in the earlier epistles.

Nevertheless, it cannot be truthfully maintained that the proposition "Christ is the head of the church" was *absolutely* foreign to Paul's thinking previous to the time when he wrote his Prison Epistles. Is not a *body* supposed to have a *head?* Besides, had not the apostle written, "The head of every man is Christ" (I Cor. 11:3) ? Now if Christ is the head of every man in the church, is he not also the head of the church?

As head Christ causes his church to live and to grow (Col. 2:19; cf. Eph. 4:15, 16) . He is its *Organic Head.* As head he also exercises authority over the church; in fact, over all things in the interest of the church (Eph. 1:20-23) . He is its *Ruling Head.* It is doubtful whether either of these two ideas is ever completely absent when Christ is called head of the church, though sometimes one connotation and then again the other receives the greater emphasis, as the context indicates. And in such a passage as Eph. 5:23, 24 both ideas (*growth* and *guidance*) are brought to the fore.

Now if the Son of God is the Organic and Ruling Head of the church, then the church is in no sense whatever dependent on any creature, angel or otherwise. This is the clear implication over against the teachers of error. Does not the church receive both its growth and guidance from its living Lord? Is it not energized by his power and governed by his Word and Spirit? Hence, is it not true that in Christ it has all it needs, and also that without him it can accomplish nothing? Cf. John 15:5, 7.

> "Thou, O Christ, art all I want;
> More than all in thee I find." (Charles Wesley, in "Jesus,
> Lover of My Soul")

And what could be a better illustration of the relation of Christ to his church than the underlying idea of the relation of the human head to the body? Advance in scientific knowledge has confirmed the adequacy of the figure used by the early church and by Paul. In a human individual it is to the head that the body, in large measure, owes its *vigorous life* and *growth* (the organic relationship) . From the pituitary gland, housed in a small cavity located in the base of the skull, comes the growth hormone (and several other hormones) . This hormone is known to be closely related to the health and growth of connective tissue, cartilege, and bone.

Consider also the other functions of the head, those related in large measure to *guidance.* It is in the head that the organs of special sense are mainly located. The brain receives impulses from the outside world (indirectly) and from inside the body. It organizes and interprets these impulses. It thinks. It reacts, and this both voluntarily and involuntarily. Thus it *guides and directs* the actions of the individual. In the *cerebrum* are located, among other things, the areas that control the various parts of the body. The *cerebellum* has been called "the co-ordinator and harmonizer of muscular action." The *medulla* controls such actions as winking, sneezing, coughing, chewing, sucking, swallowing, etc. Here also the cardiac center regulates the rate of heart-beat, while the respiratory center is in charge of the activity of the respiratory organs.

Thus, indeed, when the triune God created the human body with its *organic and ruling head,* he so constructed that head that it could serve as an excellent symbol of the Organic and Ruling Head of the church, the Lord Jesus Christ.

With reference to the latter the "hymn" now continues, **Who is the beginning, the firstborn from the dead.** By his triumphant resurrection, *nevermore to die,* Christ laid the foundation for that sanctified life, that hope and assurance in which his own rejoice (Col. 3:1-17; I Peter 1:3 ff.). This resurrection is also the beginning, principle, or cause of their glorious physical resurrection. Hence, from every aspect the statement is true, "Because I live y o u too will live" (John 14:19). He is the path-breaker, who holds the key of Death and Hades. He has authority over life and death (Rom. 8:29; I Cor. 15:20; Heb. 2:14, 15; Rev. 1:5). It is he who "on the one hand, utterly defeated death, and on the other hand, brought to light life and incorruptibility through the gospel" (II Tim. 1:10). All this is true in order **that in all things he might have the pre-eminence.** It stands to reason that One who is Firstborn, Point of Reference, Agent, Goal, Forerunner, and Sustainer — Governor (verses 15-17) in the sphere of Creation; and Head of the Body, Beginning, and Firstborn from the dead in the realm of Redemption (verse 18), has the right to the title, "the One who has the pre-eminence — the divine sovereignty — *in all things,* that is, among all creatures."

19. Note, however, the words, "that he might have." These words show that this high honor possessed by the Son was a matter of design, the Father's good pleasure. Hence, the text continues, **For in him he [God] was pleased to have all the fulness dwell.**[55]

---

[55] With the majority of translators, ancient and modern, I would make "God" or "the Father" (understood) the subject of the verb *was pleased.* Reasons:
(1) In another poetic line (Luke 2:14) the related noun *good pleasure* means "God's (understood) good pleasure." Cf. also Phil. 2:13, where *"the* good pleasure" similarly means *"his* [God's] good pleasure." Also in Eph. 1:5 the clear reference is to the good pleasure of "the God and Father of our Lord Jesus Christ."
(2) The mental insertion "God" or "the Father" is, after all, not too difficult, for in the preceding context *the Father* has been referred to in relation to the Son (see verses 12, 13, 15). In verse 13 the latter was called "the Son of *his* love," and in verse 15 this Son was described as "the image of the invisible *God.*"
The *alternate rendering,* favored by some (including R.S.V., Abbott, Lenski, C. F. D. Moule, Ridderbos), namely, "for in him all the fulness was pleased to dwell" (or something similar) is certainly possible grammatically. My hesitancy to adopt this rendering is based on the following considerations:
(1) Nowhere else in the New Testament does Paul *thus* personify this fulness. Have we the right to ascribe to Paul — or to the very early church, if the apostle is here quoting a hymn — the style of Clement of Alexandria or of Irenaeus?
(2) It is hardly correct to maintain that in Col. 1:19 (alternate rendering) we have an exactly similar construction as in Col. 2:9, that is, that here in Col. 1:19 just as in Col. 2:9 *fulness* is the subject of a form of the verb *to dwell.* On the contrary, when Col. 1:19 is rendered "for in him all the fulness was pleased to dwell" the

This delight of the Father in the Son was evident even during the old dispensation, yes, even before the world was founded (Ps. 2:7, 8; John 17:5; Eph. 1:9). During the period of Christ's sojourn on earth it manifested itself again and again (Matt. 3:17; 17:5; John 12:28). It was indeed God's good pleasure that in his Son *all* the fulness should dwell. The powers and attributes of Deity were not to be distributed among a multitude of angels. The divine supremacy or sovereignty, either as a whole or in part, was not to be surrendered to them. On the contrary, in accordance with God's good pleasure, from all eternity the plenitude of the Godhead, the fulness of God's essence and glory, which fulness is the source of grace and glory for believers, resides in the Son of his love, in him alone, not in him and the angels. It dwells in him whom we now serve as our exalted Mediator, and it manifests itself both in Creation and Redemption.

Explanatory passages are:

John 1:16, "For out of his fulness we have received grace upon grace."

Col. 2:3, "in whom all the treasures of wisdom and knowledge are stored up."

Col. 2:9, "For in him all the fulness [56] of the godhead dwells bodily."

---

noun *fulness* becomes the subject not directly of a form of the verb *to dwell* but of *was pleased,* and this concept (fulness) is thus invested with a more definitely personal attribute. If any argument can be derived from Col. 2:9 it would rather be in the opposite direction, for in Col. 2:9 *fulness* is, indeed, subject of a form of the verb *to dwell,* just as it is also in Col. 1:19 when the latter is rendered, "For in him he [God] was pleased to have all the fulness dwell." The noun πλήρωμα is then subject to the infinitive κατοικῆσαι.

[56] Much has been written about this term *fulness* (πλήρωμα). The sense of the word must be determined in each separate case by the context. In accordance with this rule the following shades of meaning, each according to its own setting, can be recognized. At least, the following resultant meanings deserve consideration:

Matt. 9:16 and Mark 2:21: the patch that fills up the rent in a garment.

Mark 6:43 and 8:20: basketfuls.

John 1:16: infinite plenitude from which believers receive grace upon grace.

Rom. 11:12: total number of elect Jews (cf. Rom. 11:2, 5).

Rom. 11:25: total number of elect Gentiles.

Rom. 13:10: love as law's fulfilment; that is, love considered as that which fully satisfies the requirements of the law.

Rom. 15:29: the sum-total or abundance of blessings imparted by Christ.

I Cor. 10:26 (in a quotation from Ps. 24:1; LXX 23:1): the sum-total or abundance of that which the earth produces.

Gal. 4:4: the full measure of the time of Christ's first coming as predetermined in God's plan, in accordance with the imperative *need* which this coming satisfied, the Messianic *hope* which it fulfilled, and the golden *opportunity* which it provided.

Eph. 1:10: the fulness of the seasons, the new dispensation.

Eph. 1:23 (very controversial). Among the many interpretations are these three:

   (1) the church as that which Christ completes.

   (2) the church as that which completes Christ, he himself being incomplete without it, as the bridegroom is incomplete without the bride.

   (3) Christ as the fulness of God, the All-Filler.

A more detailed discussion would belong to a Commentary on Ephesians.

20. Now both in Col. 2:9, 10 and here in 1:19, 20 the fulness which dwells in Christ is mentioned with a practical purpose. It is a source of blessing. Thus here in Col. 1:19, 20 we are told that it was the good pleasure or delight of God the Father that in the Son of his love all the fulness should dwell **and through him to reconcile all things to himself,**[57] **having made peace**

Eph. 3:19 and 4:13: the full fruit of the work of Christ imparted to believers by
    God; the full maturity intended by God; spiritual maturity.
Col. 1:19 and 2:9: fulness of the divine essence and glory considered as the source
    of unending blessings for believers.

The theory that Paul's *frequent use* of the term (though *not* the term itself) was due, at least in part, to its employment by the false teachers may well be correct. The noun *fulness* is found no less than six times in the ten chapters of Ephesians and Colossians, as often as in the seventy-seven chapters of all of Paul's other epistles. Moreover, the number of times the verb *to make full, fill,* or *fulfil* is used in Colossians, Ephesians, and Philippians (closely related Prison Epistles) contrasts sharply with its far lower frequency in the other epistles (as was stated earlier). Was one of the reasons why the apostle included this line of the "hymn" the fact that it contained the word *fulness* in connection with Christ? And did he, perhaps, intend to convey the meaning, "The fulness of God, and consequently the true source of his people's fulness, about which those who proclaim error are always talking, is found in Christ, in him alone"? The probability that this was one of the reasons why Paul quoted these lines in combating the Colossian heresy must be granted, even though we cannot be sure. Lightfoot is of the opinion that Essene Judaizers derived the word *fulness* and its cognates from a Palestinian source, and that it probably represents the Hebrew root *ml'*, of which it is a translation in the LXX, and the cognate Aramaic root, as the Peshito seems to indicate.

Three additional facts should be mentioned in this connection:

(1) For *the term* πλήρωμα *itself* Paul or the early hymn-writers were by no means dependent upon false teachers. The early Christians were steeped in the terminology of the Old Testament, in which the term *fulness* is used again and again; for example in Ps. 24:1 (LXX 23:1); 50:12 (LXX 49:12); 89:11 (LXX 88:12); 96:11 (LXX 95:11); 98:7 (LXX 97:7). (To that extent I can agree with E. Percy, *op. cit.*, p. 76 ff.)

(2) The theory that the *frequency* of the term in Ephesians and Colossians had something to do with its use by the false teachers by no means indicates that as early as this it already had the sense that was ascribed to it in the elaborate speculations of *second century* Gnosticism.

(3) Since the meaning of a word depends on its use in a given context lengthy arguments with respect to the question whether basically πλήρωμα means *that which is filled* or *that which fills* are not very fruitful.

For further discussion see the following:

J. B. Lightfoot, *op. cit.*, pp. 257-273; J. A. Robinson, "The Church as the Fulfilment of the Christ: a Note on Ephesians 1:23," *Exp*, 5th series, 7 (1898), pp. 241-259; C. F. D. Moule, *op. cit.*, pp. 164-169; and Delling, Th.W.N.T., Vol. VI, pp. 297-304.

[57] εἰς αὐτόν to be written (or with the sense of) εἰς αὐτόν. It was customary for Paul to say that reconciliation is *to God* (Rom. 5:10, twice; II Cor. 5:18, 19, 20). The fact that in these passages (as also in non-theological I Cor. 7:11) the verb καταλλάσσω is used, to which corresponds the noun καταλλαγή (Rom. 5:11; 11:15; II Cor. 5:18, 19), while here in Col. 1:20, 21 and in Eph. 2:16 (nowhere else in the New Testament) the compound verb ἀποκαταλλάσσω occurs, does not detract from the force of this argument. Moreover, *God the Father* is the implied subject in verse 19 (see footnote 55 above).

through the blood of his cross; through him,[58] whether the things on the earth or the things in the heavens. Not only were all things *created* "through him," that is, through the Son of God's love (verse 16), but all things are also (in a sense to be explained) *reconciled* "through him" (verse 20). In both cases *all things* has the same meaning: all creatures without any exception whatever:

> "There rustles a Name O so dear 'long the clouds,
> That Name heaven and earth in grand harmony shrouds."

This is the nearly literal translation of the first lines of a Dutch hymn:

> "Daar ruist langs de wolken een lieflijke naam,
> Die hemel en aarde verenigt te zaam."

Some have objected to the lines for theological reasons.[59]

Personally, I see no reason for rejecting the idea expressed in this poem. One might as well reject Col. 1:20! It is all a matter of interpretation. Thus, it is true, indeed, that heaven and earth are not now united, and are not going to be united, in the sense that all rational beings in the entire universe are now *with gladness of heart* submitting themselves, or will at some future date joyfully submit themselves, to the rule of God in Christ. This universalistic interpretation of Col. 1:20 is contrary to Scripture (Ps. 1; Dan. 12:2; Matt. 7:13, 14; 25:46; John 5:28, 29; Phil. 3:18-21; II Thess. 1:3-10; and a host of other passages). It was Origen who was probably the first Christian universalist. In his youthful work *De Principiis* he suggested this thought of universal, final restoration for all. In his later writings he seems to imply it here and there, but obscures it somewhat by the suggestion of a constant succession of fall and restoration. He has, however, had many followers, and among them some have expressed themselves far more bluntly. Some time ago a minister told his audience, "In the end everybody is going to be saved. I have hope even for the devil."

The real meaning of Col. 1:20 is probably as follows: Sin ruined the universe. It destroyed the harmony between one creature and the other, also between all creatures and their God. Through *the blood of the cross* (cf.

---

[58] The phrase "through him," here repeated, though lacking in important manuscripts, is probably genuine. It may be considered a repetition for the sake of emphasis. The very fact that it is a repetition probably accounts for its omission from some texts.

[59] Could that be the reason why the otherwise excellent and very popular rendering by Rev. W. Kuipers, as found in No. 199 of *The New Christian Hymnal*, is as follows:

> "I hear in the air, 'neath the canopy blue,
> Sweet notes of a Name, most resplendent and true"?

This, though probably excellent poetry, is obviously not a true translation of the Dutch lines.

Eph. 2:11-18) , however, sin, in principle, has been conquered. The demand of the law has been satisfied, its curse born (Rom. 3:25; Gal. 3:13) . Harmony, accordingly, has been restored. Peace was made. *Through Christ and his cross the universe is brought back or restored to its proper relationship to God in the sense that as a just reward for his obedience Christ was exalted to the Father's right hand, from which position of authority and power he rules the entire universe in the interest of the church and to the glory of God.* This interpretation brings the present passage in harmony with the related ones written during this same imprisonment. Note the expression "the things on the earth or the things in the heavens" (or something very similar) not only here in Col. 1:20 but also in Eph. 1:10 and Phil. 2:10.

There is, of course, a difference in the *manner* in which various creatures submit to Christ's rule and are "reconciled to God." Those who are and remain evil, whether men or angels, submit ruefully, unwillingly. In their case *peace,* harmony, is *imposed, not welcomed.* But not only are their evil designs constantly being over-ruled for good, but these evil beings themselves have been, in principle, stripped of their power (Col. 2:15) . They are brought into subjection (I Cor. 15:24-28; cf. Eph. 1:21, 22) , and "the God of *peace* (!) will bruise Satan under y o u r feet shortly" (Rom. 16:20) . The good angels, on the other hand, submit joyfully, eagerly. So do also the redeemed among men. This group includes the members of the Colossian church as far as they are true believers, a thought to which Paul gives expression in the following verses.

---

21 And y o u, who once were estranged and hostile in disposition, as shown by y o u r wicked works, 22 he in his body of flesh through his death has now reconciled, in order to present y o u holy, faultless, and blameless before himself; 23 if, indeed, y o u continue in the faith, founded and firm, and are not moved away from the hope that is derived from the gospel which y o u have heard, which was preached among every creature under heaven, and of which I, Paul, became a minister.

1:21-23

IV. *The Son's Reconciling Love toward the Colossians*
and
Their Resulting Duty to Continue in the Faith

21, 22a. And y o u, who once were estranged and hostile in disposition, as shown by y o u r wicked works, he in his body of flesh through his death has now reconciled.[60]

---

[60] Because of its length this footnote has been placed at the end of the chapter, page 96.

With joy of heart the apostle now testifies that the Colossians, too, had become recipients of this marvelous gift of reconciliation, a reconciliation which for men whose hearts receive Christ has a far more beautiful and intimate meaning than it has for the world in general. Paul reminds the Colossians of the great change that had occurred in their lives, in order that this reminder may cause them to dread the very suggestion of returning to their former manner of life (cf. Col. 3:7). Meaning: "Y o u were separate from Christ, alienated from the commonwealth of Israel, and strangers from the covenants of the promise, having no hope and without God in the world . . . far off . . . darkened in understanding, alienated from the life of God" (Eph. 2:12, 13; 4:18). This state of estrangement, moreover, was not due simply to ignorance or innocence. *There are no innocent heathen!* On the contrary, they were estranged *and hostile in disposition*. It was *their own fault* that they had been and had remained for a long time "far off," for they had actually *hated* God; and when God through conscience and through his revelation in nature and history had made himself known to them to a certain extent, they in their hostility had "suppressed the truth by their wickedness" (Rom. 1:18-23). Such inexcusable human hostility, which is the sinner's condition *by nature,* merits God's wrath (Rom. 1:18; Col. 3:6). By nature sinners are therefore "children of wrath" (Eph. 2:3). Moreover, the inner disposition of aversion to God and antipathy to the voice of conscience which formerly had characterized these Colossians had revealed itself in *wicked deeds,* such as those that are enumerated very specifically in Col. 3:5-9.

But all this was past now, at least basically. Through the blood of the Son of God's love peace had been made. He, meaning this Son of God's love,[61] in his *body of flesh* (that was the *sphere* of the reconciliation), and through his *death* (that was the *instrument*) had brought about a return to the proper relation between the Colossians and their God. A *return,* not as if there had been a time, many, many years ago, when these Colossians had been Christians, but rather in this sense, that the establishment of peace between the Father-heart of God and the soul of the sinner is for the latter a *going back* to *the state* of rectitude in which God originally created man. (The *condition* to which grace brings the rescued sinner is, of course, far better than that before the fall.) By God's sovereign grace the prodigal returns to his home from which he had been *estranged* (see verse 21; also Luke 15:11-24). That is the meaning of *reconciliation.* By Christ's atoning death God is reconciled to the sinner, the sinner to God. "The reconciled God justifies the sinner who accepts the reconciliation, and so operates in his heart by the Holy Spirit that the sinner also lays aside his wicked aliena-

---

[61] The modifiers "in *his* body of flesh through *his* death" make it clear that the subject of the sentence (verses 21-23) is not *God* (as Lightfoot maintains) but Christ. Thus also F. W. Beare, *op. cit.,* p. 175, and Lenski, *op. cit.,* p. 70 very emphatically.

tion from God, and thus enters into the fruits of the perfect atonement of Christ." [62]

Note once more that expression "in his body of flesh," a Hebraism meaning *Christ's human body,* and thus by extension, *his entire physical existence on earth,* in which he satisfied the demands of the law and bore its punishment. (Cf. Luke 22:19; I Cor. 11:27; Heb. 10:10; I Peter 2:24.) It is probable that "body of flesh" [63] is here contrasted with "body, the church" of verse 18. It should be added, however, that the Holy Spirit who inspired Colossians (as well as the rest of Scripture) foresaw the time when the Docetics would be teaching that Jesus Christ appeared to men in a *spiritual* body, and since he had no physical body only *seemed* to suffer and die on the cross. Col. 1:22 gives the lie to that theory.

22b. The purpose of the Son's reconciling work as it affected the Colossians is now stated: **in order to present y o u holy, faultless, and blameless before himself.**[64] Note: *holy,* that is, cleansed from all sin and separated entirely to God and his service; *faultless:* without any blemish whatever (Phil. 2:15), like a perfect sacrifice; and *blameless:* completely above reproach (I Tim. 3:10; Titus 1:6, 7).

The *presentation* here referred to must be viewed as definitely eschatological, that is, as referring to the great consummation when Jesus returns upon clouds of glory. This follows from the conditional clause, "if, indeed, y o u continue in the faith. . . ." It is comforting to know that not only *the apostles* looked forward with joyful anticipation to the time when they would present the fruit of *God's* grace and of *their* labor (they being God's co-workers, I Cor. 3:9) as a pure virgin to Christ the Bridegroom (II Cor. 11:2; Phil. 1:10; 2:16; I Thess. 2:19, 20; I John 2:28), but so does also Christ himself (Eph. 5:27). To him, too, the words of Zeph. 3:17 are applicable, "He will rejoice over you with joy; he will rest in his love; he will joy over you with singing." This glorious *presentation* is here referred to as the purpose of the *reconciliation.*

---

[62] L. Berkhof, *Systematic Theology,* p. 373.

[63] On the meaning of the word *flesh* see N.T.C. on Philippians, p. 77, footnote 55.

[64] Agreement with the subject of the sentence (see footnote 61 above), as well as comparison with the very similar passage Eph. 5:27, inclines me to the conclusion that here in Col. 1:22b "before him" means "before himself" (that is, before the Son of God's love), just as in verse 20 (see footnote 57 above) "to him" means (or may even be written) "to himself" (that is, to God). Note, in this connection, that while it was customary for Paul to say that *reconciliation* was *to God,* he describes *presentation* as being either *to Christ* (Eph. 5:27; II Cor. 11:2) or *to God* (Rom. 14:10); and sometimes does not clearly indicate the One *to whom* believers are to be presented (Col. 1:28; II Cor. 4:14). Of course, in view of such passages as John 14:9 and I John 2:23, it makes very little difference whether Christ is viewed as presenting his children to himself or to God. He cannot do the one without doing the other.

23. Now in connection with this glorious presentation at the Lord's return a condition must be fulfilled. Hence, Paul continues: **if, indeed, y o u continue in the faith, founded and firm. . . .** Divine preservation always presupposes human perseverance. Perseverance proves faith's genuine character, and is therefore indispensable to salvation. To be sure, no one can continue in the faith in his own strength (John 15:5). The enabling grace of God is needed from start to finish (Phil. 2:12, 13). This, however, does not cancel human responsibility and activity. Yes, *activity*, continuous, sustained, strenuous effort (Heb. 12:14). It should be noted, however, that this is distinctly the activity of *faith* (cf. I Tim. 2:15), a faith not in themselves but in God. Thus they will be "founded and firm," that is, firmly established upon the one and only true foundation, the foundation of the apostles (through their testimony). Of this foundation Christ Jesus is the cornerstone (I Cor. 3:11; Eph. 2:20; Rev. 21:14, 19, 20). The conditional clause continues: **and are not moved away from the hope that is derived from the gospel which y o u have heard.** Danger was threatening; and it was of a twofold character, as pointed out earlier (see Introduction, III B; IV A). Hence, the apostle by implication is here warning the Colossians against relapse into their former state with all its soul-destroying vices (Col. 3:5-11) and against the "solution" urged upon them by those who refused to recognize Jesus Christ as the complete and all-sufficient Savior. Let them not allow themselves to be dislodged or shunted away from the *hope* — ardent expectation, complete confidence, watchful waiting — of which the gospel speaks and to which the gospel gives rise, that gospel which the Colossians "have heard," that is, to which they have not only listened but to which they have also given heed. See above on Col. 1:6-8. That gospel, moreover, was not meant for a select few — the Colossian errorists may well have considered themselves an exclusive set! — nor was it confined to any particular region; on the contrary, it was the gospel **which,** in obedience to the Lord's command (Matt. 28:19; especially Mark 16:15), **was preached among every creature under heaven.** It recognized no boundaries whether racial, national, or regional. It is always the "whosoever believeth" gospel. Having reached Rome, from which Paul is writing this epistle, it had actually invaded every large center of the then-known world. More on this under verse 6 above. With deep emotion and humble gratitude the apostle concludes this section and links it with the next paragraph by adding: **and of which I, Paul, became a minister.** The real depth of these words can only be understood in the light of such passages as I Cor. 15:9; Eph. 3:8; and I Tim. 1:15-17. A *minister* [65] of the gospel is one who knows the gospel, has been saved by the Christ of the gospel, and with joy of heart proclaims the gospel to others. Thus he *serves* the cause of the gospel.

---

[65] Obviously the word διάκονος is not here used in the technical sense of *deacon*. For the use of this word see N.T.C. on I Tim. 3:13 and 4:6.

24 I am now rejoicing amid my sufferings for y o u, and what is lacking in the afflictions of Christ I in his stead am supplying in my flesh, for his body, which is the church, 25 of which I became a minister, according to the stewardship of God given to me for y o u r benefit, to give full scope to the word of God, 26 the mystery hidden for ages and generations but now made manifest to his saints; 27 to whom God was pleased to make known what (is) the riches of the glory of this mystery among the Gentiles, which is Christ in y o u, the hope of glory; 28 whom we proclaim, admonishing every man and teaching every man in all wisdom, in order that we may present every man perfect in Christ; 29 for which I am laboring, striving by his energy working powerfully within me.

1:24-29

V. *The Apostle's Share in Proclaiming "the Mystery,"*
namely, "Christ in y o u, the hope of glory"

24a. Expanding the personal reference begun in verse 23 the apostle continues: **I am now rejoicing amid my sufferings for y o u.** The word *now* probably refers to the fact that right at this moment Paul is not making missionary journeys nor *by his presence* ministering to the Colossians, as he hopes to do later (Philem. 22), but is enduring the many details of suffering and hardship — note the plural "my sufferings" — that pertain to his present *imprisonment* (Col. 4:10, 18; Eph. 3:1; 4:1; Philem. 1, 9, 23). But instead of complaining *he rejoices,* for do not these trials confirm his apostleship? Remember Acts 9:16! And is not suffering in behalf of Christ a great privilege also for other reasons? See N.T.C. on Phil. 1:29, 30. And will not his endurance in the midst of many hardships strengthen the Colossians, and in fact believers everywhere, in their faith? Paul has every right to say, "my sufferings *for y o u.*" See also on 2:1.

24b. This positive aspect of enduring sufferings, namely, that such sanctified cross-bearing will be of blessing to the church is brought out meaningfully in the much discussed words which follow, namely, **and what is lacking in the afflictions of Christ I in his stead am supplying in my flesh for his body, which is the church.**

Closeness to Christ causes Paul to write as he does. He is even now reflecting on the afflictions which the Savior endured when he was on earth. Paul knows that he himself in his transitory earthly existence is, in a sense to be explained presently, *filling in* or *supplying* what was lacking in Christ's sufferings. The apostle is undergoing these hardships in the place of Jesus, since Jesus himself is no longer here to endure them. Not as if Paul were doing this all by himself, but he is contributing his share. Other believers contribute theirs. Paul is also convinced of the fact that his afflictions are be-

86

ing borne for the benefit of Christ's glorious body, the church (see above, on verse 18). He knows that by his calm endurance and clear testimony during trial the church will be established in the faith.

In the foregoing paragraph I have made it clear that it is my considered opinion that the apostle is actually saying that he, as one among many, is in a sense supplying what was lacking in *the afflictions which Jesus suffered while on earth.* Percy, *op. cit.,* p. 130, calls this "the only possible interpretation." Ridderbos writes, "Our conclusion can be no other than this, that the expression *the afflictions of Christ* points to the historical suffering of Christ" (*op. cit.,* p. 158).

Of course, this does not mean that there was anything lacking in the atoning value of Christ's sacrifice. It does not mean that good works, the suffering in purgatory, faithful attendance at mass, the purchase of indulgences, or any other so-called merits can be or need be added to the merits of our Lord. Among the many passages that would refute such a theory are Col. 2:14; John 19:30; Heb. 10:11-14; and I John 1:9. But we have no right, in the interest of Protestantism in its struggle with Roman Catholicism, to change the clear grammatical and contextual meaning of a passage. We should bear in mind that although Christ by means of the afflictions which he endured rendered *complete* satisfaction to God, so that Paul is able to glory in nothing but the cross (Gal. 6:14), *the enemies of Christ were not satisfied!* They hated Jesus with insatiable hatred, and wanted to add to his afflictions. But since *he* is no longer physically present on earth, their arrows, which are meant especially for *him,* strike his followers. It is in that sense that all true believers are in his stead supplying what, as the enemies see it, is lacking in the afflictions which Jesus endured. Christ's afflictions overflow toward us. This interpretation is supported by passages such as the following:

"If they called the master of the house Beelzebub, how much more them of his household" (Matt. 10:25).

"Y o u shall be hated of all men for my name's sake" (Mark 13:13).

"If the world hates y o u, know that it has hated me before it hated y o u. . . . But all these things will they do to y o u for my name's sake, because they do not know the One who sent me" (John 15:18-21).

"Saul, Saul, why do you persecute me? . . . I am Jesus, whom you are persecuting" (Acts 9:4, 5).

"The afflictions of Christ overflow toward us" (II Cor. 1:5).

". . . always bearing about in the body the putting to death of Jesus" (II Cor. 1:10).

"I bear on my body the marks of Jesus" (Gal. 6:17).

". . . that I may know him . . . and the fellowship of his sufferings" (Phil. 3:10).

"And when the dragon saw that he had been thrown down to the earth, he persecuted the woman because she had brought forth the male child" (Rev. 12:13) .[66]

25. Paul has indicated that his sufferings are for the benefit of the church. He continues, **of which I became a minister, according to the stewardship of God given to me for y o u r benefit.** Harassed by men who tried to lead them astray, the Colossians must bear in mind that Paul, who is now addressing them and to whom indirectly they owe their knowledge of salvation, was their divinely appointed *steward.* The office of "administrator of spiritual treasures" had been entrusted to him and to his helpers (I Cor. 4:1, 2; 9:17; I Tim. 1:4; Titus 1:7) . And this, says Paul, is *for y o u r benefit.* In their case that was true in a special sense, for they had been won over from the Gentiles (Col. 1:27; 3:5-11) , and it was *especially* (not exclusively) to the Gentiles that Paul had been sent (Acts 13:47; 22:21; Rom. 11:13; 15:16; Gal. 2:8, 9; Eph. 3:1, 2, 8; I Tim. 2:7; II Tim. 4:17) . The stewardship of God had been given to him, moreover, **to give full scope to the word of God,** that is, to proclaim the Christ in all his glorious fulness to everyone, regardless of race, nationality, or social position.

26, 27. That word of God centers in Christ, God's glorious mystery. Hence, the apostle continues, **the mystery hidden for ages and generations but now made manifest to his saints.** Paul uses the term "mystery," but *not* as indicating *a secret teaching, rite, or ceremony, having something to do with religion but hidden from the masses and revealed to an exclusive group,* the sense in which the term (generally in the plural: *mysteries*) was at that time being employed outside of the circles of true Christianity. On the contrary, in the Pauline literature a *mystery* [67] *is a person or a truth that would have remained unknown had not God revealed him or it.* Such a mystery is said to have been *revealed in the fullest sense* only then when its significance is translated into historical reality. The mystery of which the apostle is thinking here in Col. 1:26, 27 had been *hidden;* that is, for ages and generations (lit. "since the ages and since the generations") it had not been historically realized. It was present, to be sure, in the *plan* of God and also in *prophecy,* but *not in actuality. Now,* however, that is, in this present era which began with the incarnation, and even more specifically with the proclamation of the gospel

---

[66] Because of its length this footnote has been placed at the end of the chapter, page 97.
[67] The word *mystery* occurs 28 times in the New Testament: 3 times in the Gospels (Matt. 13:11; Mark 4:11; Luke 8:10) ; 4 times in the Book of Revelation (Rev. 10:7; 17:5; also 1:20 and 17:7 with a sense differing from that in which it is used by Paul; probably "symbolical meaning") ; and 21 times in Paul's letters (Rom. 11:25; 16:25; I Cor. 2:1, 2:7; 4:1; 13:2; 14:2; 15:51; Eph. 1:9; 3:3; 3:4; 3:9; 5:32; 6:19; Col. 1:26; 1:27; 2:2; 4:3; I Tim. 3:9; 3:16; II Thess. 2:7) . See the entry μυστήριον in L.N.T. (A. and G.) , and the extensive literature there given.

to the Gentiles, it was made manifest to his *saints,* that is, to the entire church of this new dispensation, none excepted. It was there for all to see! To describe more fully what he has in mind Paul continues: **to whom God was pleased to make known what (is) the riches of the glory of this mystery among the Gentiles, which is Christ in y o u, the hope of glory.** The mystery, accordingly, is Christ himself, just as in I Tim. 3:16; cf. Eph. 3:3, 4, 9. It is *Christ in all his glorious riches actually dwelling through his Spirit in the hearts and lives of the Gentiles.* In all the preceding ages this had never been seen, but now every child of God ("saint") could bear witness to it. The Colossians themselves offered proof. To be sure, even during the days of the old dispensation there were *predictions* which, with ever-increasing clarity, foretold that the Gentiles would one day constitute part of God's people (Gen. 22:18; 26:4; 28:14; 49:10; Ps. 72:8; 87; Isa. 54:2, 3; 60:1-3; Micah 4:1, 2; Mal. 1:11, to mention only a few), but in the divine good pleasure the realization of these predictions did not arrive until this present Messianic Age. "Christ in y o u, the hope of glory" had to wait until now. "Christ in y o u" means Christ in y o u *Gentiles,* and that on a basis of perfect equality with Israel, the "middle wall of partition" having been completely removed (Eph. 2:14)!

Christ in y o u, the hope of glory, an Easter theme [68]

1. *Its meaning*

Christ in y o u is here proclaimed as the hope or *solid basis for the expectation of* future, eschatological glory. The content of this glory is set forth in the context: "the inheritance of the saints in the light" (verse 12), "the presentation" of the bride to the Bridegroom (verses 22, 28); see also Col. 3:4, 24; Rom. 5:2; 8:18-23; I Cor. 15; Phil. 3:20, 21; I Thess. 2:19; 3:13; 4:13-17; II Thess. 1:10; II Tim. 1:12; 4:8; Titus 2:13. While the apostle included the intermediate state in this concept of glory (II Cor. 5:1-8; Phil. 1:21, 23), his horizon was Christ's second coming and never-ending bliss.

2. *Hopes that deceive*

In all ages men have tried to establish their own basis for belief in immortality and even in a future state of perfection.

a. Some reason from the premise of *unsatisfied desire*. We desire to see a perfect landscape. Yet when, standing on a hill, we think we see one, the descent into the valley with its rotting logs and decaying fruit, disillusions us. Nevertheless, the desire persists. This guarantees future realization.

b. Others derive their proof from *the unheeded voice of conscience*. A voice within me is constantly saying, "Thou shalt do this, that." Yet, no

---

[68] Cf. G. Matheson, "The Pauline Argument for a Future State," *Exp,* first series, 9 (1879), pp. 264-284.

one has ever *fully* obeyed this categorical imperative. Is not this unrelenting demand a prediction of a future state of strict compliance, a state of perfection?

c. There is also the argument from *the enduring character of the self within me*. In a steady line of progress I as a person have already survived successive stages of being. I was an embryo. When that stage ceased my *self* persisted. I was born, became an infant. I survived that stage too. And so after boyhood I became a young man, then a man of middle age, etc. Consequently, as I have survived every one of these stages, will I not also survive the last stage, namely, physical death, and rise to an immortality of bliss and glory?

A moment's reflection is all that is necessary to show the weakness of this type of reasoning in any of its forms. Persistent yearning for the ideal in the realm of beauty, inner compulsion to obey the moral law coupled with the realization that in the here and now one can never obey it fully, and also the self's leapfrogging of biological stages, these facts do not guarantee immortality, much less perfection in a future existence. As to the last argument, even a dog, in proportion to its own life span, passes through and survives various stages, yet does not thereby attain to immortality!

3. *Christ . . . the hope of glory*

Now over against these fallible reasonings Paul proclaims Christ as the one and only solid basis for the expectation of *immortality* not only, but of future, eschatological *glory*. The evidence, moreover, which Christ gave to the world of a future state of perfection lay not only in his words or deeds but in *himself*. Our persistent yearning for the ideal in the realm of true, spiritual beauty is realized in him. And because his soul is beautiful, words of grace and beauty fell from his lips.

> "Fair are the meadows,
> Fairer still the woodlands,
> Robed in the blooming garb of spring:
> Jesus is fairer, Jesus is purer,
> Who makes the woeful heart to sing."
>   Crusaders' Hymn

As to the persistent demand of conscience, he was the only one who satisfied it in every respect. He was able to say, "Who of y o u convicts me of sin?" (John 8:46) .

> "Weak is the effort of my heart,
> And cold my warmest thought;
> But when I see thee as you art,
> I'll praise thee as I ought."
>   John Newton

And finally, as to surviving every stage of earthly existence, even the last one, he did that very thing! Easter proclaims in every land, "Hallelujah, Christ arose." In Paul's day there were witnesses — *many* of them, in fact — who had seen him alive after his resurrection (I Cor. 15:6). And was not the apostle himself also a witness? (I Cor. 15:8).

> "Death cannot keep his prey —
> Jesus, my Savior;
> He tore the bars away —
> Jesus my Lord.
> Up from the grave he arose,
> With a mighty triumph o'er his foes.
> He arose a Victor from the dark domain,
> And he lives forever with his saints to reign.
> He arose! He arose!
> Hallelujah! Christ arose!
>
>   Robert Lowry

4. *Objection*

But granted that Christ does indeed satisfy the desire for beauty, for moral and spiritual perfection, and for ultimate survival, is not he an exception to the rule, an interruption in the race of Adam? How can *his* adequacy satisfy my inadequacy? How can he really be the solid basis for the hope of future bliss for the entire church, and particularly, in the present context, the Gentiles' hope of glory?

5. *Objection answered*

Christ *in y o u*, the hope of glory.

"This Christ through his Spirit is dwelling (and this not passively but energetically) *in y o u*," says Paul. Hence, "If the Spirit of him who raised Jesus from the dead dwells in y o u, he who raised Christ Jesus from the dead will give life to y o u r mortal bodies also, through his Spirit who dwells in y o u" (Rom. 8:11).

28, 29. In connection with "Christ in y o u, the hope of glory," Paul continues, **whom we proclaim, admonishing every man and teaching every man in all wisdom.** Whether Paul, Timothy, etc., proclaim *the gospel* (cf. I Cor. 9:14), *the testimony of God* (I Cor. 2:1), or whatever else it may be called, in any case it is ever *the Christ himself* (thus also Phil. 1:17) whom they proclaim. This proclamation took the form of *admonishing* and *teaching*. The apostle had been carrying on this blessed activity before his imprisonment, but even now in his bonds he makes use of every opportunity, both in person (Acts 28:30, 31; Phil. 1:12-14) and by letter, to make known far and wide the riches both present and future, which believers possess in their Lord and Savior. And so do his helpers. Paul was ever emphasizing the need of pastoral labor. For him to *admonish* meant *to warn, to stimulate,* and *to encourage.* He would actually *plead* with people to be reconciled to God (II Cor. 5:20). He would at times even shed tears (cf. Acts 20:19, 31; II Cor. 2:4; Phil. 3:18). See N.T.C. on Philippians, p. 181. His proclamation of the Christ was a marvelous combination of the true gospel and the most affectionate presentation. He was able to write to the Thessalonians, "But we were gentle in the midst of y o u, as when a nurse cherishes her own children: so being affectionately desirous of y o u, we gladly shared with y o u not only the gospel of God but also our own souls, because y o u had become very dear to us . . . just as y o u know how, like a father (dealing) with his own children (so we were) admonishing each and all of y o u, and encouraging and testifying that y o u should live lives worthy of God, who calls y o u into his own kingdom of glory."

It should be stressed in this connection that there was no wide gulf between Paul's *admonishing* and his *teaching.* For him *abstract* doctrine did not exist. Neither did Christian ethics suspended in mid-air. On the contrary, Paul's teaching was done with a view to admonishing; his admonishing was rooted in teaching. Accordingly, the apostle never proclaimed a Christ who was a Savior but not an Example, nor a Christ who was an Example but not a Savior. Christianity for Paul was, indeed, a life, but a life based on a doctrine. And for those — for those alone! — who embrace Christ as being, by God's sovereign grace, Lord, Savior, and thus Enabler, he can also be Example.

It is remarkable how often Paul links his *admonishing* with his *teaching* concerning the person and work of Christ. A few illustrations must suffice:

Reference	Admonition, in substance	Link to teaching concerning Christ's person and work
Rom. 15:2, 3	Please the neighbor	"for Christ also pleased not himself."
Rom. 15:7	Extend a hearty welcome to each other. (Receive one another.)	"just as Christ also welcomed (received) y o u."
II Cor. 8:7-9	Abound in the grace of giving to the needy	"for y o u know the grace of our Lord Jesus Christ, that, though he was rich, yet for y o u r sake he became poor, that through

Reference	Admonition, in substance	Link to teaching concerning Christ's person and work
		his poverty y o u might become rich."
Eph. 5:2	Walk in love	"just as Christ also loved y o u, and gave himself up for us."
Phil. 2:3-8	Be humble and unselfish	"which (disposition) is also in Christ Jesus, who . . . emptied himself . . . took on the form of a servant . . . humbled himself and became obedient even to the extent of death; yes, death by a cross."
Col. 3:13	Forgive	"just as Christ has forgiven y o u."

And because this *proclamation* of the Christ by means of *admonishing* (*putting* people *in mind,* as is the literal meaning of the word) *and teaching* is ever *Christ*-centered, it is, of course, *God*-centered, that unto the triune God through Christ his Son may be the glory forever and ever (Rom. 11:36; I Cor. 8:6; 10:31; Col. 3:17). It is being carried out, moreover, *in all wisdom,* that is, in a truly practical manner, for in strict compliance with the will of God his ambassadors use the best means to reach the highest goal, expressed by Paul in these words: **in order that we may present every man perfect** [69] **in Christ;** naturally "in Christ," in the closest possible union with him, a union which is brought about by the Holy Spirit, and which is kept alive by the exercise of a faith that is not only God-given but is in its every expression being constantly sustained by God. When all guilt has been imputed to Christ, and all pollution has been cleansed by his Spirit, the church will be perfect, indeed, and will thus be presented to God in the day of the consummation of all things. See further on verse 22b above, where the same theme is discussed. Note, however, that while there and in Eph. 5:27 it was *Christ* to whom this task and honor of the presentation of believers is ascribed, and while in II Cor. 4:14 it is *God the Father,* here in Col. 1:28 it is *Paul himself and his fellow-workers.* Cf. Phil. 2:16; I Thess. 2:19. With a reference to himself Paul continues, **for which I am laboring,** that is, *toiling* to the point of weariness and exhaustion. Cf. Gal. 4:11; Phil. 2:16; I Tim.

[69] or *mature, full-grown, complete.* For full discussion see N.T.C. on Philippians, footnote 156, p. 176.

4:10. Let anyone read II Cor. 11:24-33, and let him add II Cor. 6:4-10 and II Tim. 4:7, 8 to see what it meant in those days to be a missionary, especially *the* missionary, Paul! It implied an unflinching fight against Satan and his hosts.

Paul knew what it had meant to oppose with all his might fanaticism among the Thessalonians; contention, fornication, and litigation among the Corinthians; and right now, as if his imprisonment did not bring trouble enough all by itself, the twofold danger of vice and heresy among the Colossians. See Col. 2; 3:1-17. What fightings without and fears within! Yet, constrained by the love of Christ for him, he is willing, even anxious, to give his all to the cause, and this not just in order to be an instrument in God's hand to rescue souls from hell, but to *perfect* them, and thus perfect in soul and body to *present* them to God in the day of days. To describe more fully what is implied in such labor or toil Paul adds the word **striving**. See footnotes 70 and 71. Such striving implied earnest prayers (*striving* in prayer, Col. 4:12, 13; cf. Rom. 15:30), listening to God, careful planning, letter-writing, giving direction — even from prison! — to the missionary program, bidding defiance to Satan, official gospel-proclamation (whenever possible), personal witness-bearing, and living an exemplary Christian life even in the midst of great pressure and affliction.

The question has often been asked, "How was it possible for *one* man (and a man with a thorn in the flesh!), even with the help of fellow-workers, to accomplish so much?" The answer is contained in the words of Paul himself: (striving) **by his energy working powerfully within me.**[70] Day by day, yes even moment by moment Christ's enabling Spirit was at work within Paul's entire person, bestowing strength upon body and soul. Moreover, at times in the apostle's missionary career there were even special signs and wonders (Rom. 15:19; II Cor. 12:12). Therefore, by implication, to the never-failing Christ the apostle ascribes all the glory and honor! Cf. Phil. 2:12, 13; 4:13.

Summary of Colossians 1

Epaphras, charged with the spiritual care of the Colossians, is visiting Paul, the prisoner, in Rome. He has given the apostle a full report of conditions in the Colossian church and its twofold danger: a. of relapse into pagan vice, and b. of endeavoring, in obedience to the advice of false teachers, to supplement its faith in Christ by having recourse to man-made remedies against fleshly indulgence. He has also informed Paul about the

---

[70] Literally, "striving by means of (or: according to) his energy energizing within me with power." Here *striving* is an athletic term, from which we have derived our word *agonizing*. The participle ἀγωνιζόμενος is reflected in the noun ἀγῶνα in Col. 2:1. The participle *energizing* is best taken as a middle, as in Gal. 5:6, "faith *working* through love." And from the word *power* we derive our noun *dynamite*.

loyalty to Christ which characterized the church as a whole. The prisoner, his heart filled with genuine love for the Colossians, decides to write them a letter. In this letter he takes the positive approach, so characteristic of him, and after a Christ-centered opening saluation, tells the addressees that he is continually thanking God for their *faith* in Christ Jesus and their *love* for all the saints, both of these (faith and love) strengthened by the *hope* laid up for them in the heavens, that is, the inheritance of the saints in the light. That prospect does, indeed, intensify *faith* in the Giver and *love* for all the fellow-recipients.

The hope of obtaining this inheritance is firmly grounded in the world-conquering gospel that has also made its presence felt among the Colossians, through the ministry of ever-faithful Epaphras.

Encouraged by answers to previous prayers, Paul is constantly praying that God may multiply his favors upon the Colossians, so that, while living among those whose doctrines would lead them astray, they may receive an ever clearer insight into the will of God, and may, as a result, live lives that will be spiritually fruitful in every way, and will abound in evidences of sincere and humble gratitude to God. Let them ever bear in mind that it was God who rescued them out of the domain of darkness and transplanted them into the kingdom of the Son of his love.

By means of a ringing testimony — perhaps a hymn which he is quoting — the apostle proclaims Christ as all-sufficient Savior, sovereign in both realms: creation and redemption. Therefore let the Colossians not place their confidence in anything other than Christ, for apart from him no creature has any strength either to help or to hurt. Through Christ the universe is restored to its proper relationship to God, for from his position at the Father's right hand Christ rules the entire universe in the interest of the church and to the glory of God. He who died on the cross to save sinners holds in his hands the most distant star.

If the Colossians will keep clinging to the gospel that proclaims this sovereign and all-sufficient Christ who rescued them from their former wicked life, they will not slip back. On the contrary, this Christ will one day present them holy, faultless, and blameless before himself. Of this glorious gospel Paul had been privileged to become a minister. Because of his loyalty to that gospel he is now a prisoner in Rome, supplying in his flesh what was lacking in the afflictions of Christ. Yes, the afflictions which Christ endured were overflowing to him. But he rejoices in his God-given stewardship, and intends, by God's grace, to give full scope to the word of God, the long-hidden but now revealed mystery, which is "Christ in y o u, the hope of glory." The fact that one day Christ would be living through his Spirit in the hearts and lives of the Gentiles had been long predicted but had now become a reality. This indwelling was itself the guarantee of a glorious future. With reference to the indwelling Christ, Paul concludes the chapter by saying, "whom we proclaim, admonishing every man and teaching every man in all wisdom, in order that we may present every man perfect in Christ; for which I am laboring, striving by his energy working powerfully within me."

---

⁶⁰ In connection with the accusative pronoun ὑμᾶς (y o u), the one at the beginning of verse 21, and the verbal form, if any, with which it is connected either as object or otherwise, the following main possibilities require consideration:

(1) This pronoun is modified, in verse 22, by the nom. pl. aor. pass. participle ἀπαλλαγέντες. Hence, one should read, "And y o u, who once were estranged and hostile . . . but now having been reconciled . . ."

Objections: a. In that case the accusative, rather than the nominative form of the participle would be more natural. b. The textual support for this reading is not very strong (D* G it Ir). c. The question would remain: of what verbal form is this pronoun and its modifying participle the object? This question recurs under (2); hence, may be omitted here.

(2) This pronoun is the object of the aor. inf. παραστῆσαι in verse 22. Therefore, the rendering should be, "to present y o u." The sentence which began in verse 9 continues to the end of verse 23. Verse 22a (νυνὶ . . . θανάτου) is a parenthesis in this sentence. Hence, ". . . for in him he [God] was pleased to have all the fulness dwell, and through him to reconcile all things to himself . . . and y o u, who once were estranged and hostile in disposition, as shown by y o u r wicked works (but now y o u have been reconciled in his body of flesh through his death), to present y o u holy, faultless, and blameless before himself . . ." It is evident that here the first y o u, the one at the beginning of verse 21, is repeated in verse 22, in order to disentangle the construction. It is also clear that the verb which indicates the work of reconciliation and which is included in the parenthesis is ἀποκατηλλάγητε: y o u have been reconciled, 2 per. pl. aor. ind. pass.

Objections: a. It is improbable that the very lengthy sentence (verses 9-20) would be lengthened some more by three additional verses. b. It has been shown that verses 15-20 are a literary unit, probably an ancient hymn, a unit of which verses 21-23 are not a part. c. The main idea of verses 15-20, namely, the pre-eminence of the Son in Creation and Redemption, is not continued in verses 21-23. The attention is shifted rather to the share which the Colossians have in this redemption and to the responsibility this imposes upon them.

(3) This pronoun is the object of the aor. inf. ἀποκαταλλάξαι in verse 20. Therefore, the translation should be, "to reconcile y o u." The sentence ends at the close of verse 21. Hence, ". . . for in him he [God] was pleased to have all the fulness dwell, and through him to reconcile all things to himself . . . whether the things on the earth or the things in the heavens, and (to reconcile) y o u, who once were estranged and hostile in disposition, as shown by y o u r wicked works."

Objections: see b. and c. under (2) above; also a. to a certain extent. Moule, *op. cit.*, p. 72, is correct when he states that this reconstruction makes of verse 21 "a clumsy afterthought to the sentence of verse 20."

(4) The pronoun is not connected with any verbal form. It is left hanging. The apostle wanted to say, "And y o u he has reconciled," but he never actually said ("dictated") it. He used instead the aor. indic. pass., "Y o u have been reconciled" (ἀποκατηλλάγητε), verse 22.

The following arguments have been presented in favor of this theory:

a. For Paul it was not unusual that before an idea had been fully expressed it was already being crowded out by another. He had a fertile mind.

b. This reading ("Y o u have been reconciled") has strong textual support (p⁴⁶ B 33 Ephr).

c. It is much easier to explain the substitution of "He has reconciled" (which would eliminate the anacoluthon) for "Y o u have been reconciled," than vice versa.

These are formidable arguments.

(5) The pronoun is simply the object of the 3 per. sing. aor. ind. act. verb ἀποκατήλλαξεν, *he has reconciled.*

Grounds:

a. This reading is supported by the majority of the manuscripts and versions. — The question may be raised, however, whether such evidence should not rather be weighed than counted.

b. This reading solves the grammatical problem. There is no longer any break in grammatical sequence. — This argument carries very little weight, for objection (4)c still holds. Hence, No. 5 could be simply a *solution* (?) for the sake of ease, a cutting of the Gordian knot.

c. The somewhat similar acc. pronoun ὑμᾶς in Eph. 2:1 ("and y o u being dead through y o u r trespasses and sins"), which also for a while is left hanging, is "rescued" by the aor. *active* ind. *"he made alive together with* Christ," of verse 5. If Paul used the *active* indic. there, why not also here in Colossians? — This argument probably has some value.

Conclusion

The choice lies between (4) and (5). In either case Paul said or at one time intended to say, "He has reconciled y o u." The more usual rendering, which avoids anacoluthon, may therefore probably be allowed to stand, though it does not solve the difficulties mentioned under (4) b and c. Accordingly, the distinct possibility that the rendering should be based entirely upon (4), retaining the anacoluthon, must be granted.

A.

[66] This interpretation is also supported by the following, more technical considerations:

(1) It does justice to the meaning of the prefix ἀντί. There is no justification for taking this prefix-in-composition, as here used, in any other than the substitutionary sense, as I believe I have proved in my doctoral dissertation, "The Meaning of the Preposition ἀντί in the New Testament," pp. 76, 77, Princeton Seminary, 1948. Photius has stated the case very aptly, "For he does not simply say *I fill up,* but *I fill up instead;* that is, instead of the master and teacher, I, the servant and disciple," etc. (Amphil. 121). See Lightfoot's comment on this, p. 165 of his Commentary.

(2) It is in harmony with the meaning of the expression *to fill up* (or *to supply*) *the deficiencies* (or *what is lacking*), as used elsewhere in the New Testament: I Cor. 16:17; Phil. 2:30 (see N.T.C. on that passage). In both of these cases the verb ἀναπληρόω is used. The double compound ἀνταναπληρόω occurs only here in Col. 1:24. A different double compound προσαναπληρόω (II Cor. 9:12; 11:9) also lends support to the interpretation given.

(3) It also gives the most natural meaning to the genitive τοῦ Χριστοῦ, interpreting it to mean *endured by Christ.* And according to the context the reference is distinctly to the humiliation experienced by the historical Jesus during his earthly ministry and death. See verses 20 and 22, which speak of *the blood of the cross* and of *the death* of Jesus.

B.

Accordingly, to be rejected are the following theories:

(1) Christ's vicarious atonement must be supplemented by good deeds, etc., as if its merits were otherwise insufficient.

Answer. This has been refuted in the text: Heb. 10:11-14, etc.

(2) The expression *the afflictions of Christ* indicates the sufferings which "the Mystic Christ," "the Messianic Community," or "the Corporate Christ" undergoes and must undergo during this entire dispensation until the end of the world. Along this line, though cautiously, Moule, in his very interesting and helpful Commentary, *op. cit.,* p. 76.

Answer. This violates A (3) above.

(3) *The afflictions of Christ* are those *laid upon* Paul, etc., by Christ.

Answer. This also violates A (3) above.

(4) (This is closely related to, though not identical with, No. (2).) *The afflictions of Christ* are those suffered by the exalted Mediator in heaven. The risen and ascended Christ suffers in his members. Because of the intimate bond of unity between the exalted Christ and his church the latter's sufferings may be called "the afflictions of Christ." Thus John Calvin in his *Commentary;* also Augustine and Luther. A. S. Peake, *op. cit.,* pp. 514, 515, concludes similarly.

Answer. Again a violation of A (3) above.

(5) What has been rendered "what is lacking in the afflictions of Christ" should be interpreted as "the leftover parts of the afflictions of Christ." Thus Lenski, *op. cit.,* p. 73. These "leftover parts" he also simply calls "the leftovers." Though on p. 72 he does not hesitate to use the expression "what is lacking" in his translation, yet on p. 74 he objects to calling these leftovers "deficiencies" or "something that was lacking." I honor him (his memory) for the theological position which in all probability led to his objection, but cannot agree with his reasoning at this point.

Answer. The word ὑστέρημα as used in the New Testament means (sing.) *want, lack, what is lacking, need, absence* (see Luke 21:4; I Cor. 16:17; II Cor. 8:13, 14; 9:12; 11:9; Phil. 2:30; I Thess. 3:10; and so, plur., also here in Col. 1:24). The interpretation *leftover, when it is said that this cannot mean lack or deficiency,* is hard to reconcile with the verb *to supply* (literally *to fill up,* or as we would say *to fill in*). Also if the noun used in the original means *leftover but not lack* we might have expected it (plur.) in such passages as Matt. 14:20; Mark 6:43; 8:8, 19, 20; Luke 9:17; John 6:12, 13. It does not occur in these passages.

See also, in addition to the various Commentaries listed in the Bibliography, Ernst Percy, *op. cit.,* pp. 128-134; Delling, Th.W.N.T., Vol. VI, p. 305; P. J. Gloag, "The Complement of Christ's Afflictions," *Exp,* first series, 7 (1878), pp. 224-236; W. R. G. Moir, "Col. 1:24," *ET,* 42 (1930-1931), pp. 479, 480; Josef Schmid, "Kol.1,24," *BibZ,* 21 (1933), pp. 330-344; and the dissertation of Jacob Kremer, *Was an den Leiden Christi noch mangelt. Eine interpretationsgeschichtliche und exegetische Untersuchung zu Kol.1,24b* (in Bonner, *Biblische Beiträge*), 1956.

Outline of Chapter 2

Theme: *Christ, the Pre-eminent One, the Only and All-Sufficient Savior*

I. This Only and All-Sufficient Savior is the Object of the Believers' Faith, chapters 1 and 2

    B. This Truth Expounded not only Positively but now both Positively and Negatively, chapter 2, the latter over against "the Colossian Heresy" with its:

2:1-10   1. Delusive Philosophy

2:11-17 2. Judaistic Ceremonialism

2:18-19 3. Angel-worship

2:20-23 4. Asceticism

CHAPTER II

COLOSSIANS

2 1 For I want y o u to know how greatly I strive for y o u, and for those at Laodicea, and for all who have not seen my face in the flesh, 2 in order that their hearts may be strengthened, they themselves being welded together in love, and this with a view to all the riches of assured understanding, with a view to the clear knowledge of the mystery of God, namely, Christ; 3 in whom all the treasures of wisdom and knowledge are hidden. 4 I say this in order that no one may mislead y o u by persuasive argument. 5 For, although in the flesh I am absent, yet in the spirit I am with y o u, rejoicing to see y o u r good order and the firmness of y o u r faith in Christ.

6 As therefore y o u accepted Christ Jesus the Lord, (so) in him continue to live, 7 rooted and being built up in him and being established in the faith, just as y o u were taught, overflowing with thanksgiving. 8 Be on y o u r guard lest there be any one who carries y o u off as spoil by means of his philosophy and empty deceit, according to the tradition of men, according to the rudiments of the world, and not according to Christ; 9 for in him all the fulness of the godhead dwells bodily, 10 and in him y o u have attained to fulness, namely, in him who is the head of every principality and authority.

2:1-10

I. *Warning against Delusive Philosophy*

1. It is immediately evident that Col. 2:1 is a clear continuation of the thought expressed in 1:29. Paul was writing *one letter, not four "chapters."* The continuation is: **For I want y o u to know,** the "for" constituting proof for the statement made in the preceding verse. The opening formula, "I want y o u to know," here and in I Cor. 11:3, is substantially the same in meaning as the somewhat differently worded one in Phil. 1:12. Similar is also the expression, "I (or *we*) do not wish y o u to be in ignorance" (Rom.1:13; 11:25; I Cor. 10:1; 12:1; II Cor. 1:8; I Thess. 4:13) . By the use of this formula the apostle stresses the importance of the matter under discussion. He regards the Colossian Heresy, which he is about to refute, as being a very serious danger, and therefore continues: **how greatly I strive for y o u** [71] **and**

---

[71] The rendering of the A.V., "what great conflict I have for you," is more literal, but fails to show the closeness of the connection between Col. 1:29 (A.V. "striving according to his working") and 2:1. In the original for these two verses the apostle uses two words derived from the same stem, which could almost be rendered *agonizing* (1:29) , and *agony* (2:1) . See footnote 70.

101

for those at Laodicea, and for all who have not seen my face in the flesh.
The nature of this *striving* need not be repeated (see on Col. 1:29 above).
What Paul means is, "For, in substantiation of what I have just said, I want
y o u to know how greatly I strive for y o u, Colossians, and for those at Laodicea, and for all who, *like yourselves,* have never seen me." It is well-nigh
certain that the phrase "and for all who" also includes the membership of
the church at Hierapolis (see Col. 4:13). As has been shown (see Introduction II A), so close to each other were the three cities that a spiritual danger
that affected *one* of them was almost bound to affect the other two also,
though not necessarily in the same degree.[72]

Two misconceptions must be avoided at this point:

(1) The view of many that the apostle here implies that he had never
been in Colosse.

Answer: Church and *town* must not be confused. It should be borne in
mind that when Paul on his third missionary journey was headed for
Ephesus there was as yet no church at Colosse for him to visit. On the question, "Was Paul ever in Colosse?" see Introduction II A; III A. The situation, as I see it, may well have been as follows:

On his way to Ephesus, Paul followed the natural route which via Colosse
led to Ephesus. He passed through Colosse, and may even have spent a night
there. Whether or not he did we simply do not know. His aim, however, was
to confirm the churches already established and to reach Ephesus, not to
establish new churches on the way to his destination. During his lengthy stay
at Ephesus, enquirers from the surrounding region came to hear him (Acts
19:10). Among those who came were also some people from *the three cities,*
one of those individuals being Epaphras from Colosse (cf. Col. 4:12). Upon
their conversion these men — including Epaphras — carried the great news
of salvation back to their respective towns. Thus churches were established.
Speaking in general terms, Paul could truly say that these congregations had
never seen him.

(2) The idea that the apostle was a total stranger to every member of the
three churches.

Answer: Nearly all commentators — even those that cling to No. 1, just
refuted — are careful to point out that Paul was, indeed, personally acquainted with *some* of the members of the Colossian church, and perhaps
also with some of those that belonged to the other churches in the Lycus
Valley. As to the apostle's personal acquaintances and friends in or from
Colosse see on Col. 4:12, 17; Philem. 1, 2.

The main idea of Col. 2:1 is, accordingly, that Paul, having received ample information from Epaphras (and perhaps also from others) regarding
prevailing conditions in the churches of the Lycus Valley, wants the entire

---

[72] Clearly ὅσοι *here,* as in Acts 4:6; Rev. 18:17, includes those previously mentioned. This ὅσοι is reflected in αὐτῶν of verse 2 and even in ὑμᾶς of verse 4.

membership — also that large majority that has never seen him — to know how much he loves them and how thoroughly he is concerned about them when spiritual danger threatens.

Now both in chapter 1 and in chapter 2 the apostle proclaims Christ as the only and all-sufficient Savior, the Object of the believers' faith. In both chapters, moreover, the predominant tone is *positive:* Christ is set forth in all his majesty and riches as the source of whatever believers may need and especially as the object of their trust and adoration. There is, however, a marked difference between the two chapters. While in chapter 1 the negative element — refutation of error — is merely *implied,* in chapter 2 it is definitely *expressed* (see verses 4, 8, 16, 18, 20-23), and forceful warnings are issued. Even here, however, as stated, it is Christ who is proclaimed (see verses 2, 3, 6, 7, 9-15).

Now though the heresy is *one,* the apostle views it here from a fourfold aspect (cf. Introduction III B). These four divisions, however, are not watertight compartments. There is overlapping, as will be shown as the individual passages are discussed.

2, 3. The purpose of Paul's striving is: **in order that their hearts may be strengthened.** The *heart* of all true pastoral activity is to be an instrument in God's hand to bring the *hearts* of those entrusted to one's care to the *heart* of Christ. The reason is this: once a man's heart has been thoroughly won over and established in grace, the entire person has become the object of God's marvelous transforming power, for the heart is the fulcrum of feeling and faith as well as the mainspring of words and actions (Rom. 10:10; cf. Matt. 12:34; 15:19; 22:37; John 14:1). It is the core and center of man's being, man's inmost self. "Out of it are the issues of life" (Prov. 4:23). "Man looks on the outward appearance, but Jehovah looks on the heart" (I Sam. 16:7). Over against the attack of false teachers these hearts must be *strengthened.*[73] In unity there is strength; hence the continuation is: **they themselves being welded together**[74] **in love.** Not *knowledge,* certainly not *conceit* (see Col. 2:18), but *mutual love* is "the bond of perfection" (Col. 3:14). Such love springs directly from the heart of God in Christ and leads back to him, for God is love (I John 4:8). Now when believers, welded together in love,

---

[73] The basic meaning of the verb παρακαλέω is *I call to my side;* hence, *I summon* (cf. Acts 28:20). But a person may be summoned for various purposes. Hence, the word has a great variety of derived meanings, the exact sense in any given case to be determined by the context. When used, as here in Col. 2:2, with *hearts* it is best translated *strengthen, encourage* (here passive; in Col. 4:8; Eph. 6:22; II Thess. 2:17 active). Cf. also Phil. 2:1: "if therefore (there is) any encouragement in Christ."

[74] Basic meaning of the verb συμβιβάζω is *I cause to come together; I bring, hold, knit,* or *weld together, unite* (Eph. 4:16, literally; here in Col. 2:2 fig.). It is easy to see how this basic meaning developed into other connotations: *I teach* (thus in LXX; e.g., Isa. 40:13, 14: "Who has taught him?" quoted in I Cor. 2:16), *I prove* (cf. Acts 9:22), or *I conclude* (cf. Acts 16:10).

are confronted with the danger of errors and lies, let them unitedly pray about this and discuss it among each other on the basis of God's special revelation (cf. Eph. 3:17-19), **and this with a view to all the riches of assured understanding.**[75] Thorough, rich, gratifying *insight* (see also Col. 1:9; cf. I Cor. 1:19; Eph. 3:4; II Tim. 2:7) into spiritual matters, which implies the ability to distinguish the true from the false, must ever be the goal. Even more definitely this goal is expressed in the words: **with a view to the clear knowledge of the mystery of God, namely, Christ.** The sense in which Christ is, indeed, the mystery of God has been explained in connection with Col. 1:27. See also N.T.C. on I and II Timothy and Titus, pp. 137-141, explanation of I Tim. 3:16. This mystery, progressively revealed to believers who love one another, transcends all human comprehension (Rom. 11:33-36; I Cor. 2:6-16), and is, therefore, also in that sense a divine and very glorious mystery: "the mystery of God, namely, Christ," **in whom all the treasures of wisdom and knowledge are hidden.** The Colossians need not, must not, look for any source of happiness or of holiness outside of Christ. Do false teachers boast about their wisdom and their knowledge? Or about that of the angels? Neither man nor angel nor any other creature has anything at all to offer which cannot be found *in incomparably superior essence and in infinite degree* in Christ. In him *all* the treasures of wisdom and knowledge *are hidden,* like the "hidden treasure" of which Jesus spoke in the parable (Matt. 13:44; cf. Prov. 2:4); *hidden,* indeed, but in order to be unearthed, not in order to remain concealed.[76] That this practical purpose is also in the

---

[75] Literally, "all the riches of the assurance of the understanding." *Assurance* is the meaning that fits every New Testament passage in which πληροφορία is used (besides Col. 2:2 also I Thess. 1:5; Heb. 6:11; 10:22).

[76] The word for *hidden* is pl. of ἀπόκρυφος from which we have derived our words *apocrypha* and *apochryphal*. According to Josephus (*Jewish War* II.viii.7) before being admitted to the full privileges of the order of the Essenes the novice "was made to swear tremendous oaths . . . to conceal nothing from the members of the sect and to report none of their secrets to others, even though he should be tortured to death . . . and likewise carefully to guard the books of their sect and the names of the angels." Irenaeus (*Against Heresies* I.xx.1) reports that the Marcosians "adduce an unspeakable number of *apocryphal* and spurious writings, which they themselves have forged." And Clement of Alexandria (*Stromata* or *Miscellanies* I.15) states, "of *the secret books* of this man, those who follow the heresy of Prodicus boast to be in possession." The false teachers who vexed the Colossians with their dangerous doctrines may similarly have boasted about their *secret, hidden* writings. Lightfoot says, "Thus the word *apocrypha* in the first instance was an honorable appellation applied by the heretics themselves to their esoteric doctrine and their secret books; but owing to the general character of these works the term, as adopted by orthodox writers, got to signify *false, spurious"* (*op. cit.,* p. 174).

It is possible, therefore, although it cannot be proved, that when the apostle here refers to Christ's *hidden* treasures, and implies that they are freely offered to those who would accept them by faith (see Col. 2:9, 10), he is contrasting these real and inexhaustible treasures with the worthless secrets of the false teachers, and this glorious hiding with the concealment practised by the heretics.

apostle's mind here in Colossians is clear from verses 9 and 10. What the apostle means, therefore, is this, "In Christ all these treasures are stored away. Hence, come and discover them and enrich yourselves by means of them."

"Treasures of wisdom *and knowledge,*" says Paul, which is even better than "treasures of wisdom" of which we read elsewhere (Ecclus. 1:25). Jesus, according to his divine nature, knows all things. This knowledge, being divine, is all-comprehensive, direct, simple, unchangeable, and eternal. Peter paid tribute to it when he declared, "Lord, all things thou knowest; thou dost realize that I have affection for thee" (John 21:17). Christ's omniscience is therefore a great comfort for the believer and, via Christ's revelation in Scripture, a bank from which he draws.

But in Christ *knowledge* is never separated from *wisdom,* as it often is among men. Now wisdom is the ability, in concrete situations, to apply knowledge to the best advantage. It uses the most effective means to achieve the highest goal. In the Old Testament the work of creation is ascribed to God's wisdom (Ps. 104:24; Jer. 10:12). Job 28:23 ff. and Prov. 8:22 ff. personify the wisdom by means of which God created all things. The New Testament magnifies the wisdom of God revealed in the foolishness of the cross (I Cor. 1:18-25), in the church (Eph. 3:10), and in the work of God's providence in behalf of Israel and of the Gentiles (Rom. 11:33).

At this point it is necessary to guard against error. The word *wisdom* is used in a threefold sense in Colossians: (a) the wisdom given to Paul and his fellow-workers and to believers in general (Col. 1:9, 28; 3:16; 4:5); (b) the pretended wisdom of the false teachers (Col. 2:23); and (c) the divine wisdom that dwells eternally in Christ (Col. 2:3). These three must not be confused. Sometimes divine wisdom, such as is certainly spoken of here in Col. 2:3, is equated, as to its essence, with human wisdom, as if the former were but an enlarged edition of the latter. So, for example, in connection with *the present passage,* we are told that while *"knowledge* applies to apprehension of truths, *wisdom* superadds the power of reasoning about them and tracing their relation" (Lightfoot, *op. cit.,* p. 174). But although this may be a perfectly valid and useful distinction when we are speaking about *human* wisdom, the wisdom that is ascribed to *Christ* is more than the ability to reason and to trace. Archetypal wisdom differs from ectypal: the divine pattern and the human copy can never be identical, the reason being that God is God, and we are dealing here with Christ as God (see Col. 2:9). Divine wisdom, in a sense far more exalted than human wisdom, devises, plans, guides, directs. It is original, creative. It does what no other wisdom in the entire universe can ever accomplish. *It reconciles seeming irreconcilables.* A few examples will make this clear:

(1) In his wisdom God reconciles the Jew with the Gentile, and both together with himself, performing this great miracle by means of that alto-

gether unlikely object, namely, the cross, which to the Jew was a stumbling-block and to the Gentile foolishness! (I Cor. 1:22-25; Eph. 2:13, 14) .

(2) In his wisdom he satisfies the demands both of his *justice* which asked for the death of the sinner and of his *love* which required the sinner's salvation. The law and the gospel embrace each other on the cross (Rom. 3:19-24; 5:8, 12, 13; 16:27; cf. Ps. 85:10) .

(3) In his wisdom, which Paul extols, the very rejection of carnal Israel results, by various links, in the salvation of "all Israel": "By their fall salvation is come to the Gentiles, to provoke them to jealousy . . . that by the mercy shown to y o u [Gentiles] they [Israel] may now obtain mercy." Paul concludes, "O the depth of the riches and wisdom and knowledge of God," etc.[77]

In Christ, then, for the benefit of believers, all the treasures of this all-comprehensive knowledge and of this sublime, creative wisdom are hidden.

4, 5. With reference at least to what he has just said in verses 1-3 but more probably to all of 1:3–2:3, Paul continues: **I say this in order that no one may mislead y o u by persuasive argument.** Do not exchange *demonstrated facts,* regarding the fulness that is in Christ, for *specious reasoning.* Cf. I Cor. 2:4. The original does not bear out the view of those who think that Paul had one particular person in mind when he issued this warning. There were doubtless many false teachers. Hence, says Paul, as it were, "When someone or other comes with attractive arguments, do not be turned aside by that person and his finespun phrases." He continues, **For, although in the flesh I am absent, yet in the spirit I am with y o u.** Note in connection with this statement:

(1) the fellowship of all believers in Christ. This closeness of loving communion was felt very keenly in the early church (see N.T.C. on Philippians, pp. 51-54; 93-95) .

(2) the vividness of Paul's sense of fellowship with those who for the most part had not seen him and with whom, therefore, he was not personally acquainted. It is reasonable to assume that Epaphras had given the apostle a very graphic account of conditions in the Colossian church (see also 1:7, 8; 4:12, 13) .

(3) the plus-factor in this fellowship. What Paul meant amounted to far more than saying, "In my imagination I can see y o u now, my friends. It just seems as if I am there with y o u." It was that, to be sure, but also more than that, namely, "In heart and spirit I am with y o u, with y o u to help y o u and to rejoice with y o u, as even this letter indicates and as Tychicus and Onesimus will be telling y o u" (Col. 4:7-9) . Proof: note how the apostle, using somewhat similar language asserts himself in the congrega-

---

[77] In my 36 page booklet, *And So All Israel Shall Be Saved,* I have given what I consider to be the correct interpretation of Rom. 11:26a and its context.

tion at Corinth, actually taking part in a matter of discipline, even though he was not bodily present with them (I Cor. 5:3-5); and also how warmly he makes his spiritual presence felt in the church at Thessalonica (I Thess. 2:17: "out of sight but not out of heart").

The report which Epaphras had presented to Paul was, on the whole, favorable. Though he had not in any way minimized the dangers that were threatening the church, yet he had been careful to point out that on the whole the Colossians had not been moved from their foundation. Genuine love was present among them (1:8), and, as we now learn, also *good order* — there had been no schism and no lack of orderly discipline and behavior — and *sterling, steadfast faith,* for the apostle continues: **rejoicing to see y o u r good order and the firmness of y o u r faith in Christ.**[78]

6, 7. In close connection with the preceding sentence Paul continues: **As therefore y o u accepted Christ Jesus the Lord, (so) in him continue to live.** The chiastic or criss-cross structure of this sentence — with the verbs *accepted* and *continue to live* respectively at beginning and end; and the references to Christ, namely, *Christ Jesus the Lord* and *in him,* in the center (note forward position of "in him") — shows that all the emphasis falls on the necessity of clinging to Christ Jesus the Lord (cf. Eph. 3:11; Phil. 2:11), as the all-sufficient One, as the Lord whose commandments should be obeyed and whose word should be trusted. The meaning is, "Colossians, do not be misled. Let y o u r life (y o u r "walk" or conduct) continue to be in harmony with the fact that y o u have accepted Christ Jesus the Lord as y o u r tradition. Y o u embraced him with a living faith, just as y o u were taught to do" (see verse 7; cf. Eph. 4:20). The word *accepted* is here used in its technical sense: *received as transmitted* (cf. I Cor. 11:23; 15:1, 3; Gal. 1:9, 12; Phil. 4:9; I Thess. 2:13; 4:1; II Thess. 3:6), the line of transmission having been from God to Paul (both directly and indirectly), to Epaphras, to the Colossians.[79]

By a series of four participles ("rooted," "being built up," "being established," "and overflowing"), the first a *perfect passive* and the other three *present,* Paul now shows what this living *in Christ* (that is, *in vital union with him*) means: **rooted and being built up in him and being established in the faith, just as y o u were taught, overflowing with thanksgiving.** Mean-

---

[78] In agreement with many commentators I cannot see any good reason for accepting Lightfoot's suggestion that Paul is using a military metaphor: "y o u r orderly array and close phalanx." The context does not require this interpretation.

[79] Three kinds of *tradition* are mentioned in the New Testament: (a) the Jewish oral law. Said Josephus, "the Pharisees have handed down to the people a great many observances by succession from their fathers which are not written in the law of Moses" (*Antiq.* XIII.x.6). Jesus reflects on these man-made additions in Mark 7:8, 9; (b) "the tradition of men" (Col. 2:8; see on that verse); and (c) the true God-given gospel, as taught by Christ and his apostles, sometimes called "the apostolic tradition." The reference in Col. 2:6 is to (c).

ing: "Having then been firmly implanted in Christ (for example, in his love, Eph. 3:17), as the infinite and all-sufficient Source of salvation full and free, and so continuing, constantly avail yourselves of every opportunity of being brought to higher and still higher ground, as a building rises tier by tier,[80] of being established ever more firmly in the activity of faith,[81] as y o u were taught by Epaphras (Col. 1:7; 4:12, 13), and of overflowing with gratitude" (cf. Col. 4:2). Gratitude is that which completes the circle whereby blessings that drop down into our hearts and lives return to the Giver in the form of unending, loving, and spontaneous adoration. Moreover, such giving of thanks increases the sense of obligation (Ps. 116:12-14), so that those who overflow with this grace feel all the less ready to turn away from the abundance which they have in Christ Jesus the Lord, and to follow the advice of false teachers.

Notice that Paul does not pray that the Colossians may *begin* to be thankful, but rather that the ocean of their gratitude may constantly overflow its *perimeter*. Paul is never satisfied with anything short of perfection. Hence he loves to use this word *overflow* or *abound* (Rom. 3:7; 5:15; 15:13; I Cor. 8:8; 14:12; 15:58; ten times in II Cor.; Phil. 1:9, 26; 4:12, 18; I Thess. 3:12; 4:1, 10). See also N.T.C. on I and II Timothy and Titus, p. 75.

8-10. There is a very close connection between verses 6, 7, on the one hand, and verses 8-10, on the other. What has been stated positively in verses 6, 7, namely, "Continue to live in Christ Jesus the Lord," is stated negatively in verses 8-10, the sense of these three verses being, "Do *not* allow yourselves to be carried away by any teaching that is *not according to Christ,* for he will supply all your needs, since in him all the fulness of the godhead dwells bodily and since he is the supreme Ruler of all." We have a restatement, therefore, in somewhat different form, of what the apostle had said in verse 4, "I say this in order that no one may mislead y o u by persuasive argument." It becomes clear, therefore, that in this entire section (verses 1-10) Paul indicates that he was deeply concerned about the false teaching of those whose speculative theories, cleverly presented, might tend to undermine the confidence of the Colossians in Christ as their complete Savior. He calls this subversive system of thought and morals, of rules and regulations "philosophy and empty deceit." He uses words like "man-made tradition" and "worldly rudiments" to describe it.

---

[80] The combination *plant* and *building* is also found in Jer. 24:6 and Eph. 4:15, 16. Is it correct to speak of a mixed metaphor here? Is it not rather a case of one underlying figure following another in rapid succession? I can see no confusion here.
[81] I take τῇ πίστει to be dative of respect or reference, not (with Lightfoot) instrumental. Also, in contrast with Lenski, I believe that this *faith* is to be taken in the subjective sense, although here, as in Col. 1:23, there is a very close connection between this faith-activity and its object, as the following clause ("just as y o u were taught") indicates.

COLOSSIANS 2:8-10

There is, however, another interpretation of these verses, differing rather sharply from the one set forth in the aforegoing summarizing paragraph. It is to the effect that the apostle here sets Christ over against "the elemental spirits of the universe," the words between quotation marks being the R.S.V. rendering of the Greek phrase which in both A.V. and A.R.V. is translated "the rudiments of the world" (verse 8). For comments about this interpretation which, with due respect for the erudition of those who advocate it, I cannot adopt, see footnote 83 *at the close* of my treatment of the entire passage (verses 8-10).

The apostle, accordingly, continues as follows: **Be on y o u r guard lest there be any one who carries y o u off as spoil by means of his philosophy and empty deceit.** Let not those who were rescued out of the domain of darkness and transplanted into the kingdom of the Son of God's love (see Col. 1:13) be carried off as so much booty and become enslaved once more (cf. Gal. 5:1).

Brought under bondage by someone's "philosophy"! As Josephus has shown, any elaborate system of thought and/or moral discipline was in those days called a *philosophy* (cf. our term "moral philosophy," when the *scientific* aspect is not stressed). Thus he states, "For there are three forms of philosophy among the Jews. The followers of the first school are called Pharisees, of the second Sadducees, and of the third Essenes" (*Jewish War* II.viii.2). When it is borne in mind that in several of its traits the body of error which Paul here opposes resembles Essenism, the relevancy of this quotation from Josephus becomes all the more clear. Philo also, when speaking about Hebrew religion, uses such terms as "philosophy according to Moses" and "Jewish philosophy." Paul is warning against the kind of philosophy that amounts to nothing more than *empty deceit*. It is empty, futile. It is deceptive, for, while it promises big things to those who obey its ordinances, it cannot redeem its promises (see on verse 23). Paul continues: **according to the tradition of men** (see footnote 79 above). This was not *apostolic* tradition, nor was it tradition that belonged to the main stream of *Judaism,* though it did have something in common with Judaism and embraced some of the latter's tenets. It was rather a mixture of Christianity, Judaistic Ceremonialism, Angelolatry, and Asceticism, as verses 11-23 indicate. It was a philosophy **according to the rudiments of the world.** Rudiments are *elements,* either in the physical or in the non-physical realm. The original uses the term *stoicheia,* indicating elements or units in a row or series, like the figures (1, 2, 3, etc.) in a column, or the letters (A, B, C, etc.) in the alphabet; then also the basic elements of which the physical world is held to consist (cf. II Peter 3:10, 12). The ancients sometimes spoke of earth, air, fire, and water as elements. By an easy transition the meaning advances to *rudiments* or *elements of learning;* hence, *elementary teaching* (Heb. 5:12). We speak of "Rudiments of Grammar," "Elements of Arithmetic," etc.

109

The expression "rudiments of the world" also occurs in Gal. 4:3 (cf. Gal. 4:9). This is admittedly a very difficult passage, proving the correctness of II Peter 3:15, 16. It is true, indeed, that "our beloved brother Paul" sometimes wrote things "hard to understand." One thing should be borne in mind, however, namely, that in Galatians and in Colossians we are dealing with rudiments *of the world,* a modifier that does not occur in Hebrews and in II Peter. Now in Col. 2:8, in harmony with the immediate context which speaks about "the tradition of *men,*" the term *world* (kosmos) must probably be taken in its ethical sense (as often in Paul's epistles), as indicating "mankind alienated from the life of God." These are rudiments of worldly men. They are *worldly* rudiments. In all likelihood that interpretation of the modifier *of the world* also holds for Galatians (cf. Gal. 4:9, "weak and beggarly rudiments"). Worthy of serious consideration, in the light of the contexts (in Gal. 4:3 and 4:9), is therefore the view according to which in Galatians the expression "rudiments of the world" indicates rudimentary teaching regarding rules, regulations, ordinances, by means of which, before Christ's coming into the flesh, people (Jews and Gentiles, each in their own way) tried by their own efforts to achieve salvation. With the coming of Christ and the work of his apostles this sinful, autosoteric tendency and teaching continued, sponsored now by enthusiastic Judaists. In their teaching the latter tried to combine faith in Christ with trust in Mosaic-Pharisaic ordinances. And this same danger of trusting in ordinances to supplement faith in Christ asserted itself also at Colosse (see Col. 2:11-23), though in a somewhat different, more complicated, form. That some of these regulations dealt with angel-worship need not and should not be denied (see verses 15 and 18), just so it be borne in mind that the term *rudiments* itself does not therefore necessarily mean *angels.* It is the erroneous *teaching* that is here condemned.

It thus becomes evident that when the meaning *rudimentary instruction* is ascribed to the word *rudiments,* as used in Col. 2:8 and 2:20, this sense cannot be quickly discarded as if it were definitely out of line with the use of this same word elsewhere in the New Testament.

Now if people will but see the implications of faith in Christ in all his glorious fulness and adequacy, they will die to these rudiments, as verse 20 makes very clear. Cast aside then will be these crude notions regarding regulations and ordinances with respect to such things as circumcision, feasts, food and drink, angel-worship, etc., as means toward the achievement of salvation in all its fulness. It is evident that at least in one respect the rudiments mentioned in Galatians and those against which the apostle warns in Colossians are alike, namely, in being "weak and beggarly" (Gal. 3:9). This philosophy is definitely "of the world," as any system must be that does not give Christ all the honor. It is empty, deceitful, **and not according to Christ.** It has a tendency to take men away from Christ, to weaken their trust in him as all-sufficient Savior. It is not in harmony with the fulness which believers have in him.

Hence, Paul continues: **for in him all the fulness of the godhead dwells bodily.** For the interpretation of all but the adverb ("bodily") see also above on Col. 1:19. When the apostle thus describes Christ he has in mind the latter's *deity,* not just his *divinity.* He is referring to the Son's complete equality of essence with the Father and the Holy Spirit, his *consubstantiality,* not his *similarity.*[82] He is saying that this plenitude of deity has its abiding residence in Christ, and this *bodily.*

Many different interpretations have been given of this adverb; such as, *personally, essentially, universally* (in a manner that embraces or affects the entire universe), *ecclesiastically* (in a manner that affects the entire church), *antitypically, genuinely,* etc. Now all of these can be rejected without much argumentation since they are out of harmony with the immediate context, attach a connotation to the adverb that is out of harmony with the main clause, invest that adverb with too much meaning, and miss the main purpose which the apostle had in mind in writing as he does.

There are, however, two theories that deserve more than passing notice:
A. *The view of Lightfoot (op. cit.,* pp. 182, 183), etc.

According to him *bodily* means "with a bodily manifestation," that is, "as crowned by the incarnation." Expositors of repute have endorsed this attractive view. They appeal to such arguments as the importance which Paul attaches to Christ's incarnation (Gal. 4:4), the possible parallel in John 1:1, 14, the reference in Heb. 10:5 to Christ's body ("a body didst thou prepare for me"), etc.

Objections:

(1) Paul uses the present tense. He does not say that the Word *became* flesh but that the fulness of the godhead *dwells* or *is dwelling* in Christ. And surely that indwelling did not just begin with the incarnation. It is an

---

[82] Note what a difference a single letter makes:

(1) θεότης used here in Col. 2:9 (nowhere else in the New Testament) means *deity;* θειότης used in Rom. 1:20 (and there alone in the New Testament) indicates *divinity.* Cf. German: *Gottheit* und *Göttlichkeit;* Dutch: *godheid* en *goddelijkheid.* The difference has been expressed beautifully by E. K. Simpson in these words: "The *hand* of omnipotence may be traced in the countless orbs that bespangle the heavens, and in the marvelous coadjustments of our comparatively tiny globe; but in the Son we behold the *face* of God unveiled, the express image and transcript of his very being" (*Words Worth Weighing in the Greek New Testament.* See also R. C. Trench, *Synonyms of the New Testament,* par. ii.

(2) ὁμοούσιος, as the Nicene Creed declared, means *of the same substance* or *essence,* the Son being consubstantial with the Father, while the weaker ὁμοιούσιος, preferred by the Arians, means *similar in substance* or *essence.* Though the difference seems to be trivial — only one letter! — it is actually nothing less than that between declaring that Jesus is *God* and saying that he is *man,* a very divine man, to be sure, but man nevertheless. Was not the slogan of these heretics, "There was a time when he was not"?

eternal indwelling. Moule, who is inclined to favor Lightfoot's view, nevertheless correctly observes: "The chief objection to taking σωματικῶς [the adverb] thus, as representing a stress on the fact that the godhead became really embodied, is the present tense κατοικεῖ ["is dwelling"], which is not easy to treat as a reference to a past event in history (like John 1:14, σάρξ ἐγένετο [became flesh]" (op. cit., p. 93). That is exactly the point!

(2) Lightfoot's argument to the effect that the main clause ("for in him all the fulness of the godhead dwells") refers to the pre-incarnate Christ ("the Eternal Word in whom the pleroma had its abode from all eternity"), but that the adverb ("bodily") which modifies this clause refers to the incarnation, would seem to involve contradiction.

(3) If the adverb "bodily" is interpreted literally, and we should allow this adverb really to modify, in a natural way, the main clause with its verb "dwells" or "is dwelling," would not the objection arise that the Son of God is surely not so dependent upon a physical body (or even upon the human nature) that apart from it the godhead cannot dwell in him?

It is, therefore, not surprising that among the earliest writers few adopted this interpretation, and that even today, with some prominent exceptions, it is widely rejected by scholars.

B. *The view of Percy* (op. cit., p.77), and, in the main, also of Ridderbos (op. cit., pp. 176-178).

They interpret the adverb to mean "in a concentrated, as it were visible and tangible, form." Faith clearly sees that the fulness of the godhead dwells from everlasting to everlasting in Christ, this fact having been thus visibly and tangibly demonstrated by Christ's works both in creation and redemption. It sees that the entire essence and glory of God *is concentrated in Christ as in a body.* It is in that sense that it can be said that this fulness of the godhead *is embodied, given concrete expression, fully realized, in him.* This is but another way of saying that from everlasting to everlasting he is "the image of the invisible God" (see on Col. 1:15).

I believe that this gives the proper sense, a meaning which is also in harmony with the context, both preceding and following. Since, therefore, all the fulness of the indwelling essence of God is thus completely concentrated in Christ, there is no need of or justification for looking elsewhere for help, salvation, or spiritual perfection. Hence, the apostle immediately adds: **and in him y o u have attained to fulness;** that is, in Christ y o u have reached the Source whence flows the stream of blessings that supplies whatever y o u need for this life and for the next. Abide, therefore, in him (John 15:4, 7, 9), and y o u will continue to experience that "out of his fulness we all receive grace upon grace" (John 1:16; cf. Eph. 4:13). To the very utmost limits of human capacity the church that remains in vital union with Christ receives love, joy, peace, longsuffering, kindness, goodness, faithfulness, meekness, self-control (Gal. 5:22), yes, every Christian grace. Christ is the Fountain that never fails. Why, then, O Colossians, commit the folly of hewing out cisterns for yourselves, broken cisterns, that can hold no water (Jer. 2:13)? Why trust in circumcision when y o u have been buried with Christ in baptism (verses 11-14)? How foolish to resort to principalities and authorities when in him y o u have attained to fulness, **namely, in him who is the head of every principality and authority** (cf. verse 15). For the meaning of "principality" and "authority" see on Col. 1:16. He is their head, not in fully the same sense in which he is the head of the church (see on Col. 1:18), which is his body, but in the sense that he is supreme Ruler of all (1:16; cf. Eph. 1:22), so that apart from him the good angels cannot help, and because of him the evil cannot harm believers. It seems that it was especially this last thought which the apostle wished to emphasize (see below on verse 15).[83]

In order to show the connection of verses 11-17 with the verses that immediately precede, verses 9 and 10 which have already been explained will be reprinted here:

---

9 for in him all the fulness of the godhead dwells bodily, 10 and in him y o u have attained to fulness, namely, in him who is the head of every principality and authority, 11 in whom also y o u were circumcised with a circumcision made without hands, by the putting off of the body of the flesh in the circumcision of Christ, 12 having been buried with him in y o u r baptism in which y o u were also raised with him through faith in the operative power of God who raised him from the dead. 13 And y o u, who were dead through y o u r trespasses and the uncircumcision of y o u r flesh, y o u he made alive together with him, having forgiven us all our trespasses, 14 having blotted out the handwritten document that was against us, which by means of its requirements testified against us, and he took it out of the way by nailing it to the cross, 15 and having stripped the principalities and the authorities of their power, he publicly exposed them to disgrace by triumphing over them in him.

16 Therefore allow no one to pass judgment on y o u in questions of food or drink or with respect to a festival or a new moon or a sabbath: 17 things that were only a shadow of those that were coming, but the object casting the shadow is to be found with Christ.

2:11-17

II. *Warning against Judaistic Ceremonialism*

In verses 1-10 the warning against the Colossian Heresy was couched in general terms. With verse 11, however, right in the middle of the sentence, it begins to assume specific form. We now learn that the error that was being propagated at Colosse was basically of a Judaistic character. For a reason not definitely stated but which we can probably infer from the context and

[83] Because of its length this footnote has been placed at the end of the chapter, page 135.

from similar warnings in other epistles the teachers of false doctrine were advertising such things as circumcision, rigid adherance to dietary restrictions, and strict observance of festivals and sabbaths. That brief summary makes verses 11-17 a thought-unit. The style, however, changes from the rather easy-flowing didactic evident through verse 15 to the far more crisp, direct, and hortatory that begins at verse 16 and continues with few exceptions (the longest exception being 4:7-14) to the end of the letter. It is *subject-matter*, namely, *warning against Judaism,* that unites 2:11-17. But even this subject-matter is not altogether homogeneous. The heresy which the apostle was combating was a somewhat baffling mixture of Judaistic and Pagan beliefs propagated by men who probably posed as Christians, yes better Christians than the common lot. As has been pointed out earlier (see Introduction II C), it was exactly the type of syncretism that one could expect to find in Jewish-Pagan Colosse. It is not surprising that Paul, who had the entire picture before him all the time, in his discussions and warnings should move with ease from one element of the Colossian Heresy to another and then back again. So also here in verses 11-17 we notice that in the midst of his warnings against Judaism he briefly touches upon two subjects about which he will say more subsequently, namely, Relation to angels (verse 15) and Asceticism (verse 16). Yet, he does this not in a disconnected or rambling manner, but in such a way that verses 11-17 form a unit in which every clause leads to the next one in a very natural and organic manner, as will be indicated.

11, 12. Speaking then about Christ, "the head of every principality and authority," Paul continues: **in whom y o u were circumcized.** Paul's thought at this point can perhaps be paraphrased somewhat as follows: Colossians, do not allow these teachers of error to deceive y o u as if, in order to triumph over the indulgence of the flesh (2:23) and to attain to the full measure of salvation (2:9, 10), y o u need to be literally circumcized (cf. Acts 15:1; Gal. 5:2, 3). *Y o u were already circumcized!* Yes, y o u were circumcized with a circumcision that excels by far the rite that is being recommended so strongly by the teachers of error. Y o u were circumcized **with a circumcision made without hands, by the putting off of the body of the flesh in the circumcision of Christ.**

Note points of difference proving the great superiority of the circumcision which the Colossians had already received:

Y o u r circumcision was:	*The other was:*
(1) the work of the Holy Spirit ("made without hands")	(1) a manual operation (minor surgery!)
(2) inward, of the heart (see Rom. 2: 28, 29; also N.T.C. on Phil. 3:2, 3)	(2) outward

114

Y o u r circumcision was:	*The other was:*
(3) the putting *off* and casting *away* (note double prefix in ἀπεκδύσει) **of** y o u r *entire* evil nature ("the body of the flesh"), in its sanctifying aspect to be progressively realized	(3) removal of excess foreskin
(4) Christian ("the circumcision of Christ," that is, the circumcision which is y o u r s because of y o u r vital union with Christ)	(4) Abrahamic and Mosaic

As a further description of the circumcision which the Colossians had already received the apostle continues: **having been buried with him in y o u r baptism in which y o u were also raised with him.** Meaning:

(1) Christ suffered, died, was buried in y o u r stead and for your benefit. He bore the guilt and punishment of the law for y o u. He took upon himself the curse that rested upon y o u (Gal. 3:13). When by sovereign grace y o u embraced Christ as y o u r Savior and Lord, y o u received the assurance that y o u r former guilt-laden, damnable selves had been buried with him, and that y o u r state with reference to God's holy law had changed from that of objects of condemnation to that of recipients of justification (Rom. 8:1-4; 5:1). Accordingly, not only were y o u buried with him but y o u were also raised with him.

(2) By means of his entire work of humiliation, including burial, Christ procured for y o u the work of the Holy Spirit (John 16:7). Hence, y o u r s is not only justification but also sanctification, gradual spiritual renewal. The Spirit has implanted in y o u r hearts the seed of the new life (John 3:3, 5). "Y o u died, and y o u r life is hid with Christ in God" (Col. 3:3). Hence, also in this sense, y o u were buried with him and y o u were raised with him.

But why does Paul connect "in y o u r baptism" with this having been buried with Christ and having been raised with him? He does not do this because he attaches any magical efficacy to the rite of baptism. See I Cor. 1:14-17; cf. I Peter 3:21. In the passage now under discussion the apostle definitely excludes the idea that the act of baptizing, in virtue of the action itself, and independent of the condition of the heart of them who here and now professed to believe the gospel, has spiritual value. He carefully adds: **through faith in the operative power** [84] **of God who raised him from the dead.** The man who hears the gospel as it is proclaimed must give his heart to the almighty God whose energizing power raised Christ from the dead. He must also believe that the spiritual power that proceeds from the risen

---

[84] Objective genitive after πίστεως as in Rom. 3:22, 26; Gal. 3:22; Eph. 3:12; Phil. 3:9; and II Thess. 2:13.

Savior (Phil. 3:10) will bestow upon him all he needs for body and soul, for time and eternity.

What then is the meaning of the phrase "in y o u r baptism"? Evidently Paul in this entire paragraph magnifies Christian baptism as much as he, by clear implication, disapproves of the continuation of the rite of circumcision if viewed as having anything to do with salvation.[85] The definite implication, therefore, is that *baptism has taken the place of circumcision.*[86] Hence, what is said with reference to circumcision in Rom. 4:11, as being a sign and a seal, holds also for baptism. In the Colossian context baptism is specifically a sign and seal of having been buried with Christ and of having been raised with him. It is, accordingly, a sign and seal of union with Christ, of entrance into his covenant, of incorporation into Christ's body, the church (I Cor. 12:13). The *sign* of baptism pictures the cleansing power of Christ's blood and Spirit. That vivid portrayal is very valuable (cf. Job 42:5, 6). The *seal* certifies and guarantees the operation of this activity of love and grace in

---

[85] As to discarding circumcision Paul uses language that is definite and strong: Gal. 5:2; Phil. 3:2. In Colossians he opposes this rite *for believers from the Gentiles* in this *new* dispensation. In a religious sense circumcision was, indeed, a blessing in the *old* dispensation. For a person living in that era to receive the sign of entrance into the covenant was certainly not bad in itself. On the contrary, it was a blessing as a *sign* and a *seal* of the righteousness of faith (Rom. 4:11). It was, however, never to be regarded as being in and by itself a vehicle of grace or indispensable to salvation. It stands to reason that with the shedding of Christ's blood on Calvary these *bloody* signs and seals (circumcision and the killing of the Passover lamb) attained their fulfilment, and were rendered moribund. The grievous error of the false teachers was therefore twofold: a. the attempt to force this obsolescent rite upon believers from the Gentiles; b. the view that circumcision was in and by itself a vehicle of grace, imparting to the recipient a blessing which "mere" (?) faith in Christ could never have given him. The error was therefore *a denial of Christ's all-sufficiency!* For more about this see on verses 16, 17.

This entire discussion, however, moves in the realm of moral and spiritual values. It has nothing to do with the physical or health value of circumcision in any age. S. I. McMillen, M.D., in his most interesting book, *None of These Diseases*, published by the Fleming H. Revell Co., has high praise for circumcision as a health measure, especially in the prevention of cervical cancer (pp. 19-21). His remarks and statistics are most interesting and instructive. But that is the physical side. Paul discusses the moral and spiritual question.

[86] I am speaking here about a clear *implication.* The surface contrast is that between *literal* circumcision and *circumcision without hands*, namely, the circumcision of the heart, as explained. But the implication also is clear. Hence, the following statement is correct: "Since, then, baptism has come in the place of circumcision (Col. 2:11-13), the children should be baptized as heirs of the kingdom of God and of his covenant" (*Form for the Baptism of Infants* in *Psalter Hymnal of the Christian Reformed Church*, Grand Rapids, Mich., 1959, p. 86). When God made his covenant with Abraham the children were included (Gen. 17:1-14). This covenant, in its spiritual aspects, was continued in the new dispensation (Acts 2:38, 39; Rom. 4:9-12; Gal. 3:7, 8, 29). Therefore the children are still included and should still receive the sign, which in the present dispensation, as Paul makes clear in Col. 2:11, 12, is baptism. Surely, God is not less generous now than he was in the old dispensation! Further evidence in support of this position can be found in passages such as the following: Mark 10:14-16; Luke 18:15-17; Acts 16:15, 33; I Cor. 1:16.

the lives of all those who embrace Christ by faith. Baptism, therefore, shows us a God who tenderly condescends to the weaknesses of his people: their doubts and their fears. (Cf. Heb. 6:17; also for the sacrament of communion Luke 22:19.) Surely, Noah did not despise the rainbow (Gen. 9:12-17). Happily married couples do not think lowly of their wedding rings.

The meaning, then, of Col. 2:11, 12 would seem to be as follows (in summary) : "Y o u, believers, have no need of external circumcision. Y o u have received a far better circumcision, that of heart and life. That circumcision is y o u r s by virtue of y o u r union with Christ. When he was buried y o u — that is, y o u r former, wicked selves — were buried with him. When he was raised y o u — as new creatures — were raised with him. In the experience of baptism y o u received the sign and seal of this marvelous Spirit-wrought transformation." [87]

13. In the spirit of jubilation and solid Christian optimism Paul continues, **And y o u, who were dead through y o u r trespasses and the uncircumcision of y o u r flesh, y o u he made alive together with him.** In his great mercy God had taken pity on Gentiles as well as on the ancient covenant people. "And y o u" means, "And y o u who were formerly Gentiles, and as such morally and spiritually dead, and this not only because of y o u r individual trespasses against God's holy law but also and basically because of y o u r state before God." That state is here described as "the uncircumcision of y o u r flesh," that is, "y o u r *state* of guilt; hence, y o u r *condition* of sinfulness, impotence, and therefore hopelessness."

Being children of wrath, their physical or literal uncircumcision symbolized their moral and spiritual uncircumcision. The word *y o u* is repeated for

---

[87] This discussion would hardly be complete if nothing were said with reference to the *mode* of baptism, since it is especially upon passages such as this that immersionists base their claim that baptism by immersion is the only valid baptism. They see in the words "having been buried with him in y o u r baptism" an endorsement of immersion into the water; and in the words, "in which y o u were also raised with him" solid support for emersion out of the water. With all love and respect for our brothers in Christ I venture to say, however, that in connection with baptism Scripture also uses other expressions which, on the basis of this kind of reasoning, would then also have to be regarded as indicating the proper *mode* of baptism. If *being buried with Christ* (Col. 2:11, 12; Rom. 6:4) means that baptism must be by immersion, why should not *being crucified with Christ* (Rom. 6:6) indicate that baptism should be by crucifixion, *being planted with him* (Rom. 6:5 A.V. and original) that it should be by implantation, and *putting on Christ* (Gal. 3:27) that it should be by habilitation? As I see it, John Murray is right when he says, "When all of Paul's expressions are taken into account we see that burial with Christ can be appealed to as providing an index to the mode of baptism no more than can crucifixion with him. And since the latter does not indicate the *mode* of baptism there is no validity to the argument that burial does. The fact is that there are many aspects to our union with Christ. It is arbitrary to select one aspect and find in the language used to set it forth the essence of the mode of baptism" (*Christian Baptism*, p. 31).

the sake of emphasis, as if Paul were saying, "Ponder this! Continue to reflect on it that on y o u, yes even on y o u, so deeply fallen, so hopelessly lost, so utterly corrupt in state and condition, such grace was bestowed." Cf. Eph. 2:1, 5. The predominantly Gentile origin of this church is clear also from such passages as Col. 1:21, 22, 27; 3:5-7 (similar passages in Ephesians are: Eph. 1:13; 2:1-3, 11, 13, 17, 22; 3:1, 2; 4:17, etc.). But the same God, who raised Christ from the dead, also and in that very act made the Colossians alive.

In verses 13, 14, and 15 the apostle in orderly arranged participial modifiers shows us what was implied in this *making alive*. It implied:

(1) granting forgiveness to *us:* "having forgiven us all our trespasses" (verse 13).

(2) blotting out *a writing:* "having blotted out the handwritten document that was against us" (verse 14).

(3) disarming *spirits:* "and having stripped the principalities and the authorities of their power" (verse 15).

In the work of salvation the guilt of our sins must be removed first of all. Hence, when Paul describes how we were made alive together with Christ he begins by saying: **having forgiven us all our trespasses.** Note the striking transition from y o u to *us*. If it be true that *"all* (both Jew and Gentile) have sinned and fall short of the glory of God" (Rom. 3:23), then all alike need forgiveness. And Paul, who regards himself as "chief of sinners" (I Tim. 1:15) was unable to write about a subject like this without being deeply moved in his own soul, having experienced what God did for him in rescuing him from inevitable damnation.

Forgiveness

1. *Why is it emphasized?*

It is worthy of special attention that the apostle speaks about forgiveness in each of the first three chapters of Colossians. May there not have been a special reason for this? Remember that this letter was going to be read aloud to the assembled congregation of Colosse, yes, to the very church gathered in Philemon's house. And Philemon was the master of Onesimus, the returned runaway whom Philemon must forgive! It is as if I am present when this letter is being read, and as if I hear the lector reading the precious words:

"The Father rescued us out of the domain of darkness, and transplanted us into the kingdom of the Son of his love, in whom we have our redemption, *the forgiveness of our sins. . . .* And y o u who were dead through y o u r trespasses and the uncircumcision of y o u r flesh, y o u he made alive together with him, *having forgiven us all our trespasses. . . .* Put on, therefore, as God's elect, holy and beloved, a heart of compassion, kindness, lowliness, meekness, longsuffering, enduring one another, and if anyone has a complaint against anyone else *forgiving each other*. Just as the Lord *has forgiven y o u,* so do y o u also *(forgive)*" (Col. 1:13, 14; 2:13; 3:12, 13) . And it is as if I can hear the Holy Spirit whisper in the heart of the host of this house-church, "Philemon, if the Lord did all this for *you,* should *you* not, with gladness of heart, forgive Onesimus, and fully *accept* him as a beloved brother?"

But surely not only for Philemon were these words intended but for the entire Colossian congregation, and in fact — as Paul reminds us so beautifully by saying "having forgiven *us* all our trespasses" — for each and every believer both then and now.

2. *What are its characteristics?*

The evidence shows that this forgiveness is:

a. *gracious.* The word used here in the original stresses this fact (see on 3:13, footnote 131) . It is completely unmerited by man (Rom. 3:24; Titus 3:4-7) . It is God's precious *gift* in Christ. May not this be the very reason why the sinner must become as a little child to receive it? Cf. Matt. 18:1-3. The story is told of a man who at a Fair offered $10 gold pieces. Accompanying a pile of these valuable coins there was a sign: "Free, Take one." All day long people passed by. Their smile said, "You can't fool me." The pile remained untouched. Just before closing time a child saw the sign, reached out his hand and took a coin!

b. *bountiful.* When God gives or forgives he does not do so merely *of* his riches but *according to* his riches (Eph. 1:7) . His pardoning love superabounds (Rom. 5:20) . Cf. Isa. 1:18; Ps. 103:12.

c. *eager.* God "entreats" men to be reconciled to him, "not counting their trespasses against them" (II Cor. 5:19, 20) . Cf. Ps. 86:5.

d. *certain.* When Paul received his commission he was sent to the Gentiles "to open their eyes, that they may turn from darkness to light and from the power of Satan to God, *that they may receive remission of sins. . . .*" When Festus expressed his doubt about this heavenly vision and the commission given to Paul, the apostle answered, "I am not mad, excellent Festus, but I am telling *the sober truth*" (Acts 26:16-18, 25) . Cf. Ps. 89:30-35.

e. *basic.* When a sinner is rescued out of the domain of darkness and transplanted into the kingdom of the Son of God's love, he receives *forgiveness* first of all. Moral and spiritual cleansing ("holiness") *follows* (Col. 1:13, 14, 22) . Thus also here in Col. 2:13 the very first blessing that is mentioned in connection with making the dead sinner alive is forgiveness. Cf. Rom. 3:24. Note emphasis on *justification* in Rom. 5, *followed by* emphasis on *sanctification,* Rom. 6. "How can a sinner become righteous in the sight of God?" is still basic.

3. *How do we receive it?*

What is the way along which God leads his children toward the full possession and enjoyment of this basic blessing?

a. There must be *genuine sorrow for sin* (God-wrought sorrow, II Cor. 7:10). Cf. Mark 1:4.

b. There must be *a yearning desire to forsake sin.* Those who are eager by the grace of God to put to death their evil nature (Col. 3:5-11) are pronounced forgiven (Col. 3:13). Cf. Prov. 28:13. When the Sunday School teacher asked the class, "What does it mean to repent?" a little boy answered, "To repent means to be sorry enough to quit doing what is wrong."

c. There must be *the disposition of the heart to forgive others* (Col. 3:13; Eph. 4:32). Cf. Matt. 6:14, 15.

14. But, in making us alive (see on verse 13), not only has God in mercy pardoned our transgressions against his holy law, he has even blotted out the law itself viewed in its demanding and curse-pronouncing character, that law which, because of its many rigid requirements and regulations, condemned us all. As a way of salvation and as a curse suspended above our heads God by means of his Son's substitutionary sacrifice abolished it. Says Paul: **having blotted out the handwritten document that was against us, which by means of its requirements** [88] **testified against** [89] **us.** This handwriting or handwritten document is clearly the law (cf. Eph. 2:15).[90] In a

---

[88] The original has given rise to various interpretations, and is difficult. The difficulty concerns two phrases: καθ' ἡμῶν and τοῖς δόγμασιν. If καθ' ἡμῶν is rendered "against us" and τοῖς δόγμασιν is construed with "handwriting" the result may be a translation that is open to the charge of tautology: "the handwriting with its ordinances that was against us, which was contrary to us" (cf. somewhat similar rendering in A.V. and A.R.V., text). J. A. T. Robinson avoids this difficulty by taking καθ' ἡμῶν to mean "in our name" (*The Body*, p. 43 n.). But it is difficult to find substantiation for that meaning. E. Percy (*op. cit.*, pp. 88, 89), followed by Ridderbos (*op. cit.*, pp. 186, 187), construes τοῖς δόμασιν with the *following* clause; hence, "the handwriting that was against us, which by means of its ordinances testified against us." This rendering, in substance, I can adopt. Bruce (*op. cit.*, p. 237) states his objection to it in these words: "It is rather awkward to construe τοῖς δόγμασιν with the following adjective clause, in spite of the parallels which he [Percy] adduces." It cannot be denied, however, that there are these parallels, adduced not only by Percy (*op. cit.*, p. 88, footnote 43) but also by Gram. N.T. Bl.-Debr., par. 475,1. Though placing a modifier in front of the relative clause to which it belongs may be regarded as exceptional, it is not so *very* exceptional, as the evidence which Percy and Bl.-Debr. supply, indicates. Besides, is there not, after all, a good reason for this advanced position of the modifier? Is it not true that, over against the false teachers with their love for ordinances and still more ordinances, the apostle desired to stress the idea that it was exactly because of these ordinances that the law had become our adversary, constantly testifying against us, transgressors? If that be borne in mind, the word-order does not seem so strange.

[89] ὑπεναντίον, where ἀντί has the adversative sense. In Heb. 10:27 τοὺς ὑπεναντίους means *the adversaries.* Also in the LXX this ἀντί-compound is the equivalent of the Hebrew 'ōyēbh (enemy) and çar (adversary, foe). Apart from Christ, the law is the sinner's adversary, bearing testimony *against* him.

[90] It is true that χειρόγραφον, which basically means *handwriting,* and so in its general sense, any *document,* frequently has the technical meaning *bond, certificate of*

sense that law was an adversary, an accuser of transgressors. It confronted men with the stern dictum, "Cursed is every one who does not abide by all things that are written in the book of the law to do them" (Gal. 3:10; cf. Deut. 27:26). Moreover, it contained ever so many rules and regulations of a ceremonial nature, with reference to fasts, feasts, foods, offerings, etc. Since no one was ever able to keep the law either in its moral or ceremonial aspect, it continued for a long time its mission as accuser. With the coming of Christ, born to die, a great change took place. Paul tells the Colossians, harrassed as they were by false teachers who were trying to enforce their Judaistic ceremonies upon them and were even adding rules of their own, "God has completely obliterated [91] the document with its legal demands." How had this been accomplished? Paul answers, **and he took it out of the way by nailing it to the cross.** God annulled the law when his Son satisfied its demand of perfect obedience, bore its curse, and fulfilled its shadows, its types and ceremonies. It was nailed to the cross with Jesus. It died when he died. And because of the substitutionary nature of Christ's sacrifice believers are no longer under the law but under grace (Rom. 7:4, 6; 6:14; Gal. 2:19). This does not mean that the moral law has lost significance for the believer. It cannot imply that he should now forget about loving God above all and the neighbor as himself. On the contrary, the law of love has eternal validity (Rom. 13:8, 9; Gal. 5:14). It is the believer's supreme delight. He obeys it out of gratitude for the salvation that he has already received as a gift of God's sovereign grace. But he has been discharged from the law viewed as a code of rules and regulations, a means of obtaining eternal life, a curse threatening to destroy him.

---

indebtedness. See A. Deissmann, *Light from the Ancient East,* pp. 331, 332. Taken in the latter sense "the Jewish people might be said to have signed the contract when they bound themselves by a curse to observe all the enactments of the law" (Deut. 27:14-26; cf. Ex. 24:3). Thus Lightfoot (*op. cit.,* p. 187). But since the apostle speaks about a handwriting that testified against *us,* and he is obviously writing to Christians from among the *Gentiles,* a way must now be found to make this technical sense of the term fit the Gentiles also. Lightfoot offers as a solution "the moral assent of the conscience which, as it were, signs and seals the obligation." Many commentators, in one way or another, follow this line of interpretation. It is a very attractive theory and lends itself beautifully to sermonizing. It is, however, very difficult to fit into the present context which has in view *a document containing regulations or ordinances.* Moreover, in the clearly parallel passage (Eph. 2:15) what has been abolished through the cross is not "a certificate of indebtedness with our signature on it" but "the law of commandments with its requirements." I agree, therefore, with Beare when he states (*op. cit.,* p. 198), "It represents simply the law as a written code." Cf. also Gal. 3:13, "Christ redeemed us from the curse of the law"; and Rom. 7:6, "But now we are discharged from the law."

[91] The synonymous expression, "he took it out of the way," meaning "he has completely abrogated it" indicates that the literal sense of ἐξαλείφω must not be pressed. Not the literal washing out of a signature or of an acknowledgment of debt is meant here but *the complete destruction of the law, regarded as a code of rules and regulations.*

15. Here follows the last of three important acts whereby God grants to his children the joy of salvation (see on verse 13) , the three being: (1) forgiveness of sins, (2) the setting aside of the law (in the sense explained) , and now (3) the disarming of the principalities and authorities. Says Paul: **and having stripped the principalities and the authorities of their power, he publicly exposed them to disgrace by triumphing over them in him.**[92] These "principalities and authorities" are angelic beings (see on Col. 1:16) , who are here (2:15) pictured as resisting God. It is not exactly clear just why Paul makes mention of them in the present connection. It is possible, nevertheless, that the immediately preceding statement of the abrogation of the law as our *impersonal* accuser may have led to this reference to *personal* accusers, namely, the evil angels.[93] That would certainly be a very natural transition. It also reminds us of the apostle's argumentation in Rom. 8. There, too, having pointed out how the demand of *the law* was satisfied (Rom. 8:1-4) , the apostle asks in verse 33, *"Who* shall lay anything to the charge of God's elect?" and in verse 34, *"Who* is he that condemns?" Would anyone say that Paul, well-versed in the Old Testament as he was, did *not* include Satan among those personal accusers? The idea that Satan is the arch-accuser is, indeed, decidedly biblical (Job 1:9-11; Zech. 3:1-5; Rev. 12:10) . Of course, the work of Satan and his hosts in their attempt to destroy believers is not confined to that of *accusation*. The baseness of these hordes of evil appears especially in this that first they tempt men to sin, and then, having succeeded in their sinister endeavor, they immediately accuse these same people before God, charging them with those very sins which *they,* these sinister spirits, devised.

Now in the midst of this terrific struggle (cf. Eph. 6:12) the Colossians receive a word of comfort. Says Paul, as it were, Y o u need not be afraid of these hosts of evil, for in principle the battle has already been won. It has been won *for* y o u. God himself has disarmed [94] these principalities and powers. Did he not rescue us out of the domain of darkness? (Col. 1:13) .

---

[92] Note the symmetrical structure of verses 14 and 15, in both of which in the original the leading verb occurs between two modifying participles.

[93] Ridderbos rejects this idea as being unsupported by the context (*op. cit.,* p. 189) . I would rather leave room for this possibility, for the reasons stated in the text.

[94] Here I agree with Ridderbos as against Lightfoot and others. See Lightfoot's lengthy argumentation to the effect that ἀπεκδυσάμενος must be translated as a true middle, so that the sense would be that Christ *divested himself of* the powers of evil "which had clung like a Nessus robe about his humanity" (*op. cit.,* p. 190) . Over against this note:

(1) In the New Testament the middle is occasionally used where the active is expected. See Gram. N.T. Bl.-Debr., par. 316.

(2) In Eph. 6:11, 14; I Thess. 5:8 the verb ἐνδύω is used in the middle voice with the meaning *I put on armor.* Hence, here in Col. 2:15 ἀπεκδυσάμενος middle voice, could well mean *disarming.*

(3) The subject of this sentence is still *God.* It is difficult to think of God as divesting himself of the evil angels as if they were clinging about him like a cloak.

Is not his Son *the head of every principality and authority?* (Col. 2:10). And is it not true that principalities and authorities (as well as thrones and dominions) are but creatures, having been created in him, through him, and with a view to him? (Col. 1:16). Remember, therefore, that, by means of that same Son, God stripped these principalities and authorities of their power. He utterly disarmed them. Did not Christ triumph over them in the desert of temptation? (Matt. 4:1-11). Did he not bind the strong man? (Matt. 12:29), casting out demons again and again to prove it? Did he not see Satan fallen as lightning from heaven? (Luke 10:18). When the devil and his hosts asserted themselves from Gethsemane to Golgotha (Luke 22:3, 53; cf. Ps. 22:12, 16), did not Christ by his vicarious death deprive Satan of even a semblance of legal ground on which to base his accusations? Was not *the accuser of the brothers* cast down, and this not only by means of Christ's vicarious death but also by his triumphant resurrection, ascension, and coronation? (Rev. 12:10; Eph. 1:20-23). Is it not true, then, that by these great redemptive acts God publicly exposed these evil powers to disgrace, leading them captive in triumph, chained, as it were, to his triumphal chariot?[95] Yes, in and through this Son of his love, this triumphant Christ, God has achieved the victory over Satan and all his hosts. And that victory is y o u r life and y o u r joy. Whatever y o u need is in Christ.

16, 17. In line with what he had been saying with respect to the persuasive argumentation (2:3), philosophy, empty deceit, man-made tradition, and worldly rudiments (2:8) that characterized the thinking and propaganda of the false teachers, and the *requirements* of the law (2:14) upon which they superimposed their own *regulations,* Paul now continues, **Therefore allow no one to pass judgment on y o u in questions of eating or of drinking or with respect to a festival or a new moon or a sabbath . . .**

The Jewish aspect of the Colossian Heresy stands out clearly here. Nevertheless, it is also evident that the error went beyond that mixture of Jewish religion and Christianity which is called Judaism, for the Colossian errorists passed judgment not only with respect to *eating* but also with respect to *drinking,* though with respect to the latter subject the Old Testament contains rather few prohibitions (Lev. 10:9; Num. 6:3; Judg. 13:4, 7, 14), though lack of moderation is strongly condemned (Isa. 5:11, 12; Amos 6:6; Prov. 20:1). As to *eating,* the false teachers seem to have superimposed their own regulations upon the Old Testament laws regarding clean and unclean animals (cf. Lev. 11). They also tried to impose restrictions in connection with *festivals* — think of Passover, Pentecost, Feast of Tabernacles, and perhaps others (cf. Lev. 23) —, *new moon* (cf. Num. 10:10; 28:11), and *sabbath* (cf. Ex. 20:8-11; 31:14-16). There was evidence, therefore, of a distinctly ascetic tendency. The main purpose of placing such stress on all such regula-

---

[95] Cf. Eph. 4:8, and for a favorable application of the metaphor see II Cor. 2:14.

tions was to convince the Colossians that strict observance was absolutely indispensable to salvation, or if not to salvation as such, at least to *fulness,* perfection in salvation (see on verses 9, 10). Paul issues a strong warning against this implied denial of the all-sufficiency of Christ, by continuing, **which things** — even in their legitimate Old Testament context — **are a shadow of those that were coming, but the object casting the shadow is to be found with Christ.**[96]

Why regard as indispensable ordinances as to eating, when the One foreshadowed by Israel's manna is offering himself as the Bread of Life (John 6:35, 48)? How can the observance of the Passover (cf. Ex. 12) be considered a means unto spiritual perfection when "our Passover has been sacrificed, even Christ" (I Cor. 5:7)? What justification could there be for imposing upon converts from the Gentile world the observance of the Jewish sabbath, when the Bringer of eternal rest is urging every one to come unto him (Matt. 11:28, 29; cf. Heb. 4:8, 14)? To be sure, for the time being a shadow that is cast by an approaching person may prove to be of some real value. For example, it is possible that one is eagerly expecting this person but happens to be so situated that, at his approach, for a moment his shadow alone is seen. However, that shadow not only guarantees the imminent arrival of the visitor but even provides a dim outline, describing him. Thus, too, the Old Testament regulations had served a real purpose. But now that Christ and salvation in him had arrived, what further use could such shadows serve? Though it was not wrong for *the Jew,* trained from his infancy in the law, for a period of transition to observe some of these customs as mere *customs,* having nothing whatever to do with salvation, it was certainly wrong to ascribe to them a value which they did not have, and to try to impose them upon the Gentiles. And if this was true with respect to Old Testament regulations, it was certainly even far more true with respect to man-made regulations of an ascetic character that were being superimposed upon, added to,

---

[96] On the basis of the rendering, "But the body is Christ," some are of the opinion that the meaning is, "But it is the body of Christ (the church) that must pass judgment in all such matters." However, the words σκιά (shadow) and σῶμα (*body* or *object*) clearly belong together, and to introduce the church at this point is wholly arbitrary. Also, the reading of the original is: τὸ δὲ σῶμα τοῦ Χριστοῦ, literally, ". . . but the body (or: the object) . . . of Christ," probably meaning, ". . . but the object is to be found with Christ."

The translation, "But *the substance* — or *the reality* — is Christ" is very popular. It may not be missing the truth by much. Nevertheless, it would seem to me that because of the close relation between σκία and σῶμα, which are counterparts, Paul was thinking of *a shadow* and *an object casting the shadow.* The real contrast drawn by the apostle is not precisely between that which was *unreal* and that which is *real* — the Old Testament regulations regarding these matters, and also the matters themselves, were real enough —, but rather between that which was *passing* and should therefore be discarded and that which is *abiding.* The shadow preceded the object casting it: the law with its regulations concerning foods, feasts, etc., foreshadowed salvation in Christ. Why cling to the shadow when the shadow-casting object has itself arrived?

and in some cases perhaps even substituted for the law of God. Thus the all-sufficiency and pre-eminence of Christ was being denied. And that, after all, was the basic error.

---

18 Let no one disqualify y o u by delighting in humility and the worship of the angels, taking his stand on the things he has seen, without cause puffed up by his fleshly mind, 19 and not keeping firm hold on the Head, from whom the entire body, supported and held together by joints and ligaments, grows with a growth (that is) from God.

2:18, 19

III. *Warning against Angel-Worship*

18. Turning now to the subject of angel-worship, which was one of the characteristics of the Colossian Heresy, Paul writes, **Let no one disqualify y o u.**[97] Let no ritualist tell y o u, "Since y o u, Colossians, are not following my rules and regulations, y o u are not in the race or contest at all. Y o u are unfit, unworthy." Particularly, do not begin to feel inferior when such a person, in addition to stressing the importance of all those restrictions as to eating, drinking, etc., tries to put y o u to shame by his attempt to draw a sharp contrast between yourself and himself. Let him not *disqualify* y o u **by** his **delighting** [98] **in humility** . . . Now sincere humility, is, indeed, a precious virtue (cf. Col. 3:12, and see N.T.C. on Phil. 2:3), but the humility of which this false teacher boasted was nothing but a thin disguise for insufferable pride, as is clear also from verse 23. This person was as "umble" as Uriah Heep in *David Copperfield*.

Paul continues, **and** (also delighting in) **the worship of the angels.** The question arises, Just what is the relation between *humility* and *the worship of angels?* The answer is not given. Perhaps the suggestion that has been offered by more than one commentator is correct, namely, that the teacher of error was trying to create the impression that he considered himself too insignificant to approach God directly, hence sought to contact Deity through the mediation of angels, and since the angels were willing to per-form this service for him — or, in order that they might oblige — worshiped them.

---

[97] The word καταβραβευέτω is related to βραβεύς, judge, umpire, referee. Though the verb is rare, and in the New Testament occurs only here (see, however, Col. 3:15 for the simple βραβεύω), there seems to be no good reason to depart from the etymological meaning: *to make an umpire's decision against* a person, *to judge against* someone, *to declare* (someone) *disqualified*. Thus also R.S.V., N.E.V., and Moule.
[98] For the meaning of θέλων ἐν cf. I Sam. 18:22 (LXX), "The king *delights in* you." Cf. also I Kings 10:9; Ps. 112:1 (LXX 111:1).

With respect to the words here translated *the worship of the angels* there is much difference of opinion among commentators. Some prefer the rendering, "angelic piety" or "worship as practised by angels." But the fact that Paul in this epistle constantly emphasizes Christ's pre-eminence above all creatures, including the angels (Col. 1:16, 17, 20; 2:9, 15) and that he says "of *the* angels," seems to indicate that he was combating angel-worship. Not only this, but there is evidence tending to support the theory that angel-worship was practised in the general region in which Colosse was located. Did not the Holy Spirit through John, the disciple whom Jesus loved, strongly condemn angel-worship? See Rev. 19:10; 22:8, 9. And did not John, during a considerable portion of his ministry, have *Ephesus,* only a little over one hundred miles to the west of Colosse, as his headquarters? Moreover, as has been pointed out in footnote 76, the Essenes, whose doctrine in certain respects resembled the one here attacked (though the Colossian errorists may not have been Essenes!), required of those who were about to be admitted to full membership an oath "carefully to guard . . . the names of the angels." The Synod of *Laodicea* — one of the three cities of the Lycus Valley; see Introduction II A — in the year A. D. 363 declared, "It is not right for Christians to abandon the church of God and go away to invoke angels" (Canon XXV). A century afterward Theodoret, commenting on this very Scripture-passage (Col. 2:18), states, "The disease which St. Paul denounces, continued for a long time in Phrygia and Pisidia." Irenaeus, himself from Asia Minor but widely traveled, in his work *Against Heresies* (A. D. 182-188), implies both the widespread presence of angel-worship in the camp of the emissaries of error and the firm stand of the primitive church against this evil practice, when he states, "Nor does she [i.e. the church] perform anything *by means of angelic invocations,* or by incantations, or by any other wicked curious art; but directing her prayers to the Lord who made all things . . . and calling on the name of our Lord Jesus Christ, she has been accustomed to work miracles for the advantage of mankind, and not to lead men into error" (II.xxxii.5). It is known that Michael, a leader of the host of angels, was worshiped widely in Asia Minor, and this worship, too, continued for centuries. So, for example, as late as A. D. 739 the scene of a great victory over the Saracens was dedicated to him. His worship is also implied in inscriptions found in Galatia. And he was given credit for miraculous cures. [99]

From all this it would seem that the rendering "the worship of the angels" is correct. For the theory according to which these angels were "astral spirits," "rulers of the planetary spheres," see footnote 83 above. And for Paul's own teaching respecting angels see not only above, on Col. 1:16, 17; 2:15, but also N.T.C. on I and II Timothy, and Titus, pp. 183-185.

---

[99] Cf. W. M. Ramsay, *The Church in the Roman Empire,* pp. 477-480.

Paul continues, **taking his stand** [100] on the things he has seen.[101]

This man *pretends* (perhaps even *believes*) to have seen something, and he presumes on this experience he has had. He makes the most of it. If any one ventures to contradict him or to question the truth of his theories, he will answer, "But I have seen such and such a vision." In saying this and in relating the vision he will, of course, assume an air of deep insight into divinely revealed mysteries. He prides himself on what he regards as his superior knowledge. He forgets that "Knowledge puffs up but love builds

---

[100] The words ἃ ἑόρακεν ἐμβατεύων have led to well-nigh endless discussion. Lightfoot fairly gives up the attempt to explain them. He states, "The combination is so harsh and incongruous as to be barely possible; and there was perhaps some corruption in the text prior to existing authorities." By detaching κεν from the word ἑόρακεν, prefixing it to ἐμβατεύων, and making a slight change in the word from which κεν was subtracted, he arrives at the result: ἐώρᾳ (or αἰώρᾳ) κενεμβατεύων, "treading the void while suspended in air," that is, "indulging airily in vain speculations." J. R. Harris, in his article, "St. Paul and Aristophanes," *ET* 34 (1922, 1923), pp. 151-156, saw a parallel between Col. 2:18 and line 225 of *The Clouds* of Aristophanes, where Socrates, suspended in a basket, when asked what he was doing, replies, "I tread on air and contemplate the sun." According to this view Paul, having read *The Clouds*, is here ridiculing the Colossian philosophizers as Aristophanes had satirized Socrates.

The question may well be asked, however, whether such and similar interpretations, all of them based on emendation of the text, are necessary. After all, the basic meaning of ἐμβατεύω seems to be *I step upon, set foot upon* (for illustrations of this use see Liddell and Scott, *Greek-English Lexicon*, Vol. I, p. 539); hence, *I enter into, go deeply into, investigate,* and so *take my stand on.* See G. G. Findlay, "The Reading and Rendering of Colossians 2:18," *Exp*, first series, 11 (1880), pp. 385-398. W. M. Ramsay, on the basis of an inscription from the temple of Apollo of Klaros, dating from the second century A. D., accordingly translates Col. 2:18b, 19a as follows, "taking his stand on what he has seen (in the mysteries), vainly puffed up by his unspiritual mind, and not keeping firm hold on the Head." See *The Teaching of Paul in Terms of the Present Day*, pp. 283 ff. This explanation of the expression is favored by M.M., pp. 205, 206, by Bruce, *op. cit.,* pp. 248-250, and also by R.S.V., A.R.V. (margin), and the *New American Standard Bible.* I believe it also is clearly supported by the context: the man who *takes his stand on* — hence, *brags about* (as the Berkeley Version puts it) — what he has seen, is described as being vainly inflated ("puffed up") by his fleshly mind. Cf. also the entry ἐμβατεύω in L.N.T. (A. and G.), p. 253. Ridderbos (*op. cit.,* p. 194), on the other hand, favors (though with commendable caution) the rendering: "as an initiate entering into that which he claims to have seen." This *entering into* may be compared with the rendering *intruding into* of the A.V. Though by no means denying the possibility that Ridderbos is right, since there is definite evidence in support of this use of the word, I regard the translation *taking his stand on* as probably more nearly in harmony with the context in this instance, as has been indicated.

[101] The insertion *not* (A.V. "which he hath not seen") does not rest on *the best* textual evidence in the original. Perhaps some copyist who did not understand that when Paul said, with reference to this false teacher, "taking his stand on the things he has seen," he meant, "on the things he *pretends* (or even *believes*) to have seen," inserted this *not* in his copy, thinking that otherwise the ritualist would receive too much credit. But the idiom which the apostle uses is very transparent. We may compare Paul's expression "the things he has seen" with Christ's ". . . that those that see may become blind" (John 9:39b), meaning, "that those who *pretend* to see, and are constantly saying, *We see,* may become blind" (cf. John 9:41).

up" (I Cor. 8:1). He is, continues Paul, **without cause puffed up by his fleshly mind.** Note "without cause," that is, though he is filled with an exalted opinion of himself, he has no good reason to feel this way. His mind, moreover, is distinctly the mind *of the flesh,* the attitude or disposition of heart and mind *apart from regenerating grace.*[102] It is important in this connection to observe that for the mind to be "fleshly" or "of the flesh" it is not necessary that it be "fixed on purely physical things." [103] On the contrary, it is "of the flesh" if it bases its hope for salvation on *anything apart from Christ,* as verse 19 clearly indicates. Whether the ground on which it bases this confidence be physical strength, charm, good works, or, as here, transcendental visions, makes no difference. It is "the mind of the flesh" all the same. Note how Paul exposes this individual who pretends to take such pleasure in *humility* or *self-abasement.* He says, as it were, "This man who pretends to be so very *humble* is in reality unbearably *proud.* His mind is *inflated* with the sense of his own importance, as he brags about the things he has seen." Contrast this *tawdry* behavior with respect to *questionable* visions with Paul's own *sensible* reaction in regard to *real* visions (II Cor. 12:1-4).

19. The trouble with this combination philosopher-ritualist-angel wor-shiper-ascetic-visionary is that he is taking his stand on the things he has seen . . . **and not keeping firm hold on the Head.** He does not cling to Christ. He fails to see that Christ is all-sufficient for salvation, and that all the treas-ures of wisdom and knowledge are hidden in him (Col. 2:3, 9, 10). Hence, Paul continues, **from whom the entire body, supported and held together by joints and ligaments, grows with a growth (that is) from God.** It should not be necessary to defend the proposition that when the apostle, having just referred to Christ as *the Head,* now speaks about *the entire body,* he is think-ing about *the church.* That, *in such a connection,* this is the only possible meaning is clearly implied in such passages as Col. 1:18, 24; 3:15; Eph. 1:22, 23; 4:16. [104]

The underlying figure in this passage is that of the growth of the human body. The aptness of Paul's metaphor has been questioned, and this for two reasons:
Objection No. 1. The apostle implies that in a human body the head is the source of growth. This is faulty, ancient physiology.
Answer. As was indicated in connection with Col. 1:18, the hormone that is

---

[102] See summary of the meanings of σάρξ in Paul's epistles, N.T.C. on Philippians, p. 77, footnote 55. Meaning g. is indicated here.
[103] As L.N.T. (A. and G., p. 547), wrongly interprets this word as used here in Col. 1:18.
[104] It is, indeed, somewhat amazing that Dibelius tries to defend the theory that *the body* is here *the cosmos.* See his interpretation of this passage (and also of Col. 1:18 and 2:10) M. Dibelius-H. Greeven, *An die Kolosser, Epheser, An Philemon,* 1953 (in *Handbuch zum Neuen Testament*).

closely related to the growth of connective tissue, cartilage, and bone structure of the body originates in the pituitary gland which is housed in a small cavity in the base of the skull. And that is only one of several ways in which the head influences the growth of the body.

Objection No. 2. According to Paul "nourishment is ministered" (A.V.) to the body by joints and ligaments. Lightfoot similarly states that one of the two functions of the joints and ligaments is "to supply nutriment" (*op. cit.,* p. 200). But we now know that it is not joints and ligaments but the bloodstream that carries nourishment to the various cells and tissues of the human body. Therefore, Paul was in error.

Answer. The proper rendering is "the entire body *supported and held together* by joints and ligaments." [105] Now the fact that the body is, indeed, thus supported and held together is common knowledge. It is not refuted by the most up to date science. Therefore, instead of hinting that the apostle is basing his argument on "loose physiology" (Moule, *op. cit.,* p. 107), the question may well be asked whether the rendering according to which joints and ligaments "supply nutriment" (or "nourishment") to the body is not "loose translation."

So much for the underlying figure. Now as to the real message which the apostle is here conveying, in the light of the context it is clear that the main idea is that to Christ the entire church owes its growth. *The church need not and must not look for any other source of strength to overcome sin or to increase in knowledge, virtue, and joy.* Just as the human body, when properly supported and held together by joints and ligaments, experiences normal growth, so also the church, when each of its members supports and maintains loving contact with the others, will, under the sustaining care of God, proceed from grace to grace and from glory to glory (cf. I Cor. 12; Eph. 4:16).

---

20 If with Christ y o u died to the rudiments of the world, why, as though y o u were (still) living in the world, do y o u submit to regulations, 21 "Do not handle, Do not taste, Do not touch" — 22 referring to things that are meant for destruction by their consumption — according to the precepts and doctrines of men? 23 Regulations of this kind, though to be sure having a reputation for wisdom because of their self-imposed ritual, humility, and unsparing treatment of the body, are of no value whatever, (serving only) to indulge the flesh.

---

[105] See L.N.T. (A. and G.), p. 305, entry ἐπιχορηγέω, which furnishes the evidence for the use of the word in that sense. And see also N.T.C. on Philippians, p. 74, footnote 50 with reference to the meaning of the simple verb.

2:20-23

IV. *Warning against Asceticism*

20-22. In this paragraph Paul condemns the program of austerity recommended by the proponents of error. The connection between these verses and the immediately preceding warning against the worship of the angels (vss. 18, 19) is obscure. Did the impostors perhaps use their presumed contact with the angelic world as a basis for imposing ascetic restrictions on themselves and on others? Did they say, "It must be true that by following these rules y o u will achieve the victory over fleshly indulgence and obtain fulness of salvation, for an angel showed me this in a vision"? We do not know. One fact is certain. It is this, that the apostle teaches that asceticism, no less than the worship of the angels, does more harm than good. Instead of being a remedy against fleshly indulgence, it fosters and promotes the latter.

The apostle has already warned against the *persuasive arguments* of the deceivers (Col. 2:4). He has described this type of propaganda as *philosophy and vain deceit according to the tradition of men* (2:8). He has shown that if even the law *of God*, as a code of ceremonial ordinances and rules and as a means unto salvation, was blotted out and nailed to the cross, then surely *man-made* instructions regarding eating, drinking, etc., must be discarded (2:14, 16). Such added rules and regulations and the teachings of which they are the outgrowth are nothing but puerile notions, *worldly rudiments.* They amount to no more than high-sounding nonsense that is distinctly worldly in its origin and character. Continuing, therefore, along this line, and directing his attention now to an extreme form of this error, namely, to rigid abstinence, Paul says, **If with Christ y o u died to the rudiments of the world, why, as though y o u were (still) living in the world, do y o u submit to regulations.** "If y o u died with Christ, as, of course, y o u did," for y o u were buried with him (see on verse 12 above) and y o u were raised with him (verse 12 again; also 3:1), then y o u have also in that very act made a complete break with all such rudimentary instruction that bases its hope upon anything apart from Christ and fulness of salvation in him. (For the meaning of the expression "rudiments of the world" see on verse 8; also footnote 83.) What is, perhaps, the most beautiful explanation, in Paul's own words, of the basic meaning of this passage is found in Gal. 2:18-21. There Paul is speaking about *building* (verse 18). He is building by faith, "the faith that is in the Son of God, who loved me, and gave himself up for me." He continues, "I do not nullify the grace of God: for if righteousness [or: justification] were through the law, then Christ died to no purpose." And surely if basing one's hope upon the law was contrary to the principle of salvation *solely* on the basis of the redemptive merits of Christ, then this would be true all the more with respect to trusting in purely human ordinances. By reliance on them the Colossians would be acting as though they were still living in the world, that is, in the sphere of life that is separated from Christ. But to this world Paul and all true believers have been crucified. Says he, "But far be it from me to glory except in the cross of our Lord Jesus Christ, through which the world has been crucified to me, and I to the world" (Gal. 6:14). Away, therefore, with all such weak and beggarly rudiments, such teachings and regulations which draw the heart away from Christ as the only Savior (cf. Gal. 4:9)!

With scornful and stinging ridicule Paul now summarizes these regulations, using for this purpose pithy, sparkling, proverbial language: **Do not handle, Do not taste, Do not touch.** He says, as it were, Why submit to a series of Dont's, as if by adding enough negatives y o u would ever obtain a positive, or as if victory over sin and progress in sanctification would ever be achieved by basing all y o u r confidence in sheer *avoidance*. Says Lightfoot, "Some [of these prohibitions] were doubtless re-enactments of the Mosaic law; while others would be exaggerations or additions of a rigorous asceticism, such as we find among the Essene prototypes of these Colossian heretics; e.g., the avoidance of oil, of wine, or of flesh-meat, the shunning of contact with a stranger or a religious inferior, and the like" (*op. cit.,* p. 203). Of course, in reality we do not know exactly what ascetic rules Paul had in mind when he issued this warning, nor do we know precisely what was their background.[106] That restrictions as to the use of foods and beverages were included is implied in the terse commands. Note especially "Do not taste." It is also clear from the parenthetical statement which follows in verse 22. Whether marriage was also forbidden (cf. I Tim. 4:3) or at least subjected to rigorous restrictions we do not know. It would seem, however, that the prohibitions concerned themselves especially with eating and drinking, for the apostle continues . . . — **referring to things that are meant for destruction by their consumption — according to the precepts and doctrines of men?**[107]

---

[106] What really was the origin and background of this asceticism? For a discussion of this question see the Introduction III B 2. Whether the Colossian errorists had at one time been Essenes we do not know. Resemblance does not necessarily mean identity or even descent.

[107] With most translators and commentators I take the question to be, "If with Christ y o u died to the rudiments of the world, why, as though y o u were (still) living in the world, do y o u submit to regulations, Do not handle, Do not taste, Do not touch, according to the precepts and doctrines of men?" (vss. 20, 21, 22b). The clause — "referring to things that are meant for destruction by their consumption" — (verse 22a) is then construed as a parenthesis within the question. It shows that the regulations — in this case prohibitions — refer mainly to that which is consumed by the body. Therefore, the phrase "according to the precepts and doctrines of men" (verse 22b) is construed as modifying verses 20, 21. Others, however, would connect this phrase with the immediately preceding words, which are then no longer construed as a parenthesis. The result then reads as follows: ". . . refer-

What Paul stresses here is that it is certainly most foolish to base one's hope for victory over sin and for complete salvation on anything pertaining to that which in the process of nature is doomed to destruction. Food and drink regulations (here probably especially the former), having as their purpose the betterment of man's moral and spiritual condition, are based on purely human precepts and doctrines. The parenthetical clause — "referring to things that are meant for destruction by their consumption" (cf. I Cor. 6:13) — corresponds exactly to the teaching of Jesus in Matt. 15:17: "Do y o u not understand that whatever goes into the mouth passes into the stomach, and is discharged into the latrine?" The description of the regulations as being "in accordance with the precepts and doctrines of men" also immediately reminds one of what Jesus said as reported in another verse of that same chapter of Matthew, namely, "teaching (as their) doctrines precepts of men" (Matt. 15:9), which, in turn, is a quotation from Isa. 29:13. The point of all this teaching, both in Isaiah and in the words of Jesus, is not only to show that such man-made ordinances and the doctrines from which they spring are *worthless,* but also and emphatically that they are worse than worthless, that is, actually harmful. Hence, according to the Isaiah passage a woe is pronounced upon those who substitute the commandment of men for the heart-centered fear of Jehovah, and in the context of the Matthew passage Jesus sharply denounces those in his day who nullified the word of God for the sake of their tradition (Matt. 15:6).

23. Entirely in line with this the apostle concludes this section as follows: **Regulations of this kind,**[108] **though, to be sure, having a reputation** [109] **for wisdom because of their self-imposed ritual,**[110] **humility, and unsparing treatment of the body, are of no value whatever, (serving only) to indulge the flesh.**[111]

---

ring to things that are meant for destruction by their consumption, along with (or: as happens also to) the precepts and doctrines of men." Foods and human regulations are both doomed to perish. Cf. H. Ridderbos, *op. cit.,* p. 197, though he adds that the connection is rather loose. The reason I favor the more widely held view is that the words "by their consumption" can hardly be considered to apply not only to foods *but also to the precepts and doctrines of men.*

[108] Literally, *such as,* but the reference is to the regulations and the teaching from which they spring.

[109] The meaning of λόγος depends on the context. Here it seems to have the connotation *reputation,* which is akin to that which it frequently has, namely, *report.*

[110] The compound ἐθελοθρησκία has been called a Christian term. Paul may have coined it himself. No examples of its use before Paul have been found. It reminds one of ἐθελοδουλεία, *voluntary service,* but in the present context the word used by Paul probably means *self-chosen worship, self-imposed cult* or *ritual, self-made religion* (hence, in reality, *would-be religion*).

[111] Meaning: "but serve only to indulge the flesh." Lightfoot, followed by Moule, has serious objections to this and similar adversative renderings. His main objections are: (1) there is no indication that an adversative clause begins with πρὸς πλησμονὴν κ.τ.λ.; and (2) it makes the apostle say what he could not have said.

Here "self-imposed ritual" refers to the worship of the angels of which Paul had spoken in verse 18, and "humility" repeats what he said in that same verse about the sham self-abasement of the teachers of error. The "unsparing treatment of the body" has been explained in verses 20, 21. The home-made piety of these cultists made a deep impression on some people. How serious and godly these propagandists seemed to be, and how humble! Perhaps by copying their example the Colossians, striving against sins of the flesh such as are mentioned in 3:5, 8, 9, would be able to achieve the moral and spiritual victory they were seeking. "Not at all," says Paul. Neglect of the body will never cure the soul. Man's body as well as his soul is dear to the Lord, being a temple of the Holy Spirit (I Cor. 6:19). The soul-body contrast, as if the body were evil and for that reason had to be punished, while the soul was divine, smacks of gnostic dualism or hellenism. The worship of the angels reminds one of polytheism. The humility is definitely faked. In reality these teachers of falsehood are proud. If people are deceived by them and accept their worse than worthless advice, this will flatter the pride of these "philosophers." Any system of religion which is unwilling to accept Jesus Christ as the only and all-sufficient Savior is an indulgence of the flesh, a giving in to man's sinful conceit, as if he, by his own contrivances, were able to perfect Christ's imperfect (?) work. It makes matters worse instead of better.

Again and again Paul condemns sinful pride. In addition to Col. 2:18, 23, see also Rom. 1:21, 22, 30; 12:16; I Cor. 8:1, 2; I Tim. 3:6; 6:4. Cf. James 4:6; I Peter 5:5. It is the haughty spirit that goes before a fall (Prov. 16:18). Not only those who actually swagger before men (Matt. 6:1, 2), nor only those who strut in the presence of the Almighty (Luke 18:10-12), but also those

---

"Such language would defeat its own object by its extravagance." He renders πρός "to check," so that the meaning of the sentence becomes, "All such teaching is powerless to check indulgence of the flesh."

Along with H. Ridderbos (*op. cit.*, p. 198) and many other commentators I believe, however, that the adversative sense is correct, and that we have here a μέν ... δέ (*implied*) sequence. In favor of this rendering and in opposition to Lightfoot's arguments I present the following:

(1) When the contrast is easily supplied from the context, μέν need not always be followed by δέ (*expressed*). L.N.T. (A. and G., p. 504) cites the following New Testament instances of this omission: besides Col. 2:23 also I Cor. 6:7 and II Cor. 12:12. This answers Lightfoot's first objection.

(2) This translation is in line with what the apostle has already said in verse 18, where he spoke about the *fleshly* mind, that is, the mind inflated or puffed up with sinful pride. The language of verse 23, when the adversative rendering is adopted, is therefore not much more "extravagant" than is that of verse 18. This in reply to Lightfoot's second argument.

(3) The preposition πρός is far more naturally translated *with a view to* (the indulgence of the flesh); hence, *serving* (to indulge the flesh).

(4) As was pointed out in connection with verses 20-22, both in Isaiah 29:13 and in Matt. 15:9 such man-made teaching and the regulations which flow forth from it are described as being definitely harmful. They are not only powerless to check indulgence, but they actually promote the desires of the flesh.

who conceal their revolting conceit behind a mask of humility are an abomination to Jehovah (Prov. 16:5; cf. 3:5; 16:18; 26:12; 29:23; Ps. 101:5b) . Is there a danger that the Colossians will slip back into their former *fleshly* life? There is a far better solution than that which is offered by the false teachers. In harmony with all that Paul has so far been saying — see especially 1:9-23, 27, 28; 2:2, 3, 6-10 — that solution is pointed out in Colossians 3.

Summary of Colossians 2

Paul concluded the last paragraph by saying, "I am laboring, *striving* by his energy working powerfully within me." In a new paragraph which begins in what we now call Chapter 2 he once more picks up this idea of *striving,* and writes, "For I want y o u to know how greatly I *strive* for y o u," etc. He is wrestling in prayer, in planning, in dictating this letter, and perhaps in other ways, being deeply concerned over the dangers that are threatening the churches located in the Lycus Valley. These dangers do not touch merely the intellect; no, they touch the heart! Paul writes, "I strive for all who have not seen my face in the flesh . . . that their *hearts* may be strengthened." Heresy is usually a matter of the heart, and so is true soundness. Fully realizing that impostors are placing great stress on such matters as "knowledge," "philosophy," (abstract and worldly!) , Paul emphasizes *love.* He fervently hopes and prays that the Colossians and their neighbors may be "welded together in love." Such a unity results in praying together, discussing matters together, worshiping together, the result being that the entire company of believers will obtain a clear knowledge of the mystery of God, even Christ. Having discovered this mystery, no further discoveries need be attempted. *Christ cannot be supplemented,* for in him, *"all* the treasures of wisdom and knowledge are hidden"; hidden, yes, but with a view to being *revealed* to every believer and fully *appropriated.* Continue to cling to Christ Jesus, the Lord, says Paul, just as y o u sometime ago made that wonderful decision to accept him. Continue in what y o u were taught, and let no one carry y o u off as spoil "by means of his philosophy and empty deceit, according to the tradition of men, according to the rudiments of the world, and not according to Christ." Watch out for those "worldly rudiments," those puerile notions advanced by worldly people. Remember that not only *divinity* dwells in Christ but *deity.* Being God in the fullest sense of the term, he is able and eager to supply y o u r *every* need. He is higher than all the angels in the sky, and overrules every sinister device of Satan and his helpers.

In order to gain victory over sin and fulness of salvation it will not be necessary for y o u to be circumcised. In fact, y o u have already received a circumcision that far excels the literal kind. Y o u received the circumcision of the *heart.* It is y o u r s because of y o u r vital union with Christ, having been buried with him and having been raised with him. Y o u received the sign and seal of this in y o u r baptism. Let not the law of Moses with its many ordinances frighten y o u. When Christ died, the law, with all its ceremonial regulations, died with him. It was nailed to his cross! Both the law and Satan have lost all legal claim against y o u. By means of Christ's death on the cross the law lost its hold on y o u (as a means of salvation), and the principalities and powers (angels) that might wish to accuse y o u were openly exposed to disgrace. This holds too with respect to regulations concerning food or drink, festivals, new moon, and sabbath. When once the object that projected its shadow arrives, it is foolish to keep clinging to the shadow. The types are fulfilled in Christ.

Don't be impressed by those people who make a show of their humility, pretending that they are too unworthy to contact God directly and must therefore seek to reach God by the mediation of angels whom they adore and worship. [It is not certain, however, that this was their real reason for worshiping the angels. It is a suggestion that has been offered by many.] Do not allow those pretenders to disqualify y o u, as if y o u r manner of worshiping God (or Christ) is not good enough. Remember, instead of being *really* humble, these impostors are "puffed up by their fleshly mind." They are "not keeping firm hold on the Head, from whom the entire body, supported and held together by joints and ligaments, grows with a growth (that is) from God."

And finally, if with Christ y o u died to the world's puerile notions, why then do y o u submit to ordinances, "Do not handle, Do not taste, Do not touch." Such man-made regulations have merely a show of wisdom. If y o u obey them, thinking that conquest over evil and fulness of salvation lies in that direction, y o u will be worse off than ever before. Such self-imposed ritual serves only *to indulge the flesh*. It feeds man's pride. It will but lead y o u *away from* Christ and fulness of salvation in him.

---

[83] In astrological literature *stoicheia* ("rudiments") is frequently used in the sense of *elemental* (or *astral*) *spirits* or *elemental beings*. It is held by many that this is also the meaning here in Col. 2:8. Bible translators have adopted this rendering: R.S.V., N.E.B., Moffatt, etc. Among the many commentators who favor it are F. W. Beare, *The Epistle to the Colossians* (in *The Interpreter's Bible*, Vol. XI), pp. 191-193: "astral divinities which control the spheres and are thus masters of human fate"; F. F. Bruce, *Commentary on the Epistle to the Colossians* (in *The New International Commentary on the New Testament*), pp. 228-232: "rulers of the planetary spheres"; A. S. Peake, *The Epistle to the Colossians* (in *The Expositor's Bible*, Vol. III), pp. 521-524: "astral spirits"; E. F. Scott, *The Epistles of Paul to the Colossians, to Philemon, and to the Ephesians* (in *The Moffatt Commentary*), pp. 41-43: "personal agencies, angelic beings"; and see also E. Percy, *Die Probleme der Kolosser- und Epheserbriefe*, pp. 156-167: "spiritual beings who stood in relation to the elements of nature."

Arguments that have been used in favor of this rendering, in one form or another, are the following; together with my counter-arguments:

(1) There is a good deal of evidence for the widespread use of the word in this sense.

Answer. "For the sense *elemental beings* the evidence, apart from what may be deduced from the contexts of the word in the New Testament, is later than the

Classical and, in all determinable cases, later than the New Testament, and belongs to the astrological sorts of writings" (C. F. D. Moule, *The Epistles of Paul the Apostle to the Colossians and to Philemon*, in *Cambridge Greek Testament Commentary*, p. 91. Again, "Apparently, therefore, there is no definite evidence, that στοιχεῖον meant 'spirit,' 'angel,' or 'demon,' earlier than Test. Sal., which in its present form is post-Christian, and may not be earlier than the third or fourth century" (E. de Witt Burton, *A critical and exegetical commentary on the Epistle to the Galatians*, pp. 510-518.

Besides, if the word has this meaning in Paul's letters, how is it that in his lists of angels (I Cor. 15:24; Col. 1:16; 2:10, 15; Eph. 1:21; 3:10) he never uses it?

(2) When the apostle says, "according to the *stoicheia* of the world and not according to Christ" he is evidently thinking of Christ as a person. Hence, logic requires that these *stoicheia*, who are here represented as opposing Christ, must also be viewed as personal beings.

Answer. By that same reasoning *tradition* also becomes a person, for it stands in exactly the same relation to Christ as do these *stoicheia*. Note: "according to the tradition of men, according to the rudiments of the world and not according to Christ."

(3) In Galatians 4:3, 9 these *stoicheia* are associated, if not identified, with the angelic powers. Now if that be true in Galatians, why not here in Colossians?

Answer. The appeal to Galatians is not justified. Gal. 4:10, considered as an interpretation of 4:9, rather indicates that Paul was thinking of rudimentary teaching regarding observances. Besides, is it at all reasonable to believe that Paul in Gal. 4:3, 9 (notice how he includes himself in verse 3) would be saying that before his conversion he, the Pharisee, had been in bondage to weak and beggarly angels in control of heavenly bodies and of earth, air, fire, water, etc.? Was Paul an animist before his conversion? A polytheist, perhaps, filled with fear and dread because of these astral spirits who supposedly tyrannized mankind in the period of its minority?

(4) But Paul does indeed say something about the angels in Gal. 3:19: "the law was ordained through angels." Is it not true then that with the coming of Christ these angels became as it were competitors of Christ, and tried to maintain the law, and that Paul now warns against putting oneself in bondage again to these angels? If Paul was not warning against the astral spirits of paganism, may he not have been warning against the law-mediating angels of Judaism?

Answer. The idea that Paul regarded the keeping of the law to be a bondage to angels is devoid of every shred of evidence. Paul never makes the angels responsible in any way for the idea of salvation through law-works. He maintains that the law as such is not an obstruction to the work of Christ but on the contrary is holy and good. And in Gal. 3:19 he clearly represents the angels as adding luster to the law. He does not fight those angels. He favors them.

In addition to the works already cited see also H. N. Ridderbos, *The Epistle of Paul to the Churches of Galatia* (in *The New International Commentary on the New Testament*), pp. 152-154, 161; and H. Fransen, "Enkele Opmerkingen over de exegese van Kol. 2:8 en 9," *GTT* (1952), pp. 65-89.

It is not surprising, therefore, that *many* commentators (although probably still a minority) refuse to adopt this rendering, and interpret *stoicheia* to mean *rudimentary instruction*:

Clement of Alexandria, writing about the year A.D. 200, and clearly basing his interpretation on the context, states that Paul figuratively calls Hellenic philosophy the *stoicheia* of this world (*Stromata* VI.viii).

Tertullian, about the same time, and again in complete harmony with the context, writes that Paul warned the Colossians to beware of subtle words and philosophy, as being vain deceit, such as is according to the *stoicheia* of the world, "not understanding thereby the mundane fabric of sky and earth, but worldly learning, and the tradition of men subtle in speech and in their philosophy" (*Against Marcion* V.xix).

Also, much closer to our own day, C. R. Erdman calls these *stoicheia* "the ritual observances of the Jews" (*The Epistles of Paul to the Colossians and to Philemon*, pp. 67, 68) ; J. B. Lightfoot calls them "rudimentary instruction" (*Saint Paul's Epistles to the Colossians and to Philemon*, pp. 178-181) ; C. F. D. Moule defines them as "elementary teaching — teaching by Judaistic or pagan ritualists . . . contrary to the freedom of the Spirit" (*op. cit.*, p. 92) ; Herman Ridderbos, as "elementary knowledge" and as "the basic principles of the sinful world of mankind" (*Aan De Kolossenzen*, in *Commentaar op het Nieuwe Testament*, p. 171) ; and A. T. Robertson, as "the specious arguments of the Gnostic philosophers with all their aeons and rules of life" (*Word Pictures in the New Testament*, Vol. IV, p. 491) .

Among the objections that have been advanced against this interpretation the following two are, perhaps, the most outstanding, my answer being added in each case:

(1) Col. 2:8 implies a sharp contrast between these *stoicheia* and Christ. But when these *stoicheia* are interpreted to mean rudimentary instruction regarding rules, regulations, and observances there is no real contrast. Says Percy, "In addition, there is especially this consideration that the expression τὰ στοιχεῖα τοῦ κόσμου, according to Col. 2:8, 10, as well as according to Gal. 4:3, 9, concerns something that is absolutely opposed to Christ, which does not suit the meaning *religious first principles*, which as such are the 'abiding foundations of all religion,' and will retain their validity when a more advanced stage has been reached" (*op. cit.*, p. 157) .

Answer. There is, indeed, a sharp contrast here, for these are the rudiments *of the world*, the world apart from Christ, in which sphere these people had formerly lived. These rudiments are not retained when people turn to Christ. On the contrary, we are distinctly told that believers *have died* to them (Col. 2:20) .

(2) The interpretation *rudimentary instruction* regarding rules and regulations is not in harmony with the context. Percy, having pointed out that *stoicheia* has of itself no other meaning than *element, rudiment*, continues, "When in so doing it concerns the rudiments of knowledge, this meaning must arise from the context, which is not true in the present case" (*op. cit.*, p. 157) .

Answer. In each case where Colossians uses the word *stoicheia* it is exactly the immediate context which by means of the synonyms *philosophy, empty deceit, the tradition of men* (verse 8), *ordinances, precepts and doctrines of men* (verses 20 and 22) , would seem to establish the correctness of this interpretation. Clement of Alexandria and Tertullian gave a basically correct explanation. And it does not speak well for the objectivity of the R.S.V., a Bible-translation which in some respects is excellent, that it did not consider *rudimentary instruction* or a similar rendering *worthy at least of a footnote* (contrast N.E.B.) ! Had R.S.V. retained the rendering of the A.V. ("rudiments") and had it left the elucidation to the Commentaries, instead of foisting its "elemental spirits of the universe" on an unsuspecting Bible-reading public, that procedure would have been even more commendable, and this all the more so because on its title page are printed the words "being the version set forth A. D. 1611," etc.

Outline of Chapter 3:1-17

Theme: *Christ, the Pre-eminent One, the Only and All-Sufficient Savior*
II. This Only and All-Sufficient Savior Is the Source of the Believers' Life, and Thus the Real Answer to the Perils by Which They Are Confronted, chapters 3 and 4
    A. This Truth Applied to All Believers, 3:1-17
3:1-4   1. Believers should be consistent. They should live in conformity with the fact that they were raised with Christ, who is their life
3:5-11   2. Therefore, they should "put to death" and "lay aside" the old vices; and
3:12-17 3. They should "put on" the new virtues

CHAPTER III

COLOSSIANS

3 1 If then y o u were raised with Christ, seek *the things that are above,* where Christ is, seated at the right hand of God. 2 On the things that are above set y o u r minds, not on the things that are upon the earth. 3 For y o u died, and y o u r life is hid with Christ in God. 4 When Christ (who is) our life is manifested, then y o u also will be manifested with him in glory.

3:1-4

I. *Believers Should Be Consistent*

1. Consistency requires that believers *live* in conformity with the fact that they were raised with Christ, who is not only the Object of their faith (chapters 1 and 2) but also the Source of their life (chapters 3 and 4). Of course, the line between these two divisions is not sharp. There is considerable overlapping. There is, however, a difference in emphasis.

Between Colossians 3 and that which precedes there is a close connection. The opening words of Col. 3, **If then y o u were raised with Christ,** resume the thought already expressed in 2:12, 13, "raised with him . . . made alive with him," and are the counterpart of 2:20, "If with Christ y o u died to the rudiments of the world. . . ." The Colossians, it will be recalled, were beset by the danger of relapsing into paganism with its gross sensuality, etc., as is clear from 2:23 and 3:5 ff. The wrong solution of their problem was refuted in chapters 1 and 2, especially the latter. It was indicated that there is no material cure for a spiritual ill, that neglect of the body will never heal the soul's sickness but will aggravate it, that heaven-born individuals cannot gain satisfaction from earth-born remedies. *Christ, he alone,* is the answer, Christ in all the fulness of his love and power, as already implied in both chapters 1 and 2, and set forth with even greater clarity and directness now (chapter 3), in a series of pastoral exhortations. If, then, the Colossians were corporately raised *when* Christ was raised and *with* him, as previously explained (see on 2:12, 13, 20), why should they seek salvation or fulness anywhere apart from him? Why should they resort to broken cisterns when the Fountain is at hand? Christ's resurrection, followed by his ascension and coronation, guarantees their pardon and provides for their purity. To this Savior they had surrendered themselves when they had embraced him by

139

faith. The cleansing power of Christ's blood and Spirit had been signified and sealed to them in baptism. The supply of grace remains plentiful. *Right now* — they need not wait until the day of the Parousia! — they are raised with Christ. They possess within themselves the life of the resurrection. Let the power of Christ's resurrection, therefore, be experienced by them in an ever increasing degree. Let their union with the exalted Christ transform their entire life: mind, heart, and will (Phil. 3:10). Let them seek *the things that are above,* **where Christ is.** The verb *seek* implies persevering effort; hence, the rendering, "Be constantly seeking," is not incorrect. This seeking, moreover, is more than a seeking *to discover.* It is a seeking *to obtain* (cf. Matt. 6:33; 13:45). The emphasis, though, is not on the seeking but on the object sought. A precise rendering would be, "the things that are above [placed forward for emphasis] be constantly seeking." Seeking to obtain is a common activity, but seeking to obtain *the right treasures* is not nearly so common, and therefore requires emphasis. These things that are above are the spiritual values embedded in the heart of the exalted Mediator in glory, whence, without loss to himself, they are bestowed upon those who humbly ask for them and diligently seek them (Matt. 7:7; I Cor. 12:11; Eph. 1:3; 4:7, 8). As the context indicates, the apostle has reference to such realities as tenderheartedness, kindness, lowliness, meekness, longsuffering, patience, the forgiving spirit, and above all *love* (3:12 ff.). Surely, if the hearts of believers are filled with such bounties there will be no room for fleshly indulgence. Here, then, is the true solution.

The Colossians can be assured of the fact that their exalted Christ has both the right and the power to bestow whatever gifts are needed, for he is **seated at the right hand of God** (Ps. 110:1, a phrase applied by Christ to himself in Matt. 22:41-46; 26:64; Mark 12:35-37; 14:61, 62; Luke 20:41-44; 22:66-70), clothed with majesty and honor.

This comforting truth of the ascension of the Lord and his coronation at the Father's right hand, as a Fountain of blessing for his people, was foreshadowed in the Old Testament (Ps. 8, as interpreted in Heb. 2:1-8; Ps. 68:18, as explained in Eph. 4:7, 8; Ps. 110:1, as has been shown; Isa. 53:12). It was frequently referred to by the Lord himself (see, in addition to the Gospel-passages in the preceding paragraph, John 14:1-4; 14:13-18; 16:7; 17:5; 20:17). It was from the very beginning one of the basic themes in the preaching of the church (Luke 24:50-53; Acts 1:6-11; 2:33-36; 3:21; 5:30, 31; 7:56; Rom. 8:32-34; Eph. 1:20-23; 4:7, 8; Phil. 2:9-11; 3:20, 21; I Tim. 3:16; Heb. 1:1-3, 13; 2:1-8; 4:14-16; 8:1, 2; 9:11, 12, 24; 10:12; I Peter 3:21, 22; Rev. 1:12-18; 12:5-12).

Those that seek to obtain these "things that are above" are not chasing phantoms but are gathering priceless treasures. They are not the kind of people who forget about their duty in the here and now. On the contrary, they are very practical, for the graces that have been enumerated enable them not only to gain victory upon victory in their struggle against fleshly indulgence but also to be truthfully "the salt of the earth" and "the light of the world" (Matt. 5:13, 14).

2. In similar vein Paul continues, **On the things that are above set y o u r minds, not on the things that are upon the earth.**[112] This admonition is very practical. It means that the Colossians are urged to *ponder and yearn for* [113] the things that are above, as previously defined. Now a minister who seeks to help his people in their struggle against immorality should not preach a *series* of sermons on the theme *Immorality,* going into all its sordid details. If he does, his sermons might do more harm than good. Instead of banishing the evil he may be creating a taste for it. Let him, instead, preach *one sermon* on Immorality but *an entire series* on *The Glory of Service Rendered to Christ and His People.*

This *positive* method of overcoming sin is characteristic of Paul's teaching. Note the following:

"Overcome evil with good" (Rom. 12:21);

"Put on the Lord Jesus Christ and make no provision for the flesh" (Rom. 13:14);

"Walk by the Spirit, and y o u will not gratify the desires of the flesh (Gal. 5:16); and

"For the rest, brothers, whatsoever things are true . . . honorable . . . just . . . pure . . . lovely . . . of good report . . . be thinking about these things . . . and the God of peace will be with y o u" (Phil. 4:8, 9).

The same truth is illustrated in Col. 3:12-17. This is the only effective way to "put to death the members that are upon the earth" (3:5-9a), as is also clear from 3:9a, 10.

3. Accordingly, the apostle continues, **For y o u died, and y o u r life is hid with Christ in God.** In the sense already explained (see on 2:11, 12) the Colossians are dead and buried. It is no longer they that live but Christ that lives in them. They are dead to their old selves and to the world governed by sin. Their life is bound up in the bundle of the living with their Lord and Savior Jesus Christ (cf. I Sam. 25:29). From eternity they were comprehended in him (Col. 3:12; cf. Eph. 1:4). In time they were *from God's side* ingrafted in Christ by the Spirit (John 3:5; Rom. 6:5; II Cor. 3:16; Eph. 2:22), and *as a result* were *from their side* united to Christ by a living faith (Gal. 2:20). Their new life *is hid* with Christ. It is concealed to the world

---

[112] In verse 2 the word-order of the original can be retained without any difficulty. In verse 1, because of the modifier "where Christ is," the emphasis of the original can be best retained by means of italics.

[113] For the verb φρονέω see N.T.C. on Phil. 3:19; cf. Rom. 8:5; 12:16.

(I Cor. 2:14; I John 3:2), and is indestructible, everlasting (John 3:16; 10:28; Rom. 8:31-39). And since, as to essence, Christ is in the Father, and the Father is in Christ (John 1:18; 10:30; 17:21; I Cor. 3:23; Col. 1:15), it is evident that Paul is fully justified in saying "Y o u r life is hid with Christ *in God.*"

4. Though the world will never be able to see the closeness of the *inner* relationship between believers and their Lord, the *outward* expression of this inner relationship, *the glory,* will one day become clear to all: **When Christ (who is) our** [114] **life is manifested, then y o u also will be manifested with him in glory.** "Christ (who is) our life." This cannot mean identity. To say that our life is "the extension" of Christ's life is ambiguous. Christ and we are not the same in *essence,* as are the Father and the Son. The life of Christ — hence, Christ himself — is, however, the Source and Pattern of our life. Moreover, through the Holy Spirit and Spirit-given faith, Christ is most closely united with us, and we with him. The expression "Christ, our life" must, therefore, be explained in the light of similar ones such as the following:

"Because I live y o u too will live" (John 14:19);

" (We are) always bearing about in the body the dying of Jesus, that the life also of Jesus may be manifested in our body" (II Cor. 4:10);

"It was the good pleasure of God . . . to reveal his Son in me" (Gal. 1:15, 16);

"Christ lives in me" (Gal. 2:20);

"My little children, with whom I am again in labor, until Christ be formed in y o u" (Gal. 4:19);

"But we all . . . are transformed into the same image from glory to glory as from the Lord the Spirit" (II Cor. 3:18); and

"For to me to live (is) Christ, and to die (is) gain" (Phil. 1:21).

When, on the day of his second coming, a day known only to God (Matt. 24:36; I Thess. 5:1, 2), Christ, our life, *is manifested,*[115] his attributes of

---

[114] Though the external evidence for ὑμῶν is at least equally strong as for ἡμῶν, the latter may, nevertheless, be correct. It is not unusual for Paul, a deeply emotional writer, who writes about truths he has himself experienced or himself holds dear, to change from the second to the first person (cf. Col. 1:9 with 1:13; 2:13a with 2:13b; and see on Philem. 6).

[115] In the New Testament the verb φανερόω occurs with great frequency in the writings of John (Gospel, First Epistle, Revelation) and of Paul. For a classification of its meanings in John's Gospel and First Epistle see N.T.C. on the Gospel of John, Vol. II, p. 476, footnote 294. Apart from its occurrences in John and Paul it is found only in the following New Testament passages: Mark 4:22; 16:12, 14; Heb. 9:8, 26; and I Peter 1:20; 5:4. In the letters of Paul the word is used 22 times, as follows:

a. in connection with the display of glory in the words and works of Jesus at his

majesty and power being publicly displayed, then the Colossians too will be manifested *with him* (cf. Rom. 8:32). *Their* public vindication and glory will coincide with *his*. Among the many New Testament passages (in addition to Col. 1:27) which shed further light on the meaning of this glory which God's children will share with their Lord in the day when they will be "like him" and will "bear the image of the heavenly" are especially the following: Matt. 25:31-40; Rom. 8:17, 18; I Cor. 1:7, 8; Phil. 3:20, 21; I Thess. 2:19, 20; 3:13; 4:13-18; II Thess. 1:10; II Tim. 4:7, 8; I Peter 1:13; I John 2:28; 3:2; and Rev. 17:14.

---

5 Put to death therefore y o u r members that (are) upon the earth: immorality, impurity, passion, evil desire, and greed, which is idolatry; 6 on account of which things the wrath of God is coming; 7 in which things y o u also walked at one time, when y o u were living in them. 8 But now y o u, too, lay them all aside: wrath, anger, malice, slander, shameful language from y o u r mouth. 9 No longer lie to one another, seeing that y o u have put off the old man with his practices, 10 and have put on the new man, who is being renewed for full knowledge according to the image of him who created him, 11 where there cannot be Greek and Jew, circumcision and uncircumcision, barbarian, Scythian, slave, freeman, but Christ (is) all and in all.

3:5-11

II. *Therefore, They Should "Put to death" and "Lay Aside" the Old Vices*

5. In close connection with the immediately preceding paragraph Paul continues, **Put to death therefore y o u r**[116] **members that (are) upon the earth.** Note the paradox, "Y o u died" (verse 3) . . . "Put to death therefore y o u r members . . ." (verse 5). A superficial judgment would be that the apostle is here contradicting himself. Some interpreters have, in fact, reached that very conclusion. It is as if on the one hand Paul is saying that the Colossians have already died, yet on the other hand is telling them that they must put themselves to death. How can both be true? The answer is

---

first coming (II Cor. 2:14; I Tim. 3:16; II Tim. 1:10), and the life of Jesus manifested in believers (II Cor. 3:3; 4:10, 11).

b. in connection with the disclosure and realization of *the mystery* of God in the fulness of time (Rom. 16:26; Col. 1:26; and cf. Titus 1:3 "manifested his *word*").

c. in connection with the display of glory of Christ at his *second coming* (Col. 3:4a), in which glorious display believers share (Col. 3:4b), and at which time the works and motives of men will be publicly laid bare (I Cor. 4:5; II Cor. 5:10).

d. in connection with *the divine attributes* made known to men (Rom. 1:19; 3:21).

e. in *a more general sense,* in connection with anything else that is hidden or dark and is brought to light or made visible or plain (II Cor. 5:11; 7:12; 11:6; Eph. 5:13 twice; Col. 4:4).

[116] Though the reading without ὑμῶν deserves the preference, y o u r is clearly *implied*.

that as long as believers are still living on earth their *condition* and their *state* do *not wholly* coincide. As to their *state* they are even now perfect, without any sin, wholly justified! Their old self is dead and buried (Col. 2:11-13). Now it is true that their *condition* is in harmony with this, but only *in principle*. In the words of the Heidelberg Catechism, "Even the holiest men, while in this life, have only a small beginning of this obedience [that is, of obedience to God's commandments]; yet so that with earnest purpose they begin to live, not only according to some but according to all the commandments of God" (Lord's Day XLIV, Answer to Question 114). This *progressive* character of sanctification is also clearly taught by Paul (see below, on verse 10, and cf. II Cor. 3:18; Phil. 1:6; 3:12, 13) and is in harmony with the rest of Scripture (Ps. 84:7; Prov. 4:18; Mark 9:24; also implied in I John 1:8-10). While with respect to *the new life* which was imparted to them by the Holy Spirit believers are so closely united with Christ that they are said to be with him in heaven (Col. 3:3), yet *the old life* is still *of* the earth as well as *on* earth. But there is no reason for despair. The very presence of the new life, the life "in Christ," enables believers progressively to put to death [117] the members that are upon the earth.

When the question is asked what is meant by *the members* that must be put to death the answer is: **immorality, impurity, passion, evil desire, and greed, which is idolatry.** But how can *members* be *vices?* Some expositors regard this to be impossible. They suggest various solutions.[118] Yet it would

---

[117] "Put to death" is the proper translation here, not "Reckon as dead." The command "Put to death" of verse 5 does not have exactly the same meaning as "Consider yourselves to be dead" (Rom. 6:11). And the *passive* νενεκρωμένου in Heb. 11:12 ("as good as dead"; cf. Rom. 4:19) does not change the fact that the *active* νεκρώσατε as used here in Col. 3:5, means *put to death;* for, (a) the active meaning intended here is clearly synonymous with "lay aside" in verse 8, which is not a matter solely of mental reflection or consideration (reckoning) but of voluntary, strenuous effort and exertion; and (b) the real parallel of Col. 3:5 is not so much Rom. 6:11 as Rom. 8:13 (*"put to death* the deeds of the body"), though the verb used there in the original is not the one used here in Col. 3:5 but θανατοῦτε. Hence, I cannot agree here with Bruce (*op. cit.,* p. 267) when he says, " 'Put to death,' or, as we might put it, 'reckon as dead.' "

[118] Thus Lightfoot (*op. cit.,* p. 211) puts a heavy stop after the word *earth.* He then treats the vices ("immorality, impurity," etc.) as "prospective accusatives, which should be governed by some such word as *lay aside.*" Moule (*op. cit.,* p. 116) says "This may well be right." But there is not any need for such a forced reconstruction. Had Paul meant to *imply* the verb *lay aside* he would in all probability have *expressed* it, as he does in Rom. 13:12; Eph. 4:22, 25; Col. 3:8.

Similarly objectionable is Charles Masson's solution (*Commentaire du Nouveau Testament* on this passage). Completely out of line with the context he views "members" as referring to "church-members," and as a vocative, so that the meaning would be, "Y o u, members of Christ's body, must therefore," etc.

Finally, there is Lenski's view (*op. cit.,* p. 157), according to which the words "fornication [= immorality], uncleanness," etc., are "adverbial accusatives of specification," and must be rendered, "as to fornication," etc. So construed the translation becomes needlessly difficult, and the construction lacks clarity. The idea, moreover, that since the imperative νεκρώσατε is an aorist it must refer to one fell blow

seem to me that the difficulty is not nearly as great as some would make it appear to be. John Calvin may be on the right track when he states that these *vices* are called *members* "since they adhere so closely to us." Another very similar way of solving the difficulty, a way which does not imply a rejection of Calvin's view but is clearly in line with it, would be to regard the use of the word *members* (= vices) to be an instance of the figure of speech called *metonymy* ("change of name"), in which, for example, the name of the *cause* or *source* is substituted for the *effect* it produces, the *consequences* that flow forth from it, the *fruit* or *product* it yields. Thus in Num. 3:16 (in the original) the word *mouth* is in the Hebrew substituted for the word *command* that *issued* from the mouth; or just as in American slang the expression, "I'll have none of your *lip*" means, "I will not tolerate any saucy remarks that *issue* from your lips." So here also the command, "Put to death therefore y o u r members that (are) upon the earth: immorality, impurity," etc., means, "Put to death therefore the *effects* produced by, and associated so closely with, the members of y o u r body, such effects, products or works, as immorality, impurity," etc. I am therefore in agreement with Bruce (*op. cit.*, p. 268) when he says, "In Rom. 7:23 Paul speaks of 'the law of sin which is in my members'; here [in Col. 3:5] he goes farther and practically identifies the readers' members with the sins of which they were formerly the instruments. But what he is really thinking of is the practices and attitudes to which his readers' bodily activity and strength had been devoted in the old life." Thus also Ridderbos (*op. cit.*, p. 207) states, "The 'members' are here identified with the sins committed by these members, which in a similar connection in Rom. 8:13 are called 'the deeds of the body.'"

Lists of vices are of frequent occurrence in ancient literature, both pagan (moralistic) and anti-pagan. The recently discovered Dead Sea Scrolls also have such lists.[119] In the letters of Paul they occur in the following passages: Rom. 1:18-32; I Cor. 5:9-11; 6:9, 10; Gal. 5:19-21; Eph. 5:3-6; I Thess. 4:3-7; I Tim. 1:9, 10; II Tim. 3:2-5; Titus 3:3. The difference between the Christian and the non-Christian treatment of these vices is that apart from Christ and the fulness of grace imparted by his Spirit there is no power in all the universe to overcome them. Christ, he alone, supplies that power.

As to arrangement, it is rather obvious that verse 5 lists five vices, and so does verse 8. However, whether there is any significance in this number five as here used is questionable, and if any special meaning attaches to it we must confess that we do not know what it is.[120] It is true, nevertheless, that

---

by which the members are struck dead, cannot be substantiated. The aorist does not always nor necessarily refer to *one* — and only one — deed. In any mood it denotes one *fact* or one *idea*, which in actual historical realization may at times be spread over a lengthy period of time (cf. John 2:20 in the original). *It summarizes!*
[119] See M. Burrows, *The Dead Sea Scrolls*, pp. 375, 386, 387.
[120] Not all agree. Thus Lenski sees in the number five "the half of completeness expressed by ten . . . five is also secular, these are vices" (*op. cit.*, pp. 157, 158).

the first list enumerates vices that describe the sinner as he is in himself, while the second characterizes him in his relation to the neighbor. It is also possible to see in the first list a movement from the surface of life to its center, and in the second the reverse. This will become evident as the various items are studied one by one.

Of the five vices mentioned here in Col. 3:5 the first four are also listed in I Thess. 4:3-7, the last four also in Rom. 1:24-29. The first is *immorality* ("fornication"; see I Thess. 4:3; cf. Matt. 5:32; 15:19; 19:9; John 8:41, etc.). Though referring basically to unlawful sexual intercourse, it probably includes illicit, clandestine relationships of every description. The emphasis, however, is on evil in the sexual realm, particularly evil *deeds.*

These evil *deeds* spring from evil *thoughts,* that is, from *uncleanness,* which is mentioned next (Rom. 1:24; I Thess. 4:7; cf. Matt. 15:19; Mark 7:21, etc.). It is not necessary, however, to limit uncleanness to that which is filthy in *thoughts.* The *intents* of the heart are undoubtedly also included (cf. Heb. 4:12).

That it is the evil *disposition* of the heart and will of man which is *the source* of his wicked thoughts and deeds is clear from the two vices that are mentioned next, namely, *passion* and *evil desire.* It is not easy to distinguish between these, though there may be some merit in Lightfoot's suggestion that the former describes this vice more from its passive, the latter more from its active side. For *passion* see also Rom. 1:26; I Thess. 4:5 ("passion of lust"), etc.; for *evil desire,* Rom. 1:24; I Thess. 4:5, etc. The word *evil* is added because *desire* as such is not necessarily wrong. The word used in the original may also refer to legitimate desire, for example, Christ's desire to eat the Passover with his disciples.[121] But *evil* desire is the inordinate craving for sexual satisfaction, or for other things, such as idol-worship, material possessions, renown, etc. The *emphasis,* in the present context, is, however, on illicit sex relationships, but not to the exclusion of other wicked yearnings. Out of this evil craving arise all kinds of sins. It is therefore *basic,* and is so regarded by Paul himself in Rom. 7:7. In this connection it is also interesting to note that in the Decalogue the sin of *coveting* is mentioned last (Ex. 20:17), as being the source of all the others, and that Jesus, too, considers the lustful heart, that is, the heart filled with evil desire, to be the root whence springs the evil deed, for he says, "Every one who looks on a

---

But even when it is granted that in certain types of literature the number five might have a symbolical significance, it is very doubtful whether such a meaning can be ascribed to it in Colossians. Besides, though it is true that verse 8 (as well as verse 5) lists *five* vices, verse 9 adds another to the list, making *six* in all, or eleven as the sum of both lists. It is therefore better to refrain from dubious numerology.

[121] On the word ἐπιθυμία see N.T.C. on I and II Timothy and Titus, pp. 271, 272, footnote 147.

woman to lust for her has already in his heart committed adultery with her" (Matt. 5:28).

But though by mentioning passion and evil desire the apostle has, as it were, reached the very bottom of every sin, he adds one more vice, one in which all the others are summarized, namely, *self-seeking* or *greed* (cf. Rom. 1:29, etc.). Every sin is basically selfishness, the worship of self instead of the worship of God, the substitution of self for Christ, in one's affections (cf. Col. 3:1-3). It is for this very reason that Paul adds, "which is idolatry" (cf. Eph. 5:5). The young man who gets a girl in trouble may call this "love." He is mistaken. It is self-seeking, greed, at least to a considerable extent. This young man wants "to have more than his due." He is over-reaching, going beyond what is proper (see N.T.C. on I and II Thessalonians, pp. 100, 101). However, the apostle is not thinking particularly about a *young* man but rather about "the *old* man," (see 3:9) that is, the carnal nature of *any* man, regardless of age, the nature of man as it is apart from saving grace.

6, 7. Having listed the vices which formerly characterized the Colossians and by which they are still being tempted, the apostle continues, **on account of which the wrath of God is coming.**[122] By means of what is sometimes called "a prophetic present tense" (cf. John 4:21; 14:3) Paul stresses the fact that the coming of the wrath of God, to be visited upon those who live in such sins, is so certain that it is as if that wrath had already arrived. These sins attract God's displeasure like a magnet attracts iron or like a high steeple on an isolated hill draws lightning. The reference, no doubt, is to the revelation of God's wrath in the coming judgment day (cf. Rom. 2:5-11; Eph. 5:6; II Thess. 1:8-10). Calvin very appropriately observes that the real purpose of this prophecy about the inevitability of God's wrath being visited upon confirmed evildoers is "that we may be deterred from sinning." Accordingly, even such a wrath-statement is filled with mercy!

By God's sovereign grace, however, the Colossians have, in principle, renounced this kind of conduct. For them it belongs to the past. Says Paul, **in which things y o u also walked at one time, when y o u were living in them.** Note, "y o u also," that is, "y o u, like other heathen." *Living* and *walking* are almost identical. Nevertheless, in certain contexts, as here, there is a dif-

---

[122] Although the textual support for the additional phrase "upon the sons of disobedience" is not weak, the context pleads against its insertion. It is probably an interpolation from Eph. 5:6. Its inclusion here in Col. 3:6 leads to the rendering "among whom" at the beginning of verse 7, and to the strange conclusion that Paul rebukes the Colossians for having walked among the sons of disobedience, an inference which would be contrary to his own teaching (I Cor. 5:10; cf. Titus 2:12) as well as the Lord's (John 17:15; cf. Matt. 5:13, 14).

ference. *Walking* here indicates behavior; *living,* disposition. Thus also Gal. 5:25, "If we live by the Spirit, by the Spirit let us also walk." The Colossians having become "new creatures," are no longer absorbed in these vices of former days. They have become ashamed of their earlier ways. By the power of the Holy Spirit they have been sanctified, cleansed. Their life "is hid with Christ in God" (see above, verse 3). Nevertheless, as pointed out previously, this does not mean that even now the victory has been *fully* won. The flesh is still lusting against the Spirit, and the Spirit against the flesh (Gal. 5:17; cf. Rom. 7:15-24). Hence, the command which follows in verses 8, 9a is very much to the point:

8, 9a. But now y o u, too, lay them all aside: wrath, anger, malice, slander, shameful language out of y o u r mouth. No longer lie to one another. The former vices had not only wrought destruction in the lives of men as individuals, viewed separately (see on verse 5 above), but had also disrupted the relationship between neighbors. This must not continue. Accordingly, *wrath* (Latin: *ira*), that is, settled indignation, when the heart is like a roaring furnace; *anger* or *fury* (Latin: *furor*), the tumultuous outburst, like fire in straw; [123] *malice,* not merely "mischief" but the evil inclination of the mind, the perversity of disposition which bodes ill for man's fellow-man; *slander* or *reviling;* [124] and *shameful language out of y o u r mouth,* that is, abusive speech, all of these *must be laid aside.* Note here the progress in vice, from *wrath* inside the heart, through various stages, to the bitter outward manifestations: slander and abusive language. *Lying,* too, must be discarded (cf. I Tim. 2:7). It must no longer be in evidence in the lives of believers. All manner of hypocrisy and deception has always marked the heathen world. That is true even today. A missionary told us that in answer to his question why a certain enquirer had failed to keep her promise to attend a midweek meeting, the woman answered, "I'm very sorry that I was unable to attend, but, you see, I had to go to the funeral of my mother-in-law in a distant city." Afterward the missionary discovered that the mother-in-law in question had died years ago and that the woman who had invented the excuse had not even been out of the village on the day of the midweek meeting. He added, "They will tell you anything that occurs to their minds just to save face."

Lay aside all these vices, says Paul, just as one *discards* a worn-out garment

---

[123] See C. Trench, *Synonyms of the New Testament,* par. xxxvii. Also N.T.C. on the Gospel according to John, Vol. I, p. 151.

[124] The Greek word used is *blasphemy.* But in Greek this word has a somewhat broader meaning than in English. While in our language it refers to abusive language with respect to God or things religious, that is, to *defiant irreverence,* in the original it refers to insults directed either against God or against men. In the present instance, as the context indicates, the latter is clearly meant: scornful and insolent language directed against a neighbor, slander, defamation, detraction.

or one that no longer fits the person who has been clothed with it. For literal use of the expression "Lay aside" in connection with robes see Acts 7:58. The apostle, well-versed in the Old Testament, knew that the figure of a garment was frequently used in the sacred scriptures to indicate *character*. Sometimes it referred to God-glorifying character, consisting of the fruits of grace, such as righteousness, justice, joy, faithfulness (Job 29:14; Ps. 132:9; Isa. 11:5; 61:10); sometimes to evil character: pride, violence (Ps. 73:6); or to the latters's result: shame and dishonor (Ps. 35:26; 109:29). The garment of righteousness and salvation is ascribed to Jehovah himself (Isa. 59:17). It is therefore understandable that Paul makes use of this figurative manner of speaking (so do other New Testament authors; see Heb. 12:1; James 1:21; I Peter 2:1). It is clearly implied in Rom. 13:12a, 14; Gal. 3:27, "did put on Christ"; Eph. 4:22, 25. With a slight modification of the figure the apostle sometimes speaks of the Christian's duty to *put on* his spiritual *armor* (Rom. 13:12b; II Cor. 6:7; Eph. 6:13-18; and I Thess. 5:8).

9b-11. When Paul urged the Colossians to lay aside the vices that had marked their previous manner of life he was using consistent reasoning. He was, as it were, saying, "Continue to do in practice what y o u have already done in principle." He says, **seeing that y o u have put off** [125] **the old man with his practices, and have put on the new (man).**[126]

As has been shown (see on 2:11, 12), when they were baptized the Colossians had decisively renounced — *put off* and *cast away* — "the old man" (Rom. 6:6; Eph. 4:22), that is, "the body of the flesh," their former manner of existence, their earlier wicked selves, "with its practices," the very practices listed in 3:5, 8, 9a, and had *put on* the new man, Christ (Gal. 3:27), that is, the new nature which believers have as members of Christ. Hence, let them now adorn their baptismal profession of faith with a godly life. Let them "put to death" (verse 5) and "lay aside" (verse 8) all their former vices. Says John Calvin, "The old man is whatever we bring from our mother's womb, and whatever we are by nature. It is called *the old man* because we are first born from Adam, and afterward are born again through

---

[125] Oepke (Th.W.N.T., Vol. II, p. 319) and Lightfoot (*op. cit.*, pp. 214, 215) ascribe an imperative sense to the participles "putting off" and "putting on." However, (1) in this very letter (2:11) the apostle has already mentioned "the putting off of the body of the flesh" as something pertaining to the past, an accomplished fact; and (2) the immediate context (3:2, 3) appears to be a close parallel to 3:8, 9. Both mean, "Do this, *for* y o u have already done that. Do in practice what y o u have already done in principle."

[126] Though it is true that basically the adjective νέον as used here in Col. 3:10 means *new* as to *time* (new versus old), while καινόν as found in Eph. 4:24 indicates *new* as to *quality* (*fresh* versus *worn out*), this distinction cannot be pressed here, for the idea of freshness and vigor which might be lacking in the adjective νέον is supplied by the participle ἀνακαινούμενον.

Christ." And Thomas Goodwin, "There are but two men that are seen standing before God, Adam and Jesus Christ; and these two men have all other men hanging at their girdles." Cf. Rom. 5:12-21; I Cor. 15:22, 45-49.

It should be stressed that it is only *in Christ* (by means of vital union with him) that this new man is formed in the believer; also that, because of this very fact, all those who have become new men, whether Jews or Gentiles, can also be called, in their corporate existence, "one new man" in him, as it is expressed in Eph. 2:15, "that he might create in himself of the two one new man." Cf. Gal. 3:28.

Now in each believer this new man is a progressively developing entity, as Paul indicates by continuing, **who is being renewed for full knowledge.** In slightly different language an analogous, though not entirely identical, thought is expressed in II Cor. 4:16, in the words: "Accordingly, we do not lose heart, but (are confident that) though our outer man is decaying, yet our inner man is being renewed day by day." From both of these passages it is evident that the believer's new nature resembles a growing plant. It is being constantly renewed by the Holy Spirit and increases in vigor with a definite goal in mind. The fact that the new man is, as it were, an expanding reality and that salvation means progress is clear not only from these passages and from the references given earlier, in the discussion of verse 5 above (beginning with II Cor. 3:18), but also from the following, to which many others could be added: II Cor. 9:10; 10:15; Eph. 2:21; 4:16; Phil. 2:12, 13; I Thess. 3:12; I Thess. 4:10; II Thess. 1:3; I Tim. 4:15; II Tim. 2:1. When a man is led through the waters of salvation, these are ankle-deep at first, but as he progresses, they become knee-deep, then reach to the loins, and are finally impassable except by swimming (cf. Ezek. 47:3-6). The same thought occurs in Colossians (1:9, 10; 2:19).

The new man is being renewed "for full knowledge" (to which Eph. 4:24 adds "righteousness and holiness"). This knowledge excels by far any so-called knowledge in which the false teachers who disturbed the churches of the Lycus Valley were glorying (see on Col. 2:2, 3, 18). It pertains to both heart and mind, is experiential, and has God's holy will as its object (Rom. 12:2). A true discernment of that will, particularly with reference to its "good pleasure" (Eph. 1:5), is very rewarding. It is a means toward a fuller, richer measure of salvation's joy and peace. A contrast will make this clear. While it is true that here on earth a person's experience with his neighbor will at times cause him to say, "The better I know him and understand his intentions, the less I trust him," in the kingdom of heaven the very opposite truth prevails, namely, "The more we know *him* — that is, the triune God or our Savior Jesus Christ —, and *his* purposes of grace, the more we trust and love him." Paul continues, **according to the image of him who created him.** The standard or yardstick and the aim of the renewal is God's image, the likeness of the very One who created this new man in the hearts and live⁊ of believers, just as he once created the first Adam as his own image (Gen. 1:26, 27) . Nevertheless, the new man is not simply the restoration of whatever pertained to the first Adam before the fall. (To mention only one point of difference between the original creation and the new creation: in the state of rectitude Adam had no inkling of knowledge concerning God's redemptive love.) Rather, "Just as we have borne the image of the earthly one, so we shall also bear the image of the heavenly One" (I Cor. 15:49) , in whom redemptive love is wholly centralized.

Now this glorious progressive transformation into the image of God recognizes no racial-religious, cultural, or social boundaries. Paul continues, **where there cannot be Greek and Jew, circumcision and uncircumcision, barbarian, Scythian, slave, freeman.**

All racial bigotry, chauvinism, and snobbery is condemned here. Here the truth that before God "all men are equal" receives its best — because infallibly inspired — expression. To be sure, by divine illumination there have always been men who have grasped this truth, at least to a degree. Yet, the vast majority among all races have denied it, if not in theory at least in practice. There was, for example, the Assyrian who considered his gods to be mightier than those of any other nation, stronger even than the God of Israel (II Kings 18:33-35) . There was the Jew who knew no fear because, in distinction from the men of other nations, he had "the" temple (Jer. 7:4) , and was able to say, "We have Abraham as our father" (but see how Jesus answers him, Luke 3:8) . The Edomite considered himself to be superior to other men because he was living in "the cleft of the rock" (Obad. 3) . There is also the red man who considers the white man "underbaked," the black man "burnt," but himself "just right," and is sure that the village in which he lives occupies the very center of the earth's surface; the white man who considers himself to be a member of the "superior" race, is sure that a special curse of God rests on those who belong to the opposite race, and that it is his privilege and duty by means of enslavement to perpetuate this curse; and the Negro who says that not the white man but he himself is "superior" and should assert this superiority if need be by force. Of course, not *every* member of any race or class is guilty of this exclusivism and clannishness, but there are many who are. Hindus are by no means the only ones who believe in the caste-system!

In the early days of American history there were men of distinction who regarded the white settlements as representing God's chosen people, destined, because of their extraordinary virtue, to rule the world. There are Germans who put their whole heart into singing, "Deutschland, Deutschland über alles," and Dutchmen who believe that there exists a special covenant between "God, The Netherlands, and the House of Orange." There are fine, evangelical people, "brothers and sisters in Christ," who feel certain that even in the present dispensation national distinctions have value before God (all this in spite of Col. 3:11; cf. Eph. 2:14, 18, 19), and that the Jews will one day rule over the entire world from Jerusalem. And there are males who believe that superiority is somehow linked with sex, and that "Woman is the lesser man."

Now it is not Paul's intention to deny every ethnic, cultural, or social distinction. That there are, indeed, *differences* is freely admitted, and, in fact, sometimes even emphasized. All members of the human body do not have the same function. Thus it is also with Christ's body, the church (Rom. 12:4; I Cor. 12:12-31). Let all work together harmoniously. Similarly, not all have had the same opportunities or advantages (Rom. 3:1, 2). Let the specially privileged recognize their added responsibilities (Rom. 2:9, 12; 3:12; cf. Amos 3:2; Luke 12:47, 48). In certain respects, therefore, it is by no means true that all men are alike. But in two important points they are, indeed, equal! First of all, "all have sinned, and fall short of the glory of God" (Rom. 3:23; cf. 2:11; 3:9-18; 5:12, 18). Secondly, "the same Lord is Lord of all, and is rich to all that call on him" (Rom. 10:11, 12). Those who, by God's sovereign grace, are led to believe in the Lord Jesus Christ are saved regardless of race, culture, or social position (see also Rom. 3:22b, 23, 24; 4:11, 12; 5:18b; 11:32; Gal. 3:13, 14; 3:9, 27-29; Eph. 2:11-22).

Now the present passage (Col. 3:11) is not the only one in which the apostle contrasts certain groups. See also Rom. 1:14, and especially Gal. 3:28. But in each letter the particular contrast which he draws is in keeping with the purpose he has in mind for that letter. Thus, in Galatians, in harmony with its background and intent, the distinctions enumerated are racial-religious ("neither Jew nor Greek"), social ("neither bond nor free"), and sexual ("no male and female"). It reminds one of the prayer of thanksgiving uttered by a *male* Jew who blesses the Lord each morning because he did not make him "a Gentile, a slave, *or a woman!*" Paul says that "in Christ" those distinctions, when they are regarded as marks of preferment by God, are definitely *out*. In our present passage, the contrasts and the reason for stating them thus and not otherwise are as follows:

(1) *racial-religious:* "where there cannot be Greek and Jew, circumcision and uncircumcision." [127] This is stated to counteract the teaching of the ceremonialists (see above, on 2:11-14).

(2) *cultural:* "barbarian, Scythian." Though these two designations both refer to the supposedly uncultured, there is an *implied* contrast here between the cultured and the uncultured. "Knowledge" and "philosophy" are of no help in creating within the heart "the new man." Yet, it was on such human attainments that the false teachers who were troubling the Colossian church placed the emphasis. See on 2:4, 8, 18.

---

[127] Note chiastic arrangement here, very frequent with Paul. The first term, *Greek,* corresponds with the fourth, *uncircumcision;* the second, *Jew,* with the third, *circumcision.* See on Philem. 5.

(3) *social:* "slave, freeman." It is as if Paul were saying, "O Colossians, do not look down on slaves. *Accept Onesimus as y o u r very own, y o u r brother in Christ.* As far as standing before God is concerned there is no distinction between bond and free."

Grace bridges all chasms. Though the Greeks divided mankind into two categories, Greeks and "barbarians"; and though the Romans, after conquering the Greeks politically but having been conquered by them culturally, drew a similar contrast between Greeks-Romans, on the one hand, and "barbarians," on the other; and though the Jews, unconverted to Christ, set Greek over against Jew, grace recognizes no such distinctions, for both Gentile and Jew are reconciled to each other by being reconciled to God through the cross (Eph. 2:13) .

Similarly, since the only circumcision that has any value before God is the circumcision of the heart, it stands to reason that before him the question whether or not one has been literally circumcised or has not been literally circumcised has no meaning. See N.T.C. on Phil. 3:2, 3.

And since the world by its "wisdom" did not come to know God (I Cor. 1:21) , the cultural distinction also has no value in a person's standing before God. Academic degrees do not make any one a new man. Refinement in customs and manners, in itself not to be despised, is not saving grace. And, on the other hand, being a *barbarian* (Acts 28:4; Rom. 1:14; I Cor. 14:11 twice), a mere "stammerer" to the ears of the more sophisticated, cannot, in and by itself, prevent one from becoming a new man, not even if this barbarian happens to be of the reputedly lowest class, namely, a *Scythian.*

In the seventh century B. C. these Scythians, savage and warlike nomads from the northern steppes, had deluged the countries of the Fertile Crescent, including Palestine, and, having subsequently been repulsed, had left a memory of dread and horror.[128] The account of Herodotus with reference to them is as follows (in part) :

---

[128] Lightfoot (*op. cit.,* p. 219) states that "the terror inspired by these invaders has found expression in the prophets." He then refers to Ezek. 28 [38?] and 39, and to Jer. 1:13 ff. and 6:1 ff. Others, too, have identified the Scythians with "Gog and Magog" of Ezek. 38 and 39. Thus Josephus states, "Magog founded those that from him were called Magogites, but who are by the Greeks called Scythians" (*Antiquities of the Jews* I.vi.1). And see J. F. McCurdy's article "Gog and Magog" in *The New Schaff-Herzog Religious Encyclopedia,* Vol. V, pp. 14, 15. Close exegetical study of the Jeremiah and Ezekiel passages has convinced several exegetes, however, that this identification is questionable. In Judg. 1:27 LXX inserts *Scythopolis* as the equivalent of Beth-shean. (Cf. Judith 3:10; II Macc. 12:29.) It is rather commonly supposed, therefore, that a company of Scythians, after their invasion of Palestine, established residence here, and that from this circumstance the place was called "City of the Scythians." For the rest, the only undisputed reference to the Scythians in Scripture is the present passage, Col. 3:11.

"They invaded Asia, after they had driven the Cimmerians out of Europe . . . and made themselves masters of all Asia. From there they marched against Egypt; and when they were in that part of Syria which is called Palestine, Psammetichus, king of Egypt, met them and with gifts and prayer persuaded them to come no farther. . . . They ruled Asia for twenty-eight years; and all the land was wasted by reason of their violence and their arrogance. . . . The greater number of them were entertained and made drunk and were then slain by Cyaxares and the Medes" (I.103-106). "They drank the blood of the first enemy killed in battle, and made napkins of the scalps, and drinking bowls of the skulls of the slain. They had the most filthy habits and never washed with water" (IV.64, 65, 75). Cf. Tertullian, *Against Marcion* I.1, "Marcion was born there, more filthy than any Scythian." Josephus states, "The Scythians delight in murdering people and are little better than wild beasts" (*Against Apion* II.269). In II Macc. 4:47 we read, "Menelaus, the cause of all the evil . . . sentenced to death those unfortunate men who would have been set at liberty uncondemned if they had pleaded even against the Scythians." That "even against the Scythians" speaks volumes! Cf. III Macc. 7:5. And Origen (*Against Celsus* I.1) speaks of "Scythian laws, or more impious even than these, if there be any such."

Nevertheless, even though a man be a Scythian, that as such cannot hinder him from becoming a new man in Christ. That is what Paul is here saying. Or, as Justin Martyr put it so strikingly, "But though a man be a Scythian or a Persian, if he has the knowledge of God and of *his* [God's] Christ, and keeps the everlasting righteous decrees, he is circumcised with the good and beneficial circumcision, and is a friend of God, and God rejoices in his gifts and offerings" (*Dialogue with Trypho,* ch. 28).

And finally, as to "slave, freeman," since "If therefore the Son will make y o u free, y o u will be free indeed" (John 8:36), any bondage that pertains to merely earthly social relationships can have no relevance for salvation. For more extensive discussion of Slavery see on Col. 3:23–4:1; also Commentary on Philemon in this volume, and *Scripture on Slavery,* pp. 233-237.

Paul concludes this paragraph with the words, **but Christ (is) all and in all.** *Christ, as the all-sufficient Lord and Savior, is all* that matters. His Spirit-mediated indwelling *in all* believers, of whatever racial-religious, cultural, or social background they be, guarantees the creation and gradual perfection in each and in all of "the new man, who is being renewed for full knowledge according to the image of him who created him." Thus, most appropriately, the very theme of the entire letter, namely, "Christ, the Pre-eminent One, the Only and All-Sufficient Savior," climaxes this passage.[129]

---

[129] The conjunction "and" in "Christ (is) all *and* in all" shows that "both parts of the phrase must be given recognition" (Moule, *op. cit.,* p. 122). Hence, I Cor.

12 Put on, therefore, as God's elect, holy and beloved, a heart of compassion, kindness, lowliness, meekness, longsuffering, 13 enduring one another, and forgiving each other if anyone have a complaint against anyone. Just as the Lord has forgiven y o u, so do y o u also. 14 And above all these things (put on) love, which is the bond of perfection. 15 And let the peace of Christ, for which y o u were called in one body, rule in y o u r hearts, and be thankful. 16 Let the word of Christ dwell among y o u richly; in all wisdom teaching and admonishing one another, (and) by means of psalms, hymns, and spiritual songs singing to God in a thankful spirit, with all y o u r heart. 17 And whatever y o u do in word or in deed, (do) all in the name of the Lord Jesus, giving thanks to God the Father through him.

3:12-17

III. *They Should "Put On" the New Virtues*

As the calmness of the inland lake, reflecting the beauty of the rising sun, follows the turbulence of warring winds and tempestuous billows, so, in principle, "the peace of Christ" (verse 15) had displaced the restlessness which formerly characterized the Colossians, when they lived apart from Christ, as described in the previous paragraph (see especially verses 5-9). For beauty of style and direct appeal to the heart the present section is unsurpassed. The same can be said about its practical value. If the Colossians will only live the life that is portrayed in such a graphic and yet simple manner in these few lines, their problems will be solved. Of course, only by strength imparted by God and by means of complete reliance on the sustaining power of his sovereign, transforming grace, will they be able to heed the directions given. These directions are introduced as follows:

12, 13. Put on, therefore, as God's elect, holy and beloved. "Put on" is repeated from verse 10. And the word "therefore" means (amplified), "Since y o u have in principle taken Christ into y o u r hearts, *therefore* actually *be* in practice — yes, *be fully* — what y o u have professed to be, and what I, Paul, actually believe y o u have begun to be." Be this "as God's elect." For a twelve-point summary of the doctrine of election in the epistles of Paul see N.T.C. on I and II Thess., pp. 48-50. Note especially the following statements, taken from points 7, 10, and 12: "Election affects life in all its phases, is not abstract. Although it belongs to God's decree from eternity, it becomes a dynamic force in the hearts and lives of God's children. It produces fruits. It is an election not only unto salvation but definitely also (as a link in the chain) unto service. It has as its final aim God's glory, and is the work of his delight" (Eph. 1:4-6).

15:28 and Eph. 1:23 ("all in all" in both cases, omitting "and") are not really parallel.

In apposition with the expression "God's elect" are the ascriptions "holy and beloved." As God's chosen ones, these people, both individually and collectively as far as they are true believers, are *holy,* that is, "set apart" for the Lord and for his work. They have been cleansed by the blood of Christ from the guilt of their sins, and are being delivered, more and more, from sin's pollution, and renewed according to the image of God (see on verse 10 above). They are, moreover, "beloved," and this *especially* by God (I Thess. 1:4; cf. II Thess. 4:13).

Thus, the qualifying designations of honor that were formerly applied to the ancient covenant people of Israel (see I Peter 2:9; then Isa. 5:1; Hos. 2:23; cf. Rom. 9:25) are here used in connection with the members of the church of the new dispensation. The church is the new Israel. Paul continues. (Put on) **a heart of compassion, kindness, lowliness, meekness, long-suffering.** It is immediately evident that these qualities overlap. A person with "a compassionate heart" will also be "kind." One who is lowly or humble

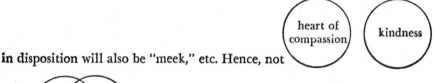

in disposition will also be "meek," etc. Hence, not

but   and so for the others. The expression *heart of compassion* [130] indicates a very deep feeling, "a yearning with the deeply-felt affection of Christ Jesus" (Phil. 1:8). As to the depth of this feeling one thinks of the reaction of Joseph upon seeing Benjamin (Gen. 43:30), or in revealing himself to his brothers (Gen. 45:1-4). Another example would be the tender relationship between David and Jonathan (I Sam. 18:1; 20:4, 17).

The next quality is *kindness.* This is Spirit-imparted *goodness* of heart, the very opposite of the *malice* or *badness* mentioned in verse 8. The early Christians by means of kindness commended themselves to others (II Cor. 6:6). God, too, is kind (Rom. 2:4; cf. 11:22), and we are admonished to become like him in this respect (Luke 6:35). Examples of human kindness would be the same persons already mentioned in connection with "heart of compassion." To avoid repetition, let us add the Good Samaritan of the well-known parable (Luke 10:25-37), Barnabas (Acts 4:36, 37; 15:37), and the apostle Paul himself (I Thess. 2:7-12).

Lowliness or *humility* — a virtue despised by the heathen (as noted earlier) — is also mentioned as a quality which believers should more and more strive to acquire. The person who is kind to others generally does not

---

[130] For a discussion of the word used in the original see N.T.C. on Philippians, p. 58, footnote 39.

have too high an estimate of himself. A happy condition arises when in a church each member counts the other to be better than himself (Phil. 2:3). Of course, there is also such a thing as "feigned humility" (see on 2:18, 23). Good examples of true humility would be the centurion who said, "I am not worthy that thou shouldest come under my roof" (Luke 7:6), and the publican who, in a striking parable, pours out his heart by sighing, "God, be merciful to me, the sinner" (Luke 18:13). According to the entire context, however, it is modest self-appraisal in relation to *the neighbors*, especially to *fellow-believers*, that Paul has in mind. Of course, these two — humility toward God and the same disposition toward men — far from being mutually exclusive, belong together.

Meekness, mentioned next, is definitely not weakness or spinelessness, the characteristic of the person who is ready to bow before every breeze. It is submissiveness under provocation, the willingness rather to *suffer* injury than to *inflict* it. A striking example is Moses (Num. 12:3).

For *longsuffering* see on 1:11. What a longsuffering hero was Jeremiah during his lengthy period of prophetic activity. Think also of Hosea who, instead of rejecting his unfaithful wife, slips away to the haunt of shame, redeems Gomer with fifteen pieces of silver and a homer and a half of barley, and mercifully restores her to her position of honor! [131]

Continued: **enduring one another.** The Colossians are urged to bear with one another in love (cf. Eph. 4:2). Paul was able to say, "Being persecuted we endure" (Cor. 4:12). The example of Job comes to mind (James 5:11). Paul adds, **and forgiving** [132] **each other if anyone have a complaint against anyone. Just as the Lord** [133] **has forgiven y o u, so do y o u also.** For the divine forgiveness see on 2:13. Christ, while on earth, had taught his disciples to pray, "Forgive us our debts, as we also have forgiven our debtors" (Matt. 6:12). It is possible that the expression "Just as the Lord has forgiven y o u, so do y o u also" is a conscious echo of the just quoted petition of the Lord's Prayer, showing that Paul knew that prayer. Anyway, it is identical in spirit and meaning. Jesus had also instructed Peter to forgive "not up to seven times but up to seventy times seven times" (Matt. 18:22), and had added a touching parable ending with the words, "So also my heavenly Father will do to y o u, if each of y o u does not forgive his

---

[131] Of course, this is true only if "the wife of whoredom," namely, Gomer (Hos. 1:2, 3), is to be identified with the "adulteress" mentioned in Hos. 3:1-3.

[132] Here again a form of the verb χαρίζομαι is used, as in 2:13. It stresses the full and gracious character of forgiveness. The noun ἄφεσις, used in Col. 1:14 and Eph. 1:7, (cf. the verb ἀφίημι, let go, send away) places greater stress on the thought that the sin is completely *dismissed* (cf. Ps. 103:12).

[133] Textual variants here are "God," "God in Christ" (very likely after Eph. 4:32), and "Christ." The textual support for the reading "the Lord" is, however, clearly the strongest. On the basis of Col. 1:13, 14 and 2:13 (see the explanation of these passages) the reference is to God rather than to Christ, though the difference is minor. When God forgives he does so "in Christ" (Eph. 4:32; cf. Matt. 18:35).

brother from the heart" (Matt. 18:35; cf. Mark 11:25). Moreover, the Lord had underscored these precepts with his own example. While being crucified he had implored, "Father, forgive them, for they know not what they do" (Luke 23:34). When Stephen, while he was being stoned to death, prayed "Lord, lay not this sin to their charge," he was following the example of Christ.

This would seem to be the proper place to point out that Paul here links his admonitions to Christ's person and work, as has been indicated also in connection with Col. 1:28. See the three columns there. The qualities which, according to Paul's teaching here, mark the new man are also ascribed to *Christ*. For his "heart of compassion" and his kindness see Matt. 9:36; 14:14; 15:32; 20:34. His lowliness and meekness are exemplified in Matt. 11:29; 21:5; John 13:1-15; Phil. 2:8; his longsuffering and endurance or forbearance, in Matt. 17:17; John 14:9; I Peter 2:23; and his forgiving spirit, in Matt. 9:2; Luke 7:47; 23:34. Accordingly, when a believer manifests these virtues in his association with his fellow-men he has "put on" Christ (Rom. 13:14). And it is comforting to know that he who has seen Christ has seen the Father (John 14:9; cf. 1:18), and that he who is an imitator of Christ (I Cor. 11:1; I Thess. 1:6) is also an imitator of God (Eph. 5:1).

14. This holds also with respect to *love,* as Eph. 5:2 clearly indicates. The apostle continues, **And above all these things (put on) love, which is the bond of perfection.** This supremacy of love — note "above all these things" — is clear also from I Cor. 13:13. Love heads the list of "the fruits of the Spirit" (Gal. 5:22). In Paul's prayer for the Philippians the petition mentioned first of all is "that y o u r love may abound more and more" (Phil. 1:9). Love dominates the writings of John, where it is mentioned scores of times. With Peter, too, love is supreme (I Peter 4:8). How highly the anonymous author of Hebrews regards it is evident from Heb. 10:24; 13:1. Love is the lubricant that enables the other virtues to function smoothly (Gal. 5:6, 13). It is *intelligent and purposeful self-giving* that Paul has in mind, the fulfilment of both the law and the gospel. In the present context it is especially *mutual* love, love for one another within the Christian community, that is thought of, though it is true that such love overflows its boundaries (I Thess. 3:12). That is of the very essence of love: to overflow. It was this love for one another, as brothers and sisters in the Lord, of which Jesus spoke when he issued his "new commandment" (John 13:34; I Thess. 4:9). See also on Col. 1:8.

Now this love is called "the bond of perfection." This has been interpreted to mean that love is "the grace that binds all these other graces together" (Bruce, *op. cit.,* p. 281). Though this may be correct, and a sensible connotation is thereby ascribed to the expression, it is probably better to interpret it in the light of what Paul himself says in this very epistle, namely, "they themselves being welded together in love" (2:2). *Love, then is "the bond of perfection" in the sense that it is that which unites believers, causing them to move forward toward the goal of perfection.* This interpretation is also in line with the apostle's purpose in writing this letter. It is as if he were saying, "Not *knowledge* or *philosophy* — the kind of knowledge and philosophy of which false teachers boast — or *obedience to human regulations,* but *love* for one another, the spontaneous response to God's love for y o u, is that which will strengthen and unite y o u, and will lead y o u toward the attainment of y o u r spiritual ideal." For the meaning of this ideal see also on 1:28.

15. Paul continues, **And let the peace of Christ, for which y o u were called in one body, rule in y o u r hearts.** This peace is the condition of rest and contentment in the hearts of those who know that their Redeemer lives. It is the conviction that the sins of the past have been forgiven, that the present is being overruled for good, and that the future cannot bring about separation between Christ and his own. Concerning this peace the apostle says in Phil. 4:7, "And the peace of God that surpasses all understanding will keep guard over y o u r hearts and y o u r thoughts in Christ Jesus." It is the peace *of Christ* because it was merited for believers by Christ, is through his Spirit bestowed upon them, and is fostered by this same Lord and Savior (John 14:27; 16:33; 20:19, 21, 26). It is, moreover, patterned after the peace that dwells in the Savior's own heart.

Now this peace also has its social aspect, on which the emphasis falls in the present passage (cf. Eph. 4:3, 4), as is evident from the phrase "for which y o u were called in one body." When men were called out of the darkness into the light they, as seen by God, were not drawn out of their sinful environment as pebbles are picked up from the beach. On the contrary, they were called as a body, for from eternity they had been viewed as a corporate entity "in Christ." In time they were "called" in order that they might promote this spiritual oneness in every way. Now this purpose can be accomplished only when the peace of Christ *rules* [134] in each heart. Let each individual, therefore, constantly ask himself, "Will I have peace within if I do this or do that?" Let him be sure to be at peace with God, for only then can he expect to live in true harmony with his brothers (cf. James 4:1).

Paul adds, **and be thankful.** It is worthy of note how frequently in this brief epistle the apostle refers to the privilege and duty of being thankful (1:3, 12; 2:7; 3:15, 16, 17; 4:2). Gratitude makes for peace and excellent public relations. When a person is overpowered by the feeling of warm and

---

[134] Basically the meaning of βραβευέτω is *let it be umpire.* Since the umpire's decision is very important, it is easy to see how the meaning *let it rule* arose. See also on 2:18, footnote 97.

deep appreciation for benefits received from God he will hardly be able to grudge someone else his wealth or superior talents. Hence, this admonition fits splendidly into the immediate context. Gratitude promotes peace. The exhortation also suits the broader context which mentions some of the blessings believers have received. They are "hid with Christ in God," have received the forgiveness of sins, and are experiencing daily spiritual renewal. Moreover, the apostle is about to mention the further blessings of the indwelling word and of psalms, hymns, and spiritual songs. For all these favors thanksgiving is in order. Though all men *should* give thanks, the Christian *can be expected* to do so. Ingratitude marks paganism (Rom. 1:21). In all probability it also marked the fearfilled alarmists who were vexing the addressees (Col. 2:16-23). Having therefore been rescued from paganism let the Colossians also turn their backs upon these so-called "philosophers." Let them in newness of spirit be joyful and praise the Lord every day. Thus they will be truly and serenely blessed, and in turn will be a blessing to others.

16. Paul has just been saying, "Let the peace of Christ rule in y o u r hearts." At first glance a believer might well ask, however, "If I do this am I not building the edifice of my hope and trust upon a rather insecure, subjective foundation?" After further thought, however, he answers, "Not at all, for I have peace when in my inmost being I, by God's sovereign grace, resolve to live in accordance with the objective word of Christ." Verses 15 and 16 must therefore not be separated. By obedience to the gospel peace is conveyed to the heart. So Paul continues, **Let the word of Christ dwell among** [135] **y o u richly.** The objective, special revelation that proceeds from (and concerns) Christ — "the Christ-word" — should govern every thought, word, and deed, yes even the hidden drives and motivations of every member, and thus should bear sway *among them* all, and this *richly,* "bearing much fruit" (John 15:5). This will happen if believers heed the word (Matt. 13:9), handle it rightly (II Tim. 2:15), hide it in their hearts (Ps. 119:11), and hold it forth to others as being in truth "the word of life" (Phil. 2:16). Though when the apostle wrote this, "the word of Christ" had not yet been entrusted to the written page in the form and to the extent in which we now have it, this does not cancel the fact that for Paul and for all believers in his day as well as, in broader scope, for us today, "All scripture (is) God-breathed and useful for teaching, for reproof, for correction, for training in righteousness, that the man of God may be equipped, for every good work thoroughly equipped" (see N.T.C. on II Tim. 3:16, 17). The logical con-

---

[135] Or "in" with most of the English translations. The immediately succeeding context would seem somewhat to favor the rendering "among," however. Thus also N.E.B., Bruce, Ridderbos. Lightfoot favors "in." The difference is not very important, for only when the word dwells *within* the hearts will it dwell *among* the people.

tinuation is: **in all wisdom** [136] **teaching and admonishing one another.**[137]

For the explanation of these words see on 1:28, where essentially the same thought is expressed in an almost identical statement. The differences are as follows: (1) in 1:28 the apostle relates what he, Timothy, etc., are doing; here (in Col. 3:16) he admonishes the Colossian believers what they should be doing. In both cases the content is the same: admonishing and teaching. Believers, by virtue of their "office" as believers — let them not forget that they are clothed with that *office!* — should do what Paul and his associates are doing by virtue of *their* office, respectively as apostle and apostolic delegates. Each person must do it in accordance with the rights and duties of his particular office. (2) In 1:28 the object is somewhat broader, "every man." Here (Col. 3:16) the emphasis is rather on *mutual* teaching and admonition. And (3) in 1:28 the phrase "in all wisdom" is placed last. In the Colossian passage it is placed first, perhaps to underscore the thought conveyed in the immediately preceding adverb "richly," as if to say, "If the word of Christ is to dwell among y o u *richly,* then *in all wisdom* y o u should admonish and teach each other."

There is something else that should also be done if the word of Christ is to dwell among the Colossians richly. It is stated in these words: **(and) by means of psalms, hymns, and spiritual songs** [138] **singing to God in a thankful spirit,**[139] **with all y o u r heart.**

---

[136] For me the fact that in Col. 1:28, in an almost identical clause, the phrase "in all wisdom" modifies "teaching and admonishing" shows that it should be so construed here also, and not (with Lightfoot) attached to the preceding clause.

[137] Not "themselves." The pronoun ἑαυτούς is not only *reflexive* but can also be *reciprocal.* See L.N.T. (A. and G.), p. 211. In Col. 1:28 the thought is similar: admonishing *every man* and teaching *every man,* not "teaching themselves." Cf. Eph. 5:19. So also in the Colossian context, 3:13 can hardly be rendered "forgiving themselves." This is my answer to Lenski's contrary assertion (*op. cit.,* p. 177), though in 3:13 he, too, renders the pronoun: "each other."

[138] As to the construction there are two main possibilities: (1) Construe "by means of psalms, hymns, and spiritual songs" with the words that precede. Paul would then be saying, "teaching and admonishing one another by means of psalms, hymns, and spiritual songs." This is favored by A.V., A.R.V. (both the old and the new), Moffatt's New Testament Translation, Berkeley Version, and by the commentators Bruce, Lenski, Lightfoot, etc. (2) Link the phrase with the words that follow (see my translation). With minor variations in translation this alternative, which is in agreement with N.N.'s punctuation, is accepted by R.S.V., Amplified New Testament, Dutch Bible (Nieuwe Vertaling), Beare (in *The Interpreter's Bible*), Ridderbos, etc. I agree with the last-mentioned author when in opposing theory (1) he states, "The idea that this mutual teaching and admonishing must be carried out by means of song seems rather unnatural to us" (*op. cit.,* p. 222). I might add that Eph. 5:19, to which the supporters of theory (1) appeal, is, in my estimation, hardly sufficient proof. It is one thing to speak to one another in song. It is something else again to say that *teaching and admonishing* must be done by means of song.

[139] Whether ἐν τῇ χάριτι or ἐν χάριτι is the best reading is not certain. Each has strong textual support. On the basis of I Cor. 10:30, and in line with the immediate context (see verses 15 and 17) the most probable meaning here would seem to be

Paul clearly recognizes the edifying nature of God-glorifying singing. As to the meaning of the terms *psalms, hymns,* and *spiritual songs* (see also Eph. 5:19) a little investigation quickly shows that it may not be easy to distinguish *sharply* between these three. It is possible that there is here some overlapping of meanings. Thus, in connection with *psalms* it is natural to think of the Old Testament Psalter, and, in support of this view, to appeal to Luke 20:42; 24:44; Acts 1:20; 13:33. So far there is no difficulty. However, expositors are by no means agreed that this can also be the meaning of the word *psalm* in I Cor. 14:26 ("When y o u assemble, each one has a psalm").

As to *hymns,* in the New Testament the word *hymn* is found only in our present passage (Col. 3:16) and in Eph. 5:19. Augustine, in more than one place, states that a hymn has three essentials: it must be sung; it must be praise; it must be to God. According to this definition it would be possible for an Old Testament psalm, sung in praise to God, to be also a hymn. Thus when Jesus and his disciples were about to leave the Upper Room in order to go to the Mount of Olives, they "hymned" (Matt. 26:30; Mark 14:26). It is held by many that what they hymned was Psalm 115-118. According to Acts 16:25 in the Philippian prison Paul and Silas were *hymning* to God. Is it not altogether probable that some, if not all, of these *hymns* were *psalms?* Cf. also Heb. 2:12. But if Augustine's definition is correct there are also hymns that do not belong to the Old Testament Psalter; such hymns as the *Magnificat* (Luke 1:46-55) and the *Benedictus* (Luke 1:68-79). Fragments of other New Testament hymns seem to be embedded in the letters of Paul (Eph. 5:14; Col. 1:15-20; I Tim. 3:16, and perhaps others).

The word *song* or *ode* (in the sense of poem intended to be sung) occurs not only in Eph. 5:19 and Col. 3:16 but also in Rev. 5:9; 14:3, where "the new song" is indicated, and in Rev. 15:3, where the reference is to "the song of Moses, the servant of God, and the song of the Lamb." These are not Old Testament Psalms. Moreover, a song or ode is not necessarily a *sacred* song. In the present case the fact that it is, indeed, sacred is shown by the addition of the adjective *spiritual.*

All in all, then, it would seem that when here in Col. 3:16 the apostle uses these three terms, apparently distinguishing them at least to some extent, the term *psalms* has reference, at least mainly, to the Old Testament Psalter; *hymns* mainly to New Testament songs of praise to God or to Christ; and *spiritual songs* mainly to any other sacred songs dwelling on themes other than direct praise to God or to Christ.[140]

The point that must not be ignored is this, that these songs must be sung in a thankful spirit. The songs must be poured forth sincerely, rising from

---

thankfully or *in a thankful spirit,* rather than a. "with grace in y o u r hearts," or b. "charmingly."

[140] See also Trench, *op. cit.,* par. LXXVIII.

within the humbly grateful hearts of believers. It has been said that next to Scripture itself a good Psalter-Hymnal is the richest fountain of edification. Not only are its songs a source of daily nourishment for the church, but they also serve as a very effective vehicle for the outpouring of confession of sin, gratitude, spiritual joy, rapture. Whether sung in the regular worship-service on the Lord's Day, at a midweek meeting, in social gatherings, in connection with family-worship, at a festive occasion, or privately, they are a tonic for the soul and promote the glory of God. They do this because they fix the interest upon the indwelling word of Christ, and carry the attention away from that worldly cacophony by which people with low moral standards are being emotionally overstimulated.

The passage under discussion has often been used in support of this or that theory with respect to what may or may not be sung in the official worship-service. Perhaps it is correct to say that the appeal is justified if one is satisfied with a few broad, general principles; for example, (1) In our services the psalms should not be neglected. (2) As to *hymns*, in the stricter sense of songs of praise, "It is probably true that a larger proportion of the religious poems which are used in public praise should be 'hymns' in the stricter sense. They should be addressed to God. Too many are subjective, not to say sentimental, and express only personal experiences and aspirations which are sometimes lacking in reality" Charles E. Erdman (*op. cit.*, p. 91).

For the rest, it is well to bear in mind that Paul's purpose is not to lay down detailed rules and regulations pertaining to ecclesiastical liturgy. He is interested in showing the Colossians and all those to whom or by whom the letter would be read how they may grow in grace, and may manifest rightly the power of the indwelling word. His admonition, therefore, can be applied to every type of Christian gathering, whether on the Sabbath or during the week, whether in church or at home or anywhere else.[141]

17. A fundamental principle for Christian life and conduct summarizes and climaxes this priceless paragraph, namely, **And whatever y o u do in word or in deed, (do) all [142] in the name of the Lord Jesus, giving thanks to God the Father through him.**

For the expression "Whatever y o u do" see also verse 23 and I Cor. 10:31. In connection with "Do all in the name of the Lord Jesus" it should be

---

[141] That Paul's teaching with respect to this subject was given this wide application in the early church is clear from such references as the following: Clement of Alexandria, *The Instructor* II.4; Tertullian, *Apology,* ch. 39; *To His Wife* II.8.

[142] With respect to the wording of the original two points are in order: $\pi\tilde{\alpha}\nu$ should in all probability be viewed as a nominative absolute, replaced later by the accusative $\pi\acute{\alpha}\nu\tau\alpha$ considered as the object of an implied verb. The implied verb is $\pi o\iota\epsilon\tilde{\iota}\tau\epsilon$, viewed as a present imperative.

noted that *the name* indicates the Lord Jesus himself as he has revealed himself.[143] "In the name" means, accordingly, "in vital relation with him," that is, in harmony with his revealed will, in subjection to his authority, in dependence on his power. The clause "giving thanks to God the Father through him" (in connection with which see especially Eph. 5:20; then also John 14:6; 15:5b; Rom. 1:8; 7:25; 16:27; I Cor. 1:20) is explained by the fact that it is on the basis of the Son's atonement that sinners are accepted by the Father, and that they ("together with him") receive every blessing. Hence, it is altogether just and fair that *through him* thanksgiving be given to the Father.

The main lessons of this closing paragraph should not escape us. As I see it they are the following:

(1) "Whatever y o u do" is very general. In contrast with the many specific rules and regulations which false teachers were trying to impose upon the Colossians (Col. 2:16-23), Paul simply enunciates a comprehensive principle, and permits believers to work it out for themselves in perfect freedom. After all, the child of God of the new dispensation is not under bondage. Let the Spirit within him rule him.

(2) This Spirit (hence also the Spirit-indwelt believer) operates in connection with the word, that is, the revelation ("name") of the Lord Jesus. Man is "free" only when he abides in Christ. Let him therefore always ask himself, "What shall I do, Lord?" (Acts 22:10). Let him diligently and prayerfully study Scripture. It is in that sense that (1) above is to be understood.

(3) In connection with any and every word and deed the believer should ask himself, "Am I able to thank God the Father for having given me the opportunity to say or do this?" (Cf. Bruce, *op. cit.,* p. 286).

(4) The sovereignty or pre-eminence of the Lord Jesus in relation to the entire universe with all its events and in relation to the believer himself should be joyfully acknowledged. Therefore, too, he should do everything "in the name of the Lord Jesus."

We notice, therefore, that the present paragraph closes as did also the preceding one (see on 3:11), with a reminder of the theme of the entire epistle, Christ, the Pre-eminent One, the Only and All-Sufficient Savior.

Summary of Colossians 3:1-17

By accepting the counsel which Paul here offers, the Colossians will not only win victory upon victory in their battle with "the flesh" (see 2:23; 3:5-9), but will live a life of usefulness for the edification of the church and the benefit of their fellowmen, to the glory of God. Let them, accordingly, be consistent. Having been "raised with Christ" let them seek the things that

---

[143] For proof see N.T.C. on Philippians, p. 117, footnote 98.

are above, not those that are upon the earth, for their *life* (and this section of Colossians concerns the believers' *life*) "is hid with Christ in God." It was heaven that gave them birth, for they were born from above. Their names are inscribed in heaven's register. Their rights are secured in heaven. Their interests are being promoted there. Hence, since they belong to heaven, let their lives be governed according to heavenly standards, and to heaven let their thoughts and prayers ascend, and their hopes aspire. Let them seek to obtain for themselves those heavenly gifts mentioned in verses 12-17. And since Christ "in them" is "the hope of glory" (1:27), it must be true that when Christ (who is) *"our life"* is manifested, then they too "will be manifested with him in glory."

A radical break with former vices is therefore in order. These must in fact be "put to death." Once and for all they must be "laid aside." Since at their baptism the Colossians had publicly repudiated the old man with his evil deeds and had put on the new man, let them therefore now continue to do *in practice* what they had already done *in principle*. The Creator of the new man will enable them to do this. And this applies to *all* true believers. Here every class-distinction disappears completely, for Christ is "all and in all."

In order to bid defiance to the forces of evil let them, however, not concentrate on evil. Let vice be conquered by virtue. Let evil be overcome with good. Let them therefore, having accepted Christ as their Lord and Savior, become imitators of him, so that all his marvelous virtues — a heart of compassion, kindness, lowliness, *above all love* — may also be seen in *them*. Thus, they will be welded into a strong, spiritual unity. Let, therefore, Christ's peace rule in their hearts. Let his word dwell among them, so that in all wisdom they will teach and admonish each other. Let them be so filled with joy and gratitude as to pour forth their very hearts in jubilation, singing not only the psalms of "the sweet singer of Israel" but also hymns of praise and other spiritual songs.

Paul concludes this paragraph by laying down not a set of detailed rules and regulations but a basic principle (which is far better), "And whatever y o u do in word or in deed, (do) all in the name of the Lord Jesus, giving thanks to God the Father through him." Thus once more, as often in this letter, Paul is directing the minds and hearts of the addressees to the only and all-sufficient Savior Jesus Christ, and via that sovereign Mediator, to God the Father.

Outline of Chapter 3:18–4:1

Theme: *Christ, the Pre-eminent One, the Only and All-Sufficient Savior*

II. This Only and All-Sufficient Savior Is the Source of the Believers' Life, and Thus the Real Answer to the Perils by Which They Are Confronted, chapters 3 and 4

B. This Truth Applied to Special Groups, 3:18–4:1

    3:18, 19 1. Wives and their husbands

    3:20, 21 2. Children and their fathers

    3:22–4:1 3. Slaves and their masters

18 Wives, be submissive to y o u r husbands, as is fitting in the Lord.
19 Husbands, love y o u r wives, and do not be harsh toward them.

3:18, 19

I. *Wives and Their Husbands*

A new paragraph begins here. The sublime yet very practical truth that Christ is the only and all-sufficient Savior and as such the source of the believers' life is now going to be applied to special groups. Paul is thinking of *household* groups. What we have here, therefore, is a kind of "table of household duties," sometimes simply called "house-table." Now it is true that even in the writings of non-Christian moralists we find codes of domestic behavior.[144] But the notion that the apostle is simply copying their tables, and coating them with a thin varnish of Christianity — merely (!) adding "in Christ" — misses the point entirely. Between these pithy directives as presented here in Colossians — also in Eph. 5:22–6:9; I Tim. 2:8-15; 6:1, 2; Titus 2:1-10; I Peter 2:12–3:7 — and the maxims of the Stoics and other moral philosophers, there is, indeed, at times a superficial resemblance, but there are at least three main differences:

(1) Christianity, as proclaimed by Paul, etc., supplied the *power* to carry out the commands, that power being the grace of God, mentioned in that very connection at the close of the list in Titus (Titus 2:1-10, then verse 11; cf. Phil. 4:13). All other moral philosophies, the very best of them, are trains lacking engines!

(2) Christianity also presented a new *purpose*. That purpose was *not* simply "to try to live in agreement with Nature," but "to do everything to the glory of God" (I Cor. 10:31), that is, "in the name of the Lord Jesus, giving thanks to God the Father through him," as stated in the Colossian context (3:17). The only proper way to explain Col. 3:18–4:1 is in the light of Col. 3:17. And finally,

(3) Christianity, as originating in Christ, supplied the only true *pattern* for God-glorifying conduct on the part of the very groups here discussed, namely, wives and their husbands, children and their fathers, servants and their masters. Christ himself, as the bridegroom, in his matchless love for

---

[144] See Seneca, *Epistles* XV.2; Th.W.N.T., pp. 949-959; 974-978; and Stobaeus, *Anthologies* IV.

the church, his bride, furnished the standard for the love of *Christian marriage* (Eph. 5:25, 32).

In his obedience to his parents (Luke 2:51), in the wonderful manner in which he, in the midst of the tortures of hell, provided for his earthly mother (John 19:25-27), and in fact in his entire life of obedience to his heavenly Father, culminating in a death in which that obedience was climaxed (Phil. 2:8), he gave to all an example of patient submission. That example was certainly intended also for *the children*. (He also had a lesson for *the fathers*, Luke 15:20-24.)

Last of all, in his willingness to stoop very low, which he proved by washing the feet of his disciples and by his death on the cross, he gave an object-lesson intended for all, certainly also for *masters and slaves*, as plainly indicated in John 13:13-17.

18. The first admonition is, **Wives, be submissive to y o u r husbands, as is fitting in the Lord.** Suffragists have said that it is positively wicked to use the word "obey" in the marriage contract. They have loudly affirmed that the marriage service in its present "Form" compels the bride to take a vow which she has no intention of keeping. A Prayer Book has eliminated the word "obey" from its Marriage Form. All this, however, does not "eliminate" Col. 3:18! Moreover, a little searching will quickly show that what the passage teaches is the consistent doctrine of Scripture anent this point. See the following passages: Gen. 3:16; Rom. 7:2; I Cor. 14:34, 35; Eph. 5:22-24, 33; I Tim. 2:11-15; Titus 2:5; I Peter 3:1-6. And the reason given here in Col. 3:18 is that such obedience is (and always has been) "fitting in the Lord," being in harmony with his will as revealed in Scripture. A Christian wife will therefore gladly strive to regulate her conduct in harmony with this command. She will not begin to think that her equality in spiritual standing before God and the great liberty which has now become her portion as a believer (Gal. 3:28) entitles her to forget about the fact that in his sovereign wisdom God made the human pair in such a manner that it is natural for the husband to lead, for the wife to follow; for him to be aggressive (in the most favorable sense), for her to be receptive; for him to invent, for her to use the tools which he invents. The tendency *to follow* was embedded in Eve's very soul as she came forth from the hand of her Creator. Hence any attempt to reverse this order is displeasing to God. Why should a woman be encouraged to do things that are contrary to her nature? Her very body, far from preceding that of Adam in the order of creation, was taken out of Adam's body. Her very name — Ish-sha — was derived from his name — Ish (Gen. 2:23). It is when the wife recognizes this basic distinction and acts accordingly that she can be a blessing to her husband, can exert a gracious, very powerful, and beneficent influence upon him, and can promote not only his but also her own happiness.

In connection with this command that wives be submissive to their husbands the following should also be noted:

(1) *It does not imply the wives' inferiority to their husbands.* In non-Christian circles wives (in fact, women in general) were regarded as being inferior beings. Among the Greeks, in spite of their high degree of culture, wives, as a rule, were not considered to be the equals or even the companions of their husbands. The Romans, too, regarded women as being intrinsically inferior. Philo, a Jewish philosopher who was greatly influenced by Greek philosophy, regarded *women* as being selfish, jealous, and hypocritical, and *married men* as being no longer free men but slaves.

The status of women in the Qumran community, which has given us the Dead Sea Scrolls, was not enviable. There seem to have been both celibate and non-celibate groups in the Qumran sect (see Miller Burrows, *More Light on the Dead Sea Scrolls,* pp. 358, 383). "One of the most conspicuous differences between the church and the Qumran sect . . . was the entirely different status of women in the two communities" (same author, *The Dead Sea Scrolls,* p. 333; cf. pp. 233, 244, 291; also H. Mulder, *De vondsten bij de Dode Zee,* p. 35).

Christianity changed all this (Gal. 3:28), and is still changing it among those who are being led to accept it.[145] Jesus made some of his most startling revelations to women (John 4:13, 14, 21-26; 11:25, 26; 20:11-18). For the dignity of women in Paul's epistles see N.T.C. on I and II Timothy and Titus, pp. 113, 114.

(2) *It is not absolute.* If a husband should ever ask his wife to do something which in her conscience (illumined by Scripture) she knows to be wrong, she has the right and the duty to disobey her husband (Acts 5:29).

(3) *It is issued in a context of love,* of which wives must be the objects, for Paul continues:

19. Husbands, love [146] **y o u r wives, and do not be harsh toward them.** The best commentary is Paul's own, in Eph. 5:25-33. A discussion of the

---

[145] For the status of woman for many centuries under Islam see S. M. Zwemer, *Across the World of Islam,* chapters V and VI, especially p. 135. For her status outside Christendom in general see J. S. Dennis, *Christian Missions and Social Progress* (3 volumes), especially Vol. I, pp. 104-125. Credit for more recent progress in her status must be given, at least in part, to the influence of Christianity.

[146] The verb used is a form of ἀγαπάω. Paul uses φιλέω only twice (I Cor. 16:22; Titus 3:15). The verb ἀγαπάω is pushing out the verb φιλέω, taking over its functions and (at least in the present case) retaining its own as well. Full, Christian love is what is here meant, a love which sublimates all other. On the relation between the two verbs see N.T.C. on the Gospel according to John, Vol. II, pp. 494-501, footnote 306.

contents of that magnificent passage does not belong here but in a Commentary on Ephesians. The love of a husband for his wife is *sexual,* to be sure, but also rises above the sexual. It is *natural affection,* but it is also far more than that. It is the love for one's wife as "a sister in the Lord." This love acts as a moderating influence upon the husband's exercise of authority. It is true that the primary responsibility for the final decision with respect to a matter rests with the husband, but the method of reaching that decision leaves ample room for mutual deliberation and gentle persuasion, in the course of which, perhaps, at times the *husband's* tentative conclusion may finally prevail, at other times the *wife's,* her partner having come to see that she was right. Thus, the husband, having fully committed himself to the principle that his love for his wife must be a true reflection of the deep, sacrificial love of Christ for the church (Eph. 5:25, 32), acts toward her as a man of understanding, is never "harsh" or "cross," but is considerate toward her,[147] and honors her in every way (I Peter 3:7). In such a marriage each seeks to please and benefit the other (Prov. 31:12; I Cor. 7:33, 34), and to promote the other's welfare, and this not only physically and culturally but also, and in fact mainly, spiritually. The husband views his wife as his equal in the sense that she is "a joint-heir of the grace of life" (I Peter 3:7). See also Gen. 24:67 (Isaac's love for Rebekah) and 29:20 (Jacob's love for Rachel).

---

20 Children, obey y o u r parents in all things, for this is well-pleasing in the Lord. 21 Fathers, do not exasperate y o u r children, in order that they may not lose heart.

3:20, 21

II. *Children and Their Fathers*

20. Children, obey y o u r parents in all things, for this is well-pleasing in the Lord.[148] This admonition is completely in line with such passages as Ex. 20:12; 21:15-17; Lev. 20:9; Deut. 5:16; 21:18; Prov. 1:8; 6:20; 30:17; Mal. 1:6; Matt. 15:4-6; 19:19; Mark 7:10-13; 10:19; 18:20; Eph. 6:1-3. Disobedience to parents is one of the vices of paganism (Rom. 1:30). It marks the ever-increasing wickedness of "the last days" (II Tim. 3:2). The soul-destructive falsehood that would abolish all parental authority — the very word "authority" being anathema in certain educational circles! —, so that children no longer need to pay any attention to their father's instruction or

---

[147] Lenski is right when he states, "This negative [do not be harsh toward them] is on the order of a litotes: ever be considerate toward them . . ." (*op. cit.,* p. 182).
[148] The reading *"to* the Lord" has slight support.

to their mother's teaching, is directly contrary to the clear teaching of Scripture, both Old and New Testament. Godly parents do not inflict upon their children the cruelty of telling them that they should do "just as they please." According to both Scripture and experience children are not only immature but also sinful by nature, wholly incapable *by nature* to choose the good (Ps. 51:5). And because of this the admonition in the form in which it is found here is very comprehensive: the children are exhorted to obey their parents "in all things," always subject to the limitation of Acts 5:29.

Such obedience is *well-pleasing*. This word is generally (though *not* expressly here in Col. 3:20) modified by "to God" or "to the Lord" (Rom. 12:1; 14:18; II Cor. 5:9; Eph. 5:10; Phil. 4:18; cf. Heb. 13:21). This modifier may certainly also be viewed as *implied* in our present passage. That God is pleased with this obedience is clear from the fact that he himself in the Decalogue pronounced a special blessing upon it (Ex. 20:12; Deut. 5:16), to which the apostle refers in the parallel Ephesian passage (Eph. 6:2, 3). For that matter, obedience to God's commandments is always well-pleasing to him! That it is carried out "in the Lord," that is, in fellowship with and dependence upon him, is understood by every child, whether older or younger, who from the heart is able to sing:

> "When we walk with the Lord
> In the light of his Word,
> What a glory he sheds on our way!
> While we do his good will
> He abides with us still,
> And with all who will trust and obey.
> Trust and obey, for there's no other way
> To be happy in Jesus,
> But to trust and obey."   (J. H. Sammis)

21. One of the most striking characteristics of these brief admonitions is their *reciprocal* character. In enjoining God-glorifying domestic relationships they do not stress the duty of wives at the expense of that of husbands, of children at the expense of that of fathers, or of slaves at the expense of that of masters. Outside of special revelation there is very little of this balance. Often the duty of the first member in each group is stressed, and little or nothing is said about the second. In ancient times when things went wrong *all* the blame was heaped on wives, children,[149] and slaves. But Paul, having admonished husbands as well as wives, and having just now reminded the children of their obligation to their parents, in all fairness proceeds to

---

[149] *Today* in civilized (?) countries, on *parents!* Or on *society*, the *environment*. Do these deserve *all* the blame?

issue a directive to the fathers also: **Fathers,**[150] **do not exasperate** [151] **y o u r children, in order that they may not lose heart.**

Fathers should create an atmosphere which will make obedience an easy and natural matter, namely, the atmosphere of love and confidence. They should bring up their children in the discipline and instruction of the Lord (Eph. 6:4).[152] When fathers are unjust or overly severe, a spirit of sullen resignation is created in the hearts of their offspring. The children "lose heart," thinking, "No matter what I do, it's always wrong." There should be no nagging, no *constant* "Don't do this" and "Don't do that." Though the negative admonition ("Don't") cannot and must not be avoided and is at times definitely in place (note the repeated "Thou shalt not" of the Decalogue, in the teaching of Jesus, and in Paul's epistles, including this very passage!), the *emphasis* must be on the positive (Rom. 12:21). A good father spends time with his children, teaches, entertains, and encourages them, and by his example as well as by outright, verbal instruction, points them to Christ. Though the rod of correction may at times be necessary, it must be used with discretion, since wise reproof is generally better than a hundred stripes (Prov. 13:24; 23:13, 14; then 17:10). Paul's admonition not to embitter the children — hence, to be kind to them — is quite different from the advice given to fathers by Ben Sira: "He who loves his son will whip him often. . . . Bow down his neck in his youth, and beat his sides while he is young" (Ecclus. 30:1, 12). How friendly and fatherly!

---

22 Slaves, obey in all things those who according to the flesh are y o u r masters, not with eye-service as men-pleasers but with singleness of heart, fearing the Lord. 23 Whatever y o u do, put y o u r soul into the work, as for the Lord and not for men, 24 knowing that from the Lord y o u will receive the recompense, namely, the inheritance. (It is) the Lord Christ (whom) y o u are serving. 25 For, the wrong-doer will receive (the consequences of) what he has wrongly done. And there is no partiality.

1 Masters, render to y o u r slaves that which is fair and square, knowing that y o u also have a Master in heaven.

---

[150] The possibility that the word "fathers" has here the meaning "parents" must be granted (see also Heb. 11:23). However, the fact that in the preceding verse the more usual word for *parents* is used would rather seem to indicate that in the present passage "fathers" means just that. Though the responsibility for the education of the children rests on both parents, and father will consult mother, the probability is that the father is here regarded as the head of the family.

[151] The verb is ἐρεθίζετε, meaning *stir up*. One can stir up for good (II Cor. 9:2) or for evil (as here in Col. 3:21). In the latter case the resultant meaning is *exasperate, embitter*. In the present passage there is also considerable textual support for the synonym παροργίζετε, *provoke to anger*. There is very little difference in meaning. Perhaps the latter verb was inserted here from Eph. 6:4.

[152] For a 15-point discussion of *Principles and Methods of Education in Israel* see N.T.C. on I and II Timothy and Titus, pp. 296-301.

3:22–4:1

III. *Slaves and Their Masters*
See also *Scripture on Slavery, pp. 233-237*

22. Slaves, obey in all things those who according to the flesh are y o u r masters . . . Nowhere in Scripture is it stated that slavery *as such* is a divine ordinance, such as marriage (Gen. 1:18, 24), the family (Gen. 1:27, 28), the sabbath (Gen. 2:3), and human government (Gen. 9:6; Rom. 13:1). In and by itself it is not pleasing to God that one man should *own* another man. The fact, moreover, that Paul addresses slaves and their masters on a basis of equality is significant, and implies their spiritual equality before God.

The Roman world was full of slaves. It has been estimated that in Rome itself at one time about a third of the inhabitants belonged to this social class. They had become slaves as prisoners of war, or as convicts, or through debt, kidnaping, purchase, or birth from slave-parents.

Now Paul did not recommend outright revolt by the slaves against their masters. On the contrary, he took the social structure as he found it and endeavored by peaceful means to change it into its very opposite. His rule, in summary, amounted to this, "Let the slave wholeheartedly obey his master, and let the master be kind to his slave." Thus the ill-will, dishonesty, and laziness of the slave would be replaced by willing service, integrity, and industry; the cruelty and brutality of the master, by considerateness and love. And a new and gloriously transformed society would replace the old.

The Pauline material dealing with this subject is found mainly in the following passages: Eph. 6:5-9; Col. 3:22–4:1; I Tim. 6:1, 2; and Titus 2:9, 10. With this should be compared what Peter says in I Peter 2:18-25. Of these five little paragraphs only the first two mention the reciprocal duties of slaves *and their masters*. One of the reasons why more attention is paid to the slaves than to the masters could well be that among those addressed there were many more of the former than of the latter (see I Cor. 1:26). The probable reason why *in Colossians* the apostle devotes far more attention to a. slaves and their masters than to b. wives and their husbands, and children and their fathers (combined) has been pointed out in the Introduction IV A 4 (Onesimus and his master Philemon).

Now when Paul instructs the slaves to obey their masters "in all things," he probably means, "not only in matters pleasant and agreeable but also in matters unpleasant and disagreeable." He cannot have meant, "in *absolutely* all things" (see Acts 5:29). As Paul says elsewhere, by means of this obedience they would "adorn the doctrine of God our Savior" (Titus 2:10). The expression "those who according to the flesh — that is, those

173

who as concerns earthly relationships [153] — are y o u r masters" implies, "Y o u r *real* Master is in heaven," a thought on which Paul will expand presently.

Now this obedience must be **not with eye-service as men-pleasers but with singleness of heart, fearing the Lord.** They must not obey simply "to catch the eye" of their master for selfish purposes. Instead of striving to please men, with the ulterior motive of seeking profit for themselves, they should "with singleness of heart," that is, with an *undivided* mind, hence, with sincerity and uprightness (cf. I Chron. 29:17), render service to their earthly masters, and in so doing show reverence for their Lord.

23, 24. Whatever y o u do (cf. with verse 17), **put y o u r soul into the work** (literally, "work from the soul"), **as for the Lord and not for men . . .** In spirit people cease to be slaves as soon as they begin to work for the Lord, and no longer in the first place for men. This was, accordingly, the most helpful advice anyone could ever have given a slave. Moreover, by means of his *wholehearted* cooperation with his master, rendering obedience to him in every way, and doing this while his master was fully aware of the fact that the service was being rendered by a Christian, the slave was promoting the cause and honor of his Lord. The master would begin to think, "If the Christian religion does this for slaves, it must be wonderful." Paul continues, **knowing that from the Lord y o u will receive the recompense, namely, the inheritance.** Even though from his earthly master the slave may receive far less than he should, yet from his heavenly Lord he will receive *the full amount* which *by God's grace* has been allotted to him.[154]

Though salvation is entirely "by grace" and definitely not "of works" (Eph. 2:8, 9; Titus 3:5), yet this gracious *recompense of eternal life* will be given "according to works" (II Cor. 5:10; Rev. 20:12, 13; then also Eccl. 12:14; I Cor. 3:10-15; 4:5; Gal. 6:7). The recompense is, moreover, "the inheritance," probably implying the following ideas: a. it is *a gift* (a person does not *earn* an inheritance), b. it is *inalienable* (I Kings 21:3; Heb. 9:15), c. it *was willed* to the person who receives it, and in that sense, is therefore his *by right* (cf. Isa. 1:27); and it implies *the death of the testator* (Heb. 9:16).

---

[153] On the various meanings of the word *flesh* see N.T.C. on Philippians, p. 77, footnote 55. Meaning c. is indicated here.

[154] The word rendered *recompense* is acc. of ἀνταπόδοσις, in the New Testament occurring only in this one passage. Here ἀντί expresses the idea of *full, complete return.* The noun ἀνταπόδομα means *requital,* used in a favorable sense in Luke 14:12; unfavorably in Rom. 11:9. The cognate verb ἀνταποδίδωμι, used in favorable sense (Luke 14:14; Rom. 11:35; I Thess. 3:9), in unfavorable sense (Rom. 12:19; II Thess. 1:6; Heb. 10:30), has the root-meaning *I render a full return for something received.* See my doctoral dissertation "The Meaning of the Preposition ἀντί in the New Testament," in the library of Princeton Seminary, Princeton, N.J., pp. 83, 84.

Now slaves, as a rule, are not heirs (Gen. 15:3; Rom. 8:15-17; Gal. 4:7). But the slaves to whom Paul is here referring *do* inherit, for their Master is Christ: **(It is) the Lord Christ (whom) y o u are serving.**[155] Let them therefore always live "as under the eye" of their Lord! For the expression "the Lord Christ" see also Rom. 16:18. These are the only two occurrences in the New Testament. The anointed Lord is the slave's employer. What a privilege and honor!

25. Paul continues, **For,** implying, perhaps, "Y o u should obey these instructions, for" **the wrong-doer will receive (the consequences of) what he has wrongly done. And there is no partiality.** According to Ridderbos this has reference solely to *the master* of the slave. It means that even though the slave may at times have to suffer an injustice from the hand of his master, that master will not be left unpunished (*op. cit.,* p. 230). Lenski, on the other hand, refers it solely to *the slave,* "The wrong done remains on the slave's back, and he will carry it to judgment." He points out that "masters are not mentioned until later" (*op. cit.,* p. 185). Lightfoot's opinion differs from both. Says he, "It seems best to suppose that both are included" (*op. cit.,* p. 229). I believe that this last position is the right one. My reason is that an almost exactly parallel idea is expressed in Eph. 6:8, only now with respect to the *right-*doer (instead of *wrong-*doer, as here in Col. 3:25), in a context in which it is definitely mentioned that the statement concerns *both bond and free.* The sentence in Ephesians is as follows, ". . . knowing that whatever good anyone does, he will receive the same again from the Lord, whether he be a slave or free." Says Lightfoot, commenting on Col. 3:25, "The warning is suggested by the case of the slave, but it is extended [in the next verse, Col. 4:1] to the case of the master."

If the slave fails to heed the admonitions that have been issued, he will reap what he has sown. No one in the church of Colosse must begin to think that since the apostle has dealt so kindly with Onesimus he also approves of what the latter did to his master. The rule (Gal. 6:7) is universal. It applies to every slave, no matter who he is. And it applies even to every master. With God there is no *partiality* (Lev. 19:15; Mal. 2:9; Acts 10:34;

---

[155] Some prefer to render this as an imperative, "Serve the Lord Christ," giving as a reason that otherwise the word "for" which introduces verse 25 has no meaning. However, whether one renders the verb as an imperative or as an indicative, in either case something has to be supplied in order to obtain a reasonable thought-connection. This is a case of "abbreviated expression." See N.T.C. on John 5:31. Besides, the difference is rather insignificant, as, in either case, the point is that Paul wants these slaves ever to bear in mind that they are really serving not first of all and most of all an earthly but a heavenly Master, and that this should be their attitude. The preceding "knowing that" would seem to point to the indicative here. Thus also A.V., A.R.V. (old and new), R.S.V., Berkeley.

Eph. 6:9; James 2:1) ; literally "no acceptance of face" (hence, "respect of persons") .[156]

4:1. By an easy transition the final admonition belonging to this table of domestic duties follows: **Masters,**[157] **render to y o u r slaves that which is fair and square, knowing that y o u also have a Master in heaven.** More literally translated, the first part would read, "Masters, that which is just and that which is fair,[158] to the slaves grant." The masters must remember that they, too, have a Master. The commended centurion understood this (Matt. 8:5-13, see especially verse 9) . The unmerciful servant of the parable related in Matt. 18:23-35 did not. Let the masters then realize that just as their slaves are accountable to them, so they, in turn, will have to answer to the Master in heaven. If they understand this, they will not treat their slaves harshly. They will "forbear threatening" (Eph. 6:9) , and will, instead, show the same consideration to their servants as they themselves expect to receive from the One who exercises authority over them. What we have here, therefore, is an application of the Golden Rule (Matt. 7:12) to the master-slave relationship.

The summary of admonitions addressed to separate groups ends, accordingly, with the mention of the all-sufficient, pre-eminent Master, even "the Lord Christ" (cf. 4:1 and 3:24) , for it is he who is the source of the believers' life, the One who is ever ready to enable every believer, to whatever group he belongs, to live to the glory of God.

Summary of Colossians 3:18–4:1

The all-sufficient Christ is also the source of life for household groups. They, too, must draw their inspiration from him, for it is from him that they derive *power* to do what is right and proper, the *purpose* to do all in the name of the Lord Jesus, and the *pattern* of obedience.

In the present paragraph wives are told to be submissive to their husbands; husbands to love their wives; next, children, to obey their parents; fathers, to be kind to their children; and finally, slaves to obey their masters, "not with eye-service as men-pleasers but with singleness of heart, fearing the Lord"; and masters, to render to their slaves what is fair and square, remembering that they (these masters) , too, have a Master in heaven.

---

[156] Moule has an interesting paragraph on the Greek word rendered *partiality* (*op. cit.*, p. 132) .

[157] In the original the vocatives *wives, husbands, children, fathers, slaves, masters* (3: 18–4:1) are all preceded by the generic article, a not uncommon usage (Gram. N.T., p. 757) .

[158] It is not true that ἰσότης must always be rendered *that which is equal* or *equality*. There are instances of the use of this word in the sense of *fairness* also in other authors (see M.M., p. 307) . Used in connection with the word *justice* (or "that which is just") it is natural to treat the two concepts as synonyms and to use the English idiom "fair and square" (or something similar) in the translation.

Because of their *reciprocal character* — admonitions being addressed not only to wives but also to their husbands, not only to children but also to their fathers, not only to slaves but also to their masters — these exhortations are eminently fair. That the counsel given in each case is fair also appears from its *content*. Wives are told to do that which accords with the manner in which they were created. Children, too, are not told to do whatever they please — which would be cruel advice — but to obey those who love them most and who are best qualified to judge what is best for them. Slaves are shown the only road to true, spiritual freedom, namely, to remember, in the midst of all their toil that they are really working "for the Lord." The same holds with respect to the other classes mentioned: husbands, fathers, and masters.

These admonitions were evidently addressed to household groups of *believers*. What happens when either the wife or the husband or the master is not a believer? What is the rule in such a case for, respectively, the husband or the wife or the slave? Scripture has not left us in the dark on this question. See the following passages: Acts 5:29; I Cor. 7:12-16; I Tim. 6:1 (contrast verse 2) ; Titus 2:9, 10; I Peter 2:18-21; 3:1, 2.

Outline of Chapter 4:2-18

Theme: *Christ, the Pre-eminent One, the Only and All-Sufficient Savior*

II. This Only and All-Sufficient Savior Is the Source of the Believers' Life, and Thus the Real Answer to the Perils by Which They Are Confronted, chapters 3 and 4

  C. Closing Admonitions, Greetings, etc., 4:2-18

4:2-4   1. Prayer urged

4:5, 6   2. Wise conduct and gracious speech stressed

4:7-9   3. A good word for Tychicus and for Onesimus, who have been sent with tidings and encouragement

4:10-15   4. Greetings

4:16   5. Exchange of letters requested

4:17   6. Crisp directive for Archippus

4:18   7. Closing salutation

CHAPTER IV

4   2 Persevere in prayer, keeping alert in it with thanksgiving; 3 at the same
time praying also for us, that God may open to us a door for the message, to
speak forth the mystery concerning Christ, on account of which I am in prison,
4 (praying) that I may make it clear, (and may speak) as I ought to speak.

4:2-4

I. *Prayer Urged*

2. As Paul is now approaching the close of the letter he issues certain admonitions of a general nature, as in 3:1-17; with emphasis on the positive, cf.
3:12-17. It is not surprising that, having spoken about *the word* (3:16), the
apostle now stresses the importance of *prayer,* for word and prayer belong
together: in the former God speaks to us, in the latter we to him. Says Paul:
Persevere in prayer. Prayer is the most important expression of the new life.
As such it is the means of obtaining for ourselves and for others the satisfaction of needs, both physical and spiritual. It is also a divinely appointed
weapon against the sinister attack of the devil and his angels, the vehicle for
confession of sin, and the instrument whereby the grateful soul pours out
its spontaneous adoration before the throne of God on high. Accordingly,
perseverance in prayer is urged. See also Acts 1:14; Rom. 12:12; Eph. 6:18.
This is in keeping with the teaching of Jesus in which he admonished his
disciples to persevere in prayer, and not to lose heart when a petition is not
immediately answered (Acts 18:1-8). Paul adds, **keeping alert in it.** This
admonition *to remain fully awake* in prayer reminds one of Matt. 26:41;
Mark 14:38; Luke 22:40, 46. Yet, in these Gospel passages the wakefulness
referred to is to be taken more literally, as the respective contexts indicate.
What the apostle has in mind is that, while continuing in prayer, the wor-
shiper shall be alive to such matters as: a. his own needs and those of the
family, church, country, world, b. the dangers that threaten the Christian
community, c. the blessings received and promised, and (last but not least)
d. the will of God. Cf. Acts 20:31; II Cor. 16:13; I Thess. 5:6; I Peter 5:8;
Rev. 3:2, 3. From the Greek verb which expresses this necessity of being
vigilant — a form of *grēgoréō* (I am awake, I remain alert) — the early Christians coined a favorite proper name: *Gregory.*

Now when one is deeply and humbly conscious of blessings received and promised he will express his gratitude to God. Hence, Paul continues: **with thanksgiving.** Cf. Eph. 5:20; 6:18; Phil. 4:6; I Thess. 5:18; and see also above, on Col. 3:15, 17. It is worthy of note that the apostle wedges his admonitions to particular groups (3:18–4:1) in between two reminders to give thanks to God (2:17 and 4:2), as if to say, "Wives, husbands, children, fathers, slaves, masters, obey these instructions *spontaneously*, prompted by gratitude for the many blessings received."

It should be borne in mind that the man who issues this directive is a prisoner. However, *this* prisoner is able to thank God even for his chains (Phil. 1:12-14). Surely, on the basis of the thought expressed so beautifully in Rom. 8:28 the believer can be thankful for whatever happens to him.

3, 4. In these prayers the needs of Paul and his companions must be included. Accordingly, the apostle continues, **at the same time praying also for us.**[159] Like Daniel before him (Dan. 2:18), and probably also Esther (Esth. 4:6), Paul felt the need of being remembered in prayer. Moreover, Timothy (Col. 1:1) and Epaphras (4:12) must be remembered similarly, and doubtless also those mentioned in 4:10, 11, 14. This is by no means the only time that the apostle asked to be thus remembered. See above, on 1:9, the parallel columns. See especially *Eph. 6:18-20*. This passage from Ephesians, in fact, should be constantly borne in mind in the interpretation of Col. 4:2-4 in its entirety. "Brothers, do pray for us" (I Thess. 5:25) was Paul's constant appeal. Now when he urged this upon his fellow-workers and fellow-believers he had something very definite in mind. Hence, stating the contemplated result of the prayer, and using an idiom that may have belonged to the common speech of that day,[160] as it is also a metaphor among us, he continues, **that God may open to us a door for the message.** A *door*, then as now, is an opportunity to enter, a means of approach or access. In the present context it is an opening for *the word* or *message*. Cf. I Cor. 16:9; II Cor. 2:12; Rev. 3:8. Now the apostle did not intend to say: Pray that *by my release from imprisonment* I may again be able to proclaim the message of salvation. No, he wanted that door right here and now! That this was not an absurd request, as if it would be impossible for a prisoner to have an open door, is shown by such a passage as Acts 28:30, 31. And if the objection be raised that such freedom as there presupposed did not necessarily continue, and that before his release the apostle was transferred from his "rented house" to the soldiers' barracks, or that in some other way he was placed under stricter custody, the answer is that even this added severity would not completely remove the open door, as is clearly shown in Phil. 1:12-18. As there

---

[159] It is not necessary to assume a literary or epistolary plural here, nor in I Thess. 2:18; 3:1. See N.T.C. on these passages.
[160] A. Deissmann, *op. cit.*, p. 300, footnote 2.

indicated, from a certain point of view the seeming disadvantage was in reality an advantage, as Paul's chain made it very clear that his was not a fair-weather religion, but something far more precious and real. Nevertheless, humanly speaking, circumstances could easily change. When Paul made this prayer-request was he thinking, perhaps, of a summons before the Roman tribunal for a hearing, probably not the first one? And is he now saying, in effect, "O Colossians, do pray that, when we are called to give an account before the authorities, we may speak forth very freely and that our message may also gain entrance into the hearts of those who hear"? Besides, testifying openly and clearly before every type of audience and under all circumstances is not easy. Hence, this man of God who in a sense already had an open door is not at all inconsistent when he now asks that prayer may be offered so that he may (at all times and under all circumstances) have an open door. This explanation is also in line with the parallel passage, Eph. 6:19, and with what follows immediately here in Colossians, namely, **to speak forth the mystery concerning Christ,**[161] its content being Christ himself as the source of salvation, full and free, for both Gentile and Jew, a secret no longer *concealed* but now, O glorious paradox!, a *secret* fully *revealed,* and not revealed only but *realized* in the hearts and lives of people of every class, station, and nationality. See further on 1:26, 27 and on 2:2 above. Paul continues, **on account of which I am in prison,** hence all the more in need of, and entitled to, being remembered in y o u r prayers (cf. 1:24). That it was indeed as a result of the proclamation of this mystery — especially its disclosure *to the Gentiles!* — that Paul was fettered and in custody follows from the many references in which it is clearly indicated that the Jews, filled with fury because Paul preached the gospel to Jew *and Gentile* without distinction, had accused him before the civil authorities (Acts 18:12, 13; 21:28; 22:21-30; 23:26-30; 24:1-9; 25:1, 2, 6, 7; 26:19-21, 32).

Now Paul wishes to be remembered in prayer for two reasons: a. so that he may continue to proclaim the blessed contents of the mystery, as has been indicated, and b. that he may do this in the proper manner. As to b., therefore, he continues: **(praying) that I may make it clear, (and may speak) as I ought to speak.** When a *good* message is proclaimed in a *bad* way it can do more harm than good. How often have not those who, though innocent, were imprisoned or otherwise molested, made matters worse both for themselves and for the cause which they were defending, by failing to observe this truth. When the apostle now asks to be remembered in prayer so that he may not fall into this error but may speak *as he should,* he probably had in mind some or all of the following particulars: a. Pray that I may speak *clearly* ("that I may make it clear"), b. *boldly,* that is, without fear or restraint ("telling all," see Eph. 6:19, ἐν παρρησίᾳ), c. yet also *graciously* (see

---

[161] or simply, "the mystery, namely, Christ." See N.T.C. on I Tim. 3:16. Christ is in any event the heart and essence of the mystery.

the context, Col. 4:6a), and d. *wisely*, so that I may know exactly what approach to use when questioned by groups or individuals of various backgrounds: visitors who come to see me in prison, soldiers who guard me, and the Roman authorities before whom I may be summoned.

---

5 Conduct yourselves wisely toward outsiders, making the most of the opportunity. 6 Let y o u r speech always be gracious, seasoned with salt, so that y o u may know how to answer each individual.

4:5, 6

II. *Wise Conduct and Gracious Speech Stressed*

5. In the spirit of the principles to which Paul has bound himself and in connection with which he has just now asked the Colossians to remember him and his companions in prayer (see verses 3 and 4 above) he now urges them to adhere to a similar way of life. Says he, **Conduct yourselves wisely toward outsiders.** To the Jew every non-Jew was an "outsider." And to the Christian every non-Christian is, in a sense, an outsider. See I Cor. 5:12, 13; I Thess. 4:12; I Tim. 3:7. In the days of the early church believers were often slandered by these outsiders. For example, they were called *atheists* because they served no visible gods, *unpatriotic* because they did not burn incense before the image of the emperor, and *immoral* because, of necessity, they would often meet behind locked doors. The apostle knew that the best way to defeat this slander was for Christians daily to conduct themselves not only *virtuously* instead of *wickedly* but also *wisely* instead of *foolishly*. See Appendix, *Scripture on Tactfulness*. It was then as it is now: in the long run the reputation of the gospel depends on the conduct of its devotees. It is as if the apostle were saying, "Behave wisely toward outsiders, always bearing in mind that though few men read the sacred scrolls, all men read y o u."

But not only does such wise conduct, so that believers use the best means to reach the highest goal, serve as a weapon against vilification and character-assassination, it also has a positive purpose, namely, to win outsiders for Christ. Paul was fully aware of the fact that the most effective way for Christians to spread the gospel so that it would be accepted was to conduct themselves in such a manner that the heathen would say, "Behold how they love each other, and, in spite of all we have said about them, even love us and treat us with kindness, returning good for evil." That Paul had this positive purpose in mind is also evident from the fact that he adds: **making the most of the opportunity.** If the participle used in the original has fully retained its etymological significance, the apostle literally said, ". . . *buying* *up* the opportunity." The sense then would be "Do not just sit there and wait for opportunity to fall into y o u r lap, but go after it. Yes, buy it." "Buy up the entire stock of opportunity" (Moule, *op. cit.,* p. 134) . "Count not the cost. Winning even one soul for Christ is worth it (cf. Prov. 11:30; Rom. 11:14) , and so is salvation itself" (Matt. 13:44, 45) . But in any event the minimal meaning is, "Avail yourselves of every opportunity to be a blessing to others."

One thought which, though not here expressed, may very well have been in the background is this: the days are evil and are speeding toward the great consummation of all things. "The night is far gone; the day is at hand." Therefore, make the most of the opportunity while y o u have it. Cf. Rom. 13:11, 12; I Cor. 7:29; Gal. 6:9, 10; and especially Eph. 5:16.

6. See also on Col. 3:8, 9, 16. Paul has asked the Colossians to pray that *his* manner of speaking might always be the very best (see above, on verse 4) . So, having as it were set the example, he now admonishes the addressees to be similarly careful in the use of *their* tongue: Let y o u r speech always be gracious . . . Note *always,* that is, both in addressing a group or in talking to the neighbor, both when conversing with an equal or when replying to someone in authority, to rich and poor alike, not only in proclaiming the message of salvation but also in discussing the weather. When gracious speech becomes their habit they will not use improper language when suddenly confronted with a difficult situation; for example, when summoned to appear before a worldly judge or when persecuted for the faith.

Just what is "gracious speech"? By non-Christians of Paul's day the same expression was used. However, what they meant by it was *sparkling conversation,* speech dotted with witty or clever remarks. When Paul uses the term he has reference to the type of language that results from the operation of God's grace in the heart. *Negatively,* such speech will not be abusive (Rom. 1:29-32; II Cor. 12:20; Gal. 5:19-21, 26; Eph. 4:31; Titus 3:2) . Neither will it be vindictive. It will be patterned after the example of Christ who "when he was reviled did not revile in return" (I Peter 2:23) . Positively, it will be truthful and loving. Perhaps the best *description* of gracious speech is found in the words of Paul himself: "speaking truth in love" (Eph. 4:15) , and the best *example* in the words of Jesus, "Father, forgive them, for they know not what they do" (Luke 23:34) .

A further description of this kind of gracious speech is: **seasoned with salt.** Those whom the Lord calls "the salt of the earth" (Matt. 5:13; Mark 9:49, 50; Luke 14:34, 35) must not be insipid in their language. Salt prevents corruption. It is hard to believe that this idea was absent from the mind of Paul, for in the parallel passage he says, "Let *no corrupt* speech proceed from y o u r mouth, but only such (speech) as is good for edification, as fits the need, that it may impart grace to those who hear" (Eph. 4:29) . But not only does salt have preservative power. It also has pungency and flavor. Speech flavored with salt is, accordingly, not empty or insipid, but thought-provoking and worth-while. It is not a waste of time. Also, such speech does not repel. It attracts, has spiritual charm. Accordingly, it is distinctive: a Christian is known by his speech as well as by his conduct.

Now in their conversations believers must be mindful not only of the particular occasion that evokes their remarks but also of the person addressed. Hence, the apostle continues: **so that y o u may know how to answer each individual.** In other words, they should speak the right word at the right time to the right person. This reminds us of I Peter 3:15, "But in y o u r hearts reverence Christ as Lord, always being ready to make a defense to anyone who asks y o u to give an account for the hope that is in y o u, yet with gentleness and reverence." The Holy Spirit himself will help them to do this. Hence, they need not be frightened (Matt. 10:19, 20; Mark 13:11). Christ will give them a mouth and wisdom (Luke 21:14, 15).

---

7 All my affairs will Tychicus make known to y o u, the beloved brother and faithful minister and fellow-servant in the Lord, 8 whom I am sending to y o u for this very purpose, that y o u may know our circumstances and that he may strengthen y o u r hearts. 9 (He is) accompanied by Onesimus, the faithful and beloved brother, who is one of y o u. They will acquaint y o u with everything (that has taken place) here.

4:7-9

III. *A Good Word for Tychicus and for Onesimus, Who Have Been Sent with Tidings from Rome and with Encouragement*

7, 8. All my affairs will Tychicus make known to y o u. Tychicus [162] was one of Paul's intimate friends and highly valued envoys. He hailed from the province of Asia, and had accompanied the apostle when at the close of the third missionary journey the latter was returning from Greece through Macedonia and then across into Asia Minor and so to Jerusalem on a charitable mission (Acts 20:4); that is, on that trip Tychicus had traveled in advance of Paul from Macedonia to Troas, and had been waiting for the apostle in that city. And now, some four years later, having spent some time with Paul in Rome during the latter's first Roman imprisonment, Tychicus had been commissioned by the apostle to carry to their destination not only the epistle to the Colossians, as implied here in Col. 4:7, 8, and the one to Phi-

---

[162] For the meaning of the name see N.T.C. on Philippians, pp. 138, 139, footnote 116, where the explanation of many other personal names is also given. For more on Tychicus, e.g., his relation to Paul after the latter's first Roman imprisonment, see N.T.C. on Titus 3:12 and on II Tim. 4:12.

lemon, as a comparison of 4:9 and Philem. 1, 8-22, would appear to indicate, but also the letter that has been transmitted to us as the Epistle to the Ephesians (see Eph. 6:21, 22, which is almost identical with Col. 4:7, 8). The description of Tychicus as **the beloved brother and faithful minister and fellow-servant in the Lord** is nearly like that of Epaphras (though not in word-order). There is *essential* identity. Hence, see on Col. 1:7. And the reasons for recommending Tychicus so highly are also similar to those given in the case of Epaphras. It stands to reason that Tychicus, having just now spent some time with Paul and being a man of sound judgment, would be the right person to supply all the necessary information about Paul and his companions and fellow-Christians in Rome. Besides, paper was not as plentiful and cheap as it is today, the circumstances under which Paul, the "aged" prisoner (see on Philem. 9) had to dictate his letters were not altogether favorable, certain things are better *said* than *written;* hence, for such and similar reasons Paul continues: **whom I am sending** [163] **to y o u for this very purpose, that y o u may know our circumstances.**[164] Not only this, however, but also, **and that he may strengthen y o u r hearts,** probably by stilling y o u r fears (cf. Phil. 1:12-14), by delivering to y o u this very letter, and in general by orally supplying the "atmosphere" of consolation and spiritual strengthening based upon the promises of God.

9. The apostle continues: **(He is) accompanied by Onesimus, the faithful and beloved brother, who is one of y o u. They will acquaint y o u with everything (that has taken place) here.**

It is not necessary to repeat what is said about Onesimus in Introduction IV B and in N.T.C. on Philemon (see especially on verses 8-22) in this volume. The emphatic recommendation of Onesimus to the entire church of Colosse was, and no doubt was meant to be, a powerful support for the plea in behalf of him which Paul addressed to Philemon, the slave's master, one of the members of that church. What has been affirmed by many a commentator, namely, that the very preservation of the Epistle to Philemon proves that this plea was successful is probably correct. By calling Onesimus "the faithful and beloved brother" the apostle underscores before the entire church verse 16 of his personal letter to Philemon. By permitting Onesimus to stand at the side of Tychicus as an informant regarding everything pertaining to Paul and the church in Rome the apostle is telling the Colossians, including Philemon, that he regards the man who by God's transforming grace is now living up the meaning of his name — Onesimus: *profitable, helpful* — to be also *wholly reliable.*

---

[163] ἔπεμψα, epistolary aorist.
[164] Though the reading "that he may know y o u r circumstances" has the support of p⁴⁶ and other manuscripts, it must be considered inferior because of the context (see verse 9b).

10 Aristarchus, my fellow-prisoner, greets y o u; so does Mark, the cousin of Barnabas — concerning whom y o u received instructions; if he comes to y o u receive him — ; 11 and Jesus who is called Justus. Of those who are of the circumcision these are the only co-workers for the kingdom of God who have been a comfort to me. 12 Epaphras, who is one of y o u, a servant of Christ Jesus, greets y o u, always wrestling for y o u in his prayers that y o u may stand firm, mature and fully assured in all the will of God. 13 For I can testify concerning him that he has put himself to much trouble for y o u and for those in Laodicea and those in Hierapolis. 14 Luke, the beloved physician, greets y o u, and so does Demas. 15 Extend greetings to the brothers in Laodicea, and to Nympha and the church in her house.

23 Epaphras, my fellow-prisoner in Christ Jesus, greets y o u, 24 (and so do) Mark, Aristarchus, Demas, and Luke, my fellow-workers.

Col. 4:10-15　　　　　　　　　　　　　　　　Philem. 23, 24

IV. *Greetings*

This section in Colossians may be divided into two parts: a. vss. 10-14, in which three of Paul's companions of Jewish birth — Aristarchus, Mark, and Jesus Justus — , and also three of Gentile birth — Epaphras, Luke, and Demas — send greetings to the Colossians; and b. verse 15, in which the apostle requests the Colossians to forward his greetings to "the brothers in Laodicea and to Nympha and the church in her house."

A look at the parallel columns reveals the following:

(1) Due largely to the fact that in the Colossian passage Paul enlarges on Mark, on "those of the circumcision," and on Epaphras, this passage is lengthier by far than the corresponding list of greetings in Philemon.

(2) In Colossians six men send greetings, in Philemon only five. Jesus Justus is not mentioned in the smaller letter. We do not know for what reason his name is omitted. The order of the names also is different. The Colossian list mentions Aristarchus, Mark, Jesus Justus, Epaphras, Luke, and Demas in that sequence. In Philemon the order is: Epaphras, Mark, Aristarchus, Demas, and Luke.

Taking the names one by one, in the order in which they are mentioned in Colossians, we begin with

186

Aristarchus

10a. Aristarchus, my fellow-prisoner, greets y o u. The native town of this man, or at least the place with which he was mainly associated, was Thessalonica. At Ephesus, during Paul's lengthy ministry there (third missionary journey, outward bound) he was with the apostle, and, recognized by the Ephesian rioters as one of Paul's traveling companions, he, along with another man from Macedonia, Gaius, was on the spur of the moment seized by the mob (Acts 19:29). Later we again find him in Paul's company on the return from this same journey. In fact, Tychicus, from "Asia," (see above, on verse 7) and Aristarchus and Secundus from Thessalonica, are mentioned as Paul's travel-companions in the same verse (Acts 20:4). This was the trip on which delegates from various churches of predominantly Gentile origin were carrying aid to the needy in Jerusalem. We meet Aristarchus once more in the very beginning of the account of Paul's Voyage Dangerous (Acts 27:2). He started out with Paul and probably accompanied the apostle all the way to Rome. (For the idea of Lightfoot, that Aristarchus disembarked at Myra, there is no evidence whatever.) From Rome he is now sending greetings both to the Colossians and to Philemon.

Now a glance at the parallel columns above indicates a rather striking peculiarity that requires some attention. In Colossians Aristarchus is called "my fellow-prisoner," but in Philemon no such qualifying designation is added. Along with others he is designated "my fellow-worker" (see on Philem. 1). Conversely, in Philemon it is Epaphras who is described as "my fellow-prisoner in Christ Jesus," but in Colossians, though much is said about Epaphras, that specific designation is not used with respect to him. From this circumstance and from the fact that Aristarchus was not "under arrest" when Paul as a *prisoner* among other *prisoners* started on his journey to Rome, and that Epaphras, too, somewhat later, was delegated to Rome *as a free man,* the probably warranted inference has been drawn that when Aristarchus, here in Col. 4:10, and Epaphras, in Philem. 23, are called *fellow-prisoners,* this must not be taken in a *strictly* literal sense. These men may well have volunteered to share Paul's imprisonment, assisting him in every possible way. They must have been glad to do this since they, as well as Paul, were captives in Christ's train (II Cor. 2:14; cf. 10:5).[165]

---

[165] The root meaning of αἰχμάλωτος is *one caught with the spear;* hence, a *war-captive,* and so simply *a captive* or *prisoner.* See N.T.C. on II Tim. 3:6. It is not wrong, therefore, to render συναιχμάλωτος *fellow-prisoner.* Since the apostle was himself a prisoner in the literal sense of that term it is hard to believe that in speaking of "fellow-prisoners" he was using this term in an *exclusively* spiritual sense, though it must be admitted that not only in II Cor. 2:14 but also elsewhere the apostle uses military terminology with respect to the service rendered to the cause of Christ (Phil. 2:25; Philem. 2; and II Tim. 2:3). Paul's use of the word *captive* or *prisoner,* even when used in a literal sense, often has a spiritual over-

Mark

10b. So does Mark, the cousin of Barnabas.

Mark, the one whom we recognize as the writer of the second Gospel, was also associated with Paul in Rome at this time, and as such is sending greetings both to the Colossians and to Philemon. We now learn that he was a cousin of Barnabas. This could be the reason why, some twelve years earlier, the latter had treated him with such extraordinary kindness. This happened just after Mark, on Paul's first missionary journey, had deserted his senior partners and had gone home. Because of this act of disloyalty and cowardice Paul had refused to accept the suggestion of Barnabas that Mark be given another chance and be taken along on the second missionary journey (Acts 15:36-41). There had been "a sharp contention" about this matter between Paul and Barnabas. But by now, Mark seems to have redeemed himself. The apostle no longer regards him as a liability, but recommends him warmly, and even includes him among those who have been a comfort to him (see on verse 11). Moreover, this favorable attitude continued, for even in his very last letter that has come down to us Paul says, "Mark . . . is very useful to me for (the) ministry" (II Tim. 4:11).

What factors or agencies did the Holy Spirit use in bringing about this favorable change in the life of John Mark? In all probability one or more of the following:

a. "The kindly tutelage of Barnabas, that true 'son of encouragement.'" Not *entirely* was it due to this but "no doubt in great measure" (F. F. Bruce, *op. cit.*, p. 305).

b. The stern discipline of Paul, shown in refusing to take Mark with him on the second journey. Perhaps Mark needed exactly that seeming harshness.

c. The influence of Peter who calls Mark "my son" (I Peter 5:13). A consistent early tradition links these two men. Peter knew *by experience* that there was hope for those who had fallen into the sins of disloyalty and cowardice.

The Holy Spirit may well have used all three factors and others also to perform his marvelous work in the mind and conscience of "the man who came back."

Paul continues, **concerning whom y o u received instructions; if he comes to y o u receive him.**

What these instructions were and who had issued them we do not know. Either it was Paul himself, in which case he here underscores what he had previously ordered regarding Mark; or else it was Barnabas, Peter, or some other person deemed to be invested with a degree of authority, in which

---

tone. Thus, when he refers to himself as "a prisoner," he adds "of Christ Jesus." We may well assume, therefore, that here, too, the word "fellow-captive" or "fellow-prisoner" has that spiritual overtone.

case the apostle here endorses these earlier directives. The first alternative would seem the more probable. In any event it is clear that Mark, being now somewhere in Paul's vicinity, was about to make a trip to Asia Minor, and that his itinerary would include Colosse. The apostle bespeaks a whole-hearted "acceptance" for him.

There is no reason to doubt that Mark made this tour, even though there is no further specific record of it. There are, however, two lines of evidence which link Mark with the churches of the general region of Asia Minor during apostolic times:

a. We know that Peter was closely associated with the churches of this region, for he addressed his first epistle to them (I Peter 1:1, 2). Also his second? Cf. II Peter 3:1. And in Peter's letter *Mark's* greetings are conveyed to these churches (I Peter 5:13).

b. We also know that during Paul's second Roman imprisonment Mark was at a place where he could easily be picked up by Timothy, who at that time was in all probability continuing his work in *Ephesus,* province of "Asia." See N.T.C., on I and II Timothy and Titus, p. 43, 321.

Jesus Justus

11. . . . and Jesus who is called Justus. Of those who are of the circumcision these are the only fellow-workers for the kingdom of God who have been a comfort to me.[166]

The name of this Jew who had become a Christian is a combination of the Greek equivalent (Jesus) of Joshua or Jeshua, and a Latin surname (Justus), which, meaning "the just" or "the righteous," may well have been regarded by those of Jewish origin as representing the Hebrew *Zadok* (I Kings 1:32); cf. also *Zedekiah* (Jer. 1:3, "Jehovah is righteousness" or "righteousness is of Jehovah"). The same cognomen is found also in Acts 1:23, "Joseph called Barsabbas, who was surnamed Justus," a Jewish Christian, and in Acts 18:7, "Titus Justus," a Roman or Latin who had been attracted to the synagogue. The name Justus was rather common among both Jews and non-Jews, and could be used both by itself or as a surname.

About this man (not mentioned in Philemon) we have no other authentic item of information than that which is given here in Col. 4:11. However, the little that is said about him, as he joins others in sending greetings to the believers in the church of Colosse, is very favorable. We are told that of

---

[166] Though not all are in agreement with respect to the proper punctuation and grammatical construction of verse 11b, it is clear that the word *circumcision* does not end a clause. The sense is not: "Aristarchus, Mark, and Jesus Justus, who are of the circumcision; these are the only fellow-workers for the kingdom of God," etc. Paul certainly would not have denied that such men as Epaphras, Luke, and others were also fellow-workers and had also been a source of consolation to him. The idea is that *from among those of Jewish origin* these three men were the only fellow-workers who had been a comfort to him.

Jewish Christians the three persons just mentioned — namely, Aristarchus, Mark, and Jesus Justus — [167] were the only fellow-workers who had been of *comfort* — that shade of meaning of the word παρηγορία predominates here — to Paul. For the term "fellow-workers" see on Philem. 1. Note the striking modifier after the word *fellow-workers:* "fellow-workers *for the kingdom of God.*" Did the apostle thus qualify the term in order to convey the idea, "Especially among the Jews with their great emphasis upon *the kingdom* I should have received more co-operation"? Besides, had he not preached "the kingdom of God" among these very people almost from the moment of his arrival in Rome? See Acts 28:31. In that passage and also here in Col. 4:11 the term "kingdom of God" obviously has reference to the divine realm as a *present* reality. It indicates the dispensation of salvation which in its present phase began with the coming of Christ. God is using Paul and others as his agents in the establishment of this reign of God in the hearts of men. See also on Col. 1:13.

It must not escape our attention that the apostle's statement with reference to these three men as the *only* Jewish-Christian fellow-workers who had been a comfort to him implies deep disappointment with other people of his own race. Paul was painfully aware of his estrangement from his own people (Rom. 9:1-5). And he was not insensitive to the fact that the Judaists (Jews who confessed Jesus but over-emphasized the law) regarded him with suspicion (Acts 15:1, 2, 24; 21:20, 21; Gal. 2:12; Phil. 3:23). It cannot be wrong to regard Phil. 1:14-17; 2:20, 21; II Tim. 4:16 as shedding further light on the apostle's feelings anent this matter. All the more, therefore, does he appreciate the co-operation he is receiving from Aristarchus, Mark, and Jesus Justus!

Epaphras

12-13. To the greetings from three Jewish Christians Paul now adds those from three of Gentile origin, namely, Epaphras, Luke, and Demas. Verses 12 and 13 concern Epaphras, the evangelist of Colosse, Laodicea, and Hierapolis. To some extent the interpretation of these verses has already been given. With respect to this brother and the apostle's high regard for him see Introduction III A 1; see also on Col. 1:7. In his quality as "fellow-prisoner"

---

[167] The combination "Aristarchus . . . and Mark . . . and Jesus who is called Justus" (verses 10, 11) would seem to make it well-nigh certain that all three were *Jewish* Christians. Though a few modifiers are added, these three names are, nevertheless, mentioned in one breath, being linked by ". . . and . . . and . . ." I cannot agree, therefore, with A. S. Peake who, in commenting on this passage in the *Expositor's Greek Testament* (Vol. III, p. 546), states, "Aristarchus is probably not included, for he went as one of the deputation sent by the Gentile Christians with the collection for the church at Jerusalem," nor with Lenski who defends this same idea even more vigorously: "He was a Thessalonian, and thus not a Jew." Acts 17:1-4 implies that among the converts at Thessalonica there were also some Jews.

(Philem. 23) Epaphras has been discussed in connection with Aristarchus (see above on verse 10a). On the three cities to which reference is made in verse 13 see Introduction II and III. Paul writes: **Epaphras, who is one of y o u, a servant of Christ Jesus, greets y o u.** In the spiritual sense Paul uses the word *doulos* (servant) specifically only with respect to himself (Rom. 1:1; Gal. 1:10; Phil. 1:1; Titus 1:1), Timothy (Phil. 1:1) and Epaphras (here in Col. 4:12). A servant of Christ Jesus is one who has been bought with a price and is therefore owned by his Master, on whom he is completely dependent, to whom he owes undivided allegiance and to whom he ministers with gladness of heart, in newness of spirit, and in the enjoyment of perfect freedom (Rom. 6:18, 22; 7:6), receiving from him a glorious reward (Col. 3:24). Every true Christian is in a sense such a servant. See N.T.C. on Phil. 1:1 for more on this concept. It is to the church in Colosse and to Philemon that Epaphras is sending his "best regards."

Paul continues: **always wrestling for y o u in his prayers.** For "wrestling" or "striving" in prayer see also Rom. 15:30, and cf. what the apostle says about himself in Col. 2:1. Epaphras was deeply in earnest as he again and again invoked God's favor upon the Colossians and besought the Lord to help them so that they might not be led astray but might stand firm in the true faith. Further, **that y o u may stand firm, mature.** For the meaning of the word "mature" see above on 1:28; also N.T.C. on Phil. 3:15 (especially p. 176, footnote 156 there).

When Paul further defines the object or contemplated result of Epaphras' prayer by adding, **fully assured in all the will of God,** he must be using the perfect participle "fully assured" in the sense of the cognate noun in Col. 2:2 (see on that passage). Thorough, rich, gratifying insight into all spiritual matters is meant; understanding which not only penetrates the mind but also fills the heart with satisfying conviction. Epaphras does not want these churches that are dear to his heart to be deluded by error. They must remain true to their confession of faith in the all-sufficient Savior Jesus Christ. It is for that reason that he wrestles for them in prayer.

And it is exactly that wrestling in prayer which is probably the best explanation of the words, **For I can testify concerning him that he has put himself to much trouble for y o u and for those in Laodicea and those in Hierapolis.** The Colossian Heresy had undoubtedly affected all three churches founded by Epaphras. Hence, it is in connection with the danger that threatened them all that he betakes himself to the throne of grace in earnest and repeated intercession.[168]

---

[168] This explanation is in harmony with the context. Another interpretation, the one suggested, for example, by E. F. Scott, *The Epistles of Paul to the Colossians, to Philemon and to the Ephesians,* p. 90, would connect the "trouble," to which Epaphras put himself, with the earthquake which about the year A. D. 60 shook the Lycus Valley. See above, Introduction, II B. Paul, according to this theory, is conveying the idea that Epaphras had been laboring to provide financial help for the

Luke

14a. Luke, the beloved physician, greets y o u.

From a comparison with verse 11 we learn that Luke was a Christian from the Gentiles. The present passage shows that he was at Rome just now and was a doctor and a person of amiable personality, beloved by his Lord, by believers generally, and by Paul specifically. He was to become the author of the third Gospel. Note that he and Mark, who wrote the second Gospel, were together in Rome. It is not at all surprising but gratifying that in spite of lengthy arguments to the contrary, thoroughly conservative scholarship is more and more arriving at the conclusion that in composing his own Gospel Luke made use of Mark's as one of his sources.[169]

Luke was a remarkable person, always loyal to Paul, to the gospel, and to his Lord. Frequently he had been Paul's companion in travel, as is indicated by the "we" sections in Acts (16:10-17; 20:6-16; 21; 27; 28). He had been with Paul on the second missionary journey, namely, at Troas and at Philippi. He had evidently been left behind at the latter place (Acts 16:17-19). Toward the close of the third tour he seems again to have joined Paul at Philippi (Acts 20:6), and he accompanied him to Jerusalem. For a while we do not see him. But suddenly he re-appears, for he is in Paul's company on the long and dangerous sea-journey to Rome (Acts 27). And it is from Rome during this, Paul's first, Roman imprisonment, that he is sending his greetings to the Colossians and also to Philemon. Later, the apostle, experiencing his second and final Roman imprisonment, would write these touching words, "Luke is the only one with me" (II Tim. 4:11a). This would be followed by, "Pick up Mark and bring him with you. . . ."

Luke and Paul had much in common. Both were educated men, men of culture. Both were big-hearted, broad-minded, sympathetic. Both were believers and missionaries.

Demas

14b. . . . and so does Demas.

Yes, Demas, too, is a fellow-worker (Philem. 24), one of Paul's assistants in the ministry who wishes to be remembered to the church in Colosse and to Philemon. Paul does not yet know that one day this man will be a deep disappointment to him, and that with reference to this assistant in the gospel-ministry he will, during his second Roman imprisonment, write these

---

stricken inhabitants. However, there is no precise and consistent testimony with reference either to the exact date or extent of this earthquake. Besides, had the apostle meant this, we might have expected a clearer reference to it.
[169] Cf. Zahn, *Einleitung*, II, pp. 404 ff. (Eng. trans., III, pp. 101 ff.); H. J. Cadbury, *The Style and Literacy Method of Luke*, pp. 73 ff.; and N. B. Stonehouse, *Origins of the Synoptic Gospels*, p. 49.

plaintive words, "Demas has deserted me, because he fell in love with the present world, and has gone to Thessalonica" (II Tim. 4:10). And with that tragic statement Demas will disappear from sacred history.

15. Having finished the section in which six men—three of Jewish and three of Gentile birth—send their greetings to the Colossians, the apostle now asks that certain greetings be forwarded to believing neighbors. His request is: **Extend greetings to the brothers in Laodicea, and to Nympha and the church in her house.**[170]

Note that Hierapolis (see on verse 13 above) is no longer mentioned. We simply do not know what may have been the reason for this. The apostle wants the addressees to convey his greetings to the brothers in nearby Laodicea. On the *geography* of the three cities — Colosse, Laodicea, Hierapolis — in their relation to each other and to Ephesus, and on their *history*, see Introduction II A (including maps 1, 2, 3), and II B. In Laodicea Paul singles out for separate greetings Nympha and the church in her house.[171] Did he know Nympha personally? Perhaps a group of Laodiceans living close together, but separated at some inconvenient distance from the others, met at her house for worship. So special greetings are extended to them and their hostess. For the house-church idea see Philem. 2.

---

16 And when this letter has been read among y o u, see to it that it is read also in the church of the Laodiceans, and that y o u also read the one from Laodicea.

---

[170] Or, "and to Nymphas and the church in his house." Not only do the manuscripts vary between Nympha (feminine) and Nymphas (masculine), but correspondingly also between "in *her* house" and "in *his* house." Some even have "in *their* house." In the latter case it is probable that a scribe erroneously included a reference to "the brothers" and so arrived at the phrase "in *their* house." As between *her* and *his,* the textual attestation for the former is qualitatively the strongest. Besides, it is not difficult to understand that a scribe, not deeming it proper to speak of the church in *her* house, would change this to *his.* All in all, therefore, it would seem that the reading "Nympha and the church in her house" deserves the preference. For the names Nympha, Nymphas, see N.T.C. on Philippians, p. 139, footnote 116.
[171] F. W. Beare, in his comment on this passage (in *The Interpreter's Bible,* Vol. 11, p. 239) opines that it was the church of Hierapolis which met at the home of Nympha. But, after the analogy of Rom. 16:23, written from Corinth (see Rom. 16:1, 23; cf. I Cor. 1:14), and I Cor. 16:19, written from Ephesus (I Cor. 16:8), it would seem more natural that when a house-church and the owner of the house are mentioned in close connection with a city (clearly implied or even mentioned by name), this church belongs to that particular community and not to some other place on the map.

4:16

V. *Exchange of Letters Requested*

16. And when this letter has been read among y o u. The letter, after it
has been delivered to the proper ecclesiastical authorities at Colosse by
Tychicus, will be read by the lector to the congregation assembled for worship. Now when this has taken place, says Paul, **see to it that it is read also
in the church of the Laodiceans.** The believers of nearby Laodicea will not
only be *interested* in this letter coming from the beloved apostle Paul, they
will also be spiritually *benefited* by it. So it must also be read in their midst.
So far there are no difficulties. But now Paul continues: **and that y o u also
read the one from Laodicea.** Altogether too large a literature has been built
up around these few words. Countless conjectures have been made regarding this "letter from Laodicea." [172]

The main ones are as follows. Paul had reference to:

(1) *A letter written by the Laodiceans.*

According to most of the advocates of this view it was addressed to the
apostle himself.

This theory was strongly advocated, among others, by Theodore of Mop-
suestia (A. D. 350-428), classical representative of the school of Antioch.
John Calvin's defense of this view was no less vigorous. Said he, "Afflicted
with double mental aberration are those who think that it was written by
Paul to the Laodiceans. I have no doubt that it was an epistle sent to Paul,
the perusal of which might be profitable to the Colossians, as neighboring
towns usually have many things in common. However, . . . some worthless
person, I know not who, had the audacity to forge an epistle that is so insipid that it is impossible to conceive of anything more foreign to the spirit
of Paul." [173]

No doubt Calvin was influenced by eagerness to reject the spurious *Epistle
to the Laodiceans;* perhaps also by hesitancy to accept a "lost" Pauline
epistle.

Among the many objections to theory (1) are the following:

a. If Paul had this letter in his possession, why should he ask the Colossians to get it from the Laodiceans?

b. How did he know that the Laodiceans had made a copy of their letter,
before sending it to Paul? But if they had made such a copy, how did the

---

[172] See J. B. Lightfoot's summary of theories, *op. cit.*, p. 274 and his lengthy discussion that follows the summary.
[173] The original statement is found in *Commentarius In Epistolam Pauli Ad Colossenses (Corpus Reformatorum,* vol. LXXX), Brunsvigae, 1895. — The marginal explanation of Col. 4:16 in the Dutch *Staten Bijbel* (I own a copy printed in 1643!)
defends the same view.

apostle know that they would be willing to give it to the Colossians and to let them read it to the church assembled for worship?

c. Why should he place these two on a par: a letter written by himself to the Colossians, under inspiration of the Holy Spirit, and an uninspired communication supposedly sent to him by the Laodiceans?

(2) *A letter written by Paul from Laodicea; perhaps Galatians or I Timothy or I Thessalonians or II Thessalonians.*

Objections:

a. Although Paul may very well have passed through Laodicea (see Introduction III A), namely, on his way to Ephesus (third missionary journey), the design of that trip was to confirm already established churches along the route of travel, and to reach Ephesus in order to spend some time there, as he had promised. On the trip there must have been little or no time for letter writing.

b. In all probability none of the letters to which reference was made was written from Laodicea. Galatians and I and II Thessalonians seem to have been written from Corinth (N.T.C. on I and II Thessalonians, pp. 15, 16). I Timothy probably originated in Macedonia (Philippi? see N.T.C. on I and II Timothy and Titus, pp. 39-41).

(3) *A letter written by Paul to Philemon.*

Since, according to this theory Philemon lived in Laodicea, this letter when it reached Colosse via Laodicea could be called "the letter from Laodicea."

Objection:

This theory has been discussed in some detail. See Introduction IV B; and see on Philem. 1, 2. Philemon, in all probability, did not live in Laodicea but in Colosse. Accordingly, there is no solid support for this view.

(4) *The letter to the Laodiceans which today is known as "the Apocryphal Epistle to the Laodiceans."* [174]

---

[174] It is a short apocryphal writing that occurs in many manuscripts of the Vulgate. It usually follows Colossians. But it antedates the Vulgate and can be found in old-Latin manuscripts before Jerome. And even in the Greek-speaking portion of the church between the fourth and eighth centuries reference is often made to "Paul's Epistle to the Laodiceans." The conclusion is warranted that it existed in Greek as well as in Latin; and if in Greek, it must have originated not later than the first half of the third century A. D. Its genuineness was defended by Gregory the Great (sixth century), Aelfric of Cerne (tenth century), John of Salisbury (twelfth century), and many others. It is found in several older editions of the English, German, Dutch and other Bibles. "For more than nine centuries this forged epistle hovered about the doors of the sacred Canon, without ever finding admission or being peremptorily excluded. At length the revival of learning dealt its death-blow to this as to so many other spurious pretensions" (Lightfoot, *op. cit.*, p. 299). For the Latin text of this forgery see Lightfoot, *op. cit.*, pp. 287-289; for Lightfoot's reconstruction of the Greek text, *op. cit.*, pp. 293, 294; and for two forms of the letter in its old English dress, *op. cit.*, pp. 298, 299.

Objections:

a. This letter is nothing but "a cento of Pauline phrases strung together without any definite connection or any clear object" (Lightfoot) .

b. Jerome already stated that "it is rejected by all." The Council of Nicea (A. D. 787) warned against it.

c. It was obviously fabricated to satisfy curiosity with respect to Col. 4:16b.

d. Since such a disproportionately large part of this small letter was lifted from Paul's Epistle to the Philippians, it is evident that it does not even fit the Lycus Valley situation.

(5) *The canonical Epistle of Paul to the Ephesians.*

This theory has gained many adherents. It is generally linked with the "circular letter" view of Ephesians, though the latter theory is not really dependent upon it. According to this interpretation of Col. 4:16b, as soon as "Ephesians" in its circuit of the churches has been read to the church of Laodicea it must, in accordance with Paul's wishes, be sent on to Colosse in exchange for "Colossians."

Evaluation:

Conclusive proof for the correctness of this theory is lacking. It is supplied neither here in Colossians nor in Eph. 1:1. (The discussion of the latter passage would be appropriate in a Commentary on Ephesians.) On the other hand, though it is merely a theory, it is not exposed to the objections that count against the preceding four. It proceeds on the valid assumptions that both letters to which reference is made in Col. 4:16 were written *by the apostle Paul* and *to churches.* According to this theory, then, "Ephesians," reaching the Colossians from Laodicea, will thus truthfully become the letter "from the Laodiceans."

(6) *A genuine letter of Paul addressed to the Laodiceans, but now lost.*

As before (see above, under (5)) , when this letter reaches the Colossians it will be the letter "from the Laodiceans."

Evaluation:

Here, too, proof is lacking, and here, too, the theory is free from the objections mentioned as valid against the first four.

The fact that this theory proceeds from the assumption that a letter written by Paul can have been "lost," in the sense that it was not handed down to posterity, should not count as a valid objection. Not all of Paul's letters have been preserved (see I Cor. 5:9) . Those favoring this theory are of the opinion that the reason why, in God's providence, Paul's letter to the Laodiceans was not preserved may well have been that the distinctive portion of the epistle — that wherein it differed from Colossians — , though certainly of real value for the membership in the Lycus Valley (at least for that of Laodicea and Colosse) , was lacking in *abiding* and *universal* significance.

It must be borne in mind that Tychicus had to pass through Laodicea in order to reach Colosse. In all probability he traveled the road which Paul himself had used, but now Tychicus traveled it in reverse (from W. to E.). See Introduction II A, map 4. Would it not have been strange if, having delivered "Ephesians" to the elders at Ephesus, and being on his way to deliver "Colossians" to the authorities at Colosse, he would have had no missive from Paul to the church of Laodicea through which town he was passing? Both theories supply this need. According to (5) Tychicus could have told the Laodiceans, "Paul's letter which I left at Ephesus will be sent to y o u presently. Having read it, send it on to the Colossians, who will send y o u, in exchange, the letter which we are going to deliver to them." According to (6) Tychicus, welcomed by the Laodiceans, would deliver to them Paul's letter addressed specifically to them. That letter itself probably contained a request that it (or a copy of it) be sent to the Colossians in exchange for the one addressed to them.

Against (6) it is sometimes urged that Paul would hardly have asked the Colossians to convey his greetings to the brothers in Laodicea, and to Nympha and the church in her house (Col. 4:15), if at the same time he had been writing a letter addressed specifically to the Laodiceans. Others, however, answer that for a heart so filled with love and friendliness such a thing can be considered neither impossible nor unnatural. Besides, objections have also been advanced against (5), particularly against the circular letter theory.

There are times, in the course of exegesis, when a precise answer is impossible, and the choice must be left between two alternatives, in this case theory (5) and theory (6).

---

17 And say to Archippus, Attend to the ministry which you have received in the Lord, that you fulfil it.

4:17

VI. *Crisp Directive for Archippus*

17. And say to Archippus. Archippus was a member of the family of Philemon who lived in Colosse, and at whose home the church was accustomed to gather for worship. In Philem. 2 the apostle bestows on him the signal honor of calling him "our fellow-soldier." See in this volume, on Philem. 1, 2. As he was probably *the son* of Philemon and Apphia he cannot have been very old. We may, perhaps, compare him to Timothy to whom Paul, after his release from the present Roman imprisonment, was going to write, "Let no one despise your youth" (I Tim. 4:12). Those words were addressed to Timothy when he was perhaps somewhere between 34 and 39 years of age. See N.T.C. on I and II Timothy and Titus, p. 157.

Now for this companion-in-arms, Archippus, the apostle has a special message. He expresses it in language which, because of its terse, commanding character, must have sounded all the more direct and unequivocal. Paul tells the church of Colosse to say to Archippus, **Attend to the ministry which you have received in the Lord, that you fulfil it.** Nothing further is said about the nature of this "ministry." Nor are we told why Archippus had to be thus admonished. Some have thought that the reason was that he lacked diligence or energy, that he was somewhat on the lazy side, always postponing to the indefinite future ("mañana") the tasks that needed immediate attention. The objection to this theory is that in that case Paul would hardly have called him "our fellow-*soldier*." Perhaps a safer method of reaching a probable answer to the double question: a. "What was this ministry?" and b. "Why did Paul choose this method of reminding Archippus of his responsibility?" is to study the exact meaning of the expression used. Archippus must attend to the *ministry*. The word in italics is the equivalent of the Greek *diakonia*. In Paul's writings it has several meanings.[175] Prominent among these meanings is, however, the spiritual one, according to which the word has reference to the office of *the ministry*, and the service implied in that office. In the present instance we can, perhaps, proceed even farther in arriving at a reasonable conclusion with respect to the sense of the term in Col. 4:17. The latter passage has a very close parallel in II Tim. 4:5, as follows:

Col. 4:17b	II Tim. 4:5b
"Attend to the ministry which you have received in the Lord, that you fulfil it."	"Do the work of an evangelist, your ministry discharge to the full."

Now in Timothy's case that "ministry" was "the work of an evangelist" or gospel-preacher (Acts 21:8; Eph. 4:11). Timothy, who, when Paul will

---

[175] Paul uses it 22 times. Not in every instance are commentators and translators in complete agreement as to its exact, contextual significance. Thus, in I Cor. 12:5 it is rendered variously: *service, ministration, dispensation, ministry;* and similar variety obtains with respect to the meanings assigned to it in II Cor. 3:7, 8, 9 (twice). Fairly certain, however, is the meaning *relief, care* (for the poor), *contribution* (to relieve the needy), in Rom. 15:31; II Cor. 8:4; 9:1, 12, 13. *Service,* of some kind or of any kind whatever, seems to be the meaning in I Cor. 16:15 and in II Cor. 11:8. In many passages *spiritual office* (for example, that of apostle or of evangelist) and/or its *administration* ("ministry" or "the ministry") is clearly shown to be the meaning in the light of the specific context in which the word is used. It is then defined in such terms as the *diakonia* "of reconciliation," the *diakonia* "for the building up of the body of Christ" or is used as a synonym of an expression like "the work of an evangelist." Clear examples of this usage — though in a few cases even this is disputed — are the following: Rom. 11:13; 12:7; II Cor. 4:1; 5:18; 6:3; Eph. 4:12; I Tim. 1:12; II Tim. 4:5, 11. It would seem that Col. 4:17 also belongs here. As to the meaning of *the cognate verb* see N.T.C. on I and II Timothy and Titus, p. 135, especially footnote 67; and for *the cognate noun* see the same volume, p. 130, especially footnote 65.

be writing these words, will be in Ephesus as Paul's envoy, must "herald the word, being on hand in season, out of season." He must "reprove, rebuke, admonish, with all longsuffering and teaching" (II Tim. 4:2).

In Colosse, too, someone must have been in charge of the flock. When Colossians was being written and brought to its destination it could not have been Epaphras, the minister of the churches in the Lycus Valley, for just now he was with Paul in Rome, from which he is sending greetings (4:12). Who was it? In view of the striking similarity between Col. 4:17 and II Tim. 4:5b, the conclusion does not seem unreasonable that this interim-shepherd was none other than Archippus. Further, since he, too, just like Timothy, was probably rather young and somewhat diffident, wondering perhaps whether the church would give him — a man so inexperienced — its full co-operation in this important work, the apostle, very tactfully, orders *the congregation* itself to encourage him by saying to him, as it were, "Go right ahead, we are with you and we promise to help you in every way. The task you are trying to perform was given to you by the Lord, and you are discharging it with strength imparted by him." Hence, "Attend to the ministry which you have received in the Lord, that you fulfil it." All this is, of course, no more than a reasonable conjecture.

---

18 The greetings by my own, Paul's, hand. Remember my bonds. Grace (be) with y o u.

4:18

VII. *Personal Greeting, Reminder, Benediction*

18a. The greeting by my own, Paul's, hand. It was customary for Paul to write a few words of greetings with his own hand (see II Thess. 3:17; cf. I Cor. 16:21). He had a twofold purpose in doing this:

a. to mark the autographed letter as a genuine one, an authentic product of the mind and heart of Paul (II Thess. 3:17); and

b. to discourage the spread of spurious letters (see II Thess. 2:1, 2).

It is also clear from this that Paul was in the habit of dictating his letters (see, in addition to the references given above, Rom. 16:22; Gal. 6:11; and see on Philem. 19).

18b. Remember my bonds. It is a sign of Paul's true greatness that he did not deem himself to be too exalted to solicit continued sympathy and intercession in behalf of himself, a prisoner! See on 1:9; cf. 4:3.

18c. Grace (be) with y o u. In this shortest possible form the benediction is also found in I Tim. 6:21 (cf. II Tim. 4:22b). But though brief it is rich in meaning, for grace is the greatest and most basic blessing of all. It is God's favor in Christ to the undeserving, transforming their hearts and lives and leading them on to glory. The apostle, who in his opening salutation had spoken of *grace* (followed by *peace*), now closes this letter by again authoritatively pronouncing *this* grace (note the article; hence really "the grace") upon the believers in Colosse.[176]

Seed Thoughts of Colossians 4:2-18

(1) "Persevere in prayer." Sometimes the answer does not come at once because we are not as yet ready to receive the blessing; sometimes, because the blessing is not yet ready for us. Besides, if whenever we prayed God *immediately* granted the petition, would we appreciate his blessings? (verse 2a) .

(2) ". . . keeping alert in it *with thanksgiving*." Paul was *a prisoner* when he wrote this. How true are the lines:

"Stone walls do not a prison make,
Nor iron bars a cage." (Lovelace)

From his first Roman imprisonment the apostle wrote four letters that have come down to us: Colossians, Philemon, Ephesians, and Philippians. Colossians overflows with "thanksgiving" (1:3, 12; 2:7; 3:15, 16, 17; 4:2) ; Ephesians, with "grace" (1:2, 6, 7; 2:5, 7, 8; 3:2, 7, 8; 4:7, 29; 6:24) and "glory" (1:6, 12, 14, 17, 18; 3:13, 16, 21) ; Philippians, with "joy" (1:4, 18, 25; 2:2, 17, 18, 28, 29; 3:1; 4:1, 4, 10) ; and all four with "love" (see especially Philem. 1, 5, 7, 9, 16, and cf. 12) , (verse 2b) .

(3) ". . . praying also for us, that God may open to us a door for the message." The prisoner prays not for a door of *exit* from prison, but for a door for the *entrance* of the message (verse 3) .

(4) ". . . (praying) that I may make it clear, (and may speak) as I ought to speak." Not only *what* we say but also *how* we say it is important (cf. Eph. 4:15) , (verse 4) .

(5) ". . . making the most of the opportunity" or ". . . buying up the opportunity." For some "Time is *money*." For Paul it is "opportunity" to conduct oneself wisely toward outsiders (verse 5) .

(6) ". . . so that y o u may know how to answer each individual." Not only *what* we say and *how* we say it is important (see No. 4 above) but also *to whom* we say it (verse 6) .

(7) "All my affairs will Tychicus make known to you . . ." Some things are better *said* than *written* (verses 7 and 8) .

(8) ". . . Onesimus, the faithful and beloved brother"; "Mark, the

---

[176] Some manuscripts add "Amen," but this addition may stem from liturgical usage or may have been added by a scribe who happened to remember that this was the concluding word in Galatians and, according to the best reading, also in Romans.

cousin of Barnabas . . . if he comes to y o u receive him." Brother *A* is very generous in his willingness to overlook the sin which brother *B* committed against brother *C,* but not nearly as eager to forgive *D*'s trespass against himself *(A)*. Paul, however, does both. He forgives Onesimus for having wronged Philemon, but he also forgives Mark for having wronged himself, i.e., Paul (see Acts 13:13; 15:38; II Tim. 4:11), (verses 9 and 10).

(9) "Of those of the circumcision these are the only co-workers for the kingdom of God who have been a comfort to me." The most privileged individuals are not always the most profitable (verse 11).

(10) "Epaphras, who is one of y o u, a servant of Christ Jesus, greets y o u, always wrestling for y o u in his prayers that y o u may stand firm, mature and fully assured in all the will of God." The mark of a great leader is that he is eager to speak well of a person and to bolster confidence in him. Paul did this again and again (verses 12 and 13).

(11) "Luke, the beloved physician, greets y o u, and so does Demas." Here these two are mentioned favorably, in one breath. Later the contrast would become apparent, and Paul would write, "Demas has deserted me, because he fell in love with the present world . . . Luke is the only one with me." Two kingdom workers may be working side by side, doing the same kind of work, as far as men can see. God sees the heart (verse 14; cf. II Tim. 4:10, 11).

(12) ". . . and the church in her house." In a sense every home should be a house-church (verse 15).

(13) ". . . see to it that it is read also in the church of the Laodiceans, and that y o u also read the one from Laodicea." This not only because these two *letters* were important to the two churches, but also because the two *congregations* should be important to each other (verse 16).

(14) ". . . that you fulfil it." Every God-given task must be fulfilled (verse 17).

(15) "Remember my bonds." A truly great man is not too proud to ask that he be remembered in prayer (verse 18).

Paul's Epistle to the Colossians

Chapter 1

1 Paul, an apostle of Christ Jesus through the will of God, and Timothy our brother, 2 to the saints and believing brothers in Christ at Colosse; grace to y o u and peace from God our Father.

3 While praying for y o u we are always thanking God, the Father of our Lord Jesus Christ, 4 because we have heard of y o u r faith in Christ Jesus and of the love which y o u cherish for all the saints, 5 by reason of the hope laid up for y o u in the heavens, of which y o u have previously heard in the message of the truth, namely, the gospel, 6 which made its entrance felt among y o u, as indeed in the entire world it is bearing fruit and growing — so also among yourselves from the day y o u heard and came to acknowledge the grace of God in its genuine character, 7 as y o u learned it from Epaphras our beloved fellow-servant, who is a faithful minister of Christ on our behalf, 8 and has made known to us y o u r love in the Spirit.

9 And for this reason, from the day we heard it we never stopped praying for y o u, asking that y o u may be filled with clear knowledge of his will (such clear knowledge consisting) in all spiritual wisdom and understanding, 10 so as to live lives worthy of the Lord, to (his) complete delight, in every good work bearing fruit, and growing in the clear knowledge of God; 11 being invigorated with all vigor, in accordance with his glorious might, so as to exercise every kind of endurance and longsuffering; 12 with joy giving thanks to the Father who qualified y o u for a share in the inheritance of the saints in the light 13 and who rescued us out of the domain of darkness and transplanted us into the kingdom of the Son of his love, 14 in whom we have our redemption, the forgiveness of our sins.

15 Who is the image of the invisible God, the firstborn of every creature, 16 for in him were created all things in the heavens and on the earth, the visible and the invisible, whether thrones or dominions or principalities or authorities, all things through him and with a view to him have been created; 17 and he is before all things, and all things hold together in him. 18 And he is the head of the body, the church; who is the beginning, the firstborn from the dead, that in all things he might have the pre-eminence, 19 for in him he [God] was pleased to have all the fulness dwell, 20 and through him to reconcile all things to himself, having made peace through the blood of his cross, through him, whether the things on the earth or the things in the heavens.

21 And y o u, who once were estranged and hostile in disposition, as shown by y o u r wicked works, 22 he in his body of flesh through his death has now reconciled, in order to present y o u holy, faultless, and blameless before himself; 23 if, indeed, y o u continue in the faith, founded and firm, and are not moved away from the hope that is derived from the gospel which y o u have heard, which was preached among every creature under heaven, and of which I, Paul, became a minister.

24 I am now rejoicing amid my sufferings for y o u, and what is lacking in the afflictions of Christ I in his stead am supplying in my flesh, for his body, which is the church, 25 of which I became a minister, according to the stewardship of God given to me for y o u r benefit, to give full scope to the word of God, 26 the mystery hidden for ages and generations but now made manifest to his saints; 27 to whom God was pleased to make known what (is) the riches of the glory of this

mystery among the Gentiles, which is Christ in y o u, the hope of glory; 28 whom we proclaim, admonishing every man and teaching every man in all wisdom, in order that we may present every man perfect in Christ; 29 for which I am laboring, striving by his energy working powerfully within me.

Chapter 2

1 For I want y o u to know how greatly I strive for y o u, and for those at Laodicea, and for all who have not seen my face in the flesh, 2 in order that their hearts may be strengthened, they themselves being welded together in love, and this with a view to all the riches of assured understanding, with a view to the clear knowledge of the mystery of God, namely, Christ; 3 in whom all the treasures of wisdom and knowledge are hidden. 4 I say this in order that no one may mislead y o u by persuasive argument. 5 For, although in the flesh I am absent, yet in the spirit I am with y o u, rejoicing to see y o u r good order and the firmness of y o u r faith in Christ.

6 As therefore y o u accepted Christ Jesus the Lord, (so) in him continue to live, 7 rooted and being built up in him and being established in the faith, just as y o u were taught, overflowing with thanksgiving. 8 Be on y o u r guard lest there be any one who carries y o u off as spoil by means of his philosophy and empty deceit, according to the tradition of men, according to the rudiments of the world, and not according to Christ; 9 for in him all the fulness of the godhead dwells bodily, 10 and in him y o u have attained to fulness, namely, in him who is the head of every principality and authority, 11 in whom also y o u were circumcised with a circumcision made without hands, by the putting off of the body of the flesh in the circumcision of Christ, 12 having been buried with him in y o u r baptism in which y o u were also raised with him through faith in the operative power of God who raised him from the dead. 13 And y o u, who were dead through y o u r trespasses and the uncircumcision of y o u r flesh, y o u he made alive together with him, having forgiven us all our trespasses, 14 having blotted out the hand-written document that was against us, which by means of its requirements testified against us, and he took it out of the way by nailing it to the cross, 15 and having stripped the principalities and the authorities of their power, he publicly exposed them to disgrace by triumphing over them in him.

16 Therefore allow no one to pass judgment on y o u in questions of food or drink or with respect to a festival or a new moon or a sabbath: 17 things that were only a shadow of those that were coming, while the object casting the shadow is to be found with Christ.

18 Let no one disqualify y o u by delighting in humility and the worship of the angels, taking his stand on the things he has seen, without cause puffed up by his fleshly mind, 19 and not keeping firm hold on the Head, from whom the entire body, supported and held together by joints and ligaments, grows with a growth (that is) from God.

20 If with Christ y o u died to the rudiments of the world, why, as though y o u were (still) living in the world, do y o u submit to regulations, 21 "Do not handle, Do not taste, Do not touch" — 22 referring to things that are meant for destruction by their consumption — according to the precepts and doctrines of men? 23 Regulations of this kind, though to be sure having a reputation for wisdom because of their self-imposed ritual, humility, and unsparing treatment of the body, are of no value whatever, (serving only) to indulge the flesh.

Chapter 3

1 If then y o u were raised with Christ, seek *the things that are above,* where Christ is, seated at the right hand of God. 2 On the things that are above set y o u r minds, not on the things that are upon the earth. 3 For y o u died, and y o u r life is hid with Christ in God. 4 When Christ (who is) our life is manifested, then y o u also will be manifested with him in glory.

5 Put to death therefore y o u r members that (are) upon the earth: immorality, impurity, passion, evil desire, and greed, which is idolatry; 6 on account of which things the wrath of God is coming; 7 in which things y o u also walked at one time, when y o u were living in them. 8 But now y o u, too, lay them all aside: wrath, anger, malice, slander, shameful language from y o u r mouth. 9 No longer lie to one another, seeing that y o u have put off the old man with his practices, 10 and have put on the new man, who is being renewed for full knowledge according to the image of him who created him, 11 where there cannot be Greek and Jew, circumcision and uncircumcision, barbarian, Scythian, slave, freeman, but Christ (is) all and in all.

12 Put on, therefore, as God's elect, holy and beloved, a heart of compassion, kindness, lowliness, meekness, longsuffering, 13 enduring one another, and forgiving each other if anyone have a complaint against anyone. Just as the Lord has forgiven y o u, so do y o u also. 14 And above all these things (put on) love, which is the bond of perfection. 15 And let the peace of Christ, for which y o u were called in one body, rule in y o u r hearts, and be thankful. 16 Let the word of Christ dwell among y o u richly; in all wisdom teaching and admonishing one another, (and) by means of psalms, hymns, and spiritual songs singing to God in a thankful spirit, with all y o u r heart. 17 And whatever y o u do in word or in deed, (do) all in the name of the Lord Jesus, giving thanks to God the Father through him.

18 Wives, be submissive to y o u r husbands, as is fitting in the Lord. 19 Husbands, love y o u r wives, and do not be harsh toward them. 20 Children, obey y o u r parents in all things, for this is well-pleasing in the Lord. 21 Fathers, do not exasperate y o u r children, in order that they may not lose heart. 22 Slaves, obey in all things those who according to the flesh are y o u r masters, not with eye-service as men-pleasers but with singleness of heart, fearing the Lord. 23 Whatever y o u do, put y o u r soul into the work, as for the Lord and not for men, 24 knowing that from the Lord y o u will receive the recompense, namely, the inheritance. (It is) the Lord Christ (whom) y o u are serving. 25 For, the wrong-doer will receive (the conquences of) what he has wrongly done. And there is no partiality.

Chapter 4

1 Masters, render to y o u r slaves that which is fair and square, knowing that y o u also have a Master in heaven.

2 Persevere in prayer, keeping alert in it with thanksgiving; 3 at the same time praying also for us, that God may open to us a door for the message, to speak forth the mystery concerning Christ, on account of which I am in prison, 4 (praying) that I may make it clear, (and may speak) as I ought to speak.

5 Conduct yourselves wisely toward outsiders, making the most of the opportunity. 6 Let y o u r speech always be gracious, seasoned with salt, so that y o u may know how to answer each individual.

7 All my affairs will Tychicus make known to y o u, the beloved brother and faithful minister and fellow-servant in the Lord, 8 whom I am sending to

y o u for this very purpose, that y o u may know our circumstances and that he may strengthen y o u r hearts. 9 (He is) accompanied by Onesimus, the faithful and beloved brother, who is one of y o u. They will acquaint y o u with everything (that has taken place) here.

10 Aristarchus, my fellow-prisoner, greets y o u; so does Mark, the cousin of Barnabas — concerning whom y o u received instructions; if he comes to y o u receive him — ; 11 and Jesus who is called Justus. Of those who are of the circumcision these are the only co-workers for the kingdom of God who have been a comfort to me. 12 Epaphras, who is one of y o u, a servant of Christ Jesus, greets y o u, always wrestling for y o u in his prayers that y o u may stand firm, mature and fully assured in all the will of God. 13 For I can testify concerning him that he has put himself to much trouble for y o u and for those in Laodicea and those in Hierapolis. 14 Luke, the beloved physician, greets y o u, and so does Demas. 15 Extend greetings to the brothers in Laodicea, and to Nympha and the church in her house.

16 And when this letter has been read among y o u, see to it that it is read also in the church of the Laodiceans, and that y o u also read the one from Laodicea.

17 And say to Archippus, Attend to the ministry which you have received in the Lord, that you fulfil it.

18 The greetings by my own, Paul's, hand. Remember my bonds. Grace (be) with y o u.

Commentary

on

The Epistle to Philemon

Outline of Philemon

Theme: *Paul's Request for the Kind Reception of the Fugitive Slave Onesimus*

I. Opening Salutation, verses 1-3

II. Thanksgiving and Prayer, verses 4-7

III. Plea in Behalf of Onesimus, Including Request for Lodging, verses 8-22

IV. Greetings and Closing Salutation, verses 23-25

EPISTLE TO PHILEMON

PHILEMON

1 Paul, a prisoner of Christ Jesus, and Timothy our brother, to Philemon
our beloved (brother) and fellow-worker 2 and to Apphia our sister and to
Archippus our fellow-soldier and to the church in your house; 3 grace to y o u
and peace from God our Father and the Lord Jesus Christ.

1-3

I. *Opening Salutation*

*For the form or structure of Paul's letters see on Col. 1:1, 2. For a discus-
sion of the persons addressed here in Philem. 1, 2, and for all other matters
of an introductory nature see the opening section of this book, the Introduction to Colossians and Philemon.*

1, 2. The Salutation opens with the words **Paul, a prisoner.** Cf. verse 9;
also Eph. 3:1; 4:1; II Tim. 1:8. He adds **of Christ Jesus.** In every reference
to himself as a prisoner Paul always stresses the fact that as such he belongs
to his Lord, for it was while engaged in *his* service and thus for *his* sake that
he was imprisoned. Moreover, all the details of the imprisonment as well
as its outcome, whether it be the death-sentence or acquittal, are in the hands
that were pierced for this prisoner, those very hands that now control the
entire universe in the interest of the church (Eph. 1:22). Paul's imprisonment is therefore a very honorable one. The mention of himself as a prisoner
of Christ Jesus is also very tactful, probably implying, "In comparison with
the *sacrifice* that I am making is not the *favor* which I am asking you to grant
a rather easy matter?" See Summary at the close of this chapter for a discussion of the apostle's tactfulness as shown in this letter. See also in the Appendix, "Scripture on Tactfulness." Paul continues, **and Timothy our
brother.** For this addition see on Col. 1:1. For "brother" see also Philem. 7
and 20, where this designation of intimate spiritual relationship and tender
love is applied to Philemon (giving us the right to insert it parenthetically
after the words "our beloved" in verse 1), and verse 16, where it is used with
reference to Onesimus.

The letter is addressed **to Philemon our beloved (brother) and fellow-
worker.** In Christ and for his sake, Philemon, a resident of Colosse, is loved

209

by Paul, by Timothy, and by every believer who has heard of him. He is loved by Christ and has the characteristics of a brother. In the companion-letter, Colossians, Paul speaks of Epaphras as "beloved *fellow-servant*" (1:7), of Tychicus and Onesimus as "beloved *brothers*" (14:7, 9), and of Luke as "the beloved *physician*" (4:14). Philemon is also called "fellow-worker." It is not impossible that he had been assisting Paul in spiritual work during the latter's prolonged ministry in Ephesus and had continued his evangelical labors after the apostle's departure from Asia Minor. But, aside from this, would not what is recorded concerning him in Philem. 7 entitle him to be called fellow-worker? Paul had many fellow-workers. Among them were such *men* as Urbanus (Rom. 16:9), Timothy (Rom. 16:21), Apollos (I Cor. 3:9), Titus (II Cor. 8:23), Epaphroditus (Phil. 2:25), Syzygus and Clement (Phil. 4:3), Jesus Justus (Col. 4:11), Mark, Aristarchus, Demas, and Luke (Philem. 23); *the married couple* Aquila and Priscilla or Prisca (Rom. 16:3); and such *women* as Euodia and Syntyche (Phil. 4:2) and those mentioned in Rom. 16. What should be stressed in this connection is the fact that the apostle considers them fellow-workers not only in the sense that they were *his* but also in the sense that they were *God's* co-laborers. And in the latter sense Paul himself was also a fellow-worker (I Cor. 3:9).

Very closely associated with Philemon and mentioned in one breath with him as those to whom the opening salutation and in a more general sense the entire letter is addressed are two other persons. Hence, the sentence continues, **and to Apphia our sister and to Archippus our fellow-soldier.** After mentioning them and "the church in *your* (Philemon's) house," and pronouncing upon them all (*y o u*) the salutation proper (verse 3), the writer again more specifically addresses Philemon himself (using the pronouns *you* and *your*, not *y o u* and *y o u r*) throughout the entire body of the letter (verse 6b is probably no exception), returning to the plural (*y o u r*), as was to be expected, in the reference to the prayers of the congregation (verse 22) and in the closing salutation (verse 25). The inference would seem to be warranted that Philemon, who with the aforementioned exceptions, is addressed in the singular throughout, is the head of the family, and that Apphia and Archippus are members of this family. Apphia may well have been Philemon's wife, and Archippus their son. Although this view of the matter cannot be demonstrated beyond possibility of contradition, deviating theories have failed to convince many apart from those who propose them. It is not difficult to understand this use of the second person singular throughout the body of the letter. The missive is a request for the kind reception of the fugitive slave Onesimus who is being returned to his master. It is, accordingly, in the final analysis up to Philemon himself — not up to Apphia, Archippus, or even the church — whether this request will be granted. But although Philemon himself must make the decision, the others, too, must hear the letter. Let them therefore assist Philemon to do his duty. Let them also hear how Paul, by the inspiration of the Holy Spirit, would solve the important problem of the fugitive slave. Their minds, too, will thus be illumined and their sympathies broadened.

Apphia is called "our sister." This is true not *literally* or *physically*, as Mary and Martha were sisters of Lazarus (John 11:1), nor *metaphorically*, referring to a church (II John 13), but *spiritually:* Apphia is "our sister" in the sense in which Timothy is "our brother," namely, as belonging to the family of faith. She is our sister *in the Lord*. Archippus is called "our fellow-soldier," a title which in the New Testament is given to only one other person, namely, Epaphroditus (Phil. 2:25). With respect to this same Archippus the apostle has issued a crisp command (Col. 4:17). Lest anyone in hearing this command should begin to hold this young brother in low esteem, Paul, with wonderful *tact* bestows upon him this title of honor, meaning "our companion in arms." Cf. N.T.C. on Philippians 2:25.

Paul adds, **and to the church in your house.** Since in the first and second centuries church-buildings in the sense in which we think of them today were as yet not available, families would hold services in their own homes. Such services would be attended by the members of the household: father, mother, children, servants. If the house was large enough to accommodate others, they, too, were invited. The early church numbered many hospitable members, ready and eager to offer the facilities of their homes for religious purposes. Thus, in Jerusalem "many were gathered together and were praying" in the house of Mary, the mother of John Mark (Acts 12:12). Lydia graciously invited Paul, Silas, Timothy, and Luke to use her home as their headquarters (Acts 16:15, 40). Wherever Aquila and Priscilla went they would if at all possible welcome the worshipers to their home. Hence, both at Ephesus (I Cor. 16:19) and at Rome (Rom. 16:3-5) there was "a church in their house." Laodicea, too, had its house-church (see on Col. 4:15). So did Corinth, at the home of Gaius (Rom. 16:23). If the number of believers in any town was small, one house-church might be sufficient; if large or widely separated, more than one would be necessary. So it is not surprising that Philemon, too, had shown similar hospitality. Since the membership of the Colossian church was probably small numerically (see Introduction II B 4) it is entirely possible that the entire congregation gathered for worship in his home.[177]

---

[177] The transition from private house, whose owner had offered its facilities for public worship, to spacious church-edifice, built expressly for congregational services, was probably gradual. Cf. the transition from buggy to automobile. Thus the oldest known church discovered by archaeologists was in reality a modified once-private dwelling. The house had been built A. D. 232-233 at Dura Europos in eastern Syria on the Euphrates. Three of its rooms had been changed into a chapel with room for 100 people. For full description see C. Hopkins and P. V. C. Baur, *Christian Church at Dura-Europos;* cf. G. E. Wright, *Biblical Archaeology,* pp. 245-247. Even earlier is

3. The opening salutation proper follows in the familiar words, **grace to y o u and peace from God our Father and the Lord Jesus Christ.** Thus there is pronounced upon Philemon, Apphia, Archippus and the entire congregation that gathers at Philemon's house *grace,* that is, God's spontaneous, unmerited favor in action, his sovereign, freely bestowed loving-kindness in operation, and its result, *peace,* that is, the conviction of reconciliation through the blood of the cross, true spiritual wholeness and prosperity, these two blessings (grace and peace) coming from God our Father and the Lord Jesus Christ. For further details of explanation and for a discussion of the question whether this salutation is an exclamation, a declaration, or perhaps merely an expression of a pious wish, see N.T.C. on I and II Thessalonians, pp. 40-45, 153, 154.

---

4 I thank my God always, making mention of you in my prayers, 5 because I hear of your love and of the faith which you have, (the latter) toward the Lord Jesus, and (the former) for all the saints, 6 (praying) that the sharing to which your faith gives rise may be energetically stimulated for Christ by the clear recognition of all the good that is ours. 7 For I have derived much joy and comfort from your love, because the hearts of the saints have been refreshed through you, brother.

4-7

II. *Thanksgiving and Prayer*

4, 5. As usual the salutation is followed by the thansgiving and the prayer. The apostle can honestly write: **I thank my God always,**[178] **making mention of you in my prayers.** He continues, **because I hear of your love and of the faith which you have, (the latter) toward the Lord Jesus, and (the former) for all the saints.** Epaphras, the spiritual leader of the Colossian church, a Colossian himself (Col. 4:12, 13), and now with Paul (Philem. 23), must have given the apostle much valuable information about conditions in that congregation. In that connection he had also made mention of Philemon's work for the Lord and of his generosity and hospitality. The fugitive slave Onesimus in all probability supplied further details. After his conversion his attitude toward his master must have changed sufficiently to say some good things about him. And there may have been other informers. Thus the apostle had heard about Philemon's love. Had he not

---

the implied distinction in I Cor. 11:18, 22, between strictly private homes and what must have been a rather spacious gathering-place for the church. With the conversion of Constantine (A. D. 323-337) church architecture received the boost it needed.

[178] See on Col. 1:3, footnote 25, for the reason why the word *always* should be construed with "I thank my God," rather than with "making mention."

opened his house for religious services? See verses 1, 2. Had he not "refreshed the saints" in other ways also? See verse 7. This love for God's consecrated children had its root, as always, in faith directed toward the Lord
Jesus.[179]

6. Verse 6 follows naturally. It is connected not only with verse 4, because
it gives the content of Paul's prayer for Philemon, but also with verse 5. In
the latter passage mention was made of the addressee's "love for all the
saints." This was demonstrated in a willingness on the part of Philemon
to share his bounties with others. Undoubtedly he had made many valuable
contributions, both material and spiritual, to the welfare of the little community. Let him then demonstrate this same attitude of liberality, and at the
same time the genuine character of his faith, in still another respect, namely,
by showing mercy to Onesimus. This thought, which pervades the entire
letter and is about to be expressed in verses 8-21, underlies the statement
in verse 6. This is true no matter which of the following two renderings of
this admittedly difficult passage be adopted. Whether the sense be:
a. (praying) that your participation in the faith may become clearly known
by y o u r good deed, etc., or

---

[179] Some believe that both the love and the faith have the Lord Jesus and all the
saints as objects. They interpret *faith* to mean *fidelity*. As a result, these interpreters
also deny the chiastic structure of the passage. But the fact that the love is for
the saints, and the faith is directed toward *the Lord,* is clear from the parallel passages: Eph. 1:15; Col. 1:14.
Note, accordingly, the chiastic structure of the sentence:

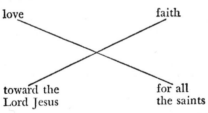

This criss-cross structure occurs frequently in Paul. See N.T.C. on Phil. 2:3, 8, 12;
on Col. 1:10; 1:16; 3:11; and on I Tim. 3:16. In the present instance the reason for
this arrangement is probably the following: the apostle wants Philemon, who has
already manifested his love to others, to show kindness to Onesimus also. Hence,
this being uppermost in Paul's mind, he mentions *love* first of all and traces it to
its source, namely, genuine faith in the Lord Jesus. This enables him to refer now to
the objects of this love: all the saints (verse 5b), which connects immediately with
the next verse (verse 6) in which he prays that this *sharing* which he has just now
commended in Philemon may become very effective. *Implied* is clearly the thought:
"Now take one more step, beloved brother; extend this same kindness and love to
Onesimus." And so, in verse 7, the apostle once more praises Philemon for the manner in which he has refreshed the hearts of the saints, adding that he (Paul) himself has been gladdened and comforted by this. It will be evident that the chiastic
structure in this instance lends itself best to Paul's purpose. *Love toward the saints*
naturally occupies the two places of greatest importance in this causal modifier
(verse 5), the first and the last place.

b. (praying) that the sharing to which your faith gives rise may be energetically stimulated for Christ by the clear recognition of all the good that is ours, in either case the basic *implication* is the same. It is a prayer that Philemon, who has already shown his unselfishness in so many ways, may take the next step also.[180]

---

[180] The differences in translation arise mainly from the fact that the passage contains several important words and phrases with different possible meanings or constructions; especially the following:
(1) Does κοινωνία as here used mean *participation* (in) or does it mean *sharing* (one's bounties with others?)
(2) Hence also: Does τῆς πίστεως mean *in the faith* or does it mean *of your faith,* that is, *springing from your faith?*
(3) What does εἰς Χριστόν mean and what does it modify?
(4) Does ἐν ἐπιγνώσει here signify *by the clear recognition* or rather *in the clear (or full) knowledge?*
(5) Does ἀγαθοῦ have reference to *the blessings* or *privileges that we enjoy* and which should stimulate us to show kindness to others, or does it have reference to *the good that we do?*
(6) And, as if this were not enough, there is the question as to which *reading* is correct: ἐν ἡμῖν or ἐν ὑμῖν. Is it *the good that is ours* or *the good that is y o u r s?*
Without going into great detail my answers are as follows: As to (1) Either meaning can be given to this word which frequently has the sense *fellowship.* For extensive discussion see N.T.C. on Philippians, pp. 51-54 and 93-95. However, if the meaning *participation* (in) be adopted, the reading ὑμῖν instead of ἡμῖν also receives the preference ("that your participation in the faith may become clearly known by your good deed"). But why the change from *your* to y o u r? Besides, there is another objection to the adoption of the reading ὑμῖν, as will be indicated under (6) below.
As to (2) The answer to the preceding determines this also. Hence, I prefer the rendering *springing from your faith* or *to which your faith gives rise.*
As to (3) The phrase εἰς Χριστόν is more naturally rendered *for Christ* than *in Christ.* As to what it modifies, it does not make much difference in the resultant meaning of the entire clause whether one translates "may be energetically stimulated (or "may become effective") for Christ by the clear recognition of all the good that is ours," or "may be energetically stimulated by the clear recognition of all the good that is ours for Christ (i.e., to his glory)."
As to (4) The rendering *in the clear knowledge* makes it difficult to arrive at an intelligible meaning for the entire sentence. On the contrary, the translation *by the clear recognition* ("by the acknowledging," R.V.) leads to a sensible result which is in harmony with Pauline thought, as indicated in the explanation.
As to (5) Though the word used in the original may indicate either *that which is morally good* (Rom. 2:10) or *blessing, privilege* (Rom. 14:16), the latter yields the better meaning in the present context, as shown in the explanation.
As to (6) It has already been shown that, with the exception of the salutations at the beginning and close (vss. 1-3, 25) and the reference to "y o u r prayers" in verse 22, the letter is specifically addressed throughout to one person, namely, Philemon (see on verses 1, 2). Even the greetings are addressed to him alone (vss. 23, 24). Therefore, the sudden appearance, here in the body of the letter (verse 6), of the second person plural (ὑμῖν) would be very strange indeed. On the other hand, that Paul, reflecting on the goodness of God in Christ toward Philemon, would immediately include himself and in fact all believers as objects of this divine love and care, and would therefore write "the good that is *ours,*" is easy to understand.
An entirely different meaning is given to the passage by E. J. Goodspeed. He renders verses 5 and 6 as follows: "I hear of the love and faith you have in the

The fact that the entrancing contemplation of the blessings of redemption — "all the good" — that are ours in Christ should evoke in our hearts the response of love and that not only God but also fellow-believers should be included in the object of this love, is not foreign to Pauline thought. The companion-epistle begins with this very idea: ". . . the love which y o u cherish for all the saints by reason of the hope laid up for y o u in the heavens" (Col. 1:4, 5). And the best commentary on Philem. 6 is probably the one found in Col. 3:13, "Just as Christ has forgiven y o u, so do y o u also forgive." Cf. Eph. 4:32; 5:2. The more thoroughly Philemon recognizes how greatly he himself has been benefited, the more inclined will he be to extend mercy and pardon to others, specifically to Onesimus. And the very fact that Philemon has manifested such a fine spirit in the past convinces the apostle that he is not writing in vain.

7. Hence, he continues, **For I have derived much joy and comfort from your love, because the hearts** [181] **of the saints have been refreshed through you, brother.** As has been indicated, this verse is closely connected with the preceding. Also, of course, with verse 4 ("I thank my God"), for verse 7, as well as verse 5, shows why Paul was so thankful. In times of hardship or need Philemon had on more than one occasion given *rest* to the weary, after the example and promise of Christ. See Matt. 11:28.[182] That such rest or refreshment had been given specifically to slaves, as some maintain, is not stated here. What Paul by means of these words *implies* but does not yet expressly *state,* is rather this, that since in the past Philemon has shown such pity and generosity to believers, let him do it again. This time let him lavish his love and sympathy on Onesimus. Paul himself will derive joy and comfort from this, as had been the case so often in the past when he had heard about the acts of kindness performed by Philemon. When the apostle writes, ". . . because the hearts of the saints have been refreshed through you, brother," this word *brother* is a fitting climax, showing how deeply the apostle loves the man whom he here addresses, how highly he esteems him, and how completely he trusts him.

Lord Jesus and all his people, and I pray that through coming to know every good thing about us as Christians they may effectually share your faith." Objections: (1) What does he mean by "the love and the faith in . . . all his people"? (2) Why should the apostle pray that "all his people" [the saints] may effectually share Philemon's faith? They already have that faith! — Other renderings or reconstructions are even less probable and require no discussion.

[181] On σπλάγχνα see footnote 39, p. 58 of N.T.C. on Philippians.

[182] In that passage, as the *Greek* has it, the Lord *twice* used a form of the word which here in Philem. has been rendered *refreshed.* It indicates *rested,* and thus *revived,* having obtained fresh courage and vigor. And in the *Syriac* translation of the Matthew passage the word, in one form or another, occurs no less than *three* times. This is an even more striking play upon words, and may reflect the actual idiom of Galilee, hence also of Jesus: "Come to me . . . and I will *rest* y o u . . . for I am *restful* [here *the Greek* has *meek*] . . . and y o u will find *rest* for yourselves."

8 Accordingly, although in Christ I am quite free to order you (to do) your duty, 9 yet for love's sake I rather appeal to you — since I am such a person as Paul, an old man, and now also a prisoner of Christ Jesus — 10 I appeal to you in the interest of my child, whom I have begotten in my bonds, Onesimus, 11 who formerly to you was useless, but now both to you and to me is useful, 12 whom I am sending back to you; (yes, even) him, that is, my very heart, 13 whom I could have wished to keep with me, in order that in your behalf he might render service to me in the bonds of the gospel; 14 but without your consent I did not wish to do anything, that your goodness might not be compulsory but voluntary.

15 Moreover, perhaps the reason why he was parted (from you) for a short period was this, that you might have him back forever, 16 no longer as a slave but something better than a slave, a brother beloved, especially to me but how much more to you, both in the flesh and in the Lord. 17 If then you consider me a partner, accept him as (you accept) me. 18 But if he has caused you any loss or owes you anything, charge that to my account. 19 I, Paul, do myself write this with my own hand, I will repay it — not to mention to you that you owe me your very self besides. 20 Yes, brother, let me have some benefit from you in the Lord. Refresh my heart in Christ.

21 Confident of your obedience I am writing to you, knowing that you will do even better than I say. 22 At the same time, prepare a guest room for me, for I am hoping that through y o u r prayers I shall be granted to y o u.

8-22

III. *Plea in Behalf of Onesimus, Including Request for Lodging*

It may seem as if this *plea* and this *request* have nothing in common, and should be treated under separate headings. The conviction that there may, nevertheless, be a subtle relation, as will be pointed out (see on verse 22), has led me to treat them under one theme.

8, 9. Accordingly, since you are the kind of person who delights in refreshing the hearts of God's people, a firm believer in loving and sharing (vss. 4-7), hence, **although in Christ I am quite free to order you (to do) your duty, yet for love's sake I rather appeal to you.** Paul is conscious of his authority as an apostle of Christ. There were times when he even laid stress on this right to rule the church in matters of faith and conduct, a commission given to him by his Lord (Rom. 1:1; I Cor. 5:3, 4; 9:1; II Cor. 10:13, 14; 12:12; Gal. 1:1; II Tim. 1:1, 11; 4:1; Titus 1:1). Yet, as he now unburdens his heart in the interest of Onesimus he prefers not to emphasize his apostolic prerogative. He would rather base his appeal on intelligent and purposeful Christian love, that very love which Philemon has been showing to all the saints (verse 5). One cannot really say that even here Paul *completely* excludes any appeal to his authority as Christ's official ambassador. If that were true, he would, of course, not even have mentioned it at all. In this respect verses 8, 9 may be compared to verse 19, where the apostle says, "not to mention to you that you owe me your very self," *but mentions it, nevertheless!* So also here in verses 8, 9, the reference to authority is made to flash before Philemon's mind for just a moment, only to recede entirely to the background when the spotlight is turned on the most dynamic motivating power in the entire universe, namely, love. In a tone of deep affection and gentle persuasion the plea continues: **since I am such a person as Paul, an old man,**[183] **and now also a prisoner of Christ Jesus.** Just how old Paul was when this was written we do not know. At Stephen's death he was "a young man" (Acts 7:58). Based on this fact and on various other data in the book of Acts and in the epistles, many are of the opinion that by now the apostle was in the neighborhood of sixty years of age. If that may not seem old to us, it must be borne in mind not only that man's average span of life was shorter in those days than it is now, but also that, as a result of all his labors and afflictions (see the stirring account in II Cor. 11:23-33, to which other hardships were added subsequently) this valiant servant of Christ had "grown old" in the service of his Lord and Master. Did he not bear in his body "the marks of the Lord Jesus"? (Gal. 6:17). Was he not the man with "a thorn in the flesh"? (II Cor. 12:7). And was he not even now also a prisoner of Christ Jesus? (see on verse 1). Surely, Philemon cannot refuse a reasonable request coming from a man who had shown his willingness at all times to surrender his all in the service of the King of Kings!

10, 11. Continues Paul: **I appeal to you in the interest of my child, whom I have begotten in my bonds, Onesimus.** That is the order of the sentence in the original. It should be preserved in the translation (cf. A.R.V.). This is not the case in A.V. and in R.S.V. The reason why this point must be stressed is that the apostle obviously has planned this statement with great care. Hence, before he ever mentions the name of the person in whose interest he is writing, he first of all seeks to create in the mind of Philemon a favorable impression of him and also sympathy for the one who is writing. Read the sentence again as Paul wrote (or dictated) it, and contrast it with what he might have written: "I am writing to you about Onesimus, that reputedly good-for-nothing slave or yours who, probably after robbing you, ran away from you." Note with what affection the apostle calls Onesimus "my child"; even more touchingly, "whom I have begotten in my bonds"; hence, "the child of my imprisonment"; *"my* child, who by God's grace was

---

[183] I cannot agree here with Lightfoot, C. F. D. Moule, and others who, with an appeal to Eph. 6:20, defend the theory that πρεσβύτης here means πρεσβευτής (ambassador). Is not this a clear violation of the context? Having just now (vss. 8, 9a) declared in unmistakable language that he does *not* wish to base his request on the authority with which his office as an apostle has invested him, he would turn right around and, almost in the same breath, appeal after all to his high prerogative as Christ's ambassador. That makes little sense.

by my personal ministry here in prison led to a saving knowledge of Christ."
We picture it thus: While still at the home of Philemon the slave had heard
about Paul, and about his gospel, zeal, loving heart, etc. Arrived in Rome as
a fugitive and in dire straits, he had taken refuge with the apostle. The
latter was used by God to change the slave into a brother beloved, the thief
into a fellow-servant. Paul continues: **who formerly to you was useless, but
now both to you and to me is useful.** Note with what tact the apostle bal-
ances the modifiers, so that the first ends with the word *useless,* the second
with *useful.* The latter, however, is the more emphatic because while Onesimus is said to have been useless with reference to only *one* person, namely,
Philemon, he is described as useful to *two* individuals, "to you and to me."
There is a play on the word *Onesimus,* meaning *profitable, helpful,* or more
precisely, on its synonym *useful* (euchrēstos) as contrasted with *useless*
(achrēstos) .[184] Onesimus who formerly to you was *useless,* not minding his
duties, a pilferer and a runaway; hence, totally untrue to the meaning of his
name, has now become *useful,* for as a Christian he will work for you with a
new attitude, striving to please you for Christ's sake, and thus pleasing me
also. Undoubtedly, there is also a reference here to the services which Onesimus, had he remained with Paul, could have rendered to him to lighten
the burden of his imprisonment, for the apostle refers to this in verse 13.

Paul has already appealed to Philemon's outgoing personality (vss. 4-7,
9a) , to his (Paul's) own age and imprisonment for Christ (9b) , and to the
fact that Onesimus has become a believer (verse 10). He now reminds
Philemon of the fact that it will be in his own interest to extend a welcome
to the returning fugitive. Will not the latter serve his master far better than
ever before?

12-14. To all this another, perhaps even more stirring, argument is added
in the words: **whom I am sending back** [185] **to you; (yes, even) him,**[186] **that
is, my very heart.**[187] Onesimus is being sent back, but by no means alone.
Big-hearted Paul sees to it that, instead of forcing this slave to beg for mercy

---

[184] Lenski's denial of this play on words is surprising. The pun is too obvious. One
is reminded of II Thess. 3:11, "not busy workers but busybodies."

[185] ἀνέπεμψα epistolary aorist. That this word should here be taken in a legal sense,
as if an accused were being "sent up" to someone in higher authority, has not been
established. The simple sense is probably the best in the present connection.

[186] "whom . . . him." This resumption of a relative by means of a pronoun occurs
frequently in Hebrew. Whether or not the present resumption must be regarded as
a Semitism is, perhaps, not as important as is the fact that obviously this repetition
is for the sake of emphasis: this very slave, who had made himself so obnoxious, has
now become the object of Paul's most tender affection.

[187] On σπλάγχνα in the sense of *heart,* both here and in verses 7 and 20, see footnote 39, p. 58 of N.T.C. on Philippians. The additional words of the A.V., "thou
therefore receive him," are based upon a reading for which the textual evidence is
definitely weak. For the idea itself see, however, verse 17, which is probably the
source of the words inserted here in verse 12.

all by himself, he returns supported by: a. Tychicus (see explanation of Col. 4:7-9), b. a letter from Paul addressed to the entire congregation of Colosse, in which love and the spirit of forgiveness is emphasized, and c. a letter dealing specifically with the case of Onesimus. Surely, never did a runaway return to his master in better company! Onesimus is "my very heart," writes Paul. So deeply does he feel himself attached to this newly won convert to the Christian faith. See also Col. 4:9. How could Philemon reject Paul's very heart?

In similar vein the apostle continues, **whom I could have wished to keep with me, in order that in your behalf he might render service to me in the bonds of the gospel.** "For an instant," says Paul, as it were, "it occurred to me that I should keep Onesimus with me to render personal service to me in my imprisonment.[188] But immediately my better judgment said, No, that cannot be. Not I but Philemon must make the final decision regarding Onesimus." Paul is speaking about help that might have been rendered to himself by Onesimus, serving in behalf of Philemon. Note "in your behalf he." Here the apostle, with marvelous generosity, is assuming that Philemon had been wishing that he himself could render such service to Paul; and also that, prevented by distance from doing so, Philemon, had he but known all the circumstances, would have been only too happy to substitute the services of Onesimus for his own. However, Paul is also convinced that it would have been wrong for him *to act* on this assumption and to have kept Onesimus with him in Rome. Why would it have been improper? Says Paul: **but without your consent I did not wish to do anything, that your goodness might not be compulsory but voluntary.** There is not even a hint here that *even now* Paul wants Philemon to send Onesimus back to Rome to be of assistance to the apostle. Such an idea is simply read into the text. On the contrary, Paul, the prisoner is rather expecting that he will be released and is already asking that at Colosse lodging be prepared for him (verse 22). Paul's actual purpose in verses 10-14 is to show Philemon what a very valuable man Onesimus has become. He is profitable, Paul's very heart, one whom Paul would have been glad to retain. "Hence, Philemon, you better forgive and forget." Cf. verse 17.

"Had I kept him with me," says Paul, as it were, "this would hardly have been fair to you. It would have placed you before an accomplished fact. In that case, your subsequent acquiescence or approval would have been a matter of coercion, not of spontaneous volition." Here Paul is imitating God as a beloved child (cf. Eph. 5:1). Was not this the reason why God had issued the probationary command in the Garden of Eden, namely, in order to give man an opportunity to serve God *of his own accord?* And had not Paul, in II Cor. 8:1-6, praised the churches of Macedonia because they had made

---

[188] For similar service see what is said about Epaphroditus in Phil. 2:25b.

their generous contributions "of their own accord"? Cf. also Ex. 35:29; 36:5. Philemon would have been deprived of the privilege of making such a spontaneous contribution — in this case consisting of the service of Onesimus — had Paul presumed on his goodness.

15, 16. Still another reason why Philemon should grant Paul's request in the interest of Onesimus is now presented: **Perhaps the reason why he was parted (from you) for a short period was this, that you might have him back forever.** Note that with a love that covers all things (I Peter 4:8; cf. I Cor. 13:7) the pleader here places the most charitable construction possible upon the case of Onesimus. He does not say, "Perhaps the reason why he ran away from you after committing larceny," etc., but "Perhaps the reason why *he was parted* (from you)," etc. In other words, Paul, though by no means clearing Onesimus of guilt, wants Philemon to see and consider God's glorious, overruling providence. "Behold *the hand of God*, in this happening," says he, as it were. God used the evil deed of Onesimus to bring about good, and this both for the runaway himself and for Philemon. The latter had been parted for a short period from *a slave;* he is joined forever to *a brother!* The bond between master and slave had been severed for the brief span intervening between the flight and the return. The bond between the two as brothers in Christ would never be severed, neither here nor in the hereafter. That was God's grand design, his marvelous plan.

Here again there is no hint of any intention on Paul's part that Onesimus be returned to him, to be of assistance to him in Rome. If anything, the very opposite: "that *you* might have him back," writes Paul.[189]

Having said, "that you might have him back forever," the apostle continues, **no longer as a slave but something better than a slave, a brother beloved.** This passage makes it clear that Paul does not consider immediate, forced emancipation the true solution of the slavery problem. He does not say, "that you might set him free," but "that you might have him back, no longer as a slave but something better than a slave, a brother beloved." When a slave becomes a "brother beloved," he ceases to be a slave, though he is still, as in this case, a servant. Paul adds, **especially to me but how much more to you.** At first glance these words seem somewhat illogical, for if it be true that by saying "especially to me" Paul is already singling out the most prominent example among all those to whom Onesimus would now be a brother beloved, how can he add, *"how much more* to you"? I have found the following solutions:

(1) The word translated *especially,* as here used, really means *exceed-*

---

[189] I am therefore in full agreement with C. F. D. Moule who states (*op. cit.,* pp. 146, 147), "But the τάχα γάρ, following what is said in v. 14, makes it difficult to interpret the present verse otherwise than as a reference to the possibility of its *not* being his master's intention (γνώμη) to part with Onesimus."

ingly or *immensely* [what about *intensely?*]. This will allow for the expression "how much more," without violating logic.[190]

(2) This is in reality an illogicality springing from enthusiasm: "most of all to me — more than most of all to you."

If either of these two solutions must be accepted I, for one, prefer the first, as the second is really no solution at all. Is there not a third possibility? It could be the following:

(3) When Paul begins to write this modifier, he is comparing his own relation to Onesimus with the relation in which believers in general would now stand to this converted man. And since to him, Paul, and to no one else, had been granted the privilege of becoming the spiritual father of Onesimus (verse 10), he is fully justified in calling him "a brother beloved *especially to me.*" However, as the apostle continues to describe the person in whose interest he is writing this stirring appeal, he now compares his own relation to him with the relation which specifically Philemon would bear to him. From a certain aspect the latter relationship would excel the former, and this for the reason which Paul immediately adds, namely, **both in the flesh and in the Lord.** The "flesh" relationship which existed between the master and the servant did not obtain between the "father" and the "child." Between Paul and Onesimus there was only a spiritual relationship, though it was, indeed, a very beautiful one. Between Philemon and Onesimus there was, in addition, also this "flesh" relationship. In both of these relationships Onesimus, it is here assumed, would now be very dear to Philemon. Inquiry into the question just what is meant by the words, "both in the flesh and in the Lord," has resulted in such answers as the following:

(1) both as a fellow-Colossian and as a brother in the Lord;

(2) both in the affairs of this world and in the affairs of the higher life.

The latter, it would seem to me, deserves the preference here, in harmony with the use of the word "flesh" ($\sigma \acute{\alpha} \rho \xi$) in such passages as Gal. 2:20; Phil. 1:22, 24.[191] Both at work and in church the new and sanctified relationship between master and servant, brother and brother, will assert itself.

17. On the basis, then, of all these grounds which Paul has presented in support of his plea, let Philemon take favorable action: **If then you consider me a partner, accept him as (you accept) me.** The original means "Take Onesimus *to yourself* just as you do me." This is more than just extending a hearty welcome to a person upon arrival. Moreover, when Paul writes, "If then you consider me a partner," he means more than, "If you look upon me as a friend." The *partner* here is the *koinōnos,* the *sharer* in

---

[190] In other words, $\mu \acute{\alpha} \lambda \iota \sigma \tau a$ is here used in an elative sense.

[191] For a classification of the various shades of meaning which this word has in the epistles of Paul see N.T.C. on Philippians, p. 77, footnote 55. Meaning c. would seem to be indicated here.

the *koinōnia* (spiritual fellowship) . This fellowship always implies *sharing* (see on verse 6) , and at times must be so rendered.[192] Let, therefore, all the rights and privileges pertaining to any one who is included in this blessed fellowship be given to the one who is now returning as a humble penitent, a sincere child of God!

18-20. All the while, as Paul was writing or dictating, there was present in his mind one final matter which might, after all, prove to be a real obstacle in the path leading to complete reconciliation. The apostle knew very well that any one traveling all the way from Colosse to Rome would need money. He also was not ignorant of the fact that lack of trustworthiness in matters relating to material things was characteristic of slaves. After his release from the present (first Roman) imprisonment he was going to write to Titus: "Urge slaves to be submissive in every respect to their own masters . . . *not pilfering, but evincing the utmost trustworthiness*" (Titus 2:9, 10) . It is possible that Onesimus had told Paul that he had committed theft. More probable, it would seem to me, is the supposition that Paul was entertaining justified suspicions that such a wrong had been committed. This would account for the use of the significant two-letter word *If* in verse 18. Paul was not sure, but suspected it! [193] This possible hindrance to the establishment of the proper, Christian relationship between master and returning servant must be removed. Therefore, gracious, big-hearted Paul continues: **But if he has caused you any loss or owes you anything, charge that to my account.** Had Paul come into an inheritance in recent years, that he was able to make this generous offer? On the basis of the fact that according to Acts 24:26 Felix detained the apostle, hoping that the latter would purchase his freedom; of Acts 28:30, which contains a reference to Paul's "own rented quarters"; and of the passage now under discussion, some have arrived at this conclusion. In any event Paul either had some money or knew where he could get it. He was entirely sincere in offering compensation for the loss which Philemon might have suffered. So, using commercial phraseology, he says, "Charge that to my account." He continues, **I, Paul, do myself write this with my own hand.** In other words, "Here is my promissory note, with my own signature attached to it." This has been interpreted to mean that the entire letter was in Paul's own handwriting. Though this possibility must be granted, it cannot be proved. All the statement actually means is that the promise to reimburse Philemon for the loss suffered was made with Paul's own hand. That the closing salutation was also by Paul's

---

[192] See N.T.C. on Philippians, pp. 51-54 and 93-95, for full discussion.
[193] I prefer this rather common interpretation to the one offered by Lenski (*op. cit.,* pp. 968, 969) , according to which the wrong done was simply this, that by fleeing Onesimus had deprived his master of his services. But in that case it is hard to explain Paul's *If*. The fact that the slave had caused his master the loss of his services was undeniable.

own hand is clear from II Thess. 3:17. Possibly the apostle himself, without use of secretary, wrote verses 18-25. But this is merely a conjecture. The offer here made is a very solemn one. It showed how intensely Paul had come to love Onesimus. Was it with somewhat of a sense of benign, fatherly humor that the pleader added: **not to mention** [but he does mention it; hence, probably meaning, not to stress the fact] **to you that you owe me your very self besides?** "Philemon, instead of my owing you this money, you really owe it to me; yes, far more besides, for you owe me your very self, your very life as a believer." [194]

Philemon had been converted either directly, through the instrumentality of Paul, perhaps while the master of Onesimus was on a visit to Ephesus and heard the apostle preach (Acts 19:10), or indirectly, through the labors of Epaphras who, in turn, was indebted to Paul. In either case Paul was able to write, "You owe me your very self." This also shows that the apostle was a firm believer in the principle of reciprocation: the obligation to make a return for favors or blessings received. He believed that this principle applied both to things received from God (see verse 6; also II Cor. 1:34; 8:7, 9; cf. Ps. 116:12) and from men (cf. I Tim. 5:4).

Reflecting then once more on the entire plea, with all the grounds so far mentioned, Paul continues, **Yes, brother, let me have some benefit** [195] **from you in the Lord.** The term of endearment, *brother* (see also verse 7), expressing love and intimate spiritual relationship, fits very well at this point. What is especially striking is the manner in which Paul all but identifies himself with Onesimus. He says, "Let *me* have some benefit from you." In other words, whatever favor Philemon grants to Onesimus is to be viewed as granted to Paul himself. We have a similar instance of the marvelous identifying power of love in the Syrophoenician woman's touching plea in behalf of her daughter. She says to Jesus, "Help *me!*" (Matt. 15:25), and, of course, in the words of Christ himself, "To the extent that y o u have done it to one of these brothers of mine, (even) the least (of them), y o u have done it to *me*" (Matt. 25:40). As a mere human being, acting apart from Christ, it might have been impossible for Philemon to pardon and restore Onesimus. Let him then do it (and thereby impart a benefit to Paul) *in the Lord,* in fellowship with him; reflecting on the blessings which he himself, the master of Onesimus, had received from fellowship with *his* Master, and by means of the grace and power derived from him. Paul adds, **Refresh my heart in Christ.** For the meaning of these words see on verse 7. The apostle is expressing the wish that he, too, may be included in the circle of those to whom Philemon in the past has given rest of heart. And this, in fellowship

---

[194] As I see it, we have here another case of abbreviated expression. See N.T.C. on John 5:31. For a different explanation see Lenski, *op. cit.,* p. 971.
[195] ὀναίμην. This could well be a play on the name Onesimus. It is the only instance of the use of the first person optative in the New Testament.

with Christ. Let him place the entire matter before Christ. If he does this, there can be but one answer. He will surely grant Paul's request. In fact, he will do even more; hence, Paul continues:

21. Confident of your obedience I am writing to you. This obedience to which the apostle refers is *gospel-obedience*. It is a hearkening to the demands of God as expressed in the gospel (cf. Rom. 10:16; Phil. 2:12; II Thess. 3:14). It is, therefore, more than heeding *Paul's* advice and granting his request. It is exactly the gospel as proclaimed by Christ that demands that those who have been greatly benefited shall also show kindness to others. Matt. 18:21-35 proves this point in a striking manner. The apostle states, as it were, that he does not even have to wait until he hears whether or not Philemon has acted according to the stirring plea that was by means of this letter presented to him. He fully trusts Philemon to do what is right and charitable. In fact, he adds, **knowing that you will do even better than I say.** Exactly what Paul may have had in mind when he added these words we do not know. To infer from this rather obscure hint that the apostle *must* have meant, "I know that you will send Onesimus right back to me," or "I know that you will at once emancipate him," is certainly rash. Besides, Paul was not thinking in terms of having Onesimus returned to him, but rather of his own liberation from imprisonment and a journey to Colosse (verse 22). Aside from emancipation, there were other ways in which Philemon was able to do even better than requested. To mention but a few: he might give Onesimus some spare-time to do evangelistic work. He might review his entire relation to his servants on the basis of gospel principles. He might, as a result, urge other masters, too, to treat their servants with greater consideration. He might send a message to Paul, saying, "You asked me to provide a guest room for you. I'll do better than that. You can stay at my own home." And so one could easily continue. But this should suffice to show that those who think that there was *only one* way in which Philemon could do even better than requested are in error.

22. Paul concludes his eloquent plea in words which, on the surface, may seem to have nothing to do with it, and to introduce an entirely new subject, but which actually stand in close connection with it, namely, **At the same time, prepare a guest room for me.** The true interpretation, it would seem to me, is the one given by Lightfoot (*op. cit.*, p. 345), who shows the connection in these words, "There is a gentle compulsion in this mention of a personal visit to Colosse. The apostle would thus be able to see for himself that Philemon had not disappointed his expectations." Paul's tactfulness surely is evident here also, as it is so strikingly throughout the letter. See the Summary which follows the exegesis of this chapter. Paul continues, **for I am hoping that through y o u r prayers I shall be granted to y o u.** Here the second person plural reappears: the prayers to which Paul refers are those not only of Philemon but also af Apphia, Archippus, and in fact of all believers in Colosse. Not only does *he* pray for Philemon (verse 4) and for believers everywhere, but *he also wants believers to pray for him* and for others who are engaged in spiritual warfare. "Brothers, do pray for us," is the language he uses elsewhere (I Thess. 5:25) ; see also on Col. 1:9, the parallel columns. Moreover, he does not say, "Through y o u r prayers I hope to be released from imprisonment," though that, of course, is implied, but phrases it far more beautifully: "I shall be granted to y o u." Here again it becomes evident that Paul, the prisoner, is conscious of that same providential guidance with respect to his own life to which he had already directed the mind of Philemon in verse 15, in order that the latter might also gratefully discern it in whatever had happened to him. Above all, Paul here displays, as he does so often, his firm conviction that God is an answerer of prayer. All the evidence points to the fact that Paul was, indeed, released from his first Roman imprisonment, and made more journeys.[196] No doubt he made use of the guest room prepared for him by Philemon, whether in his own home or elsewhere.

---

23 Epaphras, my fellow-prisoner in Christ Jesus, greets you, 24 (and so do) Mark, Aristarchus, Demas, and Luke, my fellow-workers.
25 The grace of the Lord Jesus Christ (be) with y o u r spirit.

23-25

IV. *Greetings and Closing Salutation*

A. *Greetings*

23, 24. Epaphras, my fellow-prisoner in Christ Jesus, greets you, (and so do) Mark, Aristarchus, Demas, and Luke, my fellow-workers.
For these five men and the greetings they send see on Col. 4:10-14.

B. *Closing Salutation*

25. The grace of the Lord Jesus Christ (be) with y o u r spirit. The best textual evidence supports this reading. One is reminded of Phil. 4:23; cf. also Gal. 6:18; I Cor. 16:23; I Thess. 5:28; II Thess. 3:18; and II Tim. 4:22. Upon Philemon, Apphia, Achippus, and all those who gather for worship in their home, yes, upon all Colossian believers, Paul, as God's official representative, pronounces God's grace, that is, his unmerited favor in the

---

[196] See for this evidence and for a conjecture as to the apostle's itinerary N.T.C. on I and II Timothy and Titus, pp. 23-28, 39, 40.

anointed Lord and Savior, based on his merits, conveyed by his Spirit. If this pronouncement is accepted with a believing heart, then from this basic blessing of grace all others flow forth, filling the very *spirit* (pneuma), the inner personality viewed as contact-point between God and his child, with the peace of God that passes all understanding!

No one has attached a postscript to this gem of a letter. Information as to whether Philemon acted in accordance with Paul's stirring, masterly plea is entirely lacking, though a favorable inference is inescapable. The main point is this: here is Christianity in action. Here is an actual demonstration and illustration of *faith working through love!*

Summary of Philemon

of Paul's Masterpiece of Tactful Pleading, in which he asks Philemon that the runaway slave, Onesimus, who as a penitent and converted man is now returning to the house from which he fled, be fully accepted.

(1) Listen to me, that is, to Paul, a man who has grown old in the service of his Lord (verse 9).

(2) I am now a prisoner of Christ Jesus (1, 9). Surely, compared to the hardships of my imprisonment how small is the favor I am asking of you.

(3) Besides, I am your friend, who loves you, and admires you for the manner in which you have again and again refreshed the hearts of the saints (4, 5, 7, 8, 9, 20).

(4) We are in debt to God for all his goodness shown to us (6). Also, you are in debt to me. In fact, you owe me your very life (19).

(5) Onesimus is my child, my very heart, a brother beloved (10, 12, 16).

(6) It is to your advantage to grant my request that you accept Onesimus, for the once useless one has become useful. I, for one, surely so regard him (11, 13, 14).

(7) Favorable action on your part would be in line with God's providential direction, which we should gratefully acknowledge (15, 22b).

(8) The fellowship of all believers in Christ demands this, for not only you and I are included in this but so is Onesimus (17).

(9) I have confidence in your obedience (21).

(10) I want you to prepare a guest room for me, for I hope, in answer to the prayers of God's children, to be granted to y o u (22b). Surely, you would not wish to disappoint my eyes.

These are the ten arguments Paul uses.

Paul's Epistle to Philemon

1 Paul, a prisoner of Christ Jesus, and Timothy our brother, to Philemon our beloved (brother) and fellow-worker 2 and to Apphia our sister and to Archippus our fellow-soldier and to the church in your house; 3 grace to y o u and peace from God our Father and the Lord Jesus Christ.

4 I thank my God always, making mention of you in my prayers, 5 because I hear of your love and of the faith which you have, (the latter) toward the Lord Jesus, and (the former) for all the saints, 6 (praying) that the sharing to which your faith gives rise may be energetically stimulated for Christ by the clear recognition of all the good that is ours. 7 For I have derived much joy and comfort from your love, because the hearts of the saints have been refreshed through you, brother.

8 Accordingly, although in Christ I am quite free to order you (to do) your duty, 9 yet for love's sake I rather appeal to you — since I am such a person as Paul, an old man, and now also a prisoner of Christ Jesus — 10 I appeal to you in the interest of my child, whom I have begotten in my bonds, Onesimus, 11 who formerly to you was useless, but now both to you and to me is useful, 12 whom I am sending back to you; (yes, even) him, that is, my very heart, 13 whom I could have wished to keep with me, in order that in your behalf he might render service to me in the bonds of the gospel; 14 but without your consent I did not wish to do anything, that your goodness might not be compulsory but voluntary.

15 Moreover, perhaps the reason why he was parted (from you) for a short period was this, that you might have him back forever, 16 no longer as a slave but something better than a slave, a brother beloved, especially to me but how much more to you, both in the flesh and in the Lord. 17 If then you consider me a partner, accept him as (you accept) me. 18 But if he has caused you any loss or owes you anything, charge that to my account. 19 I, Paul, do myself write this with my own hand, I will repay it — not to mention to you that you owe me your very self besides. 20 Yes, brother, let me have some benefit from you in the Lord. Refresh my heart in Christ.

21 Confident of your obedience I am writing to you, knowing that you will do even better than I say. 22 At the same time, prepare a guest room for me, for I am hoping that through y o u r prayers I shall be granted to y o u.

23 Epaphras, my fellow-prisoner in Christ Jesus, greets you, 24 (and so do) Mark, Aristarchus, Demas, and Luke, my fellow-workers.

25 The grace of the Lord Jesus Christ (be) with y o u r spirit.

Appendix

Scripture on Tactfulness

In the various textbooks of the biblical sciences this subject is generally neglected. Yet it is by no means of minor importance. Tactfulness is definitely a virtue. Though its presence, sometimes in a remarkable degree, among worldly people cannot be denied (cf. Luke 16:8), yet *in its noblest form* it is a product of special grace. Its parents are Love and Wisdom. It is that skill which, without any sacrifice of honesty or candor, enables a person to speak the right word at the right time, and to do the proper thing in any given situation. It is premeditated prudence, sanctified mother wit, consecrated savoir faire. The tactful person does not shirk his duty even when he is convinced that he must admonish or rebuke. But he has learned the art of doing this without being rude. He is humble, patient, and kind. The apostle Paul draws his picture in I Cor. 13.

God himself is the archetype or model of tactfulness to be imitated by men, as Isa. 28:23-29 teaches so strikingly. In more than one way his divine wisdom coupled with considerateness is shown; for example, in the account of the creation of Eve (Gen. 2:18-24); in his punitive yet also merciful dealing with Adam and Eve immediately after the fall (Gen. 3:9-19); in the manner in which he dealt with Cain (Gen. 4:7, 15), with Abraham (Gen. 12:1-3; cf. chapters 15, 17, 18, 22), and with Jonah (Jonah 4:10, 11). These are but a few instances among ever so many others. In fact, God *always* uses the right approach!

Jesus, during his earthly sojourn, repeatedly demonstrated this quality. The following are but a few examples of his tact in dealing with people: the raising of the daughter of Jairus (see especially Matt. 9:25 and Luke 8:55b); the sending forth of laborers into the spiritual vineyard, selecting those very men who at his suggestion had been praying for such laborers (Matt. 9:37–10:1); his illustrated teaching on the indispensability of humility (Matt. 18:1-3; John 13:1-18); his conversation with the Samaritan woman (John 4:1-42), with Thomas (John 20:24-29), and with grief-stricken Peter (John 21:15-17).

Among purely human biblical examples of tactfulness are the following:
a. in the Old Testament: Abraham's generous proposition made to Lot (Gen. 13:1-13); Joshua's challenge to the elders of Israel, in which he takes the lead in doing for himself and his family what he wants them to do for themselves and their families (Josh. 24:15); Abigail's stirring appeal to David, a supplication presented so tactfully that the latter exclaimed, "Blessed be your discretion" (I Sam. 25:14-33); Nathan's parable of "the little ewe lamb" (II Sam. 12:1-12); Solomon's wise judgment (I Kings

3:16-28); and Mordecai's earnest entreaty presented to his cousin and foster-child, Queen Esther (Esth. 4:13, 14).

b. in the New Testament: Joseph's contemplated action with respect to Mary (Matt. 1:19); John the Baptist's humble recessional (John 3:22-30); the considerate action of "the disciple whom Jesus loved" with respect to Mary, the mother of Jesus (John 27:19b); Gamaliel's advice (Acts 5:33-42); the balanced and forward-looking advice of the Jerusalem Conference (Acts 15:22-29); the irrefusable invitation extended to the missionaries by Lydia (Acts 16:15); the pacifying words of the town-clerk (Acts 19:35-41); Paul's remark to the Sanhedrin, "with respect to the hope of the resurrection of the dead I am on trial," very true and very clever (Acts 23:6-9); and his courageous conduct and inspiring words during the Voyage Dangerous in moments when all seemed hopeless (Acts 27:20-26, 33-36).

This trait in the great men of the Old Testament and of the early church must not be minimized. In fact, it is probably not an exaggeration to say that *one* of the reasons for Paul's almost unbelievable success as a missionary was his tact in dealing with men. Thus, for example, he was eager to become "all things to all men" that he might by all means save some (I Cor. 9:22). Hence, he would carefully choose *one* approach to the Jews (Acts 13:16-41), but *another* to the Gentiles (Acts 17:22-31), would not only address large audiences but would also seek out individuals to bring them to Christ (I Thess. 2:11), would work among the people with his hands in order not to burden them (I Thess. 2:9), and in his epistles would be careful, wherever possible, to speak words of praise and encouragement before presenting his reprimanding admonitions. Yet, he never used words of flattery (I Thess. 2:5), and was able, when the occasion demanded this course, to say, "O foolish Galatians! Who has bewitched y o u?" (Gal. 3:1).

Before taking leave of this subject of the use of tact it should be pointed out that this application of *discretion* or *prudence* in practical matters is as it were a theme that runs through the book of Proverbs from beginning to end. See especially Prov. 1:4; 2:1-5; 2:11; 3:1-12; 3:21; 5:2; 8:12; 10:19; 11:22; 15:1, 17, 28; 19:11; 22:24, 25; 25:11.

Scripture on Slavery

In ancient times slavery was widespread. Especially among the Greeks it was common practice to reduce captives and often criminals and debtors to the state of bondage. On the island of Delos sometimes as many as ten thousand slaves were sold in a single day. Among the Romans the lot of the slave seems to have been more cruel than among the Greeks. The slave was not considered to have any rights. The law offered him no protection. To be sure, there are recorded instances of masters who were kind to their slaves, but these are the exceptions. It is not surprising that a civilization which looked upon all foreigners as "barbarians" and upon labor as "unworthy of a free man and vulgar" (cf. N.T.C. on I and II Thessalonians, pp. 66, 67) would welcome slavery.

In the Old Testament we immediately feel the breath of special revelation. We enter a different world. It must be freely admitted that the Old Testament does not regard the possession of slaves to be *always and under all circumstances* a moral evil. Israelites were permitted to impose the punishment of slavery upon those nations whose cup of iniquity was full (Gen. 15:16; Lev. 25:44-46). A burglar who was unable to make restitution according to the law had to be sold into slavery (Ex. 22:1-3). These were divine regulations of a punitive character. But such stipulations were a far cry from divine and indiscriminate permission for any one to go man-stealing for pleasure or profit. The divine approval did not rest on the kidnaper. On this point the law was clear: "Whoever steals a man, whether he sells him or is found in possession of him, shall be put to death" (Ex. 21:16). Accordingly, when in more recent centuries some have tried to defend modern slavery by appealing to Moses they have done so without any shadow of warrant.

The insecure basis of such an appeal becomes even more clearly evident when the cruelty which in every century has been a characteristic of the slave-trade is taken into consideration. Perhaps a single day spent *as a slave* on a "slave schooner" would have changed the mind of many an advocate of slavery. It is just possible that had he himself been shackled to other slaves for sixteen hours a day in a three-feet high 'tween deck, with little — and in case of rough weather with *no* — ventilation, had he seen other slaves die at sea of dysentery, smallpox, or other disease, or, in case of safe arrival, had he — or *she* — stood upon the block exposed to every vulgarity of man's inhumanity to man, and subsequently while at work had he been flogged unmercifully by a so-called "overseer," he would probably never again defend slavery, not even "as an indispensable means of leading heathen to Christ."

It is exactly the *cruelty* of slavery which even the *Old* Testament opposes with every possible emphasis. Note the following:

(1) A man who has purchased a female slave with the intention of making her an inferior wife is not permitted to treat her as a slave (Ex. 21:7-11).

(2) Extreme cruelty to a slave must result in immediate manumission (Ex. 21:26, 27).

(3) Returning a runaway to his master to become enslaved once more is strictly forbidden (Deut. 23:15).

(4) Though there is a difference among commentators with respect to the question whether all of the kindness-to-slaves regulations applied to foreign (non-Hebrew) slaves as well as to Israelites, the preponderance of evidence is certainly in the direction of the divinely imposed mandate of at least showing fairness and mercy to all, including the foreigner. Thus, for example, definite provision was made for the incorporation of foreign slaves into religious fellowship with Israel, and this by means of circumcision (Gen. 17:12, 13, 22, 23, 26, 27) and partaking of the paschal meal (Ex. 22:44).

(5) Among the Israelites an impoverished person could "sell himself" in order thus to pay his debts. But his condition was in reality not that of slavery but rather that of mild indenture or voluntary apprenticeship (Lev. 25:39).

(6) The basic rule in Israel is laid down in Lev. 25:42, 43, namely, "They are my servants whom I brought forth out of the land of Egypt. They shall not be sold as slaves, neither shall you rule over him with harshness. You shall revere God" (Lev. 25:42, 43; cf. Neh. 5:5).

(7) For the Hebrew indentured servant the seventh year was that of emancipation (Ex. 21:1, 2), or if the year of jubilee should arrive before the seventh year then that year of jubilee meant freedom (Lev. 25:39-41).

(8) When a Hebrew had served his term he must not be sent away as a pauper or beggar. On the contrary, "When you let him go away from you into freedom, you must not let him go empty-handed. You shall furnish him liberally with provisions from your flock, from your threshing floor, and from your wine-press. As Jehovah your God has blessed you, you must give to him. You shall remember that you yourself were once a slave in the land of Egypt, and that Jehovah your God redeemed you. That is the reason why I give you this command today" (Deut. 15:13-15).

(9) In fact, the probability existed that at times an indentured servant, given permission to become a free man, would say, "I love my master, my wife, and my children; I will not go out free." Definite provision was made whereby also such a desire could be fulfilled (Ex. 21:5, 6).

We come to the New Testament. Here in the attitude of the centurion toward his slave one finds the counterpart of (9) above. When conditions were ideal, the servant's "I love my master" (Ex. 21:5), would be answered by the master's, "My servant is precious to me" (Luke 7:2), and vice versa. It fills the heart with pure delight to hear the centurion address Jesus in these words, "Say the word, and *my boy* will be healed" (Luke 7:7). Surely, such "slavery" ceased to be slavery at all! Moreover, the love proclaimed by Jesus, a love extending even to enemies (Matt. 5:43-48), has had its definite effect on the thinking of every consistent believer. Paul proclaimed the truth, "There can be neither Jew nor Greek; there can be neither bond nor free . . . y o u are all one man in Christ Jesus" (Gal. 3:28). God does not favor masters above slaves. With him there is no partiality (Eph. 6:5-9; Col. 3:11, 25). It is not surprising therefore that Paul mentions "kidnapers" or "slave-dealers" in one breath with murderers and sodomites as those against whom the law of God thunders its denunciations (I Tim. 1:9b, 10). The book of Revelation implies that one of the reasons for the fall and desolation of Babylon was the slave-trade (Rev. 18:13).

Thus Old and New Testament combine in showing that though those indeed, are wrong who attach an exclusively "social" value to Christianity, those, too, are in error who assign to it a purpose so abstractly "religious" that it loses all contact with the concrete situations of life. To be sure Christianity is a religion, but a religion that includes definite guide-lines for human action in every sphere. No Christian should ever be afraid to condemn the curse of slavery. He has Scripture, both Old and New Testament, on his side.

All this does not mean that either Jesus or Paul advocated social revolution: immediate emancipation of every slave. Such a sudden upheaval of the entire Roman economy would have resulted in indescribable misery for many a bondman who depended on his master for a living, and would have placed an insurmountable obstacle in the way of the propagation of the Christian faith.

Enforced emancipation has by no means always been appreciated even by the slaves. The booklet *Strange But True,* pp. 6, 7, relates that when imperial Russia gained control over the Caucasus territory, the viceroy of the Czar advised the local princes to emancipate their house-slaves. When the slaves heard about it, however, they protested bitterly, and insisted that slavery was their hereditary right!

Another somewhat similar scene is touchingly portrayed by Susan Dabney Smedes, one of whose essays is found on pp. 796-800 of *The Heritage of America.* This concerns the aftermath of the Civil War. She writes that even long after Lincoln had issued his Emancipation Proclamation "no apparent change took place among the Burleigh Negroes. Those who worked in the fields went out as usual and cultivated and gathered in the crops.

APPENDIX

In the house they went about their customary duties. We expected them to go away or to demand wages or at least to give some sign that they knew they were free. But, except that they were very quiet and serious and more obedient and kind than they had ever been known to be for more than a few weeks at a time of sickness or other affliction, we saw no change in them. At Christmas such compensation was made them for their services as seemed just. Afterward fixed wages were offered and accepted. Thomas called them up now and told them that as they no longer belonged to him they must discontinue calling him master. 'Yes, marster,' 'Yes, marster,' was the answer to this." [197]

Now whatever value there may be in the objection that the instances related must have been of an exceptional character, it remains true that especially this second example points in the right direction as to the true solution, and this not only of the slavery question of the past but also of similar problems today. What Paul teaches, not only in his letter to Philemon but also elsewhere, is that *love, coming from both sides* (masters and slaves) *is the only solution*. This love is the response to God's love for his child. Whether that child be black or white, bond or free, makes no difference. It is this love of God which melts cruelty into kindness and in so doing changes despots into kind employers, slaves into willing servants, and all who accept it into "brothers" in Christ. The kingship or rule of God works from within outward, not from without inward. The truth of the gospel contained in passages such as Matt. 5:43-48; 7:12; John 3:16; Acts 10:34, 35; Rom. 3:21-24; 12:9-14; I Cor. 13; Eph. 6:5-9; Col. 3:12-17, 25–4:1, will do far more to solve social questions than any number of bayonets.

Brief Bibliography on Slavery

In addition to articles on slavery in the best encyclopaedias see also the following:

J. O. Buswell, *Slavery, Segregation, and Scripture,* Grand Rapids, 1964. This book contains a good Bibliography, pp. 93-97.

H. S. Commager and A. Nevins (editors), *The Heritage of America,* especially sections 99 ("The Rev. Mr. Walsh Inspects a Slave Ship") and 183 ("Thomas Dabney Does the Family Wash").

J. C. Furnas, *Goodbye to Uncle Tom,* New York, 1956.

A. Grünfeld, *Die Stellung der Sklaven bei den Juden,* Jena, 1886.

E. Hamilton, "The Roman Way," R. Carpenter, "Ancient Rome Brought to Life," and R. Stillwell, "Greece — The Birthplace of Science and Free Speech," three articles in *Everyday Life in Ancient Times,* published by the National Geographic Society, 1951, as reprints of articles that appeared in the issues of Oct., 1941, March, 1944, Nov. 1946, and Jan. 1951.

---

[197] From *The Heritage of America,* edited by Henry Steele Commager and Allan Nevins, Copyright 1939, 1949 by Henry Steele Commager and Allan Nevins. Reprinted by permission of Little, Brown and Company, Publishers.

APPENDIX

M. Mielziner, *Die Verhältnisse der Sklaven bei den alten Hebräer*, Leipsic, 1859,
   Eng. transl, in *Evang. Review*, 1862, pp. 311-355.
P. Schaff, *Slavery and the Bible*, Mercersburg, 1860.
J. R. Spears, *The American Slave Trade*, New York, 1960.
R. Wallace, "How the Negro Came to Slavery in America," *Life*, Sept. 3, 1956.

For the older literature see the Bibliography at the close of the article "Slavery"
in *The New Schaff-Herzog Encyclopaedia of Religious Knowledge*, Vol. X, pp.
449-454.

SELECT BIBLIOGRAPHY

I would especially recommend the following:

Bruce, F. F., *Commentary on the Epistle to the Colossians* (*New International Commentary on the New Testament*), Grand Rapids, Mich., 1957.

Calvin, John, *Commentarius In Epistolam Pauli Ad Colossenses. . . . Ad Philemonem* (*Corpus Reformatorum,* vol. LXXX), Brunsvigae, 1895; English translation (*Calvin's Commentaries*), Grand Rapids, Mich., respectively, 1957, 1948.

Lightfoot, J. B., *Saint Paul's Epistles to the Colossians and to Philemon,* reprint of 1879 edition, Grand Rapids, Mich.

Ridderbos, Herman, *Aan de Kolossenzen* (*Commentaar op het Nieuwe Testament*), Kampen, 1960.

GENERAL BIBLIOGRAPHY

For other titles see List of Abbreviations and Brief Bibliography on Slavery.

Abbott, T. K., *The Epistles to the Ephesians and to the Colossians* (*International Critical Commentary*), New York, 1916.

Ante-Nicene Fathers, ten volumes, reprint, Grand Rapids, Mich., 1950, for references to Clement of Alexandria, Irenaeus, Justin Martyr, Origen, Tertullian, etc.

Barclay, W., *The Letters to the Philippians, Colossians, and Thessalonians* (*The Daily Study Bible Series*), second edition, Philadelphia, 1959.

Barnes, A., *Notes on the New Testament, Ephesians, Philippians and Colossians*, reprint, Grand Rapids, Mich., 1949; also *Thess.-Philemon*.

Barnett, A. E., *The New Testament: Its Making and Meaning*, Nashville, 1946.

Beare, F. W., *The Epistle to the Colossians* (*Interpreter's Bible*, Vol. XI), New York and Nashville, 1955.

Benoit, P., *La Sainte Bible traduite en francais sous la direction de l'École Biblique de Jerusalem*, 1949.

Berkhof, L., *New Testament Introduction*, Grand Rapids, Mich., 1916.

Berkhof, L., *Systematic Theology*, Grand Rapids, Mich., 1949.

Bible, Holy, In addition to references to Bible-versions other than English, there are references to the following English translations: A.V., A.R.V., R.S.V., Berkeley, N.E.B., New American Standard, Moffatt, Goodspeed. These are references. The *translation* which is found in N.T.C. and followed in the exegesis is the author's own.

Bieder, W., *Brief an die Kolosser*, Zurich, 1943.

Bruce, F. F., *Commentary on the Epistle to the Colossians* (*New International Commentary on the New Testament*), Grand Rapids, Mich., 1957.

Buckler, W. H., and Calder, W. M., *Monumenta Asiae Minoris Antiqua*, Vol. VI. *Monuments and Documents from Phrygia and Caria*, 1939.

Burney, C. F., "Christ as the ARXH of Creation," *JTS* xxvii (1925, 1926), pp. 160 ff.

Burrows, M., *The Dead Sea Scrolls*, New York, 1956.

Burrows, M., *More Light on the Dead Sea Scrolls*, New York, 1958.

Calvin, John, *Commentarius In Epistolam Pauli Ad Colossenses. . . . Ad Philemonem* (*Corpus Reformatorum*, vol. LXXX), Brunsvigae, 1895; English translation (*Calvin's Commentaries*), Grand Rapids, Mich., respectively, 1957, 1948.

Charlesworth, M. P., *Trade Routes and Commerce of the Roman Empire*, 1924.

Conybeare, W. J., and Howson, J. S., *The Life and Epistles of St. Paul*, reprint, Grand Rapids, Mich., 1949.

Cullmann, O., *Königsherrschaft Christi und Kirche im N.T.*, 1950.

Deissmann, A., *Light From the Ancient East* (translated by L. R. M. Strachan), New York, 1927.

Dennis, J. S., *Christian Missions and Social Progress* (3 volumes), New York, Chicago, Toronto, 1899.

Dibelius, M., *An die Kolosser, Epheser, an Philemon* (Lietzmann's *Handbuch zum Neuen Testament*), 3rd edition, revised by H. Greeven, Tübingen, 1953.

GENERAL BIBLIOGRAPHY

Dodd, C. H., *Colossians and Philemon* (*Abingdon Commentary*) , 1929.

Erdman, C. R., *The Epistles of Paul to the Colossians and Philemon*, Philadelphia, 1933.

Findlay, G. G., "The Reading and Rendering of Colossians 2:18," *Exp*, first series, 11 (1880) , pp. 385-398.

Findlay, G. G., "On Colossians 2:22, 23," *Exp*, first series, 12 (1880), pp. 289-303.

Forschungen in Ephesos veröffentlicht vom Österreichschen archäologischen Institute, 1906-1953.

Fransen, H., "Enkele Opmerkingen over de exegese van Kol. 2:8 en 9," *GTT* (1952) , pp. 65-89.

Glover, R. H., *The Progress of World-Wide Missions*, New York, N.Y., 1925.

Goodenough, "Paul and Onesimus," *HTR*, 22 (1929) , pp. 181-183.

Goodspeed, E. J., *New Solutions to New Testament Problems*, Chicago, 1927.

Goodspeed, E. J., *The Meaning of Ephesians*, Chicago, 1933.

Goodspeed, E. J., *The Key to Ephesians*, Chicago, 1956.

Greeven, H., "Prüfung der Thesen von J. Knox zum Philemon brief," *TZ*, 79 (1954) , pp. 373-378.

Greijdanus, S., *Bizondere Canoniek*, Kampen, 1949, two volumes.

Grollenberg, L. H., *Atlas of the Bible*, tr. of *Atlas van de Bijbel*) , London and Edinburgh, 1956.

Grosheide, F. W., "Kol. 3:1-4; I Petr. 1:3-5; I Joh. 3:1, 2," *GTT* 54 (1954) , pp. 139-147.

Hamilton, W. J., *Researches in Asia Minor, Pontus, and Armenia*, 1842.

Harris, J. R., "St. Paul and Aristopanes," *ET* 34 (1922, 1923), pp. 151-156.

Harrison, P. N., "Onesimus and Philemon," *ATR*, XXXII (1950), pp. 286-294.

Hendriksen, W., *Bible Survey*, Grand Rapids, Mich., sixth printing, 1961.

Hendriksen, W., *More Than Conquerors, An Interpretation of the Book of Revelation*, Grand Rapids, Mich., thirteenth edition, 1963.

Hendriksen, W., *The Bible on the Life Hereafter*, Grand Rapids, Mich., second printing, 1963.

Holtzmann, H. J., *Kritik der Epheser- und Kolosserbriefe*, 1872.

Hopkins, C., and Baur, P. V. C., *Christian Church at Dura-Europos*, New Haven, 1934.

Hurlbut, J. L., *A Bible Atlas*, New York, Chicago, San Francisco, 1940.

Johnson, Sherman E., "Laodicea and its Neighbors," *BA*, Vol. XIII (Feb. 1950) , pp. 1-18.

Johnson, Sherman E., "Early Christianity in Asia Minor," *JBL*, 77 (March 1958) , pp. 1-17.

Käsemann, E., "Eine urchristliche Taufliturgie," *Festschrift Rudolf Bultmann zum 65. Geburtstag überreicht*, 1949.

Keller, W., *The Bible as History*, New York, N.Y., 1956.

Knox, J., *The Epistle to Philemon* (Interpreter's Bible, Vol. XI) , New York, 1955.

Knox, J., *Philemon among the Letters of Paul*, Chicago, 1959.

Kraeling, E., *Rand McNally Bible Atlas*, New York, Chicago, San Francisco, 1956.

Kremer, J., *Was an den Leiden Christi noch mangelt. Eine interpretationsgechichliche und exegetische Untersuchung zu Kol. 1, 24b* (Bonner, *Biblische Beiträge*) , 1956.

Kuiper, H. J. (editor) , *The New Christian Hymnal*, Grand Rapids, Mich., 1929.

Lenski, R. C. H., *Interpretation of Colossians, Thessalonians, Timothy, Titus, Philemon*, Columbus, Ohio, 1946.

Lightfoot, J. B., *Saint Paul's Epistle to the Colossians and to Philemon*, reprint of 1879 edition, Grand Rapids, Mich.

GENERAL BIBLIOGRAPHY

Loeb Classical Library, New York (various dates), for The Apostolic Fathers, Eusebius, Horodotus, Josephus, Philo, Pliny, Plutarch, Strabo, Xenophon, etc.

Lohmeyer, E., *Die Briefe an die Kolosser und an Philemon* (*Meyers Kommentar*), Göttingen, 1930.

Lukyn, W. A., *The Epistles of Paul to the Colossians and to Philemon* (*Cambridge Greek Testament for Schools and Colleges*), Cambridge, 1907.

Marsh, F. B., *A History of the Roman World from 146-30 B. C.*, second edition, London, 1953.

Masson, C., *L'Épître de Saint Paul aux Colossiens* (*Commentaire du Nouveau Testament*, X), 1950.

Matheson, G., "The Pauline Argument for a Future State," *Exp*, first series, 9 (1879), pp. 264-284.

Maurer, C., "Die Begründung der Herrschaft Christi über die Mächte nach Kolosser 1:15-20," *Wort und Dienst, Jahrbuch der Theologischen Schule Bethel*, n.F.IV (1955), pp. 79-93.

Mayerhoff, E. Th., *Der Brief an die Colosser mit vornehmlichter Berücksichtigung der drei Pastoralbriefe kritisch geprüft*, Berlin, 1838.

Mitton, C. L., *The Formation of the Pauline Corpus of Letters*, London, 1955.

Moule, C. F. D., *The Epistles of Paul the Apostle to the Colossians and to Philemon* ("Cambridge Greek Testament Commentary"), Cambridge, 1957.

Mulder, H., *De vondsten bij de Dode Zee*, 's-Gravenhage, 1957.

Müller, J. J., *The Epistles of Paul to the Philippians and to Philemon* (*The New International Commentary on the New Testament*), Grand Rapids, Mich., 1955.

Murray, J., *Christian Baptism*, Philadelphia, 1952.

National Geographic Magazine, "Lands of the Bible Today" (Dec. 1956) ; in the same issue, "Jerusalem to Rome in the Path of St. Paul." Also published by National Geographic: *Everyday Life in Ancient Times*, 1953.

Norden, E., *Agnostos Theos*, 1913.

Paulus, H. E. G., *Philologisch-kritischer Kommentar über das Neue Testament*, Lübeck, 1800.

Peake, A. S., *Critical Introduction to the New Testament*, 1909.

Peake, A. S., *The Epistle to the Colossians* (*The Expositor's Bible*, Vol. III), Grand Rapids, Mich., 1943.

Percy, E., *Die Problem der Kolosser- und Epheserbriefe*, Lund, 1946.

Piper, O. A., "The Savior's Eternal Work; An Exegesis of Col. 1:9-29," *Int*, 3 (1949), pp. 286-298.

Pope, R. M., "Studies in Pauline Vocabulary; Redeeming the Time," *ET* 22 (1910, 1911), pp. 552-554.

Radford, L. B., *The Epistle to the Colossians and the Epistle to Philemon* (*The Westminster Commentary*), London, 1931.

Ramsay, W. M., *Historical Geography of Asia Minor*, London, 1890.

Ramsay, W. M., *The Church in the Roman Empire*, London, 1893.

Ramsay, W. M., *Cities and Bishoprics of Phrygia* (two vols.), London, 1895-1897.

Ramsay, W. M., *The Letters to the Seven Churches of Asia*, London, 1904.

Ramsay, W. M., *The Teaching of Paul in Terms of the Present Day*, London, 1913.

Rendtorff, H., *Das Neue Testament Deutsch, 8. Die Kleineren Briefe des Apostels Paulus*, Göttingen, 1949.

Ridderbos, Herman, *Aan de Kolossenzen* (*Commentaar op het Nieuwe Testament*), Kampen, 1960.

Robertson, A. T., *Word Pictures in the New Testament*, New York and London, 1931, Vol. IV, on Philemon and Colossians, pp. 464-513.

GENERAL BIBLIOGRAPHY

Robinson, J. A., "The Church as the Fulfilment of the Christ: a Note on Ephesians 1:23," *Exp,* 5th series, 7 (1898), pp. 241-259.

Robinson, J. A. T., *The Body,* 1952.

Robinson, J. M., "A Formal Analysis of Colossians 1:15-20," *JBL,* Vol. LXXVI, Part IV (Dec. 1957), pp. 270-288.

Rutherford, John, "St. Paul's Epistle to the Laodiceans," *ET,* 19 (1907, 1908), pp. 311-314.

Schille, "Liturgisches Gut im Epheserbrief," doctoral dissertation, Göttingen, 1952.

Schultze, V., *Altchristliche Staedte und Landschaften,* II, Kleinasien, 1922.

Scott, E. F., *The Epistles of Paul to the Colossians, to Philemon, and to the Ephesians (Moffatt Commentary),* New York, 1930.

Simpson, E. K., *Words Worth Weighing in the Greek New Testament,* London, 1946.

Stonehouse, N. B., *Origins of the Synoptic Gospels,* Grand Rapids, Mich., 1963.

Thiessen, H. C., *Introduction to the New Testament,* Grand Rapids, Mich., 1943.

Trench, R. C., *Synonyms of the New Testament,* edition, Grand Rapids, Mich., 1948.

Van Leeuwen, J. A. C., *Paulus' Zendbrieven aan Efeze, Colosse, Filemon, en Thessalonika (Kommentaar op het Nieuwe Testament),* Amsterdam, 1926.

Vincent, M. R., *The Epistles to the Philippians and to Philemon (International Critical Commentary),* New York, 1906.

Wiggers, F., "Das Verhältniss des Apostels Paulus zu der christlichen Gemeinde in Kolossä," *TSK* (1838), pp. 165-188.

Windisch, H., "Die götliche Weisheit der Juden und die paulinische Christologie," *Neutest. Studien für Heinrici,* 1914.

Wood, J. F., *Discoveries at Ephesus,* 1877.

Wright, G. E., *Biblical Archaeology,* London and Philadelphia, 1957.

Young, E. J., "The Teacher of Righteousness and Jesus Christ, Some Reflections Upon the Dead Sea Scrolls," *WTJ,* Vol. XVIII, No. 2 (May, 1956), p. 145.

Zahn, Th., *Einleitung in das Neue Testament,* 1897-1900.

Zwemer, S. M., *Across the World of Islam,* London and Edinburgh, 1929.